VIEWS FROM THE STREETS

STUDIES IN TRANSGRESSION

STUDIES IN TRANSGRESSION

Editor: David Brotherton
Founding Editor: Jock Young

The Studies in Transgression series will present a range of exciting new crime-related titles that offer an alternative to the mainstream, mostly positivistic approaches to social problems in the United States and beyond. The series will raise awareness of key crime-related issues and explore challenging research topics in an interdisciplinary way. Where possible, books in the series will allow the global voiceless to have their views heard, offering analyses of human subjects who have too often been marginalized and pathologized. Further, series authors will suggest ways to influence public policy. The editors welcome new as well as experienced authors who can write innovatively and accessibly. We anticipate that these books will appeal to those working within criminology, criminal justice, sociology, or related disciplines, as well as the educated public.

Terry Williams and Trevor B. Milton, *The Con Men: Hustling in New York City*

Christopher P. Dum, *Exiled in America: Life on the Margins in a Residential Motel*

Mark S. Hamm and Ramón Spaaij, *The Age of Lone Wolf Terrorism*

Peter J. Marina, *Down and Out in New Orleans*

David C. Brotherton and Philip Kretsedemas, eds., *Immigration Policy in the Age of Punishment*

Robert J. Durán, *The Gang Paradox: Inequalities and Miracles on the U.S.-Mexico Border*

Kerwin Kaye, *Enforcing Freedom: Drug Courts, Therapeutic Communities, and the Intimacies of the State*

Views from the Streets

THE TRANSFORMATION OF GANGS AND VIOLENCE ON CHICAGO'S SOUTH SIDE

Roberto R. Aspholm

Columbia University Press
New York

Columbia University Press
Publishers Since 1893
New York   Chichester, West Sussex
cup.columbia.edu

Library of Congress Cataloging-in-Publication Data

Names: Aspholm, Roberto R., author.
Title: Views from the streets : the transformation of gangs and violence on Chicago's South Side / Roberto R. Aspholm.
Description: New York : Columbia University Press, 2019. | Series: Studies in transgression | Includes bibliographical references and index.
Identifiers: LCCN 2019019479 | ISBN 9780231187732 (paperback) | ISBN 9780231187725 (cloth) | ISBN 9780231547437 (ebook)
Subjects: LCSH: Gangs—Illinois—Chicago. | Homicide—Illinois—Chicago. | Criminal justice, Administration of—Illinois—Chicago.
Classification: LCC HV6439.U7 A837 2019 | DDC 364.106/60975311—dc23
LC record available at https://lccn.loc.gov/2019019479

Columbia University Press books are printed on permanent and durable acid-free paper.

Printed in the United States of America

Cover designer: Chang Jae Lee
Cover image: © Leonard Freed/Magnum Photos, Chicago, Illinois, 1987.

CONTENTS

ACKNOWLEDGMENTS vii

Introduction 1

Chapter One
The Shattering of Chicago's Black Street Gangs 16

Chapter Two
From Street Organizations to Cliques: Black Street Gangs in Chicago Today 46

Chapter Three
The Anatomy of Contemporary Gang Violence in Chicago 78

Chapter Four
Understanding the Persistence of Gangs and Violence in Chicago 109

Chapter Five
A Critical Appraisal of Violence Prevention Failures 140

Conclusion
Reducing Gang Violence from the Streets Up 168

APPENDIX: NOTES ON POSITIONALITY, THE POLITICS OF REPRESENTATION, AND RESEARCH METHODOLOGY 197

A PARTIAL GLOSSARY OF CHICAGO GANG SLANG 205

NOTES 211

BIBLIOGRAPHY 249

INDEX 267

ACKNOWLEDGMENTS

The completion of this book was only possible with the love and support I received from the many teachers, mentors, family members, friends, and collaborators who have helped me throughout this process and throughout my life's journey more generally. First and foremost, I thank my friends and brothers Sheldon Smith and Kenny Rainey for their vital assistance with this project as well as their enduring comradeship. I am proud of them and appreciate them both more than they know. I am indebted to my advisor and dissertation chair, Mark Mattaini, for his encouragement and stewardship of this project, particularly in its early phases, and for his continued championing of my work. The support I have received from Jim Gleeson, in his capacities as both a mentor and a friend, has been indispensable and unwavering and has extended far beyond my doctoral studies. My utmost gratitude goes to John Hagedorn, who has served as a mentor, champion, and friend from the day we met, and as an intellectual inspiration for far longer. His assistance and fellowship throughout the process of writing this book have been invaluable. I am grateful to Robert Lombardo for introducing me to the world of gang research back in my undergraduate days and for his help in guiding this project. I owe a debt of gratitude to Joseph Strickland—the "one-man reentry program"—for mentoring me in my community work, putting me in with good folks in the hood, inspiring my eventual return to school, and helping shape my research.

My work has been greatly enriched by Cedric Johnson, whose course on black politics opened my eyes to new analytic perspectives that continue to shape my thinking in fundamental ways. I am grateful to Creasie Finney Hairston for her support and encouragement during my doctoral studies. I have been fortunate to enjoy the camaraderie and friendship of Arturo Carrillo, Casey Holtschneider, Aissetu Ibrahima, Jalonta Jackson, Ifrah Magan, Olubunmi Oyewuwo-Gassikia, Aslihan Nisanci, Suhad Tabahi, and Roni and Gail Wilson during our doctoral studies and beyond. I am thankful to J Breezer Rickey, Flory Sommers, and the many great teachers and coaches I have had throughout my life for their support and inspiration. My gratitude also goes to my colleagues at Southern Illinois University Edwardsville, especially Kim Carter and Jill Schreiber, for their support during the last legs of this long journey. I am appreciative of Christopher St. Vil and Robert Weide for their friendship and camaraderie beyond institutional walls.

I owe a great deal of thanks to the good people I had the pleasure of working with during my years on the South Side of Chicago. I am grateful for my Grand Boulevard/Washington Park comrades, especially Ken Davis, Cornelius Ellen, and Andrea Lee, for helping me get my footing on the South Side and for continuing to provide me with mentoring and friendship. My sincerest gratitude goes to my Woodlawn colleagues, especially Renita Austin, Warren Beard, Mattie Butler, Bryan Echols, Alex Gardner, Chuck Hayes, Erick Puckett, and Otelua Thomas, for their support and education during my many trials by fire in the hood. Thanks to Shannon Bennett, Jitu Brown, and Jawanza Malone from North Kenwood/Oakland; Juan Cruz from Albany Park; and Josina Morita (from everywhere) for the comradeship in our battles to improve the lives of young people in our city. I am also thankful to the folks from Ninety-Fifth Street, especially Lonnie Black, Angie Cummings, Tamikia DeBerry, John Hardy, and LeVon Stone Sr., for embracing me and bringing me into the family. My gratitude to Chico Tillmon for his solidarity as well.

I am fortunate to have a tremendous family that has both supported me during the process of writing this book and shaped me into the man I am today. I am especially grateful to my amazing wife, Piere Washington, for always loving and supporting me. She sacrificed a great deal to help bring this book to fruition. No words could adequately convey my gratitude and love. I am grateful for my daughters, Paris and Pilar, for bringing joy and inspiration to my life every day. I love them both beyond words. I owe a great deal of thanks to my mother and father, Beth Rademacher and Tony Aspholm, for instilling in me a deeply rooted sense of compassion and social justice. Thanks also for the last-minute editorial work on this book manuscript! I am also fortunate to have siblings, Jim Aspholm, Rose Aspholm, and Martin Aspholm, who keep me grounded and always challenge me to be the best version of myself. Thanks to my brothers Kawaskii Bacon and Abdul Omari for supporting and inspiring me by making positive moves when so many of our friends went in other directions. I am grateful to my aunts and uncles for their love and support, especially Laurel Miller and the late Patrick Kearney. Special thanks also to my extended family, especially Cynthia and the Bobo family; Marcus Davis; the Ellen family; Sommer Green; Tabaris McLaren; Paris Neal; Kathy, Joe, and the Olson family; Julio and the Puma family; Ben Thullen; Rolene Walker; and Pete, Perez, and the Washington family. I owe a great deal of thanks to all the young people I have worked with throughout the years—and who are far too many to name here—for allowing me into their lives and for the education and friendship they have provided.

At Columbia University Press, my utmost thanks to Eric Schwartz for believing in this project and to Lowell Frye for his expert assistance and coordination. I am grateful to Kathryn Jorge and Virginia Perrin for their indispensable copyediting assistance in the final stages of producing this book. My sincerest thanks also to the two anonymous reviewers who provided helpful comments on earlier drafts of the book that greatly assisted in its development. I am appreciative of David Brotherton not only for serving as an intellectual inspiration but also for seeing the value in this project and bringing it to Columbia in the first place. Thanks to the Graduate College at the University of Illinois at Chicago for financial support during the early stages of this research. My gratitude also to Nathan Aguilar for key assistance with interview transcription as well as thoughtful conversations about the project as it developed.

Most importantly, I thank the men who shared their lives with me by participating in this study. I cannot mention their names in these acknowledgments for obvious reasons, but I appreciate them all from the bottom of my heart. I have done my best to do their stories justice in these pages.

To all those who have lost their lives to the streets, especially Harold Bobbitt Jr., Daniel Gomez, Corey Harris, Marcus London, Thomas Olson, Davon Smith, Damian Turner, Darris Williams, Darris Williams Jr., Lawrence Williams Jr., Micah Williams, and Joseph Wood, may they rest in peace, and may this work honor their lives and memory.

Introduction

Chicago has long symbolized the municipal embodiment of violence, street gangs, and urban pathology within the public imagination—"first in violence, deepest in dirt," as the century-old reputation goes.[1] Over the past decade, moreover, the city has experienced a resurgence in national media coverage related to its gangs and persistently high levels of violent crime, spawning countless news stories and journalistic profiles of the city often referred to as "Chi-raq," an allusion to Chicago as a devastated battlefield akin to the war-torn nation of Iraq.[2] The city's reputation for gangs and violence has recently reclaimed a central place in popular culture as well, as award-winning filmmakers have directed acclaimed films examining these topics, television networks have churned out a profusion of new shows, and a cadre of young rappers from Chicago's South Side have propelled "drill music," their self-styled brand of gangsta rap, into the international spotlight, netting major-label record deals and fueling local gang feuds in the process.[3] Chicago has also assumed a high-profile position in the nation's political discourse, as Barack Obama addressed the violence plaguing his adopted hometown on a number of occasions during the final years of his presidency, and the topic was a notable theme in the presidential debates of 2016.[4] In short, Chicago's long-standing reputation for gangs and violence has repenetrated America's collective consciousness and public discourse in a singular, far-reaching fashion in recent years.

As with nearly every other city in the United States, levels of violence in Chicago peaked during the early 1990s before falling during the latter part of that decade and the early years of the twenty-first century as part of the "great American crime decline."[5] Following a decade of reductions, however, Chicago's homicide rate stabilized around 2004 and remained remarkably steady over the ensuing decade—a period during which nearly every other major U.S. city enjoyed further, substantial declines in killings—before skyrocketing in 2016 to levels not seen since the bloody gang wars of the 1990s.[6] The stark reality is that Chicago has led the nation in total homicides each year since 2012. Indeed, Chicago's homicide tallies have far exceeded those of Los Angeles and New York, cities with 1.2 million and 5.8 million more residents, respectively, as well as those cities most comparable to Chicago historically in terms of homicide rate (see figure 0.1). Astoundingly, Chicago recorded more homicides than New York and Los Angeles *combined* in 2016, 2017, and 2018, assuming the dubious distinction as the most violent among the twenty largest cities in the United States.[7]

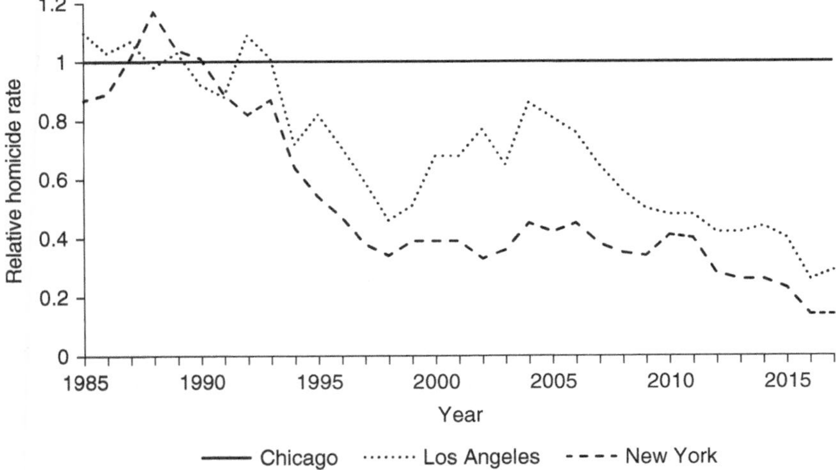

FIGURE 0.1. Homicide rates for New York and Los Angeles as a proportion of Chicago's homicide rate, 1985–2017

Source: Data from U.S. Federal Bureau of Investigation, "Uniform Crime Reports," accessed January 26, 2017, https://www.ucrdatatool.gov/; U.S. Federal Bureau of Investigation, "Crime in the U.S.," accessed July 18, 2019, https://ucr.fbi.gov/crime-in-the-u.s

Much of Chicago's violence has been attributed to its street gangs, which include many of the country's oldest, largest, and most notorious—the Black P Stones, Gangster Disciples, Latin Kings, and Vice Lords, among several others. Local and national law enforcement agencies claim that Chicago is home to as many as one hundred gangs, with a combined membership of 150,000, and that Illinois has the highest per-capita rate of gang membership of any state in the nation. The Chicago Police Department, moreover, has cited "street gang altercations" as the primary motive for homicides in the city since at least 1991, the earliest year for which such data are available.[8] While the inherently political nature of law enforcement information on street gangs demands an appropriately cautious interpretive approach, gangs and violence have been undeniably serious issues in many Chicago communities for decades.

Yet, in spite of these bleak realities and Chicago's resurgent national profile as the epicenter of street gangs and urban violence, little street-level research has been conducted exploring the nature of these realities in recent years.[9] This is disappointing, given the rich, century-long tradition of trailblazing scholarship on gangs and violence in Chicago, which provided important insights into these dynamics as the city's landscape evolved and helped shape the standards for research on these topics more broadly as well.[10] The dearth of recent research on these issues, moreover, means that the prevailing narratives on gangs and violence in Chicago have been largely shaped by law enforcement agencies, elected officials, and mass media outlets. As such, these narratives reflect the respective viewpoints and interests of these powerful entities as they pertain to these issues, interests that typically include assigning blame for persistent crime problems and justifying requests for increased police funding; consolidating public support for policy agendas, especially those involving punitive criminal justice policies and the withdrawal of public resources from low-income communities; and increasing viewership and/or readership. In each case, the pursuit of these interests is often facilitated through the creation of what social scientists call "moral panics," in which "a condition, episode, person or group of persons emerges to become defined as a threat to societal values and interests; its nature is presented in a stylized and stereotypical fashion by the mass media; the moral barricades are manned by editors, bishops, politicians and other right-thinking people; [and] socially accredited experts pronounce their diagnosis and solutions."[11] This dynamic aptly characterizes the discourse pertaining to gangs and violence in Chicago, especially in the years following the city's media-anointed "violence epidemic" in 2012.[12]

The Chicago Crime Commission, for example, paints an ominous picture of Chicago's gangs as a nebulous and omnipresent menace, claiming that "gangs constitute an entire sector of Chicago's population, yet even the law enforcement organizations that watch them daily cannot precisely gauge the extent of their presence. . . . Most residents of the city, then, live and work within feet of a gang's operations."[13] The Chicago Police Department (CPD) warns that gangs in the city have "become more violent" and that "anybody in the area is fair game, including men, women and children."[14] Former CPD superintendent Garry McCarthy has characterized the city as existing in a "state of lawlessness" due to its "very unique gang problem" and mounting public scrutiny of law enforcement.[15] Donald Trump has referred to gang members as "animals" who "[transform] peaceful parks and beautiful quiet neighborhoods into bloodstained killing fields" and has described Chicago as "a war zone" and the violence there as "carnage."[16] Richard Boykin, former commissioner for Cook County (home to Chicago), has called gang members "evildoers" and "terrorists" and promoted the notion that gang conflicts in the city amount to "a terrorist siege."[17]

Such characterizations have been employed to justify proposing and/or implementing a range of severe policy responses to street gangs and urban violence, both in Chicago and beyond. Trump's comments about gangs, for example, have been used to rationalize draconian and xenophobic immigration policies as well as proposed federal intervention in Chicago that would be "not . . . so politically correct," an apparent allusion to the trampling of civil liberties via the intensification of suppressive policing practices.[18] Boykin has advocated "charging individuals pulling the trigger and co-conspirators" in gang shootings with "domestic terrorism."[19] Mark Kirk, a former U.S. senator from Illinois, called for the mass arrest and prosecution of eighteen thousand alleged Gangster Disciples in Chicago following the 2013 murder of a teenage girl near Barack Obama's South Side home.[20] More substantively, these narratives have been used to justify generous funding for the CPD, whose 2016 budget accounted for an astonishing 39 percent of Chicago's entire general fund, placing Chicago second in an analysis of police expenditures in twelve major U.S. cities and totaling nearly five times the New York Police Department's 8 percent share of their city's budget.[21] The CPD has also enjoyed substantial annual funding increases, including a $60 million bump in 2018, despite a citywide budget shortfall of more than $259 million.[22] Chronic corruption within the department and brutality by its officers has cost Chicago taxpayers tens of millions of dollars each year as well, with the city shelling out nearly $642 million in civil damages between 2004 and 2015 alone.[23]

Costly law enforcement and criminal justice projects, moreover, often come at the expense of needed public resources and services, particularly in marginalized communities most impacted by violence. The generous and ever-increasing budget allocations for Chicago police in the twenty-first century, for example, have been accompanied by the closing of upward of one hundred of the city's neighborhood public schools, almost all of them in poor and working-class African American communities, under the auspices of "fiscal responsibility." In 2013 alone, Chicago closed nearly fifty schools, resulting in the displacement of at least twelve thousand students, nearly all of them low-income and African American.[24] In addition, the city shuttered six of its public mental health clinics in 2012 and privatized another in 2016, leaving a city of 2.7 million residents with five public mental health facilities. Three of the six centers that were closed, as well as the one that was privatized, were located in low-income areas on Chicago's South Side.[25]

Portrayals of street gangs and gang members in the media largely echo those espoused by law enforcement agencies and elected officials. In many cases, the media provide a direct outlet for these powerful social actors to promote their singular view of gangs and gang members as irredeemable criminals. News reports of investigations, crimes, arrests, prosecutions, and convictions of gang members, for example, all rely primarily on information provided by law enforcement and criminal justice officials and, thus, inherently reflect those perspectives and interests. Based on her ethnographic research centered on a federal drug case in two Los Angeles gang neighborhoods, Susan Phillips refers to these ostensibly official accounts as "narratives of precision" that problematically "censor parts of a story . . . and subsequently manufacture key images that justify the shape of police action."[26] In addition, fictional television shows that depict street gangs often do so from the perspective of police and prosecutors, and "real crime" series such as *Gangland* advance a sensationalistic view of these groups that emphasizes, with near exclusivity, violence and criminality. The first five seasons of that series profiled Chicago gangs in no less than eight episodes, which featured titles such as "Maniacal," "The Devil's Playground," and "Hustle or Die."[27]

Indeed, there is perhaps no more potent a distillation of the media's outsize impact on public perceptions of these issues than its treatment of Chicago. The city's singular reputation for gangs and violence, which has driven much of the national discourse on these topics in recent years, is largely a media-fueled sleight of hand: While Chicago's homicide rate is much higher than other U.S. cities firmly established in the twenty-first century global economy—New York, Los Angeles, Boston, San Francisco, and the like—it pales in comparison to deindustrialized rustbelt cities like St. Louis, Detroit, and Baltimore, whose homicide rates consistently surpass Chicago's by a two-to-one margin.[28] This dynamic reflects the reality that the astronomical rates of homicide found in certain sections of Chicago's South and West Sides are diluted in citywide measures via the virtual absence of serious violence in other areas of the city. Acknowledging these discrepancies between perception and statistical reality, the authors of a 2018 *CityLab* article concede: "But it's Chicago that *feels* like America's murder capital."[29] Given the media's relentless fixation on Chicago, it is little wonder why.

In spite of this widespread national attention, however, the questions that have captivated the public imagination since the middle years of the Obama presidency remain largely unanswered: What is going on with the gangs and violence in Chicago? And what might be done to address these issues? Apparently, neither City Hall nor the CPD has an effective understanding of or solution to these problems, as highly touted interventions like focused deterrence policing and the Cure Violence public health model have failed to reduce the city's stubborn homicide rate and prevent its remarkable explosion in recent years. The research presented in this book provides insights into these important questions and, in doing so, challenges much of the conventional wisdom on contemporary gangs and violence in Chicago (and beyond). As the following chapters describe, the traditional hierarchical outlaw-capitalist street gangs whose leaders once controlled violence on the city's South Side from the top down have been supplanted by horizontally organized neighborhood cliques engaged in violence that is increasingly unregulated and unpredictable. In short, today's gangs and the violence in which they are embroiled are radically different from their historical predecessors. Indeed, one of the central refrains in my interviews with Chicago gang members was "this ain't the nineties no more." These evolving realities have important implications for addressing gangs and violence in Chicago today, and the contextual approach to analysis delineated in these pages holds lessons for understanding and addressing these issues in other contexts as well.

THE STUDY

The research described in this book evolved out of my experiences living and working on the South Side of Chicago over the course of eight years, first as a graduate student intern, then as a community-based social worker, and, finally, as a doctoral student and researcher. I initially moved to Chicago from my hometown of Minneapolis to attend college and study social work. After completing my undergraduate degree, I secured a graduate internship with a grassroots community organization on the city's South Side as part of a master's program in social work and moved from the North Side to Bronzeville, the blighted and impoverished but slowly gentrifying historic South Side ghetto. The move had the intended effect of bringing me closer to my work, both literally and figuratively. During my yearlong internship I helped administer restorative justice, mentoring, and college- and career-readiness programs, and coached the previously defunct track and field team at Walter H. Dyett High School, a tough public school on the northern edge of Washington Park. Dyett became somewhat (in)famous in the years after I left, as soon-to-be rap star Chief Keef attended school there before dropping out during his sophomore year, and community activists waged a highly publicized and ultimately successful campaign—which included a thirty-four-day hunger strike—to stop then mayor Rahm Emanuel's plan to close the school in 2015.[30]

After completing my internship and master's degree, I took a position with an organization in Woodlawn, a nearby South Side community. Woodlawn had served as the historic birthplace of radical black political power in Chicago during the 1960s, when Saul Alinsky helped neighborhood residents organize The Woodlawn Organization to fight urban-renewal-minded encroachment by the University of Chicago, municipal neglect from the offices of "hizzoner" Mayor Richard J. Daley, and political disfranchisement wrought by the city's Democratic machine. During this same period, the Blackstone Rangers (later the Black P Stone Nation), widely considered the country's first "supergang," also emerged in Woodlawn, as did their bitter rivals, the East Side Disciples, who would become a cornerstone of the fledgling Gangster Disciple Nation by the early 1970s.[31] In Woodlawn, I spent two and a half years coordinating a number of youth employment, afterschool, and summer programs and helped organize initiatives and grassroots coalitions to address issues such as youth jobs, sexual health, and community violence. Many of these initiatives were run out of First Presbyterian Church, which had served as the headquarters for the Stones in the late 1960s under the supervision of social radical and Stone champion Rev. John Fry. Old-time churchgoers shared their memories from that era and pointed out to me where gunfire, once intended for the Stones, had chipped away at the church's gray stone exterior and where stained glass windows shattered by bullets had been repaired.

Many of the youth I worked with in these capacities were gang members; many others were not. Some occupied a space somewhere in the middle, as the notion of "gang membership" as a black-and-white distinction often oversimplifies the more fluid and complex realities of identity, relationships, and neighborhood dynamics that characterize daily life in many Chicago communities. Yet all of these young people were forced to navigate a social and physical world shaped in fundamental ways by gangs and violence. The blocks and neighborhoods where young people lived were largely defined by their place within the gang landscape of the wider community. This dynamic shaped peer associations both in the neighborhood and beyond, served to restrict movement based on territorial considerations, and affected community life more generally as gang members occupied public space in often-conspicuous ways.[32] If young people were not gang members themselves, their family members, friends, and neighbors often were, and the violence and incarceration that frequently accompanies gang life therefore affected these youth as well. Indeed, the responses to gangs and violence by law enforcement, city and state governments, and community organizations impacted life in fundamental ways for all community youth, from shaping policing practices that were often applied indiscriminately to black youth in these neighborhoods to helping determine the availability of community programs and resources designed to address these issues.

Some of the efforts with which I was involved seemed to have a positive impact, providing young people with critical resources and opportunities, helping them to improve their lives, and strengthening prosocial community relationships. Other efforts were perhaps less impactful; some seemed downright misguided and perhaps even harmful. Many young people I worked with were unable to escape the pitfalls of gangs, violence, incarceration, and early death. After being involved in organizing a youth-led, cross-community grassroots survey about neighborhood safety and police–community relations, I grew increasingly interested in stepping back to examine the dynamics of street gangs, violence, and community interventions from a research perspective and decided to return to school to pursue a PhD in social work at the University of Illinois at Chicago.

I dove back into the literature on gangs and violence in Chicago with which I had first become acquainted as an undergraduate student. A tremendous amount of scholarship has been published about these topics in Chicago, dating back nearly a century to the 1927 publication of Frederic Thrasher's groundbreaking book, *The Gang*, widely considered the foundation on which modern gang research has been built. Dozens of important studies of gangs emerged from Chicago in the ensuing decades, including seminal works by Gerald Suttles, Irving Spergel, Lincoln Keiser, James Jacobs, and Ruth Horowitz.[33] The more recent scholarship on Chicago's street gangs by Sudhir Venkatesh, John Hagedorn, Felix Padilla, and others primarily explores their "corporatization" in the post–civil rights era. This research describes how, during the last two to three decades of the twentieth century, Chicago's black and Latino street gangs transformed themselves from youth groups oriented primarily around identity and social support into corporate-style, outlaw-capitalist drug organizations. This shift was fueled by a number of historical factors, most prominent among them deindustrialization and endemic unemployment, intensifying urban disinvestment, mass incarceration, the crack cocaine epidemic, and a growing sense of nihilism among young people in dispossessed inner-city communities in the face of these realities. Many of Chicago's gangs were well-equipped for corporatization, having established cross-neighborhood federations, central leadership structures, and powerful sets of symbols, rituals, and ideologies during their initial development, which began, in some cases, as early as the late 1950s. The nature of gang warfare, moreover, followed the logic of corporatization, particularly during the crack epidemic of the 1980s and 1990s, when gang leaders waged wars over the control of illicit drug markets and the amassing of profits and power on the streets and in prison.[34]

Despite the richness of this scholarship, however, I found little within the literature that reflected what I had seen living and working with gang members and other youth on Chicago's South Side. Indeed, much of what I had seen stood in stark contrast to the descriptions in the existing research. It was ultimately this dissonance that shaped the questions that guided my dissertation research project. What, exactly, *were* the contemporary dynamics of gangs and violence on Chicago's streets? How did they differ from the prevailing dynamics of the 1990s, when most of the more recent existing research had been conducted? To the extent that there were differences between these eras, what had produced these apparent changes? How might an understanding of the contemporary realities on the streets help make sense of the failure of touted violence prevention models to actually reduce violence in Chicago? What might be more promising alternatives for addressing gangs and violence in the city? My research findings in relation to these questions serve as the basis for this book.

These findings are based primarily on in-depth, semi-structured qualitative interviews with thirty-five African American gang members from Chicago's South Side (see table 0.1). Thirty of these interviews were conducted with active gang members between the ages of sixteen and thirty-one from fourteen distinct gangs. These participants described a high degree of contact with the criminal justice system, with a median of nearly nine arrests among all participants and reported adult felony convictions for fifteen of them. Only six of these young men reported being formally employed at the time of their interviews, and ten described dropping out of high school and failing to complete high school or general equivalency requirements. All four of the major historic South Side street gangs—the Black Disciples, Black P Stones, Gangster Disciples, and Mickey Cobras—are represented among these study participants, as are "Outlaw" and "Insane" Gangster Disciples and the Four Corner Hustlers, a gang based

TABLE 0.1
Profile of Study Participants

Participant	Age	Gang status	Community area	Traditional street gang
Floyd	27	Active	Grand Boulevard	Black Disciples
Montrelle	23	Active	Grand Boulevard	Black Disciples
Terrence	22	Active	Grand Boulevard	Mickey Cobras
Rick	19	Active	Grand Boulevard	Mickey Cobras
Durrell	24	Active	Washington Park	Black Disciples
Memphis	22	Active	Washington Park	Black Disciples
Kevin	16	Active	Washington Park	Black Disciples
Roosevelt	31	Active	Woodlawn	Mickey Cobras
Melvin	24	Active	Woodlawn	Gangster Disciples (Outlaw)
Cassius	20	Active	Woodlawn	Gangster Disciples (Outlaw)
Lamont	25	Active	Woodlawn	Black P Stones
Rasheed	21	Active	Woodlawn	Black P Stones
David	23	Active	South Shore	None
Bibby	22	Active	South Shore	Rollin 60s Crips*
Cedric	20	Active	South Shore	Gangster Disciples (Insane)
Carlos	19	Active	Chatham	Black Disciples
Cortez	23	Active	Roseland	Gangster Disciples
Daequan	21	Active	Roseland	Four Corner Hustlers
Ronald	24	Active	West Pullman	Black P Stones
Aaron	21	Active	West Pullman	Gangster Disciples
Antonio	24	Active	New City	Black P Stones
Reggie	22	Active	Englewood	Gangster Disciples (Insane)
Javon	20	Active	Englewood	Gangster Disciples
Harold	25	Active	Greater Grand Crossing	Black Disciples
Marco	21	Active	Greater Grand Crossing	Black Disciples
Weezy	19	Active	Greater Grand Crossing	None
Zeke	18	Active	Greater Grand Crossing	Black Disciples
Bernard	24	Active	Greater Grand Crossing	Gangster Disciples
Jabari	21	Active	Greater Grand Crossing	Gangster Disciples (Insane)
James	20	Active	Greater Grand Crossing	Black P Stones
Pernell	34	Transformed	Woodlawn	Black P Stones
Daniel	55	Transformed	Roseland	Gangster Disciples
Eldridge	48	Transformed	Public housing†	Gangster Disciples
Paris	42	Transformed	Public housing†	Gangster Disciples
Lorenzo	50	Transformed	Austin (West Side)‡	Four Corner Hustlers

* Bibby had recently moved to Chicago from Los Angeles, where he was active with the Rollin 60s Crips. He retained this affiliation as his primary gang identity.

† Gang life in this neighborhood largely revolved around a public housing development, although not all members of the local gang lived in the projects.

‡ While Lorenzo hailed from the West Side, he had extensive experience working on violence reduction on the South Side as well as in other areas of the city.

primarily on Chicago's West Side. As can be seen in table 0.1 and will be discussed at length in later chapters, many of the study's participants belonged to gangs comprised of members from more than one of these traditional street gang identities. In addition, two participants belonged to neighborhood-based gangs but did not identify with any of these broader, traditional identities, and one recent transplant from Los Angeles still identified primarily with his LA gang roots.[35]

Five older gang members who had transformed their lives and were now working to reduce violence in Chicago were also interviewed.[36] These men ranged in age from their mid-thirties to mid-fifties and had extensive gang backgrounds and involvement with the criminal justice system during their adolescence and early adulthood. More recently, they had achieved notable success in higher education, with all five having earned college degrees and three holding advanced graduate degrees. These individuals had worked in a variety of capacities in both their native communities as well as throughout the city of Chicago on efforts to reduce violence, facilitate community reentry among returning prisoners, provide resources to distressed families, and build and mobilize grassroots groups to address community needs, among other endeavors. These participants provided a wide-ranging perspective that encompassed their own gang involvement during the 1980s and 1990s, their experiences transitioning out of active gang life, living through changes in the city's gang landscape over time, and working with young gang members within the context of many of these changes in the twenty-first century.

Study participants hailed from ten low-income, high-violence communities on Chicago's South Side (see figure 0.2). These communities are among the most marginalized and distressed in the city, with levels of poverty, unemployment, racial segregation, and violence as much as two to three times higher than citywide rates and up to ten times national averages (see table 0.2). These neighborhoods are also among the city's most blighted, with many having lost more than half of their housing stock over the last half-century due to public and private disinvestment, leading to widespread abandonment, decay, and landlord arson.[37] Nearly two-thirds of the schools that remain open in these communities perform below the city average, and these neighborhoods rank among Chicago's leaders in rates of mental health hospitalization.[38] (For a discussion of the study's research methodology, see the appendix.)

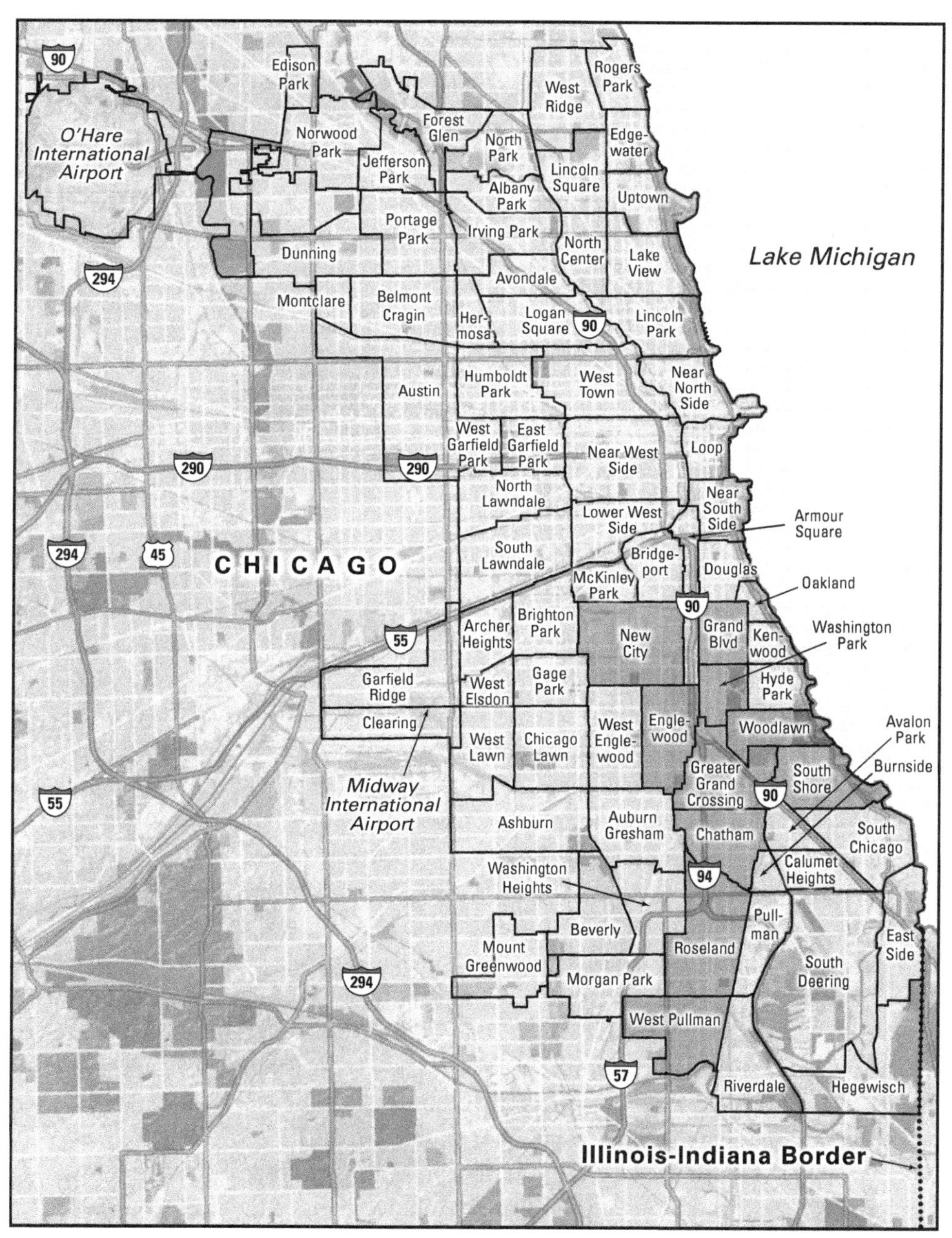

FIGURE 0.2. City of Chicago community areas and study communities
Note: Darkened areas indicate study participants' communities.

TABLE 0.2
Study Participants' Communities: Select Social Indicators

	Poverty rate	Unemployment rate	Percent African American	Homicide rate (per 100,000)*
Study participants' communities †	37	25	94‡	46
City of Chicago	22	12	31	16
United States	12	4	13	5

Sources: Data from Suniya Farooqui, *Chicago Community Area Indicators, 2015* (Chicago: Social Impact Research Center, Heartland Alliance, 2017); Chicago Police Department, "Crimes—2001 to Present," 2018, https://data.cityofchicago.org/Public-Safety/Crimes-2001-to-present/ijzp-q8t2; Federal Bureau of Investigation, "Crime in the U.S," accessed July 18, 2019, https://ucr.fbi.gov/crime-in-the-u.s.

* Figures listed represent average annual homicide rates for the years 2006–2015.

† Austin, Lorenzo's West Side community of origin, is excluded from these figures.

‡ Racial demographic data for the New City community are excluded from this figure. New City serves as a point of convergence for three highly segregated areas of Chicago's South Side: one Latino, one black, and one white. As the community remains highly segregated despite the substantial presence of three racial/ethnic groups, to include the percentage of African American residents (24 percent) in the calculation of this figure would have implied a level of integration that does not exist.

ORGANIZATION OF THE BOOK

Chapter 1 begins with a brief prelude introducing the dynamics of Chicago's traditional black street gangs, particularly during the 1990s, before it dives into the fracturing of these gangs during the first decade or so of the twenty-first century. In particular, this chapter examines the effects of a number of sociohistorical developments that served to weaken these gangs organizationally as well as the internal rebellions led by young gang members that ultimately shattered them. Chapter 2 explores how youthful gang members, in response to these new and evolving realities, have reconstructed gangs on the South Side of Chicago in radically new ways by rejecting traditional gang ideologies, practices, and forms of organization. Chapter 3 addresses the topic of gang violence and, in particular, how the changes described in the first two chapters have reshaped the nature of gang violence on Chicago's South Side, as the top-down, large-scale drug wars of the 1980s and 1990s have given way to increasingly local, expressive, and unpredictable patterns of violence. Chapter 4 explores how to account for the persistence of gangs and violence in Chicago in the wake of the transformations described in the preceding chapters. This chapter makes a case for understanding street gangs in terms of the various material and psychosocial functions that they play in the lives of young people facing desperate conditions and bleak prospects. In doing so, this chapter challenges mainstream interpretations of these groups as criminal associations and of gang members as pathological.

The final chapter and conclusion tackle the subjects of violence prevention and gang intervention. Informed by the preceding analysis, chapter 5 offers context-driven critiques of two "universal" violence prevention models, the focused deterrence policing strategy embraced by the CPD and the Cure Violence public health model, both of which have been highly touted and widely celebrated but have ultimately failed to reduce levels of violence in Chicago. Employing knowledge of prevailing patterns of gang organization, dynamics, and violence, this chapter attempts to elucidate these failures. The conclusion distills the lessons of the book and applies those lessons to delineate an alternative strategy for reducing gang violence rooted in addressing the conditions that ultimately fuel this violence and engaging gang members as active agents in efforts to that end. The conclusion also makes the case that the current moment presents a unique opportunity for bold, meaningful intervention in Chicago to address gangs and reduce violence, while calling into question the political will to pursue such an agenda.

Chapter One

THE SHATTERING OF CHICAGO'S BLACK STREET GANGS

Chicago's major black street gangs were all founded between the late 1950s and early 1970s on the city's South and West Sides. These gangs, which have historically been among the largest and most organized gangs in the country, include the Black Souls, Four Corner Hustlers, New Breeds, and various Vice Lords branches, all based primarily on Chicago's West Side, and the Black Disciples, Black P Stones, Gangster Disciples, and Mickey Cobras, based mainly on the South Side. As discussed briefly in the introduction, the most recently documented chapter in the collective history of these gangs involves their post-1960s reconfiguration as vertically organized outlaw-capitalist organizations during a period when Chicago's African American neighborhoods were ripped apart by deindustrialization and soaring unemployment, retrenchment and abandonment, the crack epidemic and the war on drugs, and skyrocketing incarceration rates.[1] Indeed, Chicago's black gangs had proven remarkably resilient in the decades since their respective inceptions, adapting to changing historical conditions and circumstances, navigating internal clashes and power struggles, and managing to remain essentially intact at the close of the twentieth century. For the black gangs on the city's South Side, however, this remarkable continuity did not survive the first decade of the new millennium.[2] While the names of these traditional gangs largely live on, today's gangs are organized very differently than—indeed, in many ways, in diametrical opposition to—their hierarchical, corporate-style predecessors.

Before delving into exactly what today's gangs look like, however, this chapter will explore how this fundamental transformation occurred. The chapter begins with a brief revisiting of the particularities of gang organization and violence during the 1990s, providing an essential context for understanding the trajectory of these gangs since that time. Following that section are detailed treatments of the various precipitating historical factors and internal processes by which the black street gangs on Chicago's South Side weakened and eventually shattered during the first decade or so of the twenty-first century. Simply put, we cannot understand today's gangs without understanding their history.

PRELUDE: CHICAGO'S BLACK STREET GANGS DURING THE 1990S

From the 1960s through the 1990s, Chicago's black street gangs were organized as cross-neighborhood gang federations that members referred to as "street organizations" and/or "nations" (e.g., the Almighty Black P Stone Nation). These gangs comprised a number of neighborhood-based chapters, or sets, each with its own local leadership hierarchy, and collectively organized under the control of a central leadership body. Most of Chicago's major gangs had at least a dozen sets, and many gangs had substantially more than that: The Gangster Disciples, long the largest gang in Chicago, had upward of one hundred sets throughout the city during their peak. Membership at the neighborhood level—that is, within each set—tended to be rather large, typically numbering several dozens, with members' ages often spanning multiple generations. Leadership structures were relatively rigid and hierarchical, with divisions of labor that often included various committees as well as demarcated roles for women and younger members. Central leadership formalized and coordinated instrumental relationships and mediated disputes between their gangs' various chapters. Organizational "literature" detailing each gang's history, values, symbols, laws, practices, and prayers served to legitimize these leadership hierarchies, delineate prescriptions for behavior, and socialize members by providing a comprehensive framework for collective identity, values, and action.

Gang scholars refer to this complex, durable form of organization as "gang institutionalization." In his examination of Chicago's black street gangs, John Hagedorn explains that institutionalized gangs can "persist for decades despite changes in leadership and police repression" because they represent "'living organisms' instilling in their members, as well as the community, a belief in the organization itself . . . handed down as tradition through generations."[3] In this sense, like the African American and Chicano gangs of Los Angeles, Chicago's traditional gangs were decidedly institutional in nature. Paris, a study participant who came of age during the organizational prime of these traditional street gangs, offers compelling support for this position, arguing that the pathologizing, perfunctory stereotypes evoked by the term "gang" work to obscure the complexity of these groups and impede the depth of analysis necessary to understand them.

PARIS: I use the word "street organization" strategically 'cause, again, I think we should abolish the word "gang." Because the word "gang" and guns change the whole dynamic of a conversation. The definition of a gang is a radical group of people. But if this was an organization, then that organization structure look like there's something to it.

RRA: There's a logic to it?

PARIS: Right. There's a methodology, there's an ideology to it. You can see it. It's substance there. If you researched it, you'd be able to identify with some of the people. You may not be part of it, but you could understand.

Lamont, one of the older active gang members who participated in this study, offers a striking illustration of this "substance" in his discussion of the workings of the Black P Stones during his adolescence:

LAMONT: Every decision that is made is made by a top leader in the Black P Stone Nation, which is a general. And if any decision is made without a general, the next person that's in charge is the mufti.[4] If the mufti have not made a decision, and somebody act on a decision that has not been agreed upon, violations will be taking place.

RRA: So there are formal leaders—people with certain ranks and positions?

LAMONT: Yes. Nobody without no rank within the Black Stones of what I'm speakin' about—I don't know what go on in other communities—but in my community, *rank* outweigh everything. . . . Headquarters dictate and control—look, they want this general to get elected. If he gettin' elected, he need to visit the body [the organization's central leadership]. The body have to question him: "You a general. What's act one?" You know, the Stones got different laws—it's called acts. If you break a act . . . it's a jury that hear that. So that separate a soldier from a mufti to a general. Because as you get up, you need certain papers [pieces of organizational literature] at certain levels. The Stones are real [*pausing*] . . . iffy on knowledge that you received and who you givin' it out to. They got they own prayer, they got they own laws, they got they own everything—they own world . . .

My duties varied because I was a young soldier. So I may be workin' on this particular committee. So what a lot of people don't know is gangs are broken up into committees. Right? So when a war is about to occur in the community or amongst two gangs, if they're structured the right way, the way that I've seen it is, it's not just gonna be someone sayin', "Oh, we're goin' to war." It's a group of guys who are in charge of those particular things . . .

RRA: What about women—were there any women that were involved?

LAMONT: A few. And we don't call 'em Stones, we call 'em Roses, right? 'Cause they're sisters. The way the Black Stones are structured is different from the Gangster Disciples. The Black Stones is brought up on such of a structure of Islam and things of that nature. And with that, it's not a woman duty to get dirty. A woman would keep drugs, guns, or, you know, cook, chill, count money, get the drugs together. They'd be your lookout people. A woman could take a pound of weed—you give it to her, put it in her purse, the police would never stop her. Things of that nature. So those are your disguises. Little kids like me were used to move certain things 'cause I wouldn't get stopped.

As Lamont alludes to here, drug distribution was the central function of Chicago's black street gangs during the 1980s and 1990s. These gangs had forcibly taken over control of retail-level drug distribution in the city's black neighborhoods from the Outfit, Chicago's mafia organization, during the late 1960s.[5] The transition from clandestine to open-air markets for heroin and other drugs over the following decade or so and the explosion of crack cocaine use in the mid-1980s created new economic opportunities for Chicago's black street gangs, whose control of neighborhood territories provided a basis for the establishment and control of these emerging public drug markets. Gang leaders, many of whom had been incarcerated since the early 1970s, perceived the economic opportunities at hand and began reorienting their organizations more fully around the illicit drug trade. Where drug crews and organizations emerged in New York and other cities independently of street gangs, in Chicago the street gangs themselves essentially became the drug organizations.[6] Daniel, who had left Chicago in the early 1980s and did a short prison bid out of state, explains these dynamics on his return to the city in the mid-1980s:

> When I moved back to Chicago at twenty-four, twenty-five, you know, of course this is the time when cocaine and crack cocaine had become an epidemic. And it was also a time where the open markets for sellin' heroin had occurred. So then you could see the spread not only of those drugs and the effects, but you could also see the strength and spread of how street organizations created and leveraged havin' territories. So then if you wanted to participate in those markets, you could only participate where you had membership—where you had a license. . . .
>
> The catalyst—everything came from jails and prisons. I mean, that was the driving force. The driving force for the structure and enforcing the structure was what was goin' on in jails and prisons. 'Cause guys were tryin' to create business opportunities for themselves while they were incarcerated that they could utilize once they came home.

Given their economic focus, the hierarchical leadership structures of these gangs approximated those of conventional corporate organizations, in function if not in form. In practical terms, gang leaders reaped a disproportionate amount of the profits from these economic endeavors and autocratically dictated gang policy. For a number of gangs, the economic predominance of gang leaders over rank-and-file soldiers even extended to mandates to participate in the periodic sale of drugs whose profits were funneled entirely to the gang's central leadership. In a study of the financial records of a black street gang operating in Chicago's notorious Robert Taylor Homes during the height of the crack epidemic in the early 1990s, Steven Levitt and Sudhir Venkatesh found that set leaders earned as much as $130,000 per year, while foot soldiers earned an average of less than $3,000 annually. Members of the gang's central leadership, moreover, collected 20 percent of all revenues from dozens of sets throughout Chicago as tribute, easily raking in hundreds of thousands of dollars each year.[7]

Failure to comply with gang policies often resulted in "violations," as Lamont alludes to in the passage quoted earlier, which consisted of various forms of physical beatings and, in some cases, financial penalties. Violations, then, were employed as a means of enforcing organizational policy and compelling members' compliance with the dictates of gang leadership. The actual or perceived mismanagement of drug operations and accounting errors were common grounds for violations. Similarly, a member's failure to carry out hits and other acts of violence against a group's opposition or to refrain from violence that had not been authorized might also result in violations. Gang leaders, in other words, largely monopolized the sanctioning of violence both internally and with respect to gang warfare. Gang literature and appeals to collectivism were employed by gang leaders to justify their inordinate power and income and the subordinate position of gang soldiers. Rank-and-file members' aspirations of gang mobility also worked to sustain these arrangements, as being an effective drug dealer and loyal soldier were generally considered the primary criteria for promotion. Taken as a whole, these dynamics promoted a distinct culture of obedience within Chicago's black street gangs during the 1980s and 1990s. Roosevelt describes these dynamics as they existed around the turn of the century:

> We'd have days where we'd have "nation packs"—where you have to serve drugs just for the nation. You wasn't gettin' paid for it, this is for our organization to make sure we had money for our parties, our guns, takin' care of our blocks, makin' sure we had taken care of our Brothers, and makin' sure we had our work [drugs] every time. So you wouldn't get paid for that, it was just for the nation. It was just makin' sure that we always had something to keep our organization going. . . . And if you was comin' up short with money, you was gon' get violated. . . .
>
> You had to be out there every day with us—during the wars, during the struggle, you know? . . . If you didn't come to the blocks to participate and come to service [gang meetings] or something like that, that was a violation. . . . When the Brothers told you to go out there and take care of your business [perform acts of violence against the gang's opposition], you had to do it. Or if you didn't do it, your ass was gettin' dealt with.

In line with their economic inclinations, the gang wars of this era were typically fought over control of illicit drug markets and economic and organizational predominance on the streets and in prison. The allure of unprecedented profits and power during this period effectively shattered Chicago's long-standing People and Folks gang coalitions, which had been organized in the Illinois Department of Corrections in 1978, as wars broke out between fraternal gangs like the Gangster Disciples and Black Disciples and the Insane, Maniac, and Almighty gang "families" of the Latin Folks' Spanish Growth and Development.[8] Dictated by powerful leaders, the gang wars of the 1990s were fought primarily by rank-and-file members and were among the bloodiest in the city's storied history of violence. Driven by these conflicts, Chicago's homicide rate hit an all-time high of 33.1 per 100,000 in both 1992 and 1994, an increase of roughly 50 percent over the city's homicide rates throughout the 1980s.[9] In short, the rampant gang violence of this era was largely directed from the top down and fueled by instrumental, especially economic, imperatives. "People with money had power. It's just like in the real world," Lorenzo explains. "But the only difference about Chicago, man, you could be the most savvy businessman, [but] if you ain't no killer, then people gon' end up takin' your shit." Recounting the bloody war fought between the once-allied Four Corner Hustlers and Unknown Vice Lords during the 1990s, Lorenzo elaborates:

> That's really one of the reasons we was into it so long with the Unknowns. Willie was extortin' Vice Lords, and Angelo was like, if any Foe give him a dime, then *he* might as well extort him. He was like, "We ain't givin' you shit." And, really, the Unknowns and Foes war was, like, a war of the old against the young. 'Cause you gotta think, me and Angelo is the same age, at that time we twenty-two, twenty-three. And Willie Lloyd in his forties.[10] So it's some old men tryin' to extort us. And we like, "Shit, we out here every day. Hell nah!" . . . If you think about it from just a natural sense and not even a gang sense: You a king. Who gon' relinquish all of their authority and come under the umbrella of somebody else?

For a number of reasons, however, the dynamics of Chicago's gang landscape during the 1990s ultimately could not be sustained. Beginning around the turn of the century, the black street gangs on the city's South Side underwent a process of destabilization that culminated in their eventual shattering. The following sections detail the contextual shifts that created this instability, their effects on internal group workings, and how youthful gang members responded to and shaped these evolving dynamics.

These developments were not sudden, and they unfolded unevenly from gang to gang and from neighborhood to neighborhood. Nonetheless, the broader contextual factors that drove these dynamics ultimately affected all of the major black street gangs on the South Side of Chicago in strikingly similar ways.

CRACKS IN THE FOUNDATION: THE CONTEXT AND BEGINNINGS OF ORGANIZATIONAL DECLINE

A number of major historical shifts created the conditions for and initiated a process of organizational deterioration within Chicago's black street gangs beginning in the late 1990s and carrying over into the new millennium. The first of these shifts involved the declining profitability of the city's drug markets, particularly those on the South Side. A variety of factors contributed to this downturn, perhaps the most salient among them being changing patterns of drug consumption. As the 1990s came to a close, the crack cocaine epidemic that had seized dispossessed urban communities across the United States beginning in the mid-1980s was in major decline, and demand for crack plummeted.[11] This trend has continued unabated into the twenty-first century: While more than half of Chicago arrestees tested positive for cocaine in 2000, less than one-fifth did so by 2012.[12] Law enforcement agencies have claimed credit for these declines, framing them as the result of their successful disruption of cocaine supply chains in South and Central America. Yet diminished demand is clearly responsible for reduced crack use, as cocaine prices have fallen by nearly 75 percent since the mid-1980s. A reduced supply in the face of consistent demand, on the other hand, would have sent prices skyrocketing.[13]

As children during the late 1980s and 1990s, most of the study participants recalled growing up during the height of Chicago's crack era, and a number of them reported that their mothers and fathers had been addicted to crack cocaine. By the time they had come of age and became involved in gang life, however, the market for crack had drastically diminished. People had seen the effects that crack addiction had on families and communities, and the drug was increasingly shunned, particularly by the young people who sold it on the streets and their peers. "Crackhead" entered the urban lexicon as a derisive term denoting a desperate, impulsive, fanatical person who lacks self-control and fails to maintain basic personal care.[14]

Crack was officially "wack" in the eyes of urban youth, who increasingly turned to marijuana as a safer, less destructive alternative. Data from the National Institute for Drug Abuse, for example, indicate that among a probability sample of male arrestees in Chicago from 2000 to 2010, two-thirds of those born before 1970 tested positive for recent cocaine use, while only 10 percent of those born after 1989 tested positive. On the other hand, approximately three-fourths of this younger group tested positive for marijuana, compared with less than one in four members of the older cohort.[15] These statistical trends are reflected in Cassius's firsthand account of evolving patterns of drug use on the South Side of Chicago:

CASSIUS: People sell crack, but these days, people work off they phone. They don't just be outside talkin' 'bout, "What's up? Rocks and blow!" People work off they phone, so if you want some crack, you gon' call a mu'fucka like, "Bring me one down."

RRA: So it's not like it was in the nineties?

CASSIUS: Like, the *nineties*? Nah. Hell nah! It was scorchin' hot for crack. Now it's, like, calmed down. It's just the basic addicts every day who call the phone and shit. . . . But weed is—shit, I don't think that's never gon' fade out, shit. If you smoke weed, you smoke weed [you're dedicated to it].

RRA: So weed is more popular nowadays?

CASSIUS: Yeah, the weed is more popular. It's more, like, a friendly zone drug. So it's a lot of more people do it.

Cassius's statements also lend insight into another dynamic that has reshaped the nature of the illicit drug trade in the early years of the twenty-first century, namely, the transformation of drug markets themselves. The open-air drug markets that dominated public housing developments, street corners, and other public space in dispossessed urban communities in the 1980s and 1990s have increasingly disappeared from these neighborhoods in recent years. Like their brick-and-mortar retail counterparts in the formal economy that have been devastated by the rise of online shopping, technological developments have rendered drug markets rooted in stable, public physical spaces increasingly irrelevant and unprofitable. In this case, this transformation is largely a result of the ubiquity of cell phones. Gang members today no longer have to stand on a street corner to sell drugs, waiting for customers that may or may not be coming, subjecting themselves to potential arrest and prison time, and exposing themselves to attacks by their opposition. Instead, they can conduct business from their cell phones and make drop-offs to familiar customers as necessary. The rise of cell phones and, more recently, the internet as tools for conducting drug sales, however, has also served to shift retail-level drug distribution points away from their traditional inner-city locales more broadly, as suburbanites and other outsiders are no longer forced to depend on the reliability of these public urban markets to purchase drugs. Instead of sojourning to the inner city to buy drugs on a street corner, suburban drug users can just text their local dealer—typically a white suburban peer—to set up transactions locally. The "use of mobile devices has quietly revolutionized drug dealing. . . . Low-income black and Latino communities are no longer needed as drug super-markets," as the authors of a 2017 article on the recent heroin epidemic conclude.[16] Indeed, by 2013, less than one in five Chicago arrestees who tested positive for or who described using cocaine reported buying crack cocaine outdoors, and nearly three-quarters purchased these drugs from a "regular source," that is, someone they knew and patronized often.[17]

What these changes in drug consumption and drug markets have meant for black street gangs on Chicago's South Side is a dramatic reduction in drug revenues, which had served as the gangs' primary economic lifeblood since the 1980s. The higher cost of cocaine as well as the shorter, more intense high of crack and its higher level of addictiveness make the potential profit margins associated with selling crack substantially higher than those for selling marijuana. The proliferation of mobile, clientele-based drug dealing, moreover, drained clients from Chicago's once-prominent, gang-controlled open-air drug markets. Combined with gangs' corporate organizational structures that funneled the bulk of drug profits to gang leaders, drastically declining drug revenues meant that gangs could no longer sustain their status as populist employers of their respective memberships. Chicago gangs' involvement in the illicit drug trade during the crack epidemic of the 1980s and 1990s had made "the gang the new hiring hall for young men" in black communities "overwhelmed by the irresistible tide of joblessness" wrought by deindustrialization.[18] But if the crack trade had once brought about new employment opportunities, then the end of the crack epidemic was akin to the loss of yet another major industry, and its workers—in this case, gang members—likewise suffered widespread occupational displacement.

As gang leaders struggled to maintain their own earnings in the face of these challenges, youthful gang members were increasingly marginalized within and even excluded entirely from the gang-controlled drug-selling operations in their neighborhoods. The drug game, then, increasingly failed to ensure even basic subsistence—or pocket change, for that matter—for growing numbers of gang members. The economic benefits that had served as a cornerstone of gang membership during the 1980s and 1990s did not apply to the generation of gang members coming of age in the early twenty-first century. Moreover, opportunities for mobility within the gangs' organizational structures, which had existed to some degree in previous decades and that had constituted a common aspiration among young gang members, were likewise evaporating alongside profit margins. Despite these considerable shifts in the gang landscape, however, youthful gang members were still expected to conform to their gangs' leadership hierarchies and follow the directives of their superiors. Yet the lack of even meager wages, diminishing avenues for and aspirations of organizational mobility, and declining moral support from gang higher-ups compromised the control that gang leaders were able to exercise over their rank-and-file members and fostered rebelliousness among young gang members. Terrence explains these dynamics as they played out in his neighborhood during his teenage years:

TERRENCE: They [older gang members] was gettin' money, [but] they didn't used to help us with nothing. They used to leave us out there stranded. . . . They didn't give us no guidance, no nothing. . . .

RRA: Why do you think that they didn't provide the type of leadership for you all that they got when they were comin' up?

TERRENCE: On the South Side of Chicago, it's not too much drug dealin' goin' on. . . . When the older generation was doin' they drug dealin', it was on the decline, so they wasn't makin' as much money as the [generation before them]. So they couldn't provide for us like they was provided for—like, people who had bought them drugs, guns, and all that. They couldn't do that for us. 'Cause the lil money they made off [selling drugs] was just for them to survive . . .

> [When] we was in age about fourteen, fifteen, sixteen, we start gettin' into it with them hard 'cause they wanted us to stop fightin', stop gangbangin' more. They was older than us, so they was more about money—gettin' they money outside. We was younger, we was fightin' every day, makin' it hot [increasing police scrutiny], and they didn't want—they didn't like that. . . . They said we used to gangbang for no reason 'cause we wasn't doin' it for no money.

Another significant factor that contributed to the declining profitability of Chicago's drug markets was the near-wholesale demolition of the city's public housing projects. Between 1995 and 2010, the Chicago Housing Authority (CHA) razed more than twenty-one thousand public housing units, with clearance efforts ramping up in earnest in 1999 with the release of the CHA's ten-year *Plan for Transformation*.[19] While a good portion of these demolitions took place on the West Side and at the Cabrini-Green projects on the Near North Side, CHA demolitions were largely concentrated in Bronzeville, the historic black South Side ghetto where city officials had originally clustered public housing projects as a means of fortifying racial segregation in the postwar era.[20] Indeed, upward of 60 percent of all public housing demolitions took place in this area, which black Chicagoans commonly refer to as the "Low End," owing both to its geographic location in the lower-numbered streets of the South Side and, as sociologist Mary Pattillo points out, "the neighborhood's lowly status."[21]

I first arrived in Chicago in the midst of these demolitions in 2004, although I was living and going to school on the city's North Side, a figurative world away from the Low End. Friends I knew from Minneapolis came to Chicago that fall for a visit and brought me to the Robert Taylor Homes on the South Side where they had grown up. They talked about the dramatic changes to their old community, where only a few of the original twenty-eight sixteen-story high-rise buildings were still standing. By the time I moved to the South Side in 2008, the remaining buildings had been demolished, along with nearly all of the other nearby projects: Stateway Gardens, Clarence Darrow Homes, Madden Park Homes, 41st–Cottage Grove, Randolph Towers and various other Washington Park Homes scattered sites, and most of the Ida B. Wells Homes, Prairie Avenue Courts, and Lakefront Properties.[22] The Harold Ickes Homes and the remainder of the Wells Homes soon followed in being reduced to rubble.

The Raymond Hilliard Homes were emptied of families and converted to senior housing.

Chicago's public housing developments had long housed many of the city's most lucrative, defensible, and violently contested drug markets.[23] The gang sets based in the projects, moreover, were often among the city's most organized and powerful. "It was *unity*. It was *structure* when them projects was up," as Memphis explains. "That's exactly where it all started from: the buildings, B. Mu'fuckas makin' $100,000 a day." The demolition of nearly all of Chicago's public housing developments, then, not only served to eradicate many of the drug markets that had been the most profitable for the city's street gangs, it also served to eliminate gang strongholds and disrupt long-standing gang networks. This disruption occurred on two fronts: both within the former project developments, where local sets were effectively eradicated, and in the neighborhoods to which former project residents—including thousands of gang members—moved following their displacement. Indeed, despite political rhetoric justifying public housing demolition as a vehicle for racial and class integration, the realities of entrenched segregation and a dearth of affordable housing in most Chicago communities meant that the majority of displaced project tenants moved to neighborhoods that were among the poorest and most racially segregated in the city. More than 70 percent of former CHA residents who moved into private housing with a Section 8 voucher between 1999 and 2005, for example, relocated to sixteen Chicago communities—all on the South and West Sides—that were, on average, 91 percent African American and had an average household poverty rate of 32 percent.[24] A 2011 CHA report on relocation revealed a similar pattern, with the highest concentration of former public housing residents relocating to South and West Side communities that, with few exceptions, rank among citywide leaders in terms of segregation, poverty, unemployment, and violent crime.[25]

The arrival of thousands of gang members from demolished public housing developments into existing gang territories in other distressed black neighborhoods in Chicago in the early years of the twenty-first century frequently led to violent clashes within these receiving communities. These conflicts were fueled by a number of dynamics, more than one of which may have been pertinent in any particular situation. In many cases, for example, gang members moving from the projects into other communities hailed from rival gang organizations. In some cases, the influx of formerly project-based gang members created competition and conflict over control of drug markets in receiving communities.[26] Even in instances where rival gang affiliations and economic competition may not have been pertinent issues, broader considerations of neighborhood "ownership," relational dynamics, and ignorance of and misunderstandings over local traditions and standards of comportment often created tension and fueled conflicts, even between members of the same traditional street gangs. In the following passage, Paris describes some of these dynamics as they played out in receiving communities.

Just use one CHA property—one high-rise, like the high-rise I was born in. This was the phenomenon: you get one CHA high-rise that's got fifteen floors, ten apartments [on each floor]. So just picture, you got 5 people in every family—that's a mother, father, 3 kids. Right? So that's 50 people on one floor, times 15 'cause it's 15 floors. Now just picture displacin' 750 people. You gon' take all these families and put 'em in whatever part of the city. What happened with CHA was people who had Section 8, certain buildings and certain community people went to certain areas. So even if the people that was in that area was from that group [gang], they upbringing was different. You could be from Africa, but you come from a different tribe, your upbringing may be different . . .

So you could have that internal feudin' with the people that's from there. They feel like this they shit. And if enough of us come from the projects, shit, this our shit now. I'm bein' honest, I know this firsthand. I watched how Englewood's shit got flooded. I watched how Chatham get flooded. I watched how the East Side get flooded with project-ass people. How do I know? 'Cause I came from there [the projects] and went to the community.

Yet these transitions did not always—or at least did not *permanently*—result in violence. As participants in this study describe, gang members from the projects were often integrated into established gangs in receiving communities via existing relationships, increasing neighborly familiarity, and/or flat-out necessity. This integration happened both within and, in a stark reversal of long-established Chicago gang practices, across traditional gang lines. In previous decades, gang members would typically make efforts to avoid moving into neighborhoods or attending high schools dominated by an opposing gang. Indeed, under certain circumstances, it was difficult or even impossible for gang members to safely visit family members or friends in enemy territories. When moving into a neighborhood or school controlled by an enemy gang proved unavoidable, gang members were often forced to switch allegiances and align themselves with their former enemies for the sake of survival. Consider, for example, Lamont's response when asked if the gang members in his neighborhood growing up all identified with the same traditional gang: "Yes, sir. No other way. If you was anything else, you'd get the life beat out of you 'til you Black Stone [*laughing*]. Stone to the bone!"

With the influx of unprecedented numbers of gang members from public housing and as the structure of Chicago's black street gangs weakened in the early years of the twenty-first century, however, the will and ability of these groups to effectively enforce traditional gang allegiances within their neighborhoods diminished substantially. Thus, gang members displaced from the projects, as well as those simply moving across neighborhoods into areas dominated by rival gangs, were increasingly able to—and did—retain their original gang identities even as they were integrated into gang life in their new neighborhoods through developing and/or strengthening relationships. Below, Memphis and Harold provide examples of these dynamics as they pertain to their respective neighborhoods. Memphis, who grew up a few blocks away from the southern section of the Robert Taylor Homes and attended elementary school with many of the development's youthful residents, including many young gang members, explains how his block was a natural landing spot for many displaced gang members given their existing friendships. In this case, all parties shared a common traditional gang identity as Black Disciples. Harold, on the other hand, describes the integration of gang members with varying traditional affiliations in his neighborhood, offering a notable counterpoint to the traditional gang dynamics described in the previous quote from Lamont.

MEMPHIS: Around '98, we was goin' to John Farren, and we met up with some more guys who was from the projects—you know, the projects still was up. So I met my man and them.

RRA: So what happened to your friends when they started tearing the projects down?

MEMPHIS: Then they came back here [to our block].

RRA: So is everybody from your block a BD or is there people with different affiliations?

HAROLD: Aw, yeah. But since we grew up with 'em and they hang with us a lot, we show 'em love, we don't never disrespect them. We don't treat 'em like no opp 'cause they be with us, you know what I'm sayin'? We respect that. It's cool, we ain't ask 'em to flip or nothing. Well, we asked them, but, you know . . .

RRA: They wasn't with it?

HAROLD: If one flip, that's cool. But if one don't flip, that mean he true to it. Like, man, he ain't flip. Aw, okay, he with it, then. Like, we gotta respect him—he a Gangster, that's what it is, then. . . . We still kick it with 'em every day. They our brothers, too.

The eradication of powerful project-based gang sets through the widespread demolition of public housing and the introduction of members from those gangs into other gang territories throughout Chicago, however, were not the only factors contributing to the disruption of longstanding gang networks. The incarceration of increasing numbers of gang members and, especially, gang leaders also had the effect of weakening existing gang structures. The convergence of a number of factors during the 1990s—most notably, the crack epidemic, the escalating involvement of Chicago's gangs in illicit drug distribution, the focus of the war on drugs on retail-level drug markets, and tough-on-crime policies, including mandatory minimum prison terms and truth-in-sentencing laws—meant that gang members were being arrested and incarcerated at unprecedented rates and facing increasingly lengthy prison sentences. The use of federal drug laws and organized crime statutes, moreover, moved growing numbers of gang leaders, including many of Chicago's most powerful gang chiefs, into the federal prison system. Table 1.1 lists a number of major federal prosecutions of black Chicago street gangs over a quarter-century beginning in 1989, when the first of such investigations culminated in the indictment of sixty-five alleged members and associates of the Black P Stones (then identified as El Rukns), including Stones chief Jeff Fort. Most of these cases resulted in criminal convictions for major leaders of the various gangs listed. In short, as Memphis put it, federal authorities "went and locked all the heavies up."

The scores of Chicago gang leaders sent to federal prisons across the country drastically weakened their capacity to provide leadership and

TABLE 1.1
Major Federal Prosecutions of Black Chicago Street Gangs, 1989-2014

Street gang	Years of indictments	Total number of gang members indicted*
Black Disciples	1998, 2004, 2013	86
Black P Stones	1989, 2001	85
Four Corner Hustlers	1992, 2005†, 2005	72
Gangster Disciples	1995, 1999, 2002, 2013‡, 2014	115
Mickey Cobras	2001, 2006	62
New Breeds	2006, 2010	82
Vice Lords	1994, 1995, 2004, 2010, 2014§	148
Total	1989–2014	650

Note: This table likely omits a number of relevant cases, as I compiled these data myself through internet searches and did not have access to any official government data related to such cases.

* While not every one of the individuals indicted in these cases may have been convicted in court, a 2013 Human Rights Watch report reveals that 97 percent of federal drug defendants plead guilty. Moreover, of the 3 percent who choose to go to trial, 90 percent are convicted. Thus, these numbers are likely to be largely reflective of the numbers of alleged gang members who were actually convicted in these cases. It should also be noted that, in many of these cases, state charges were brought against both those facing federal charges as well as other individuals not included in these numbers. See Human Rights Watch, *An Offer You Can't Refuse: How US Federal Prosecutors Force Drug Defendants to Plead Guilty* (New York: Human Rights Watch, 2013).

† Indictment also included members of the New Breeds.

‡ Indictment also included members of the Black Disciples.

§ Indictment also included members of the Traveling Vice Lords, Black Souls, Gangster Disciples, and New Breeds.

dictate and enforce policy among their members on the streets. While most of Chicago's gang chiefs had been incarcerated in the Illinois Department of Corrections since the 1970s, they had long been able to maintain control of their gangs from the state's prisons. Indeed, imprisonment had actually served to strengthen their organizations, expand their ranks, and enhance their authority. As James Jacobs details in *Stateville*, his ethnography of the eponymous Illinois prison, by the early 1970s Chicago's black street gangs had become "the predominant inmate force" at the prison, completely transforming long-standing inmate patterns of organization, acting as power brokers with the prison administration, and swelling their respective memberships via recruitment within the inmate ranks.[27] Hagedorn notes that Stateville quickly became "known as the 'White House' because that is where major decisions were made" related to gang policy in Chicago.[28] In contrast, after being scattered across the country in the Federal Bureau of Prisons system, often in solitary confinement or other "supermax" conditions of custody, gang leaders were increasingly hard-pressed to maintain control of their organizations.

Further exacerbating these issues was the growing prevalence of snitching within Chicago's gang organizations, as increasing numbers of gang members turned on their comrades in exchange for judicial leniency in the face of lengthy federal sentences.[29] This dynamic further decimated the ranks of gang leadership, eroded organizational cohesion, and created uncertainty on the streets. As younger gang members increasingly dominated the street ranks due to the incarceration of their older counterparts, mechanisms of control and accountability broke down, and gang members had greater latitude to act autonomously. As Roosevelt explains:

> Over the time, people was gettin' locked up for murders, you know, and catchin' drug cases and stuff like that. That's what was slowin' most of the guys down. . . . Couldn't nobody eat 'cause the police was always comin' through the block, shuttin' the blocks down. People was snitchin', tellin' the police where we was hidin' our stuff, where we was havin' stash houses, everything. . . . And then, over time, when most of the people got killed and was locked up, that's when some of the structure was messin' up. 'Cause people wasn't around, so some of the people thought they can get away with doin' things as far as steppin' on other people turfs and goin' out of bounds, you know? And doin' things on they own without tellin' nobody.

The gang leaders who remained on—or at least close to—the streets were beginning to lose control both at the neighborhood level and, even more definitively, at the broader, cross-neighborhood level. The loss of many of the most talented gang leaders to federal correctional institutions was producing a crisis of leadership, and, lacking leaders who possessed the authority and legitimacy to mediate and settle disputes between sets, gangs increasingly lost their capacity to maintain organizational cohesion across neighborhoods. These internal conflicts, then, whether based on money, power, or personal animosities, increasingly spun out of control and fueled further organizational erosion. In some ways, the stage had already been set for this dynamic with the process of gang corporatization during the 1980s, which had refashioned social relations within Chicago's black street gangs in ways that prioritized often-competitive profit seeking over traditional ideals of brotherhood. In *The Hidden War*, a study of crime and government neglect in Chicago's public housing projects, for example, Susan Popkin and her colleagues describe the Harold Ickes Homes as a "war zone" in the late 1990s after Gangster Disciples that had been displaced from other projects slated for demolition had moved into the development and begun battling the GDs native to the Ickes for control of the local drug trade.[30] Similarly, in their book *The Almighty Black P Stone Nation*, Natalie Moore and Lance Williams describe violent competition between adjacent Stone sets over control of diminishing drug markets in the late 1990s.[31]

Participants in this study discussed similar dynamics of intragang conflict, although, tellingly, the conflicts they described in the early years of the twenty-first century did not revolve around control of drug markets. Lamont, for example, whose description of the strong central leadership of the Black P Stone Nation during his early days of gangbanging was quoted at length earlier in this chapter, recounted an incident in which an older gang member from his neighborhood, Tone, was killed in a drunken argument with another Stone from a nearby set. Lamont explains the subsequent fallout:

> The general who in my hood, [*pounding his chest*] he mad. You know, Tone come out of his hood, he raised him, been knowin' him since he was a little boy, blessed him to bring him in and everything. So I'm like, how they gon' do it? Because the guy who shot him, his uncle a general. So he's sayin', "Man, my uncle a general. Yeah, I popped his ass. [So what?] My uncle a general." Tone—nah, his uncle ain't a general, but the man who love him like a uncle a general, you see what I'm saying? So now it's really *fuck them*. So what they wind up doin' was tellin' ol' boy uncle like, "Look, we just wanna holla at your nephew for a lil bit. We ain't even gon' kill him, murk him, nothing." . . . His uncle told him, "Go down there. They ensured me you gon' be okay." He get down there. Mu'fucka get to talkin' to him, they start whoopin' him. Car pull up with some more of the guys, you know, shit get ugly . . .

Notably, while street justice appears to have been served in this instance, this justice—or, perhaps more accurately, vengeance—was not the result of transparent organizational adjudication or even centralized autocratic authority; rather, it was achieved through deceptive internecine power plays.

In summary, a number of shifts in the wider context within which Chicago's street gangs existed served to drastically weaken the organizational structures and capacities of these groups around the dawn of the millennium. Most notable among these shifts were the decline in the crack epidemic, the demolition of public housing, and the incarceration of scores of gang leaders in the Federal Bureau of Prisons. The ways in which gang leaders and rank-and-file gang members interpreted and responded to these changes, moreover, often further exacerbated their corrosive effects. Taken together, these developments set the stage for the popular rebellions within Chicago's black street gangs that followed.

THINGS FALL APART: THE DELEGITIMATION OF GANG LEADERSHIP AND RANK-AND-FILE REBELLION

Within the context of declining drug revenues, ruptured gang territories, and leadership crises, young rank-and-file gang soldiers began to call into question the structures and practices of their respective organizations and to reevaluate their position within these hierarchies. Most significantly, these gang members increasingly recognized the vertical structures of these organizations as essentially exploitive, with rank-and-file members selling drugs and committing acts of violence at the command of gang leaders who reaped an inordinate share of the money and power derived from these activities. In the course of street-level drug selling and gang warfare, moreover, gang soldiers risked arrest and bodily harm on a routine basis, while gang leaders typically assumed relatively little risk in directing these activities from the safety of the suburbs or the distant confines of the state's penitentiaries. In addition, while the failure of gang soldiers to follow orders or meet expectations typically resulted in violations—that is, violent sanctions—ranking gang leaders and others who were particularly close or useful to gang leadership were often able to defy organizational protocol without repercussion. Whatever financial support might have been available to incarcerated gang members or to those fighting criminal charges during earlier times of greater organizational profits and structure had largely disappeared as well, and young gang members became increasingly frustrated with the lack of material and social support they received from their gangs during periods of incarceration.

Although many of these dynamics had long characterized the inner workings of Chicago's street gangs, rank-and-file gang members had generally accepted these conditions as an unalterable reality. Research with Chicago gangs during the 1990s conducted by Venkatesh, Felix Padilla, and others suggests that members had two options under these circumstances:

hold out hope that they might one day rise through the ranks to a position of power within their organization or quit in disillusionment.[32] But as opportunities for internal mobility evaporated with the waning of the crack epidemic, gang structures weakened with the federal imprisonment of top gang leaders, and bloodshed on the streets wore on, young gang members accurately interpreted their marginal positions within their gangs as increasingly permanent. The dissonance between gang appeals to collective identity and interests and the realities of highly stratified organizational arrangements and coercive, exploitive leadership strategies had come into sharp focus. In short, youthful gang members deemed the status quo unjust and intolerable, and gang leaders lost legitimacy in the eyes of rank-and-file gang members. The following quotes from James, Carlos, and Jabari serve to illustrate the various dimensions of this emerging consciousness among youthful gang members and their rejection of the established culture of obedience within their gangs.

JAMES: A lot of niggas started to realize like, what are you doing for me, for me to even listen to you? Are you providing for my household? Are you takin' care of my kids or my girl if I get locked up? Is you bonding me out? Is you gon' be there when I'm out there [on the front lines during gang wars]? No. And then we out here taking the most risk and you getting all the money. . . . Why should I even listen to what you tellin' me? Why should I let you lead me, when I'm a born leader myself? . . . That's over with. . . . And then it just got to the point where, shit, they knew what we was about, and they knew they couldn't tell us shit.

CARLOS: It's the niggas that's sittin' in them big-ass cribs in the 'burbs that's really runnin' the hood, you feel me? And not even in the hood seein' what's goin' on, but they callin' shots: "Hey, man, go shoot that mu'fucka up." Don't give no fuck, you feel me? It's crackin' out there and *we* out there . . .

'Cause it's like this, shit. It can be two months straight, big Folks ain't even been out here. It been the lil Folks out here holdin' this shit down. So when big Folks and them pull up tryin' to organize some shit, Folks and them be like, "This our shit now," you feel me? "Y'all still from right here, but we got shit poppin' right now. It's our turn to get it crackin' out here." So it could be an altercation in the mob.

JABARI: You ain't gon' let nobody hit you in your mouth for something that you made a mistake. That's just like—okay, I go on a hit. I supposed to killed him, but I shot him and missed him, though—ain't hit nothing. "You ain't hit nothing? You gotta get violated." "Damn, that's my first time shootin' a gun. So you gon' hit me in my mouth? I ain't ask you to go shoot that—y'all told me to do that." You feel me? That's how it be. So you might not like that, and you gon' hit him [the leader] in his mouth. . . .

Then dude[s] just come out of jail—know everything about everything—come to you and tell you, "Man, you gotta do it this way. You gotta abide by these rules and policies." And you might not like some of these rules and policies. You like, "This what I gotta do?" "Yeah, or we gon' have to violate you," or something. You not gon' go. You not gon' honor that. You gon' be like, "Fuck these rules. Fuck this structure. Who *is* you? I don't even know you." That's how you gon' be. . . . [The older guys] get locked up, come home, [there are] new faces on the block. Then you thinkin' this still your block, whole time, it's something different.

As these passages reveal, young rank-and-file members of Chicago's black street gangs had grown increasingly disillusioned with and resistant to what they perceived as the oppressive and hypocritical conditions within their respective organizations. In turn, young gang members channeled this disillusionment into rebellions against gang leaders and other older, more established members. These rebellions typically involved verbal and physical challenges to long-standing gang arrangements and customs, as gang members refused to follow orders, challenged claims to authority, violently opposed violations, subverted inequitable economic arrangements, and developed new identities rooted in their emergent resistance. Such dynamics represented a dramatic break from historical precedent, whereby authority and violence flowed unequivocally down the chain of command, and violent clashes with gang leaders who were loath to relinquish their power and authority were widespread. Clearly, a new day was dawning on the streets of Chicago's South Side.

Consider, for example, the passage below in which Rasheed recounts a physical altercation between himself and an older gang leader in the neighborhood where both he and Lamont grew up. Following an incident in which Rasheed and a friend "did some cutthroat shit" by robbing a fellow

Stone who was not from their neighborhood but who lived in the area, the robbery victim and Rasheed's superior confronted them about the incident. During the encounter, Rasheed not only verbally challenged the authority of his superior, but beat him up when he attempted to physically reassert his authority. The contrast between the dynamics described by Rasheed and those detailed earlier in the chapter by Lamont—only five years Rasheed's senior—as he recounted his early days of gangbanging are striking and serve as a clear illustration of the tremendous shifts in gang dynamics that had taken place within a relatively short period of time. That the altercation described below occurred in a Black P Stone stronghold long known for its durable organizational structure, and as a result of a situation in which Rasheed openly admits that he was at fault, moreover, further reveal the ubiquity and enormity of these changes. As Rasheed explains:

> So after we robbed him, he come walk straight into the hallway with one of the big homies while we in there chillin'. So that shit was awkward as hell, know what I'm sayin'? He like, "These two right here." They like, "Aw, y'all out of order, woo wop the bam." . . . I'm like, "Fuck what you talkin' 'bout! We ain't tryin' to hear that shit. You can go ahead and save that shit for somebody else." He like, "What you mean, 'Fuck what I'm talkin' 'bout?' This is my building." He get to power trip now. You know me, I'm—"Shit, what? Man, this *my* building." On Chief, he *rushed* me—like, swift.[33] I ain't even know he could move that fast. He rushed me, hands around my neck. I'm shocked! I'm gettin' loose [*wrestling imaginary hands off his neck*]. I ain't gon' lie—I hope you don't think I'm lyin' 'cause we havin' this interview or whatever. . . . I whooped big homie ass, you hear me! I patched him up—*psh, psh, psh* [*slamming his fists into his palms*]. On Chief! . . .
>
> So we right up in the building the next morning. He walk past me, say some slick shit. I steal on [punch] Moe ass—*bing, bing, bing*! 'Cause he was on some "it ain't over" shit, anyway. So, shit, I'm on that shit, too! I ain't gon' let you steal on me first.

Likewise, Kevin reported witnessing a strikingly similar altercation between his older brother and a gang leader—"one of the old heads"—over claims of ownership and control of their neighborhood during his early adolescence. Although the gang leader was ostensibly able to reassert his authority in this particular situation, he was ultimately powerless to stop the erosion of the neighborhood's gang structure, which, by the time of Kevin's interview, his comrade Memphis characterized as "completely out the window."

KEVIN: He was a older mu'fucka, about thirty, thirty-four, thirty-five. . . . He was the man of the block, I guess. And my bro said, "This ain't your block." You know, shit went from there. . . . I was in the store. I just come out, nigga hittin' my brother with a bat. They get to fightin'. He beatin' my brother up and shit. . . .

RRA: What about your other brother, he wasn't out there?

KEVIN: Nah, he was locked up at the time. He was just about to get out when the shit happened. . . .

RRA: What happened when he got out?

KEVIN: They was ridin', tryin' to catch his ass. . . . He locked up [now], so, shit, we gon' wait for him when he get out.

The rebellion of youthful gang members involved not only defiance in the face of gang leaders' attempts to assert authority over or dominate them, but also challenges to the economic inequalities that defined both the structural arrangements of Chicago's corporate-style street gangs as well as the illicit drug trade more generally. One such strategy, for example, involved young gang members intentionally failing to repay gang leaders for drugs that they were given on consignment—in short, stealing from their superiors. As a relatively older member who had achieved a degree of success in the drug game and parlayed that success into a budding career as a self-employed barber and a drug supplier one level removed from the streets, Roosevelt explains his frustrations with having had to deal with such situations:

RRA: Did you have any issues with guys trying to beat you out for some money?

ROOSEVELT: Yeah, I had a couple of issues where somebody—a few of them tried to get over on me. Yeah, I did have some issues, I'm 'a be real with that. 'Cause people think they can be slick and run off with your money thinkin' I don't need it, which I do. And that's a real issue. . . .

RRA: And these were the lil homies or what?

ROOSEVELT: Yup. Some of the lil homies that I fronted something to. I probably fronted, like, $1,000 worth [of] some Kush or something, and he ain't bring my money back. So we had to go find his ass and fuck him up.

Yet it was precisely the type of arrangement described here by Roosevelt that young gang members increasingly took issue with: rank-and-file gang members having to assume all of the risk involved in retail-level drug distribution while absentee higher-ups reap the lion's share of the profits. In addition, the erosion of gang leaders' ability to control their ranks emboldened young gang members to subvert these arrangements. In short, young gang members increasingly—and, in general, correctly—doubted the ability of older gang leaders to punish such transgressions. As Rasheed put it, "They old. They ain't movin' no muscle." Weezy explains these dynamics clearly and more generally from the perspective of the rank and file:

> Most of the older guys, they don't really fuck with us no more 'cause they fronted us weed, gave us shit, and we ain't never bring them shit back, you know? 'Cause, shit, man, they ain't out here with us. They somewhere with they family and stuff, but they wanna claim something, you know? I don't know how you could ever claim something but you not out there.

Another, more aggressive, form of economic rebellion described by participants involved robbing older gang leaders outright. Similar to failing to repay money they earned from selling drugs they received on consignment, many young gang members viewed such robberies as, at the very least, an acceptable by-product of the cutthroat capitalist dynamics established by gang leaders themselves, if not a fully justified form of redistributive economics. Perhaps even more so than in other forms of rank-and-file resistance, the potential for severe violence in these incidents was particularly high. In their work on the Stones, Moore and Williams describe the dynamics of the "stickup era" in the early 2000s, noting that, within a context of diminishing drug revenues, "those who could no longer eat by selling drugs began to rob those who had either drugs or drug money."[34] As participants in this study described, in some cases this practice eventually extended to heavyweights even within one's own gang, as declining drug revenues pushed younger members further to the margins of the drug business—or even out of it altogether—exacerbating inequality within the ranks.

In the passage that follows, for example, Carlos describes the robbery and murder of Dolla, a flashy, well-paid gang leader at the hands of members of his own gang. As the man killed was one of Carlos's mentors, Carlos attributes this particular incident to the "jealousy" of the soldiers who took his mentor out. Nonetheless, these dynamics serve as a concrete example of Carlos's own comments, quoted earlier, about rank-and-file rebelliousness in the face of exploitive leadership and flagrant inequality on the streets. If, as Carlos describes, Dolla was a "get-money nigga" who prioritized profits over camaraderie and relationships, his subordinates apparently came to see things in much the same way.

CARLOS: Dolla was a get-money nigga. . . . He wasn't one of them niggas that sit on the corner with the lil Folks—nah. He don't play games. He a grown man. But he was about that money, and some niggas in the mob got him, you know, the homies. Hell yeah. That shit deep, boy.

RRA: What happened with that?

CARLOS: I don't really wanna speak on they situation or nothing, 'cause some niggas that's still in jail right now [for] forty, forty-five years for that situation that's goin' on in that whole lil mob right there. But it was jealousy, you feel me? Like, everybody was gettin' money, but some had more than others. And, I guess, it was sometimes when he [Dolla] can do something you couldn't do at the time. You got three thou' in this pocket, but he walkin' around with twenty thou'. You got seven thou', he got thirty thou', you feel me? You just can't even win in his boat right now.

In some cases, participants described disputes between young gang members and gang leaders as giving rise to the wholesale splintering of neighborhood sets and to wars between the resulting factions. These divisions were often the manifestation of pervasive intergenerational hostilities within a set, although in some instances deepening rifts between a few individuals eventually forced all members to choose sides between the quarreling factions. Under these circumstances, loyalties might have been determined by not only generational allegiances but also by personal relationships and, within larger sets, geographic considerations. Indeed, in some cases, bigger sets splintered simply due to the growing inability of gang leaders to maintain formal cohesion among relatively large memberships with sizable geographic territories. Under such circumstances, these sets might have split into two or more factions yet maintained friendly relations. Nonetheless, in all cases, the resulting dissolution of these gangs illustrates the intensifying crisis of legitimacy faced by gang leaders and their inability to exert authority and effectively resolve internal discord. Below, for example, Aaron details the sequence of events that led to the splintering of his neighborhood gang and the resultant war between the gang's younger and older members:

AARON: It been a couple of shootings over some shit like that—younger niggas and older niggas gettin' shot from shootin' at each other type shit, robbin' each other.

RRA: Guys from the same hood?

AARON: Yup, same hood. That's why it's a war now between the two sides, you feel me?

RRA: So tell me about that. What happened with that?

AARON: A couple of years [ago], one of the big homies got killed, and they was sayin' it was another one of the [younger] guys' fault. But it really wasn't his fault. . . . But they was tryin' to make it like they was mad or some shit. So he like, "Aw, you mad, and you wanna tell everybody it's my fault?" So him and one of the lil homies, they had robbed [the big homie] for some loud or some shit—took that shit and was like, "Man, you lucky we ain't kill you." . . .

But it's more than that lil story. Mu'fuckas got into it with some niggas off 103rd Street, and they felt like one of the older heads was supplyin' them with guns. . . . So they caught him over there in the hood, and they killed him.

RRA: The lil homies killed him?

AARON: Some of the lil homies killed one of the older homies, yup. So that's what really started the feud. Once he died, that's what started the gang-on-gang shit. Mu'fuckas just got to choosin' sides from there—who you gon' be with? Either you rockin' with them niggas or you not, shit.

From the perspective of gang leaders themselves, the dynamics described in this chapter contributed to a fundamental transformation in the risk-benefit analysis that made holding such leadership positions increasingly less appealing. On one hand, the monetary profits that accompanied gang leadership roles had generally declined precipitously by the early years of the twenty-first century. In other words, compared to the crack era of the 1980s and 1990s, the material benefits of being a gang leader had substantially diminished. In addition, the pressures and rebellions from disgruntled rank-and-file members challenged the very existence of these positions. Gang leaders were not only faced with external conflicts with other gangs but besieged by internal ones within their own organizations. Finally, the unenviable prospect of being a central target of a federal drug or organized crime case and spending decades in prison also likely figured prominently into this calculus. Taken together, the prospect of managing a declining enterprise, contending with disaffected and violently rebellious subordinates, and facing the real possibility of living out one's days in a federal penitentiary all likely contributed to the eventual acquiescence of gang leaders and their potential successors to the youthful gang rebels. As Lorenzo put it, "They made it so don't nobody *wanna* be a leader of a gang."

The internal rebellions waged by young gang members against gang leaders ultimately proved successful, and gang leaders lost control of the organizations they had long ruled with an iron fist. These rebellions, however, did not materialize out of thin air; they were precipitated by a number of major historical circumstances that, in combination, set the stage for these intragang conflicts. If just one of those ingredients had been missing—if the demand for crack had not declined, the projects had not been demolished, or scores of gang leaders had not gone to federal prison—perhaps things would have played out differently. As it happened, however, the collective weight of these circumstances effectively shattered the black street gangs on Chicago's South Side during the first decade of the twenty-first century.

The older gang members interviewed for this study expressed two conflicting, yet not incompatible, views and feelings about these dynamics. Having been brought up within the traditional gang structures and ideologies and having experienced their youthful primes during their organizations' heydays understandably gave these individuals an affinity for the halcyon glory days, so to speak. They pointed out that the older generations of gang members and leaders against whom youthful members had rebelled had earned their stripes by "putting in work" on the streets to build their respective organizations, effectively laying the foundation for those younger members. Thus, in many ways, they understandably lamented the demise of this era and the historical disconnect that they perceived among the younger generations.[35] On the other hand, these older individuals—a number of whom held prominent leadership roles within their respective organizations—also admitted in their interviews that sound and fair leadership during the era of hierarchical gang structures was often compromised by ego, nepotism, exploitation, and manipulation of the rank and file. In part, they interpreted these dynamics as a by-product of the prioritization of economic imperatives within their organizations, which sometimes worked to privilege effective earners over quality leaders, as well as the removal of more talented and committed gang leaders via federal prison. Roosevelt and Eldridge offer insights into each of these respective perspectives:

ROOSEVELT: Most of these young cats don't know that the older guys is the reason why they can stand out there. 'Cause if it wasn't for the older guys to put the work in and make the organization strong, they wouldn't even be out there doin' what they doin' now! So they have to realize where they come from. . . . They only live the fast life and be gone quick 'cause they don't have no history. They don't know they background. And they think they know everything [*laughing*]. But they don't have no structure behind it.

ELDRIDGE: Some people get in play and be in power strong and not thinkin' with a clear mind. You know, they had a lil money so somebody could put 'em in play. They was somebody favorite, so somebody put 'em in play. And then just don't know how to handle it. You know, they say with great power come great responsibility. Or power with no perception is no power at all. So a lot of people that was in play were probably takin' advantage of it. . . . And as you get older, you start to see a lot of shit was foul. Like, damn, man, they was manipulatin' us. Man, they was takin' advantage of us. But in a manner, hey, well, we was shorties.

These perspectives point to the complex and somewhat conflicted legacy of Chicago's traditional institutionalized gangs, even among older gang members. "Gangs are more than one thing," as Hagedorn argues.[36] Indeed, perhaps nowhere has this been truer than in Chicago, where the city's traditional street gangs embodied elements of both broad-based quasi-religious brotherhoods as well as exploitive outlaw-capitalist drug organizations. In any event, the shattering of these traditional black street gangs during the first decade of the twenty-first century set the stage for the fundamental transformation of gang dynamics on the city's South Side. The particularities of this transformation are explored in chapter 2.

Chapter Two

FROM STREET ORGANIZATIONS TO CLIQUES

Black Street Gangs in Chicago Today

The rebellions within Chicago's black street gangs during the first decade or so of the twenty-first century rendered the leadership structures and organizational arrangements that had distinguished these gangs for decades effectively obsolete. In the wake of these rebellions, youthful gang members have refashioned their gangs in radically new ways that often stand in direct contrast to the traditional corporate-style gangs that they supplanted. This chapter describes these newly reconstituted black street gangs on Chicago's South Side, focusing, in particular, on their organizational configurations and leadership structures, culture and ideologies, bases of solidarity, issues related to collective and personal identity, and their involvement in drug dealing. The ways in which these gang characteristics and dynamics diverge from those that predominated during the corporate gang period of the 1980s and 1990s will also be emphasized. In general, the findings presented here signify a radically new era in the history of street gangs on Chicago's South Side during the first two decades of the twenty-first century.

FROM OBEDIENCE TO AUTONOMY: GANG CULTURE AND STRUCTURE IN THE TWENTY-FIRST CENTURY

As described briefly in chapter 1, beginning in the 1960s, the leaders of Chicago's major African American gangs had built their respective organizations into broad-based, cross-neighborhood, hierarchically structured gang nations. The neighborhood branches of these gangs fell under the jurisdiction of their respective central leadership bodies, which typically wielded autocratic power in dictating gang policy, enforcing discipline, conferring promotions, and controlling gang warfare. The rebellions explored in chapter 1, however, put an end to these long-standing arrangements, freeing neighborhood sets from this often coercive and exploitive control and restoring autonomy at the local level. Indeed, study participants were unequivocal in declaring that their gangs operate independently and govern themselves, and that the days of external oversight and authority are over. Lacking legitimate central leadership, moreover, formalized coordination between the one-time chapters of these traditional gangs has all but disappeared, as local gangs have retreated into the comfort of what they are best able to understand and manage: their immediate neighborhoods. Many larger and more geographically dispersed sets, which once may have boasted upward of one hundred members and twenty square blocks of territory, have split into two or three or four independent groups, each with as few as a dozen members and a couple of blocks to claim as their own. In short, today's gangs are not sets or even "factions" of cross-neighborhood gang organizations like their forebears, as those organizations have effectively ceased to exist as such. Marco explains these dynamics as they relate to his neighborhood as follows:

MARCO: Everybody doin' they own thing. Everybody independent. We govern ourself.

RRA: What's the relationship like between y'all and the BDs from other hoods?

MARCO: I would say we really don't got one with 'em. Not because we dislike each other, it's because my block, that's our world, you feel me? Our problems ain't they problems, just like they problems ain't our problems. . . . So it's all sixteen [friendly] between us, like, "Oh, what's up, bro?" "Yeah, what's up? Woo, woo, woo." But them dudes down there ain't bro right there [*motioning in the direction of the next room, where his friend is waiting*], you know? [The bond is] stronger between us, though.

In this sense of neighborhood independence and self-governance, today's gangs might be understood as a throwback to the adolescent street-corner groups that represented the predominant gang typology in Chicago prior to the formation of the black and Latino gang nations beginning in the 1960s. This archetype was immortalized most famously in Frederic Thrasher's foundational 1927 tome, *The Gang*. Crucial differences between these periods, however, both in terms of their historical contexts as well as the specificities of gang dynamics, preclude such simple comparisons. Importantly, for example, not only have the central leadership hierarchies of Chicago's black street gangs been rendered obsolete—if not eradicated entirely—but, in a break from all periods of the city's gang history, formal positions of leadership at the neighborhood level have also been largely, if not universally, eliminated.[1]

In place of traditional chains of command or even the established predominance of one or two local gang leaders, Chicago's youthful African American gang members have established egalitarian arrangements based on a delicate balance of collectivist ideals, mutual respect, and personal autonomy. These horizontally oriented arrangements represent an unmistakable repudiation of the vertical organization and culture of obedience that had characterized Chicago's street gangs for decades as well as the ideologies, codified in each gang's respective literature, that had legitimized them. The city's young gang rebels have been decidedly uninterested in replacing their gangs' deposed leaders and assuming their autocratic power. Rather, they have focused on reshaping their gangs in ways that are distinctly more democratic. Thus, while natural leaders may emerge organically within a neighborhood, the battles young gang members waged against former gang leaders should be understood as a rejection of conventional gang ideologies rooted in authoritarian power hierarchies and as a manifestation of new ideologies founded on egalitarianism and autonomy. Here, Carlos and Montrelle offer insights into the democratization of Chicago's black street gangs and the ways in which current gang dynamics contrast from those of past eras.

CARLOS: It's just a mutual respect now, you feel me? You still got the old heads out here, you know what I'm sayin', the big Folks . . . [but] it ain't no chief or no kings or none of that shit no more. Nah, it ain't like that no more, like in the nineties and shit. Everybody for they own, G. . . . [There] used to be structure and all that shit, but you your own man out here.

MONTRELLE: We usually come together and talk and weigh out the pros and cons of things. You know, so it's mainly mutual decisions. . . . Certain people got more influence than others because certain people been around longer and survived more, but there's no set leaders or anything. We all together. . . . He may be the man on the block 'cause he might got this amount of money or he may have did this and that, but at the same time he just like the rest of us.

Although participants often talked about their gangs as having "no structure"—a common refrain among older former group members when speaking about today's gangs as well—these egalitarian arrangements do not simply reflect an inevitable abolition of internal gang stratification, passively accepted by youthful gang members in the wake of gang fracturing. Rather, they reveal the adoption of fundamentally new ideologies among young African American gang members, the nature of which is apparent in not only these horizontal gang structures but also in how new gang members are being socialized by their counterparts. Under the premise of collectivism in service of broad-based gang nationhood, gang socialization during previous decades stressed obedience to an authoritarian and often coercive and exploitive chain of command. In direct contrast, the socialization of new gang members today emphasizes ideals of equality and autonomy alongside traditional gang principles like collectivism and loyalty. The culture of obedience that long defined Chicago's traditional black street gangs, in short, has been supplanted by a culture of autonomy. Indeed, young gang members are encouraged to consciously and vigorously resist the types of autocratic domination that pervaded the city's gangs during previous decades.

In practical terms, this means that established gang members in their late teens and twenties are telling the fourteen- and fifteen-year-old youngsters in their neighborhoods who are just "jumping off the porch" that they are their "own man" in the streets and that they should not let anyone—not even the older gang members themselves—exploit them, bully them, or otherwise control them. In contrast to previous gang dynamics, when messages of brotherhood and unity often contrasted with gang members' structural subordination to authoritarian intragroup power hierarchies, the ideologies of today's gangs are remarkably consistent with the daily experiences of gang life.[2] As such, they can be understood as behavioral prescriptions. Consider the following passage from my interview with Zeke, in which he explains the ideologies of autonomy and resistance with which he was socialized by his fellow gang members. Note the congruence between these values, his description of expectations for member behavior, and the internal group processes and structural arrangements within his gang.

ZEKE: All of us got say-so.

RRA: What do you mean by that?

ZEKE: Like, you know how the clique have that one big homie? All of us big homies. We make our own decisions, you know? Like how they be tellin' me, like, "Don't let nobody send you off [take advantage of or manipulate you]. If your gut tellin' you 'no,' listen to your gut. Don't let nobody make you be a send-off or nothing like that. Listen to what your mind tellin' you. If you think it's not right to do it, don't do it. If you think it's right, well go on 'head." You know, and stuff like that.

Only one study participant, Marco, described the existence of an official leadership title within his gang that was recognized as having legitimacy in the eyes of its current members. Unlike positions of gang leadership in previous eras, however, this position—"first Demetrius," a traditional Black Disciple leadership position—was purely symbolic and did not involve formal authority or concrete benefits of any kind. Rather, the title represented an honor the group bestowed on one of its own, as opposed to a promotion or a formalization of conferred power or authority. Indeed, that none of the other three members of Marco's gang who were interviewed for this study even mentioned this position of leadership at all—despite being asked questions on the subject—seems a clear indication of the strictly honorary and intimate nature of the position. Moreover, in contrast to the top-down approach to gang leadership development in the 1990s in which gang leaders wielded authority over promotions, the first Demetrius position described by Marco can be understood as emerging from the bottom up, as it was voted on democratically by all of the group's active members. In fact, in spite of the existence of this position of leadership, Marco and his comrades espoused perhaps the most coherent and consistent commitment to the ideologies of autonomy, democracy, and resistance of all participants in this study. Marco explains these prerogatives and their relation to symbolic leadership in his neighborhood in recounting the democratic process by which that leadership was transferred:

MARCO: It's *no* type of authority with us. All our opinion[s] count. 'Cause you one of my brothers, you know? So that's the only type of thing. On our block, ain't no "big I's" and "little you's." Like, when they was havin' a vote to who gon' have the block, you know, it's called first D—that's first Demetrius. It's a old term for it, but . . .

RRA: So when you say "have the block," what do you mean?

MARCO: Basically, the face of the block. Ain't nothing different, though. The face of the block, you the one who gon' say, "Hey, man, we gon' have a meeting on Sunday." That's all he do, you feel me?

RRA: So who was talking about doing the vote?

MARCO: My homie, Rillo, he's one of the older guys. He been with the shit since he was thirteen, you feel me, he been gangbangin' hard since he was thirteen. He said, "Man, I'm finna give the block up. Y'all have a vote." So it's just like that. . . . We had a vote. . . . My homie, Jay, ended up gettin' the block, you know, he had [the most] hands raised.

Even in Lamont and Rasheed's neighborhood, where the local Black P Stones have maintained a reputation for their traditional gang structure, the power of former gang leaders over younger members today has diminished to the point of virtual nonexistence. Many of these older individuals, perhaps recognizing their waning influence with—much less control over—younger gang members, have transitioned into jobs with local community agencies and grassroots organizations. Lamont, who had also been able to parlay his experiences and reputation as a gang member into a job with a local nonprofit organization, describes these dynamics as follows:

How has it changed? It's no structure. It's no leadership. . . . The structure in my hood amongst the older men is still there. Amongst young people like me, it's not. It's a lot of people dead, it's a lot of disloyalty, it's a lot of people that turned state's [evidence] on cases, you know, things of that nature. But as far as that older group of people who were around for the original piece, they're still around, they're still active, they're still involved in the community. Their outlook is different. They're not pushin' drugs—they're pushin' jobs, they're pushin' education, they're empowering youth. They're doin' what they should have been doin' from the jump, but except they were young men at that time, and [the streets] had them swallowed up.

This transformation from gang leader to youth advocate and community worker described by Lamont has conceivably allowed former gang leaders to maintain, to some extent, a well-defined role within the neighborhood that carries with it some degree of esteem. While such efforts by one-time gang leaders were generally respected and, in some ways, even admired by current gang members, Rasheed emphasized the generational disconnect described by Lamont and made it clear that current gang members in his neighborhood were taking no orders from the "old heads." Indeed, although his references to "order" and "keep[ing] shit tightened up" seem to suggest the maintenance of more traditional notions of gang collectivism and obedience, Rasheed ultimately describes ideologies, group structures, and processes of socialization that are nearly identical to those explained by Zeke and Marco.

RRA: So is it still directive as far as, you know, the older guys saying, "This is how it's gonna be"?

RASHEED: Nah. Now, it's like, fuck what they said, [whether] I'm right or wrong, you feel me? So if a mu'fucka bogus, they bogus, so it ain't really about what the old heads say. It's about who gon' say something when shit get out of order. 'Cause they old. They ain't movin' no muscle. So it's really up to the mu'fuckas around my age, lil bit older, to keep shit tightened up, you feel me, make sure the younger guys stay on point. 'Cause they don't got no relationship with [the younger members]. The older heads might rap with 'em every now and then, but that shit probably go right in one ear and out the other. I'm kickin' it with these lil niggas so they lookin' at me eye-to-eye, know what I'm sayin'? I'm just a couple years older than they are.

Here Rasheed contrasts the relationship between the "old heads" and the younger generations of gang members, which he describes as nonexistent, with his own relationship with his comrades a few years his junior, relationships that he characterizes in egalitarian terms as being "eye-to-eye." Rasheed goes on to describe one of the guys a few years his senior—a "crucial Brother"—who had a profound impact on him as well as the broader cultural shift within the neighborhood.

RASHEED: He like, "Man, don't let a mu'fucka trick you. Don't let a mu'fucka go on you [discipline you], woo wop the bam." . . . He the first one who put it in our head like *we* the law.

RRA: So do the younger guys take direction from y'all? Like, if you come on the block, are you tellin' somebody that's fourteen or fifteen, "Hey, look, this what you gonna do"?

RASHEED: We ain't on no—we ain't *tellin'* a mu'fucka to do nothing. . . . I think they be listenin', but they still do what the fuck they wanna do, just like we was doin' what the fuck we wanted to do. I just hope they listen for [their own benefit].

The ability to "do what [you] wanna do" represents a central organizing principle—indeed, perhaps *the* central organizing principle—of gang life for young gang members on Chicago's South Side today. This fierce ethos of personal autonomy is readily apparent in the horizontal form of organization that characterizes today's gangs. In accordance with their ideologies of autonomy and egalitarianism, moreover, these groups have abolished the practice of violations, the physical beatings long employed by gang leaders as a tool of discipline and coercion. Study participants made it clear that, while internal disputes might be resolved in a variety of ways, including fistfights, the type of authority necessary to order and carry out violations no longer exists in their gangs in any form. When asked about the use of violations today, for example, Memphis simply replied, "Man, that shit *been* over with." (The nearly boundless nature of personal autonomy and the extent of the ideological rejection of violations and other mechanisms of collective social control within today's gangs, as well as the effects of these developments on the nature of gang violence, are explored in greater detail in chapter 3.)

Alongside the eradication of central and local leadership hierarchies and the establishment of egalitarianism and autonomy as essential governing ideologies, the increasing importance that young gang members place on personal relationships, alluded to in many of the quoted passages included in this section, represents another striking new dimension in the evolution of Chicago's black street gangs. Indeed, this development has contributed not only to the further reorganization of the internal dynamics of these groups but has also fundamentally transformed intergang dynamics across much of the South Side as well.

THE DECLINING SIGNIFICANCE OF TRADITIONAL GANG AFFILIATION

Perhaps an even more stunning development than the abolition of gang leadership structures has been the declining significance of traditional gang affiliations (e.g., Gangster Disciples, Mickey Cobras) in shaping the nature of contemporary relationships among gang members on Chicago's South Side. As discussed briefly in chapter 1, gang members are now openly forging alliances and even formally unifying with members of longtime rival organizations. This dynamic, generally referred to as "cliquing up," is taking place both *between* today's independent neighborhood gangs as well as *within* these gangs. In other words, not only are gangs with historically rival affiliations developing informal cross-neighborhood alliances, but individual gangs themselves increasingly comprise members with various traditional gang affiliations. In accordance with the framing of this practice as "cliquing up," gang members today often refer to these amalgamations as "cliques." Jabari succinctly describes this new form of gang as follows: "A clique is a group of people who don't represent the same organization, but they form an organization. . . . You a Gangster, I'm a Stone, he BD. We all together."

Table 2.1, which specifies the traditional gang affiliations represented in each of the study participants' gangs, reveals the near-ubiquity of such intergang unifications. While eleven of the fourteen gangs to which participants belong have retained a traditional gang affiliation as the predominant identity within their group (represented in the table by bold text), only three of these gangs consist of members who all share the same traditional gang affiliation. The remaining eleven represent a mixture of various traditional identities.

Clearly, such affiliations no longer function as the incontrovertible basis for association among Chicago gang members. Like the breakdown of gang leadership hierarchies and the establishment of local egalitarian forms of internal gang governance, the declining significance of traditional gang

TABLE 2.1
Traditional Gang Identities in Participants' Gangs

Participant(s)	Traditional gang identities represented in gang
Floyd, Montrelle, Terrence, Rick	**Mickey Cobras**, Black Disciples
Durrell, Memphis, Kevin	**Black Disciples**
Roosevelt, Melvin, Cassius	Outlaw Gangster Disciples, Mickey Cobras, Black P Stones
Lamont, Rasheed	**Black P Stones**
David, Bibby, Cedric	**Insane Gangster Disciples**, Black P Stones, Mickey Cobras
Carlos	**Black Disciples**, Gangster Disciples, Black P Stones
Cortez, Daequan	**Gangster Disciples**, Black P Stones, Four Corner Hustlers
Ronald	Gangster Disciples, Black P Stones, Vice Lords
Aaron	Gangster Disciples, Black Disciples, Black P Stones, Vice Lords
Antonio	**Black P Stones**, Black Disciples, Gangster Disciples
Reggie	**Insane Gangster Disciples**
Javon	**Gangster Disciples**, Black Disciples, Black P Stones, Mickey Cobras
Harold, Marco, Weezy, Zeke	**Black Disciples**, Gangster Disciples
Bernard, Jabari, James	**Gangster Disciples**, Insane Gangster Disciples, Black Disciples, Black P Stones

Note: Bolded names of traditional street gangs indicate numerical and/or symbolic predominance within a particular gang. Where no street gang name is bolded, no one identity predominates.

affiliations signifies a radical departure from the city's gang customs and a fierce rejection of conventional gang doctrines by young members. These gang members generally view the city's decades-old ideological gang rivalries with disdain and openly flout these customary antagonisms by building alliances across once-unassailable gang fault lines. Participants' rejection of ideological gangbanging is apparent in the following quotes from Carlos and Rasheed, in which they characterize these traditions as impractical "bullshit" and a form of divisive "segregation," respectively. The ability to build relationships across gang lines, moreover, is simply taken for granted in these statements and can therefore also be understood as a manifestation of the emphasis on individual autonomy among contemporary gangs on Chicago's South Side. In other words, gang members today have embraced the notion that the license to determine relationships on the streets rests with individual gang members themselves, as opposed to being contingent on traditional gang affiliations.

RRA: So is everybody from your hood BD, then?

CARLOS: Nah, not necessarily. It's a lot of renegade shit goin' on—a lot of bar-none shit goin' on out here in the field right now, so it really ain't even mu'fuckas goin' by them laws, you feel me? . . . It's just really who you know. Like I say, it ain't even about, oh, I'm a Stone, he a Lord, and he a Gangster. Or he Folks, and he such-and-such. It ain't even like that no more. It's really: Is you tryin' to get to this money or you on some bullshit? It's really common sense out here now, you feel me? I fuck with everybody, man.

RASHEED: I don't really give a fuck what [traditional gang] a mu'fucka is. That shit personal. . . . Real fuck with real, so at the end of the day, that gangbangin' shit [is] really all fucked up. That's segregation. That shit real—that segregation shit real, B. They segregated us with that shit, know what I'm sayin'?[3]

RRA: Is everybody from your block Stone, then? 'Cause you know, depending on where you're at, sometimes it be a mixture.

RASHEED: Yeah, we all [*pounds his right fist over his heart, a Stone salute*]. Ain't none of that other shit. Well, it's other people that we know that's something else, but the main squad, everybody from my block, is Stone. Now, everybody got they friends that might come to the block who ain't Stone and shit. Like, my homie who locked up right now for the hit that I could've been on, he was GD.

In place of traditional gang affiliations, personal relationships have become the primary foundation through which associations are shaped within and between Chicago's street gangs. Along with the rejection of customary gang ideologies and the increasing centrality of personal autonomy among the city's youthful gang members, this shift has been driven by a number of interrelated factors. As described earlier, today's gangs have become more insular, shunning the type of high-level city and prison gang politics that had shaped Chicago's gangland since at least the 1970s and shifting their focus toward local concerns. Accordingly, the loyalties of current gang members are no longer shaped by identification with now-defunct cross-neighborhood traditional street gangs, but rather with their immediate circle of comrades with whom they share close personal relationships and much of their daily lives. In addition, the heightened insularity and diminished organizational complexity of today's gangs has reduced the need for broad-based membership, and most of the participants in this study reported having less than twenty core members in their respective groups. These shifts have also made once-essential divisions of labor unnecessary, pushing women further toward the margins of these gangs and leaving little room for members beyond their mid-twenties.[4] Indeed, study participants were essentially unanimous in reporting that their comrades were all between sixteen and twenty-five years old and exclusively male.

The near-wholesale demolition of Chicago's public housing developments, moreover, has meant that these comrades are increasingly likely to identify as members of different—and, often, rival—traditional street gangs. As thousands of project-based gang members were displaced into gang territories throughout the city's black neighborhoods, contact with and familiarity between members of longtime rival gangs rose dramatically. This dynamic was a primary catalyst for a paradigm shift that has persisted even after these demolitions and displacements largely wound down late in the first decade of the twenty-first century. The waning influence of gang leaders and conventional gang ideologies has meant that young gang members are increasingly amenable to building relationships across traditional gang fault lines, with shared experiences in the streets serving to cement these intergang bonds. In the following passages, Harold and Aaron expound on these dynamics.

HAROLD: It go off sets now, you know? It could be BDs, GDs, they just together 'cause they off that same block. That's how it be now.

RRA: So it's not whatever organization you are as much as it is who you with?

HAROLD: Basically, who you with and what set you be at, yup. . . . People stay on they block and they just get to kickin' it and then they respect them as them bein' that gang. [If] somebody get killed, they'll just name it after that person. And if you knew that person, but you a different gang, you [are going to be] with them, too. You just call it a set. Like, I'm from Tre World—we call ourself Tre World [named after a member who was killed by the police]. We BDs, but it might be some GDs that's cool with us, you know what I'm sayin', that's already been with us, though. Back in the day, it was just straight: y'all all BDs, y'all all GDs, woo, woo, woo, all Stones. But now it's cliques.

AARON: Man, it ain't no structure. It's gang-on-gang shit, really. It's just neighborhoods. Mu'fucka claim that gang shit, but it's all about your neighborhood—where you from. Like, it's Terror Town, O-Block, all that. That's what the fuck it is. It ain't no GD, BD, shit like that. That's all it is, basically: where the fuck you grew up at and who you with.

The supplanting of traditional gang allegiances with a new paradigm of loyalty rooted in individual autonomy and personal relationships has thrown Chicago's streets into a type of disarray not seen since the tumultuous early days of cross-neighborhood black and Latino gang organizing in the 1960s. Gang loyalties that had endured for decades have been called into question, dissolved, and/or imploded, and new relationships and alliances have been formed. These dynamics have routinely given rise to conflicting expectations and loyalties, forcing gang members to make difficult choices and leading to intragang violence. This process of allegiance renegotiation, in turn, has further contributed to the splintering of Chicago's traditional gang structures.

These idiosyncratic and often-complex dynamics are evident in Terrence's account of the violent fracturing of his Mickey Cobra set, Free Block, after a fierce war between two nearby gangs with whom Free Block was allied created an intergenerational rift within the gang. On one side of the war was Bang City, a Cobra set adjacent to Free Block and a longtime ally. On the other side was D-Mob, a nearby set of Black Disciples with whom younger members of Free Block like Terrence and Rick shared close friendships. In short, the young MCs from Free Block sided with their friends from D-Mob in the conflict, while the older MCs from Free Block sided with their Cobra neighbors and allies from Bang City. These divided loyalties ultimately shattered Free Block's decades-old Cobra stronghold, which devolved into open intragang warfare as an extension of the original conflict between D-Mob and Bang City. The bond between the young members of Free Block and D-Mob, moreover, eventually led to a merger of sorts in which some members of D-Mob, including Floyd and Montrelle, began claiming Free Block as their primary affiliation, while simultaneously maintaining their Black Disciple identity and their bonds with their D-Mob comrades. The salience of personal relationships, the declining importance of traditional gang affiliation, and the imperviousness of young gang members to the control of older gang leaders are all evident in Terrence's account of this process.

TERRENCE: With me, it's not really about what gang you is, it's more of how the *person* you is that makes me dislike you. That was the problem with us and the MCs, too, 'cause we associate ourself with more of the BDs. Like D-Mob,

Goodfellas, KPB, them the people we hang with. And the MCs didn't like that. And we didn't care. . . .

Basically, [that's] the story of how we got into it with Bang City. Like, I was cool with most of them [*pausing*] . . . majority of them [*pausing*] . . . cool with all of 'em! . . . The whole Indiana all the way back to Federal, [during] my brother era, all them was together. They grew up together. They was the gang—they was the MCs. We MC, but as we growin' up, it got segregated. Like, our older guys, they was still messin' with certain people down there. But as we grew up, we wasn't goin' down there talkin' to them like that. We stayed on our side, from Indiana to Wabash, [and] they stayed on they side. That's when it started separatin' like that between our neighborhood. . . . Certain people didn't get along with them. You know, Montrelle, Black [both Black Disciples originally from D-Mob], they didn't get along with 'em.

RRA: What kind of position did that put you in?

TERRENCE: Man, it put me in a bad predicament at first 'cause I was still goin' to MC meetings and all that. So, basically, all the attention was fallin' on me. After a while, I just stopped caring. So I don't like nobody now. I don't talk to none of them—none of the older guys. We actually into it with them, too. Like, we shoot at them, too. I don't talk to nobody but my crowd I know.

RRA: So what made you make the decision as far as, okay, these the guys that I'm riding with?

TERRENCE: [The older guys] started givin' Bang City guns. And, basically, they givin' them guns to shoot at us. . . . That left me with a choice: I have to pick sides. I've been knowin' Black and Montrelle almost all my life, so [I sided with them].

Even as gang members have rejected long-standing alliances based on gang affiliations and united with traditional enemies on the basis of locality and personal relationships, however, the legacy of Chicago's traditional black street gangs remains deeply embedded in the fabric of the city's gang culture. Remarkably, present-day gang members, including the study participants, have not abandoned their traditional gang identities as Black Disciples, Mickey Cobras, Gangster Disciples, Black P Stones, and the like. Even those too young to remember—much less have taken part in—the era when these gangs existed and functioned as formidable street organizations/gang nations have adopted these identities, and this practice continues unabated among subsequent generations of gang members today. Given the reorganization of gangs on Chicago's South Side as independent neighborhood-based collectives, it would have been easy and seemingly rational for these youthful gang members to simply abandon these old labels and assume new, exclusively neighborhood-based group identities. Yet they have almost universally retained these identities.[5] Clearly, association with these traditional street gangs remains an essential element of identity among the city's gang members.

The nature and implications of these identities, however, are drastically different today than during previous decades. More specifically, identifying with one of these traditional street gangs no longer entails "gang membership" in the conventional sense of the term, as, for all intents and purposes, these gangs no longer exist as organizations unified in any substantive sense—certainly not as hierarchically structured gang nations and, increasingly, not even as homogeneous neighborhood sets. Instead of functioning as a basis for formalizing and sustaining collective ideologies and bonds, then, these traditional gang identities are now viewed in largely individual terms, as gang members draw on them in fashioning their personal identities, mannerisms, styles, and ideologies. "That shit personal," as Rasheed proclaimed. The adoption of renegade gang identities as well as the rare instances in which a gang member "flips" and changes their traditional gang identity entirely push this individualistic paradigm to even further lengths. In previous eras, these practices were treated as treasonous defections; today, they are routinely regarded as a logical extension of personal autonomy and a legitimate form of individual identity construction.

Consider the following examples described by James and Jabari, who hail from the same block in the midst of one of the Gangster Disciples' largest traditional strongholds. The shattering of the gang's organizational structure had fractured their sizable neighborhood set into a number of smaller, independent gangs, which coexisted uneasily for a period of time under a façade of friendship and unity before festering tensions eventually bubbled over into open internecine warfare.[6] These dynamics created something of an identity crisis for James and Jabari. The respective ways in which they resolved this crisis reveal both the continued significance of traditional gang identities as well as the contemporary emphasis on resistance, autonomy, and individuality in the construction of these identities.

For his part, Jabari adopted an identity as an "Insane" Gangster Disciple, an example of the overtly renegade identities increasingly popular among today's young gang members. These identities typically involve the addition of "Outlaw," "Nolaw," "Insane," or "Renegade" in front of the name of a traditional street gang, a practice that allows gang members to both maintain their original gang identities as well as symbolically repudiate notions of subordination to the ideologies and hierarchies traditionally associated with these gangs. This has been a particularly common practice among disgruntled members of the Gangster Disciples, long Chicago's largest and most fully corporatized street gang, which had rebellious factions developing during the organization's 1990s peak, if not earlier.[7] Cassius, for example, describes the Outlaw Gangster Disciples as follows:

CASSIUS: The Outlaws, they ain't really got no board of directors. So they ain't really got nobody who lay the game plan for mu'fuckas. They really do what they wanna do, the Outlaws.

RRA: So what's their relationship with the traditional Gangster Disciples?

CASSIUS: They branched off from the original Gangsters and made theyself the Outlaw Gangsters. . . . They wanted they own, you know, set of laws or—which they don't have [*laughing*]. So, shit. Yeah, they wanted to do things on they own.

In practical terms, these titles no longer denote renegade factions of a broader gang organization as, again, such organizations no longer exist. Rather, they represent identities—sometimes collective, sometimes individual—that are increasingly being adopted by young gang members from a wide variety of the city's black street gangs.[8] Those who embrace these identities often assume a stance as categorical enemies of the street gangs from which they consider themselves renegades. At the very least, a central element of such identities involves a willingness, if not an outright desire, to engage members of the renegades' traditional street gangs in violent conflict. In the following passage, Jabari describes both the psychology as well as the practical implications of such renegade identities within the context of contemporary Chicago gang culture. He reports that his adoption of an "Insane" identity was essentially unremarkable in the eyes of his comrades, most of whom, nonetheless, chose to maintain their traditional identities as Gangster Disciples. As Jabari points out, however, those who embrace these renegade identities often run into problems in Illinois jails and prisons, where traditional gang structures have retained greater influence.

JABARI: Everybody renegadin' it, throwing up "L's" and "I's" and shit. . . ."I," that's Insane. I got that [tattooed] on my neck. We Insane Gangsters—IGD.

RRA: So do y'all differentiate yourselves from the regular GDs?

JABARI: We the same, but an Insane GD will get into it with other Gangsters. Like, I get into it with other Gangsters, that's why I'm Insane GD.

RRA: So are y'all still cool with some of the regular GDs, too, then?

JABARI: All of my homies regular GDs; ain't none of them "I." I'm still trying to make them "I"—put the "I" on they backs.

RRA: So what's the whole Insane thing, then?

JABARI: You can be Insane anything—it's renegades. Just like "L's." Like, if I go to the joint and I'm yellin' "Insane," the GDs gon' beat my ass. 'Cause they: "Leave that shit in the world." When you come on the deck, it's all Folks—it's Larry's guys. On my mama: seven, four, fourteen.[9] I be like, "Fuck that, I'm Insane!" They gon': "What? Take him to the back. Matter of fact, get him off the deck. Whoop him—send him to ATG." I keep fightin', I keep fightin', I'm 'a go to ATG—against the grain [a segregated unit]. That's where I'm 'a have to be. And that's where all the "L's" and them niggas be. That's how the County rockin' right now—ATG. Everybody ATG in there.

For James, the infighting and betrayals in his neighborhood fueled intense feelings of uncertainty and distrust that eventually colored his views of not only his gang's ostensible allies from adjacent blocks but of some of his closest comrades as well. Following a reflective period of incarceration, he resolved to leverage his recently forged relationship with a number of Black P Stones—the Gangster Disciples' oldest and fiercest rivals—to "flip Black Stone."[10] He explains his decision as follows:

JAMES: I was a Gangster at first. I flipped Black Stone, you know what I'm sayin', 'cause I wasn't really rockin' with the guys like that no more. And all the older niggas I fuck with, we just fuck with each other on money-wise, so really that gangbangin' shit didn't really come into hand with them, you feel me? But as far as that, I told myself I couldn't see myself saying, I'm one of the guys shaking your hand, shakin' up [performing a gang handshake] with you, and kickin' it with you outside, parlaying with you, knowin' that I'd kill you. Knowing that me and you done had bad words and knowing that certain situations that got took so far to the point where, shit, nigga, I'm 'a kill you. You a man like I'm a man, but I'm 'a kill you first. You feel me, because I done seen shit—the guys robbed the guys, the guys done *killed* the guys.

RRA: In the same mob?

JAMES: Yeah, in the same mob, same organization. So, shit, I don't want to be a part of that. I can't say you my homie if I know he gon' kill me down the line if I do something he don't like or we come across each other on bad terms, you know what I'm sayin'?

RRA: So the hood that you were originally from, that's the hood you still kicking it in now, or a different area?

JAMES: I'm still in the same area, [but] I also be in different areas 'cause by me being Black Stone. Other than that, it's still cool. I know niggas don't like what I did when I did flip, but niggas ain't gonna do nothing. 'Cause they know who I am, so they ain't gonna do nothing. They know what I can do.

Although driven by a similar desire to alter his Gangster Disciple identity within the context of organizational implosion and internecine warfare, James's conversion to the Black P Stones was interpreted among his comrades as a repudiation of this identity, whereas Jabari's adoption of the "Insane" identity was viewed as a less offensive modification. Yet, in spite of defying popular sentiment among his peers on the block, James's decision was ultimately regarded by these peers as an acceptable expression of personal autonomy and individual identity construction. The Stones that James joined up with were not direct enemies of his original Gangster Disciple neighborhood, and as long as he did not formally denounce that neighborhood, his GD peers would tolerate his conversion. Indeed, as he expresses below, Jabari even believed that this transition would ultimately prove beneficial for his friend—that being a Stone would "help him be better as a man."

JABARI: Bro just left. Like, he ain't talk to nobody. He talked to me, but he was locked up. And then I'm like, "Man, you ain't even gotta do that shit, bro. Niggas is gon' look at you different. It ain't like we gon' love you different, just respect out of a man. Like, people on the street look at that shit."

RRA: So why do you think he did that, then?

JABARI: Because he felt uncomfortable around niggas he was Gangsters with. But still, them niggas ain't never did nothing to you. At the end of the day, them niggas gon' kill somebody for you. At the end of the day, nigga, this is the hood you servin' [selling drugs] in. You could have been Insane first [as opposed to flipping to Stone]. . . .

It's just certain shit you don't do. He ain't have to do that, though. He just felt like, "Man, I don't wanna be Gangster no more. I'll kill one of them Folks." "Nah, bro. What you think you doin' now? You was just Gangster and you was just beatin' up the Folks. What you mean? It's the same thing, it's just these are our guys we know." . . . And he flipped strong. He fuckin' with some niggas who was Stonin' it. Shit, he like how them Moes move, I guess.

RRA: How did the guys on your block take it?

JABARI: They took it as, "Shit, oh well. James, he Stone? Oh well. He cool with us, shit, he still Rico World, woo, woo, woo," you feel me? Long as he ain't turn his whole back on us, like, he just gave us the [*sticking up his middle finger*]—you know? . . . But, see, this the thing when you a clique now—see, we went from a mob to a clique, right? I'm twenty-one. If this was back when we was like, let's say fifteen, fourteen, sixteen, he would have got his head knocked off. Like, they would've pumpkin-headed him, for real. That's what the GDs do—pumpkin heads. They'll take you to the back and beat your head 'til your shit literally look like Halloween. On my mama. . . .

But he good, though. I feel like the Moes gon' help him be better as a man. Folks really wasn't teaching him nothing. . . . A Moe gon' sit you down, show you how to do this and that, tell you how to be about it, be smart, woo, woo, woo. You know, they really brotherhood-ing it. We the Folks, like, it sound rugged—it sound just bad and grimy.

While young gang members have fundamentally refashioned Chicago's gang landscape in their image, localizing and democratizing governance, emphasizing autonomy and personal relationships, and rejecting traditional gang ideologies and divisions, external forces have also continued to have enormous effects on these gangs as well. Perhaps most notably, the declining urban drug economy, discussed in chapter 1 as a chief contributing factor in the weakening and eventual shattering of Chicago's traditional black street gangs, has continued to shape the city's gangs in important ways in the early twenty-first century.

ON (NOT) GETTING BY IN THE MARIJUANA-BASED DRUG ECONOMY

Chapter 1 explored the catastrophic effects that, in conjunction with several other major historical events, the waning demand for crack cocaine had on Chicago's corporate-style, outlaw-capitalist black street gangs at the dawn of the millennium. For many young rank-and-file gang members, shrinking drug revenues meant that they were increasingly marginalized within their gangs' drug-selling operations or even excluded from them entirely. The emergence of marijuana, typically a much less profitable drug from a distribution perspective, as the substance of choice among urban drug consumers during this period and its persistence as such into the present day has only exacerbated this dynamic. Thus, while selling drugs represented the focal point of gang life in Chicago during the 1980s and 1990s, the findings from this study emphatically indicate that, in the early twenty-first century, this is no longer the case. To the extent that participants in this study discussed selling drugs, it was often within a context of highlighting its decline within their communities and gangs. Few participants, moreover, described selling drugs other than marijuana, and the low levels of profitability associated with selling marijuana have left increasing numbers of gang members without even the most basic opportunities for income generation in the illicit drug trade. Their marginalization in the formal economy, in other words, now increasingly characterizes their experiences within the underground economy as well. The inability to earn money selling drugs has made basic survival increasingly difficult for many Chicago gang members, who are overwhelmingly excluded from conventional employment opportunities and whose families are typically poor.

While I had been keenly aware of these realities from my pre-research days working with young people on the South Side of Chicago, they came into even sharper focus during the course of my research. On one occasion in the field, for example, I was hanging out with some guys with whom I had previously worked outside of a corner store on a busy thoroughfare near the large apartment building where most of them live and that serves as their collective home base. It was a balmy eighty-degree summer day, and the streets were full of both car and pedestrian traffic, the latter driven in part by two nearby public train stations. The group of guys on the block grew from four or five to about a dozen or so as the afternoon wore on, and I eventually pulled a few of them away individually to conduct interviews. During one of these interviews, Memphis told me that he was the only one of his comrades on the block actively selling drugs. One of his peers later verified the veracity of this claim, which was also seemingly supported by the various phone calls that Memphis fielded from his friend whom he had left in charge of selling his drugs and who was attempting to make a sale to a haggling customer during our interview. That this was the dynamic in a neighborhood with a good amount of both car and foot traffic and proximity to both major public transportation and the Dan Ryan Expressway suggests the extent to which selling drugs has become a marginal part of gang life on Chicago's South Side. More generally, Memphis describes here the bleak realities he and his peers face in trying to survive on the streets as well as their desperate and escapist attempts to cope through their own substance abuse.

MEMPHIS: Like, right now—okay, you just seen . . .

RRA: Like, ten guys on the block.

MEMPHIS: And who you think hustlin'?

RRA: You tell me!

MEMPHIS: Me. Out of ten niggas! This what I'm sayin', everybody else just out there. It's just a typical day. And they only out there 'cause ain't no mu'fucka wanna be in no crib [house]! They ain't got no job, and a mu'fucka ain't got no money, so they just out there. Why you think everybody tryin' to jump on this [interview]? They broke—everybody broke. You know what I'm sayin'?

After you brought up in something for so long, you know, you gon' become condemned to shit. You gon' fall right in line with however the usual routine you been doin' every day. Most niggas wake up every day broke, tryin' to find a high, B. You know, that's fucked up, but it's the truth. . . . You ain't even buy yourself a fuckin' meal to eat! I'm sayin' this 'cause I witness—I done did this shit a couple of times. I done grew out the shit now, but it's fucked up that I know that's what's goin' on.

Beyond the problem of low demand, this desperate dynamic has also been fueled by the switch from open-air drug markets to the delivery-based drug-selling practices described briefly in chapter 1. Indeed, while made possible by the ubiquity of cell phones in the twenty-first century, this switch was also precipitated by the declining profitability of fixed, open-air drug markets driven by the decline of the crack era. In a mobile drug delivery model, fewer people are needed to serve as retail-level drug dealers, and the need for lookouts, security, runners, and other ancillary positions (read: jobs and attendant operating costs) associated with open-air markets are largely eliminated. The realities of rampant gang conflicts and police occupation, moreover, make selling drugs on a street corner a rather unattractive proposition in the face of a viable alternative.

That said, a number of participants made unprompted remarks about the persistence and continued profitability of open-air drug markets, particularly heroin markets, on Chicago's West Side. "The best heroin always been out West," Lorenzo, a West Side native, explains. "People came even from out South to get heroin from out West." The available evidence seems to corroborate these insights. A 2016 report from the Illinois Consortium on Drug Policy and Roosevelt University, for example, notes that the five communities that make up the core of Chicago's West Side each rank among the six communities with the highest rates of arrest for heroin possession in the city. The average rate of heroin possession in these communities, moreover, is more than four times higher than the average in the five South Side communities with the highest such rates, which include Englewood, New City, and Washington Park.[11] While a full empirical exploration of these dynamics is beyond the scope of this research, the important thing to note is that participants' references to ostensibly lucrative West Side drug markets functioned specifically to distinguish the relative poverty of their South Side counterparts. Floyd describes both the drug delivery sales model and the West Side's drug market predominance as follows:

FLOYD: Ain't no money really bein' made on no blocks, you know? All the money is in traffic, so you really not makin' no block hot from makin' money 'cause ain't no money really out there.

RRA: So when you sayin' the money is in traffic, you talkin' about dudes ridin' around, making they drop-offs and all of that?

FLOYD: Mm-hm. Pick-ups, drop-offs. You know, there's no block—well, not on the South Side. I can't speak for no other side of the city. But the South and East Sides, everybody in traffic because don't nobody wanna risk standin' on the block and gettin' shot at. . . .

> It's still out there, though. You know, I was out with some of my people out West earlier this year. And they still got money. Like, I recently seen my first brick of heroin. I didn't believe this shit was still goin' on in Chicago! I was shocked to see the shit!

Those participants in this study who reported selling drugs, moreover, admitted that their earnings from these activities were generally far below a basic subsistence wage. Indeed, as discussed in chapter 1, even during the height of the crack epidemic, when the earnings potential for retail-level drug dealers was likely at its peak, the wages for most of these dealers barely cracked the legal minimum wage.[12] Marijuana's displacement of crack as the substance of choice among most urban drug consumers, then, has only served to further erode these meager earnings. Although heroin use has made a major resurgence in recent years and selling heroin—like crack cocaine—is often much more lucrative than selling marijuana, the longtime predominance of West Side heroin markets appears to have rendered the markets on Chicago's South Side largely redundant. Thus, while a couple of participants talked about selling heroin, and their reports, as well as what I know from conversations with other individuals whom I know to sell heroin but did not interview formally, indicate that they tend to earn substantially more money than their counterparts who sell weed, the demand for heroin on Chicago's South Side simply does not appear high enough to make this an industry with broad-based employment opportunities for today's gang members. So while selling heroin provides a decent income for a relatively small number of South Side gang members, the drug's recent explosion in popularity has had little impact on the economic prospects of this population on any meaningful scale.[13]

In practical terms, many gang members today have difficulty earning enough money to ensure that they are able to feed themselves, indulge in their minor vices, and occasionally purchase a new outfit or pair of fashionable shoes. Of the thirty active gang members interviewed for this study, for example, only six owned a car at the time of their interview, and only two of these six had purchased their cars with money they earned from selling drugs; the others did so with money earned via conventional employment. In addition, as described by Memphis in a previous passage, gang members often turn to drug use, particularly marijuana, as a means of coping with their everyday experiences of marginality and despair. The fact that many gang members smoke marijuana themselves has the effect of sending whatever meager profit margins they might enjoy from their drug sales, quite literally, up in smoke. In short, although selling drugs was never very lucrative for the vast majority of Chicago gang members, contemporary patterns of drug consumption and distribution have intensified this harsh reality. In the following passage, James explains the near impossibility of effectively sustaining oneself as a retail-level marijuana dealer. Both the financial struggles associated with low-wage, menial—and, in this case, illegal—work, as well as a reliance on substance abuse as a coping mechanism in the face of such hardship are apparent in his account.

> It's a slight struggle, because you gotta understand—say if you buyin' weed. Okay, I'm finna buy a zip [an ounce] for $300, you know? I'm finna bag up $550, so I'm finna bag up fifty-five bags, all sawbucks [ten-dollar bags of marijuana for resale]. So I just spent $300. And I smoke weed, so now I'm finna smoke at least, by the time I been done sold the whole thing, if I ain't got a good line [a high demand], I done smoked $100 worth already. So now I'm goin' back to the store [mid-level drug supplier] with my $300, 'cause I'm puttin' $150 up [saving $150]. But, really, I ain't even put $150 up 'cause I'm smoking, so that mean I gotta buy Swishers.[14] And they two for a $1 or $0.75. So that's another $30 gone. You know, and I'm smokin' cigarettes, and now they, what, $12.75 a pack, $13 a pack. . . . And that depends on how many packs I go through a day. Then I'm buyin' food all day 'cause I'm high and I'm hungry. Then I gotta pay my phone bill, it's $50 a month, you know?
>
> So, really, it be hard to maintain. . . . You still gotta buy the weed, you gotta buy sandwich bags, you gotta buy a scale to weigh your weed, make sure they gave you the exact amount—the right amount for your money's worth. All that. It's a lot [of hassle], man. It's a lot.

The eradication of the organizational hierarchies of Chicago's traditional black street gangs, moreover, has made opportunities for mobility in the drug business all but nonexistent for the average Chicago gang member. As such, the few opportunities for drug business promotions that exist today are no longer attainable via traditional standards for advancement, such as "putting in work" for the gang as an effective salesperson or obedient soldier or being the beneficiary of internal gang politics. Instead, mobility in the drug game is increasingly dependent on key personal, and frequently familial, relationships with individuals in prominent positions within drug distribution networks. Crucially, these networks are no longer synonymous with the city's street gangs: Drugs are sold readily across gang lines, and drug networks, like today's gangs, often include members from a variety of traditional street gangs who are not beholden to traditional gang leadership structures. A Black Disciple from a predominantly Mickey Cobra gang might sell drugs for a Gangster Disciple. The old model of street-gang-as-drug-organization is largely, if not entirely, defunct at this point on Chicago's South Side. In the following passages, Carlos and Floyd describe a number of these dynamics. Carlos discusses the opportunities afforded him through his father's position as a drug distributor a couple of layers removed from the streets and alludes to the persistence of the drug trade as a highly stratified and fundamentally exploitive business. Floyd emphasizes the scarcity of opportunities for substantive entrée and mobility within the drug game, similarly framing these possibilities in terms of existing, often familial, relationships.

CARLOS: My daddy, he one of the big—he one of them niggas out here. . . . It's a saying. I don't know if it's the full saying, but like, it's people that do shit, and some people that [shit] gets done to them. I'm one of the people that benefit from the shit that's gettin' done, you feel me? I might not be the person that's doin' it, but I get beneficial off that shit that's happening. Just off the simple fact who I'm plugged with and who I'm related to out here.

FLOYD: [You] had to already been sellin' drugs to be in the drug game. It's kinda like a union, you gotta be grandfathered in now. So if you ain't already in it, you ain't gon' be in it. 'Cause you ain't got the clientele—you ain't known by nobody. You gotta *know somebody*, know somebody. You have to be grandfathered in to what they got goin' on and be gettin' on through they clientele.

RRA: But it ain't no gang-type shit that's runnin' the drug shit at this point, right?

FLOYD: Not on the black perspective. Maybe the Latinos. You know, the Latinos still got access to the cartels and stuff. But on the black side? You had to have already been doin' this for twenty—you have to already be plugged in, you feel me?

RRA: Like, Tito's big brother was kinda in play with that, too, right?

FLOYD: Oh, yeah. Like him, he another person—he grandfathered in from the early 2000s, late '90s. He been gettin' money, so he was able to come home [from prison], and he still seein'—he makin' a lot of money. And Tito, he was able to get put on by his big brother. But, you know, for the next person [they don't have that opportunity].

As Carlos and, especially, Floyd describe here, access to opportunities for advancement and the chance to make even decent money in the drug game are increasingly rare for African American gang members and are often based on factors beyond their control. The study participants, in the throes of the desperate struggle for daily subsistence associated with selling—or, even worse, not selling—marijuana and other drugs at the retail level, were acutely aware of this reality. They harbored no illusions about the fallacy of "fast money" so often linked to gangs and drugs in the public imagination and popular discourse. The vast opportunities and bold ambitions described by older gang members early in chapter 1 in reference to the glory days of the crack era have given way to the sober recognition among today's gang members that gangbanging and selling drugs no longer constitute a viable career path. Given the lack of profitability and nearly nonexistent potential for advancement associated with selling drugs on the South Side of Chicago today, the continued participation of the city's gang members in the underground drug economy can only be understood within the broader context of the acute un- and underemployment experienced by Chicago's black youth: Nearly 90 percent of the city's working-age black teenagers and more than half of those in their early twenties are unemployed, the highest rates for black youth among the nation's ten largest metropolitan areas.[15]

When presented with opportunities for conventional employment, no matter how menial and precarious, participants reported that they and their peers took advantage of such opportunities virtually without exception. The "guaranteed check" associated with standard employment was preferable to the inadequacy and instability of "hustling." These perspectives are consistent with my experiences running a half-dozen state- and city-funded youth employment programs that collectively employed hundreds of young people during my time working on Chicago's South Side. It would be difficult to overstate the demand among young people in these communities for these jobs, which are temporary, part-time, and typically pay just above the state's minimum wage for youth workers ages fourteen to twenty-four. In particular, I recall my surprise during my first summer running these programs, as young gang members with big reputations on the streets, who I had assumed would scoff at such menial job opportunities, desperately scrambled to secure the paperwork they needed to render them eligible for the program. *Why on earth would these guys want these jobs?* I wondered. The answer, I soon learned, was simple: They were not making much money on the streets. More generally, navigating the blitz of young people eager for work as they sought to claim slots for these programs was an unenviable challenge that, based on basic numerical realities, inevitably left many desperate youth on the outside of these programs looking in. Indeed, recent reports for the city's One Summer Chicago, a public–private youth employment initiative, show that the city turned down more than 160,000 young jobseekers between 2014 and 2017 alone, nearly 60 percent of the program's total applicants, due to inadequate funding.[16]

While study participants' perspectives on and experiences with the conventional labor market will be discussed in greater detail in chapter 4, one final illustration of the financial desperation experienced by today's gang members bears inclusion here. In the following excerpt, Marco describes the fate of Rillo, the former first Demetrius in Marco's neighborhood, whose retirement had prompted the vote for his replacement that Marco described earlier in this chapter. The most venerated member of his gang, Rillo left the streets behind at the age of twenty-five for what was, in all likelihood, a minimum-wage, dead-end job at a neighborhood convenience store. Having attained the experience and local status on the streets that once may have opened the doors of opportunity for him within a traditional drug-oriented gang structure, Rillo had hit a dead end in today's fragmented South Side gangland. Apparently unable to carve out a decent subsistence on the streets, he bitterly resigned himself to low-wage conventional employment. As Marco explains:

Folks been workin' in the store around the hood, you know, Folks couldn't really be out here all like that. . . . He didn't feel like doin' this shit no more because, I guess, he gettin' that age, and he feel like this shit is stupid. Last time I tried to talk to him about something like, "Hey, Folks, why are we—" He: "Man, listen. You said opps? Man, I don't give a fuck about that shit." That's all he would say. He was with Jay recently, though. He [told Jay], "Man, I don't care about that shit." So I stopped talkin' to Folks about what we got goin' on 'cause [if] you don't care, I ain't finna tell you, you feel me? So we just been holdin' it down and shit.

The dearth of prospects for mobility in the illicit drug trade, and in the underground economy more generally, has likely contributed to the adoption and maintenance of egalitarian gang governance over the last decade or so. While rank-and-file gang members during previous decades also faced long odds of actually making a decent living in the drug game, the gang hierarchies of that era provided the illusion of the possibility of such ascendance. Indeed, the erosion of this illusion, resulting from the increasing marginalization of young members in their gangs' drug operations, was among the chief factors that brought about the internal rebellions that shattered these traditional gang hierarchies in the first place. Gang members on the South Side of Chicago today are mostly stuck "petty hustling" in an attempt to fulfill their basic needs and desires—food, bus and train fare, cigarettes, marijuana, and the occasional new outfit. While a repudiation of the coercion and exploitation that often characterized the gang leadership of yesteryear has clearly shaped today's egalitarian gang ideologies and structures, the sober recognition that few, if any, tangible opportunities for advancement in the underground economy remain for present-day gang members has likely informed these developments as well: Within a context of near-ubiquitous dispossession, hierarchies make little sense.

Taken together, the dynamics described in this chapter and chapter 1 represent nothing less than a paradigm shift in Chicago's gang landscape, a departure from decades-old traditions in terms of leadership, organization, culture, ideology, identity, relationships, alliances, and involvement in the underground economy. While processes of gang fracturing and reorganization have played out idiosyncratically, and thus somewhat unevenly, across neighborhoods, the unequivocal trend has been a striking shift in gang culture and structure away from obedience and toward autonomy—from street organizations to cliques. Though the names of the city's traditional street gangs live on in varying forms and fashions, those names are essentially all that remain of the corporate-style street gangs of the 1980s and 1990s. Indeed, from the perspective of today's gang members, the chief legacy of those traditional gangs is how little their current gangs resemble them. As Carlos succinctly puts it, "It ain't like that no more, like in the nineties and shit. Man, hell nah."

The older, transformed gang members interviewed for this study generally responded to these developments in two related ways. On one hand, they often insisted that the traditional gang structures still exist in some capacity. Daniel, for example, points out that the Gangster Disciples "still have board members. I'm not even sure if there's a means of takin' away a board member's spot after they appointed to the board. . . . Larry Hoover's still the chairman." Indeed, many older individuals who were a part of these traditional gang structures have maintained their longtime networks of friends who were also part of those organizations, many of whom held—or hold, as the case may be—leadership positions. So it is understandable that, from the perspectives of these individuals, the traditional gang structures still exist; after all, they and their friends essentially *are* the traditional gang structure. How, in other words, can the gang structure be said to no longer exist if many of the people who made up the structure are still around keeping the legacy alive?

On the other hand, there is an unequivocal recognition among these gang traditionalists that things are very different today than they were in the 1980s and 1990s. Daniel, for example, qualified his remarks about the persistence of the Gangster Disciples' organizational hierarchy by saying that it remains relevant primarily "for those who were part of the structure," but not for the younger generations. Indeed, to whatever extent the traditional gang hierarchies might remain in existence, they have very little, if any, bearing on contemporary forms of gang organization and culture among today's youthful gang members. In this sense, transformed gang members accurately perceive the dynamics among today's gangs as profoundly different from those of previous eras. These individuals admittedly had difficulty understanding these contemporary dynamics, as they do not conform to—and, indeed, often exist in diametrical opposition to—their own experiences and expectations. As Daniel and Paris elaborate:

DANIEL: I mean, I would say, in honesty [*laughing*], it's evolved to something I don't even really understand. . . . I'll give you an example. I read an article in one of the newspapers, and it was sayin' they got these guys in Cook County

Jail who were Gangster Disciples, and when they were asked who's they leader, they said they didn't have a leader. Right? So I'm like, well, how did you become a Gangster Disciple? I mean, can I just say I'm a police officer [*laughing*], you know what I'm sayin', and go to the police station and say, "Hand me a gun and a badge. I'm an officer"? Like, what are you talkin' about? So it's the same thing, right? How can you say you a Gangster—who made you a Gangster Disciple? You just picked up the name and runnin' with it? And I'm not sayin' people can't do that, they can do whatever they wanna do. All I'm sayin' is, in my mind, that's not how it works. . . . If they sayin' that there's no structure, what did you sign up for? Why you walkin' around with that name? What does it mean? What does it mean to *you*?

PARIS: I say, you know, some of these guys are like hip-hop gangsters. They didn't take the sworn oath. They don't live by the rules. They've never paid dues or nothing. So to be part of an organization is no different than if you was a member tithing at the church, you was part of a fraternity or sorority or something—you'd be dues-payin'. That's when you part of an organization. Not the way we've gotten away from it to the point where people just say they this based on what they neighborhood is. So it was totally different then. . . .

You know, I carried myself in a manner where you gon' be able to recognize that I was in the vision based on who I was, how I was, I would be demonstrating like, I'm a part of this. Just like bein' part of a fraternity—if you say, "Man, you gotta do this, you gotta do this, you can't do this." Like bein' part of a religion—the religion say you can't do this, you can't do that. If you gon' be part of it, you gon' be part of it. Nowadays, I don't think that people understand the essence of what the real organization ideology is.

Lorenzo offered that the contemporary dynamics among Chicago's black street gangs today perhaps more closely resemble the gang dynamics in Los Angeles than they do their own historical antecedents. "If you've ever been to California, it's a thousand kind of Crips, and it go by whatever street you on. And that's really how Chicago done turned into and got so segmented." Interestingly, Bibby, a twenty-two-year-old recent transplant from Los Angeles, was able to provide a comparison of the two gang cultures based on firsthand experience with both: As a teenager, he was active with the Rollin 60s Crips back in his hometown, and he had also been hanging out with a gang in his current area of residence in South Shore after moving to Chicago. In his interview, he recounted in great detail his "put on" with the Rollin 60s, an elaborate initiation process that involved a period of regular social interaction referred to as "programming," formal sponsorship by a neighborhood "OG" (original gangster), a weeklong process during which he had to fight members of various sections of his neighborhood to prove his mettle and earn recognition, and, finally, the conferral of a "hood name," or gang moniker, as a formalization of his status as an "official" member. Conversely, Bibby expressed confusion about the relative fluidity and chaos that characterized the gang landscape in Chicago, particularly the mixing among individuals with rival traditional gang identities, a strict nonstarter in Los Angeles. "The gang culture in LA and the gang culture in Chicago is different," he observed. "They gang shit that they got goin' on [in Chicago], I don't know what's really the catch to it, but to me, this shit unorganized, bro. This shit too crazy, bro."

For their part, the Chicago Crime Commission, the civic organ of the Chicago Police Department, is apparently vaguely aware of some of the developments among the city's black street gangs. Their ideological commitment to criminalizing gang members and painting them in the worst light possible, however, appears to have precluded their ability to accurately assess the city's contemporary gang landscape: "Street gangs, both large and small, have splintered into subgroups, or factions, each with its own distinct leader. . . . Since there are fewer members in each faction, juveniles can rise through the curtailed ranks much more quickly. . . . The current disorganization of gang structure reflects [gang members'] base desire to seek positions of authority and use their fellow gang members as means towards this end. . . . Gang members are now ruled by their own greed, rather than any sort of devotion to their brotherhood or leaders."[17] Aside from their mention of gang fracturing, this research bears out that everything in this statement is erroneous, and everything, including the alleged cause of gang fracturing, is manufactured to depict gang members as morally bankrupt savages. The black gangs on Chicago's South Side today, moreover, are not really "factions" at all, as this term implies that these independent neighborhood-based groups remain part of broader, coherent gang organizations that, in reality, no longer exist. Equally misguided are the commission's continued references to the historic People and Folks coalitions that have been effectively defunct on the streets since the mid-1990s.[18] Conversely, there is no mention of emergent forms of gang identity, such as Insane and Renegade, that have supplanted these traditional coalitions as one basis for loose-knit alliances on the streets.

Like contemporary gang organization and culture, the nature of gang violence today is also markedly different from that of previous eras. The ways in which the gang dynamics explored in this chapter have transformed contemporary gang violence in Chicago are taken up in the following chapter.

Chapter Three

THE ANATOMY OF CONTEMPORARY GANG VIOLENCE IN CHICAGO

The wars waged by Chicago's street gangs during the 1990s over control of illicit drug markets and supremacy on the streets and in prison made that decade one of the most violent in the city's history. The crack cocaine epidemic that hit Chicago in the mid-1980s had ushered in a new era of unprecedented profits in the underground drug economy, and competition over these profits shattered many of the city's traditional gang alliances and triggered ferocious warfare among longtime fraternal gangs. These wars were directed by powerful gang leaders, many of whom called the shots (literally) from various prisons within the Illinois Department of Corrections. This violence was carried out, however, primarily by young, rank-and-file gang soldiers, thousands of whom lost their lives in these conflicts. The cross-neighborhood structure of Chicago's street gangs during this period, moreover, meant that these wars often transcended neighborhood boundaries. The war between the Black Disciples and Gangster Disciples, for example, was fought throughout the city—from their mutual home base of Englewood to the infamous Robert Taylor Homes to the "Wild Hundreds" of Roseland to Chicago's Cook County Jail.

The nature of gang violence in Chicago during the 1990s, then, represented a natural extension of the organizational characteristics of the city's black street gangs during that period, particularly with respect to their cross-neighborhood structure, rigid chains of command, and emphasis on the prerogatives of outlaw capitalism via the drug trade. The shattering and reconfiguration of these gangs, in turn, has transformed the nature of contemporary violence on the city's South Side in ways that mirror the trajectory of these gangs themselves. In exploring the particularities of this violence, this chapter aims to bring a level of clarity and specificity to this topic that has proven largely elusive even as gang violence in Chicago has seized the public imagination in recent years.

CONFLICT LOCALIZATION AND ALLIANCE RENEGOTIATION: THE SCOPE AND STRUCTURE OF GANG WARFARE

Just as contemporary African American street gangs in Chicago are radically different from their late-twentieth-century predecessors, the nature of violence between today's gangs is likewise radically different from the violence of the 1980s and 1990s. Among the most pronounced shifts in gang violence during this period has been the fracturing and localization of gang conflicts. On one hand, the shattering of Chicago's black street gangs and the delegitimation and eradication of centralized gang leadership hierarchies mean that the level of organizational coordination required to direct expansive, cross-neighborhood gang wars no longer exists among the city's black street gangs. On the other hand, the retreat of Chicago's now-independent neighborhood gangs from citywide and prison-based gang politics in favor of a more insular focus on local matters means that current gang members have no interest in such large-scale conflicts. Thus, the scope of today's gang wars has been dramatically reduced, as coordinated, cross-neighborhood campaigns regulated by powerful gang leaders have been replaced with distinctly parochial conflicts determined at the neighborhood level. The large-scale, top-down gang wars of the 1990s, in other words, have been superseded by a complex web of perhaps a couple hundred hyperlocal conflicts taking place at any given time throughout the city. As James states, "It really be a block-versus-block type of thing, or clique-versus-clique. It don't really be about no organization thing no more."

Accordingly, gang wars in Chicago today typically take place between gangs within a mile's distance of one another, and often much closer than that—that is, between groups whose geographic proximity brings them into regular contact with one another. The splintering of once-sizable neighborhood sets and the attendant fragmentation of gang territories, moreover, has contributed to the propinquity of these conflicts, as a geographic area that previously contained two gang sets might now be home to six independent gangs, each with a territory no larger than a handful of square blocks. Marco offers a snapshot of these dynamics as they exist in his neighborhood:

> You know, everybody got they own little oppositions. . . . We into it with niggas three blocks to the left. We into it with niggas two blocks down—that's Seventy-Seventh and Maryland. . . . And then four blocks up on Seventy-First and Langley, them some more GDs that's called Mac Block. Then the one next to us called Super City, and then the one on Seventy-Seventh, that's called Rico World. Each of them got they own set of guys and stuff. . . .
>
> We could see them every day. Like, we be on our block and look to the left, we see 'em posted up. They so close, I could be like [*cupping his hand around his mouth*], "Hey!" And they'll look, you know? And I'll probably drop the rakes at they ass, you know, they'll crack the treys or something [they'll flash disparaging gang hand signs to one another].[1] This the same people we have shootouts with. It's so crazy, though, 'cause they right there.

The shattering and restructuring of Chicago's black street gangs as smaller-scale, independent groups has made navigating the city's highly fractured gang landscape an increasingly daunting prospect for today's gang members, one often rife with uncertainty. As the passage above from Marco suggests, today's gangs, which typically "control" relatively small territories consisting of a mere handful of city blocks, are often besieged by a number of rival groups within their immediate vicinity. Yet these contemporary gangs lack the support and resources once provided by traditional street gang structures that helped local sets navigate such difficult circumstances, including the provision of firearms, money, additional manpower, strategic expertise, and diplomatic influence.[2] Independence, in other words, also has its drawbacks. To help offset the loss of support and security once provided by traditional gang structures, black gangs on Chicago's South Side today are developing new, informal alliances with one another—"cliquing up," as described in chapter 2. This practice of cliquing up can effectively double the manpower and firepower a group is able to leverage during times of crisis and generally expands the scope of territory through which gang members can move with relative comfort. Accordingly, gang members typically view such alliances as an essential survival strategy, especially since their oppositions have typically formed one or more of these alliances as well. "Niggas cliquin' up, G, tryin' to stay alive out here," as Carlos explains. "One hood ain't gon' do it on its own. Gonna need some backup 'cause if that [opposition] hood come with another hood, then they two times as strong as you are. So you gon' have to make a phone call [to another group]: 'Folks, come check it out.'"

These alliances are typically rooted in shared hostility for mutual enemies and/or preexisting personal relationships between two groups' respective members, particularly bonds derived from familial ties and childhood friendships. In some cases, then, the ancient proverb counseling that "the enemy of my enemy is my friend" provides a strategic basis for cliquing up. In other instances, the relationship between family members or friends who live in different neighborhoods may serve as the foundation for an alliance between two groups. In addition, while proximity can lead to friction and conflict between neighboring gangs, as evidenced in Marco's account above, the familiarity derived from shared geography can also serve as a basis for friendly intergang relations. Not only do gang feuds typically occur between groups in close proximity, in other words, but alliances do as well.

For example, the various sections of the Woodlawn community delimited by Sixty-Third Street, its major east-west artery, and its four major north-south thoroughfares—Martin Luther King Drive, Cottage Grove Avenue, Woodlawn Avenue, and Stony Island Avenue—each contain a handful of gangs that are generally loosely allied with one another, with the area's major gang hostilities occurring between these sections (see figure 3.1).[3] This dynamic, both in Woodlawn and elsewhere, is often bolstered by elementary school attendance boundaries that zone young people into particular schools based on their neighborhood of residence. "Growin' up, if you went to Till [Math and Science Academy], you was straight," as Cassius explains, noting that the three or four gangs housed at the school coexisted on relatively friendly terms. This dynamic contrasted sharply with these groups' shared enmity toward the "mu'fuckas west of King Drive—the Dulles mu'fuckas—or Fiske. . . . on the [east] side of Cottage

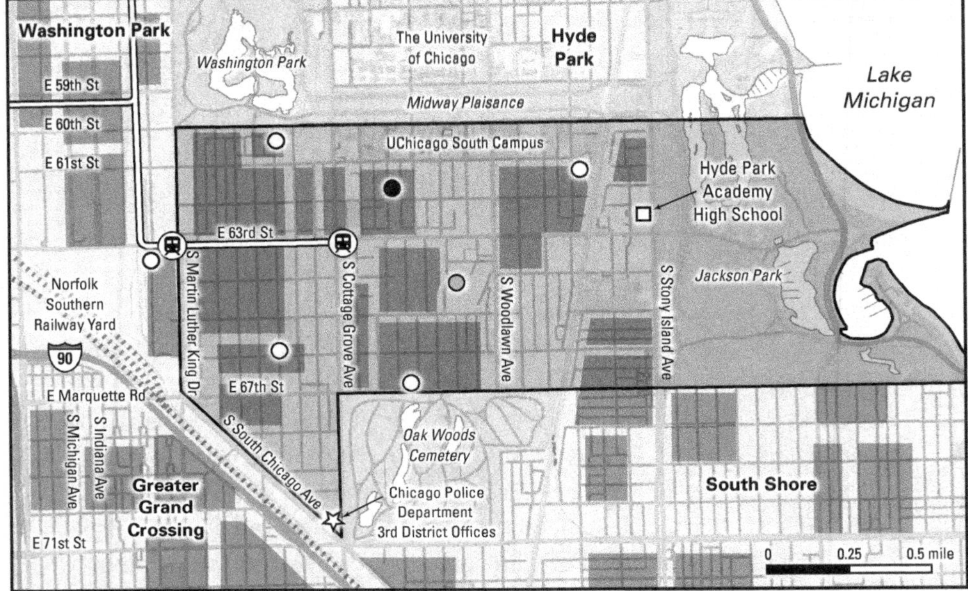

Public neighborhood elementary school (kindergarten - 8th grade)
Former public elementary school, converted to charter school
Former public elementary school, closed
Public neighborhood high school
Gang territory

FIGURE 3.1. Woodlawn community gang territories and schools

Grove," that is, with the young people from adjacent neighborhoods, schools, and street gangs, which were collectively defined by common boundaries. As figure 3.1 reveals, moreover, the elementary schools in Woodlawn are often only a half-dozen blocks away from one another, and gang territories frequently border one another directly.

While the relatively small attendance areas for Chicago's public elementary schools—as well as the relative youth of their students—generally preclude major in-school gang hostilities, the same cannot be said for the city's high schools. With larger attendance zones that bring gang members from a variety of neighborhoods together under the same roof, gang conflicts in high schools are often a serious problem. The attendance boundaries for Hyde Park Academy High School, for example, encompass nearly the entire geographic area included in figure 3.1, including approximately fifteen of the gang territories.[4] Walter H. Dyett High School, where I worked as a graduate intern, had at least nine street gangs prominently represented, as well as a handful of gangs with a notable but less substantial presence, among its then five hundred or so students. Predictably, gang tensions at the school were extremely high, and fights were a nearly daily occurrence. Such problematic dynamics have intensified in recent years with the widespread closing of Chicago's neighborhood schools as part of a concerted effort by successive mayoral administrations to replace traditional public schools with privately managed charter schools.[5] Admission to these charter schools is typically determined by lottery selection as opposed to residence in a designated attendance area, and students who are not selected in the lottery are assigned to schools in other communities.[6] In a dynamic with striking parallels to Chicago's public housing demolitions, then, young people from an increasing number of distinct neighborhoods and gang territories have been displaced from their shuttered neighborhood schools and transferred to schools in other areas. As a result of these policies, for example, the attendance zone for Wendell Phillips High School, one of the few remaining neighborhood high schools on the near- or mid-South Side, now encompasses an astounding thirteen square miles of inner-city Chicago—a footprint that also houses no less than *eleven charter high schools*.[7] The city's young people, meanwhile, are forced to negotiate these often-treacherous dynamics, both at school as well as on their way to and from school (Chicago does not have school buses).[8] Reggie, who attended the now-closed Paul Robeson High School, explains some of the challenges associated with navigating this difficult terrain:

I'm not gon' lie, like, that was kinda stressful, too, 'cause you got your opps at school. So a lot of times it's temptation where you wanna drop out. . . . You know, and then goin' to school, you could see your opps there, walkin' down the street. You see them, they'll shoot at you, then hopefully you make it. You on your way to school, though! Or for the simple fact that you get out of school, you still gotta worry about the opps. You still gotta worry about them shooting at you. So you gotta rush home now—ain't nobody pickin' you up, you walkin'. And then you gotta change your routes and the way you walk because certain parts of the block you can't walk on—your opps gon' be there, you feel me? You takin' the alleyways so that you can get a straight shot through to the house.

Yet while cliquing up can provide a crucial measure of security and support within this increasingly volatile gang landscape, such alliances also have their drawbacks. For one, receiving support in the face of a gang war requires the reciprocation of such support in the wars being fought by one's allies. Thus, while these alliances increase a group's capacity to defend itself and "turn up on" (visit violence on) its opposition, they also tend to expand this pool of opposition. In addition, cliqued-up gangs might be treated as responsible for the actions of their allies even if they did not partake in or approve of those actions. A high propensity for violence, then, can make a gang a particularly useful ally within the context of active gang warfare, but it can also make that group a liability to have as an ally due to the likelihood that its violent proclivities may function to attract a wider range of enemies as well. Below, for example, Weezy describes the impact of these dynamics on the dissolution of his gang's alliance with another group whose reckless violence thrust Weezy and his comrades into an unwanted war with a gang a few short blocks away.

WEEZY: This is why I said we don't clique up with other sets. Under our nose, they shot at the crew down the street from us. They shot at them without us knowin', though.

RRA: Who shot at them?

WEEZY: It's a clique called CMB. They shot at the GDs right down the street from us. And by us bein' so close, they thought it was us, but whole time it was them. But we already cliqued up with 'em [CMB]. So when that shit happened, we kinda parted ways with 'em like, damn, y'all just got a war started, and we not even on that with them, you know? And so the GDs, they so fluky and gay and shit, they started shootin' at us, but they know it was CMB. . . . And that's why we don't clique up with nobody no more, 'cause you don't never know what they could be doin' and then put it on us. Now we got all type of heat comin' our way that we don't need.

In short, the fracturing and localization of gang warfare and the need to renegotiate alliances in the wake of broader gang dissolutions have worked to heighten the instability and uncertainty surrounding much of the gang violence in Chicago today, relative to the wars of past decades. These dynamics have been exacerbated by policies that have closed scores of neighborhood schools and thrown tens of thousands of students, including many gang members, into schools with students from other areas and gang territories. The informality and relative tenuousness of many of today's gang alliances, moreover, as illustrated in the passage from Weezy above, adds further uncertainty to this mix. These shifts, however, represent only the tip of the proverbial iceberg with respect to the transformation of gang violence in Chicago in the early twenty-first century. The causes of gang violence today, for example, have undergone similarly radical shifts since the 1990s.

THE ETIOLOGY OF TODAY'S GANG WARS

Despite the increasing centrality of neighborhood among Chicago's contemporary black street gangs and the localization of the conflicts in which they are embroiled, these conflicts are decidedly unrelated to the types of territorial disputes over control of neighborhood drug markets that motivated much of the city's gang violence during the 1980s and 1990s. This shift away from territorial, drug-related gang violence is largely a by-product of the developments in urban drug markets discussed throughout chapters 1 and 2, namely, the declining profitability of retail-level drug distribution associated with marijuana's displacement of crack cocaine as the drug of choice among urban drug consumers and the shift away from open-air neighborhood drug markets in favor of delivery-oriented sales models. As a result of both of these trends, product demand and attendant levels of profitability are generally not high enough to justify the risks associated with maintaining open-air drug markets, which tend to draw intense police scrutiny and are more susceptible to slow-downs related to both suppressive law enforcement tactics as well as public violence related to gang wars.

These changes have rendered the control of neighborhood drug markets increasingly irrelevant, and violent competition over these markets among gangs on the city's South Side has overwhelmingly dissipated. Indeed, only two of the roughly three dozen gang wars described by the participants in this study could be classified as a conflict over ownership of drug markets. Aside from these, moreover, no other conflicts involved territorial disputes of any kind. These realities constituted points of emphasis and clarification for a number of participants during their interviews. "It was never a conflict over drugs," Lamont explains, making a point to dispute his perception of "what the news be tryin' to say." "It was never like, y'all comin' on our territory and servin' [selling drugs], so we into it. It wasn't ever that," he continued. "Really people gettin' into it because of beefs, not because of territories or drugs."

The following passage from Marco offers a striking illustration of the irrelevance of territorial conflicts, both as they pertains to drug markets and otherwise, within the scope of contemporary gang warfare in Chicago. Here, Marco describes a recent gang war that had the effect of pushing two nearby rival gangs off of their respective blocks, as their members retreated from public space in order to avoid victimization in what had become routine gang shootings from Marco's group and its one-time ally, CMB. Crucially, not only were these gang wars not driven by economic or territorial considerations, but the inadvertent annexation of rival gang territories yielded no material benefit for Marco and his peers, whose financial precarity persisted unabated. These dynamics contrast sharply with the ubiquity and intensity of drug market-related violence associated with the crack epidemic during the late twentieth century and the tremendous economic stakes associated with those conflicts. At the height of the war between the Gangster Disciples and Black Disciples for control of the lucrative drug markets in the Robert Taylor Homes, for example, more than three hundred shooting incidents were reported in the development over a single five-day period in March 1994.[9] In contrast, lacking the motivation and capacity to maintain geographic expansion, Marco's gang soon relinquished control of the blocks they had effectively taken possession of back to their opposition. In short, it makes little sense for gangs today to fight for control of corners that hold little to no value in the underground economy. As Marco explains:

When we was with [CMB], bro, we was fuckin' shit up. . . . The whole Seventy-Fifth strip—like, our opps on Seventy-Fifth and Langley call theyself Super City or whatever. But when we was with CMB doin' all them drills, man, wasn't nobody on Seventy-Fifth, you know? From Seventy-Fifth and Maryland all the way to King Drive. And then when I got out the joint, standin' on that block, it was my first time actually posted out there in a long time, it felt good. We moved they ass around. The Moes on Eberhart, we moved they ass around, too. 'Cause mu'fuckas applyin' pressure, though, you know? Doing drills, drills, drills.

But thinkin' about that, man, it's like, a'ight, we moved them around, but how does that benefit me? You know, really, though. Like, a'ight, I sell drugs, I got twenty dollars in my pocket, but this my life savings, you feel me? Like, come on, man.

Violence based on traditional ideological gang rivalries has also diminished dramatically in recent years. These traditional rivalries are perhaps best encapsulated by Paris's account of his early days of gangbanging in the late 1980s and early 1990s, when he would "be mad at a guy 'cause he was part of a different organization than mine. . . . 'cause what colors he had on. . . . 'cause what way he had his hat wearin'." Chapters 1 and 2, however, have chronicled young gang members' intensifying rejection of Chicago's traditional ideological gang enmities as well as their development of intimate alliances that subvert those longtime fault lines. In short, today's gang members no longer view these rivalries as a legitimate basis for gang warfare. On the other hand, as black street gangs on the South Side increasingly comprise members who identify with various traditional street gang affiliations, the conflicts in which these gangs are embroiled now often involve violence between individuals and/or groups who share traditional gang identities. Just as traditional gang ideologies no longer serve as the basis for intergang violence in Chicago, in other words, they also no longer preclude violence between individuals or groups with the same traditional gang identities.

Recall, for example, Terrence's account of the violent dissolution of his Mickey Cobra set discussed in chapter 2: He and his age cohort of MCs united with their Black Disciple friends in a war against an adjacent Cobra set—which also included a handful of members who identified as Gangster Disciples—and, eventually, against the older MCs from Terrence's own neighborhood. I had just moved into and begun my work in the community as this process was devolving toward all-out internecine warfare. My early conversations with some of the guys involved in this developing conflict served as one of my first introductions to the transforming gang dynamics on the South Side and challenged everything I thought I knew about gangs and violence in Chicago. *So you guys are Mickey Cobras, but your closest allies are Black Disciples?* Yup. *And you guys are into it with the other MCs from right up the street, who have historically been your closest allies?* Yup. *Because your BD friends are into it with them?* Yup. *And the MCs you're beefing with have Gangster Disciples in their set as well?* Yup. *So it's MCs and BDs at war with MCs and GDs?* Yup. *And you guys are getting into it with the big homies from your own neighborhood now as well, because they sided with the other MCs?* Yup.[10]

As a result of the fracturing and increasing insularity of the city's African American street gangs, today everyone outside the confines of one's immediate neighborhood, regardless of their traditional gang affiliation, is commonly viewed as a potential enemy. This dynamic is perhaps best captured by the adoption of "EBK" (everybody killer) and "bar-none" as increasingly popular renegade identities, mottos, and/or general dispositions among today's gangs: Both EBK and bar-none epitomize a willingness to engage in violent conflict with anyone or any group outside of one's immediate comrades. Obviously, as described earlier in this chapter, gangs from different neighborhoods can and do routinely clique up with one another. Yet, such informal and relatively tenuous alliances (generally) notwithstanding, personal relationships and neighborhood allegiances have become the sole delimiters of gang violence in Chicago. The following quotes from Jabari and Memphis illustrate this dynamic in decidedly stark terms:

JABARI: It be Gangsters gettin' into it with Gangsters. . . . I'm not gon' get into it with my own group of Gangsters, [but] even if he a Insane, I'll still get into it with this nigga, I don't care. If you ain't from my hood, fuck you. That's how it is everywhere—if you ain't from that hood, it's *fuck you.*

MEMPHIS: That's how it go, basically: If you ain't from the block, fuck you. You can be BD, GD—I don't give a fuck what you is. But that's how it is now. See, when structure was out, I don't give a fuck what block you from, if you BD and [another] BD touch you, they gon' get fucked up [violated]. It ain't like that no more.

Just as personal relationships serve as the foundation for contemporary gang allegiances, interpersonal animosities likewise tend to serve as the foundation for modern gang hostilities. These animosities might develop for any number of reasons, many of which are typical sources of conflict among adolescent males and young adults more generally, including status, jealousy, gossip, perceived disrespect, competition over the attentions of young women, disagreements over money, accusations of theft, neighborhood pride, and personality clashes. Given these dynamics, the central role of proximity in today's gang wars makes a great deal of sense, as proximity increases contact and attendant opportunities for misunderstandings and conflicts of these various types to arise. Indeed, in many cases, people on either side of a conflict know one another, likely having grown up in the same community, perhaps having gone or actively going to school together, and the like. The gang war that Terrence described earlier involving D-Mob, Bang City, and Free Block, for example, began with an allegation that a friend of Montrelle's—who was not even a gang member—had stolen a bicycle belonging to a member of Bang City. This incident sparked a series of fistfights and group brawls that eventually gave way to a protracted series of shootings that claimed dozens of casualties over a five- to six-year period. Below, Antonio offers another example of the interpersonal and idiosyncratic roots of many of Chicago's contemporary gang wars.

> The biggest situation we done had was over a girl. 'Cause one of the guys was fuckin' with one of the other dudes from across the way—one of his little sisters or some shit. Little sister went back like, "Oh, he touched [sexually assaulted] me, this, that, and the third [etc., etc.]." Come to find out, she was rockin' [having sex with] him anyway, you feel me? But by that time, shit had already escalated—mu'fuckas done already got into it. Mu'fuckas comin' on the block, sprayin' the block, [we] go back over there, do our thing or whatever.

As described in these examples, however, conflicts between members of different gangs that may begin as distinctly interpersonal do not typically remain as such; rather, these conflicts tend to evolve quickly into collective gang wars. Indeed, most of the fights and nearly all of the shooting incidents described by the participants in this study occurred within the context of such ongoing conflicts. The transformation of interpersonal and situational clashes into gang wars is largely driven by the intensity of group solidarity and relational intimacy among today's street gangs. Following the logic of the Industrial Workers of the World's famous slogan about union solidarity, these groups operate under the collectivist principle that "an injury to one is an injury to all." "You with these guys so much, every day you posted on the block with 'em, it's like they became your brothers," as Harold explains. "Somebody shoot at them, it feel like they shootin' at you. . . . You be with him more than your own family."

Indeed, because today's gangs are relatively small groups fundamentally oriented around intimate personal relationships, the loss of a member is typically experienced among his surviving comrades as profoundly sorrowful. This dynamic may have been diluted to some extent during previous eras, when gangs typically had many dozens of members within a single neighborhood and violence was often controlled by gang leaders and fueled by business considerations. Mirroring the evolving nature of today's gangs, then, contemporary gang violence tends to be motivated by expressive, as opposed to ideological or instrumental, imperatives, particularly as they relate to intimate relationships and group solidarity among gang peers. In the following passage, for example, Cedric describes how the death of his friend Telly, who "lost his life to the opps," sent Telly's closest comrade into an inconsolable rage that culminated in a brazen and devastating retaliatory shooting.

> He wasn't goin' for that shit, you know? Since that was his boy, he lost his mind when they killed him. They was best friends—every day with each other. Like, mu'fuckas spend the night at each other house almost every day. Everybody got that homie that they cool like that with—you gon' do everything with Folks. You really don't see Folks without him. [He] lost his mind. Now he locked up for the rest of his life for killin' one of the opps. I'm talkin' about broad day[light], walkin' up on they block, shootin' the whole block up. Two shot [and] wounded, one dead, you know? So he got two attempts, and he fightin' a body. And they got good evidence on him.

While many of today's gang wars developed in recent years via the processes described in the preceding pages, many others are holdovers from earlier eras of gang nation wars and outlaw-capitalist drug organizations. Yet even longstanding gang conflicts that were once driven by traditional ideological gang rivalries and/or disputes over control of drug markets have been reframed by today's gang members in terms of intimately felt collective grievances. Durrell, for example, described the perennial gang wars between his group of Black Disciples and nearby Gangster Disciple and Mickey Cobra gangs not in the ideological or economic terms on which they had been historically fought, but in terms of the comrades he had lost to these conflicts. The fact that these wars were decades old and had been originally waged under the authority of now-deposed gang leaders was ultimately unimportant to Durrell. What was important to him was that his neighbors, friends, and family members had been seriously hurt and killed in these conflicts. Indeed, Durrell himself had taken four bullets as a fifteen-year-old in one of these wars. Ultimately, then, contemporary gang wars on the South Side of Chicago are best understood as collective vendettas.[11] As Durrell explains:

> Once you already killed somebody that somebody done grew up with and you loved 'em, anytime it could go up. So it ain't really never really be because of no gang. Once you killed one of the guys or you done hurt one of the guys, you feel like you wanna get back at 'em, you know? They gon' do the same. So it just go on and on. . . . Some blocks you get into it with since forever. It'll never really be over.

Group solidarity and blood feuds, however, are not the only dynamics shaping the nature of contemporary gang violence on the South Side of Chicago. The following section explores how the prevailing culture of personal autonomy among today's gangs and the shifts in the causes of violence discussed above have transformed group processes related to contemporary gang violence.

AUTONOMY, UNPREDICTABILITY, AND VIOLENCE AS "EVERYDAY LIFE"

Just as the eradication of centralized gang leadership hierarchies has deregulated gang violence by shifting the control of gang wars to the city's now-independent neighborhood gangs, the democratization of these groups has had a similar effect on the sanctioning of violence at the personal level. The power to authorize or prohibit violence is no longer limited to a handful of designated gang leaders, as such privileged positions have been eliminated from today's gangs. Instead, the paradigm of individual autonomy embraced by black street gangs on Chicago's South Side today means that each gang member is now regarded as possessing the inherent sovereignty to make his own decisions with respect to participation in violence. On one hand, this can be interpreted as a positive development, as gang members are no longer being coerced by their superiors into committing acts of violence against their opposition. Conversely, however, no gang member has the power to constrain the use of violence beyond himself, either, as such decisions are now considered and correspondingly acted on by each member individually at any given time. As Chicago rapper and Black Disciple Chief Keef perceptively warbled on a 2013 song, "I can't control my niggas, and my niggas, they can't control me."[12]

Given the typically intimate quality of relationships between today's gang members, the sentiments of one's comrades certainly have some effect on a decision to carry out an act of violence or not within a particular situation. Yet all members acknowledge the personal autonomy of each of their counterparts to either commit or abstain from committing an act of violence, even if doing so flies in the face of broader collective sentiment within the group. (The one exception to this general rule involves failing to defend one's comrades in situations of ostensibly unavoidable violence, particularly by fleeing.) The following narrative from Marco clearly illustrates the bidirectional nature of this autonomy: His inebriated comrade, Wells, exercises autonomy in carrying out an ill-advised daytime assault on members of a rival group, while Marco exercises his own autonomy in refusing to accompany Wells on the attack. As Marco explains:

> It's ten in the morning, we at Lu-Lu crib. [Wells] was in a car, he saw the opps on Seventy-Sixth and Maryland. Now, it's ten in the morning! He like, "What's up, man? I'm finna go score." I'm: "Nah, Folks, I don't think you should do that, man, it's too bright outside, you know?" He get to: "Man, what, you scared?" I'm: "Nah." You know, but I'm smart, though. I don't let nobody dictate my pace. . . . So he called me scared and shit. A sucker would've went down there with him. I stood on my own two. I'm: "Nah, bro, I ain't finna do that, man. That's stupid, bro. It's ten in the morning. We ain't got no mask or no nothing." He: "Man, fuck that, I'm finna go down there myself." One of my bros didn't want him to go by himself so he went with him. . . .
>
> So they go down there, man, he shoot the block up, and he ended up shooting somebody. . . . Folks drunk, I don't know, he feelin' himself or whatever. But

anyway, Folks who went down there thirsty [Wells], he locked up right now. 'Cause mu'fuckas saw his face, mu'fucka tellin' on him, you know?

The intensity of this ethos of autonomy among today's gangs, moreover, extends even beyond the use of violence within the context of active gang conflicts. Participants reported, for example, that gang members are individually capable of starting wars with other groups—even those considered to be allies—and breaking peace treaties that had been established to quell violence with existing rivals. In the past, such unilateral action on the part of a gang soldier would have undoubtedly resulted in a prompt and severe violation. Black gang members on Chicago's South Side today, however, no longer regard such traditional mechanisms for controlling gang violence as legitimate, and, given the horizontal structure of today's gangs, no one holds the authority to order or carry out violations should a member's actions conflict with the will of the broader group. Indeed, gang leaders' coercive and abusive use of violations was among the chief grievances identified by participants as bringing about the popular rebellions that ousted these leaders in the first place. On an ideological level, then, current gang members are fiercely opposed to the use of violations in any capacity, and formal violations have been excised from their collective consciousness as a possibility under essentially any circumstance. Thus, although unilateral violence is not necessarily reflective of the collective sentiment, and despite the likelihood that such violence will bring about consequences detrimental to the entire group, these dynamics are simply accepted by today's gang members as a cost of membership in an egalitarian collective. The following passages from Terrence and Rasheed demonstrate both the tremendous breadth of gang members' personal autonomy as well as the obsolescence of violations implied by their omission from these excerpts.

TERRENCE: People do what they wanna do and we just follow 'em. Like, if somebody wanna get into it with [another gang], we help 'em no matter what. Just 'cause that's our friend. . . .

RRA: I mean, say it was one guy that was like, real wild and he just gettin' into it with everybody, makin' y'all hot. Would y'all respond to that like, "Man, G, you gotta chill out," or what?

TERRENCE: I mean, we have people like that already [*laughing*]. We'll tell 'em sometimes—like, if it was somebody we didn't wanna get into it with, really, like, a lot of us was cool with, we'll try to tell 'em like, "Leave it alone." But if he keep forcin' the issue, we don't have no choice. Either stop messin' with him or help him. And most of the time, like I said, I've been knowin' most of these guys all my life. I'm not just gon' stop messin' with them. So, basically, I have to pick a side.

RRA: What is it gonna take for guys that's in your type of position to then move toward that process where they like, you know what, man, we gotta put this shit [violence] aside . . .

RASHEED: Shit, mu'fuckas steady wantin' [peace]. It's just, man, once the blood drawn, though, bro, that shit be fucked up, B. 'Cause you could—put it like this: We into it [with another gang, but due to a peace treaty] all fifty of us calm. All fifty of them or however many of them, they sittin' back, they cool. You feel me, we just coexisting. It's still that one mu'fucka from probably either set or both sets—probably two mu'fuckas—who still got it in 'em like, "Fuck them niggas, man, ain't no peace with them niggas." Know what I'm sayin'? And then pull some shit, fuck the whole agreement up. And then it's like, a'ight, mu'fuckas just fucked the treaty up, it's back on. Especially if mu'fuckas scored or something—*definitely* if a mu'fucka scored. Oh, yeah, it's on! So, shit, like they say, one bad apple, B. Come on, man, it's hell on earth. It's always gon' be a bad apple.

As suggested in these narratives, the ideology of personal autonomy among gangs today has made gang violence on Chicago's South Side much more volatile than in the past. As described earlier in the chapter, moreover, very little of this violence is related to the types of explicit, instrumental causes typical of gang warfare during earlier periods, such as the campaigns waged over drug markets and organizational supremacy during the 1980s and 1990s, or even the conflicts over territory and access to scarce public accommodations during earlier periods. Those types of goal-oriented conflicts typically required concerted, persistent campaigns that endured until one side or the other proved victorious. By contrast, the gang wars of today lack such discernible goals and more closely resemble collective vendettas driven by hostilities built up over a series of violent incidents between two groups. Some of the violence described by study participants, then, was specifically retaliatory, taking place in the immediate aftermath of another violent incident or hostile confrontation. Yet much of this violence was unrelated to any specific provocation; rather, the mere existence of a gang war itself—that is, of standing hostilities—was cited as justifiable grounds for violence. Without a discrete precipitating cause, much of the violence within Chicago's contemporary gang conflicts does not conform to a readily identifiable and predictable pattern.

Consider the following accounts of gang shootings from Marco, Carlos, and Terrence that each of them had been involved in around the time of their respective interviews. Note that none of these incidents was preceded by a discernible provocation.

MARCO: Just the other day—when was this? Like, the end of last week or something . . . [I go to] slide on bro and them who be on Evans. So I hit them cuts. I got the gun on me. So as I get up there, I'm finna ring the bell, I'm like, man, fuck it, I might as well go through the opps' shit. I'm right here, this close with the gun, fuck it, let me go try to score. A'ight, now I go through the cut. Folks and them [from the window] like, "Hey, man, where you goin'?" I was like, "Man, I'm finna go [*motioning with his hands like he's shooting a basketball*]." He know what that mean: I'm finna go score, you know? He: "A'ight, man, I'll be waitin' on you when you get back."

CARLOS: Man, it been so much shooting and shit. In my hood, it's a war right now, all summer and shit. We was shootin' dice in the alley. So, shit, the opps slid through and hit a boy on the [adjacent] porch. They shot the porch up and hit a lil innocent boy . . .

RRA: So what was the issue, then? You said these are some guys y'all are at war with?

CARLOS: Yeah, these—it really wasn't even an issue. 'Cause, like I said, you don't have to have an issue. They can just slide down on you if they feel like. On a hot day, you feel me: Oh, this a good days to slide down on the opps' shit. You blowin' some shit down. You see a mu'fucka lackin' out here—you lackin', man, it's crackin'. . . . So it really wasn't even an incident. They pulled up and start shootin', you feel me, just 'cause we *been* had an incident previous times.

RRA: So what about the last time you could remember that y'all went to go do something, what was that situation?

TERRENCE: About two days ago [*laughing*].

RRA: Okay, so what happened?

TERRENCE: We drove down Champlain and shot [at members of a rival gang]. They was just outside, wasn't payin' attention, so [my friend] shot . . .

RRA: So is it just y'all at war, or . . .

TERRENCE: Yeah, we at war—it's a war. So, basically, we do it 'cause of the war. It's nothing that actually drives us that make us get up, go do it. We do it 'cause of the war . . .

RRA: How do you feel about the incident now, you know, what happened . . .

TERRENCE: I haven't thought about it 'til you brought it up [*laughing*] . . . It's just like, the moment when you step out your house, you know what you be done did, and you know people that's out here that's willin' to shoot you. So, basically, it's a everyday life. You have to keep your eyes open.

As these passages indicate, although a great deal of contemporary gang violence is unpredictable, it is also regarded as routine and often employed with a startling degree of casualness. Thus, this violence not only erupts at times of acute rage—for example, in Cedric's and Marco's accounts of their friends' ill-fated daytime shootings—but violence also occurs within the course of "everyday life." Indeed, for young people on Chicago's South Side who grew up in the midst of the city's drug wars during the 1990s and came of age during the internal rebellions and parochial gang wars of the early twenty-first century, gang violence has represented a persistent fact of life. The shattering of the city's traditional black street gangs and the decline in urban drug markets, however, have stripped much of the conventional instrumentality and purpose from this violence. There are few lucrative open-air drug markets left to fight over. There are no positions of leadership or prosperity to which gang members might ascend. There is no greater ideological cause associated with the building of one's "nation" through territorial expansion or the elimination of the opposition. Despite the fact that many of today's gangs consist of merely fifteen or twenty members at any given time, moreover, there is typically no ambition of complete annihilation of one's enemies.

While a deeper analysis of the multiple meanings and functions of gang violence today will be taken up in chapter 4, the following section turns toward an analysis of the rising use of social media and the creation of rap music among Chicago gang members, developments that have refashioned the city's gang landscape in a number of additional ways.

DRILL MUSIC, SOCIAL MEDIA, AND THE PERSISTENT POWER OF IDENTITY

An examination of street gangs and gang violence in Chicago in the twenty-first century would be incomplete without an exploration of the symbiotic role of rap music and social media in the lives of today's gang members and in the conflicts in which they are embroiled. Like the shattering of the city's black street gangs, these developments must be understood within their broader sociohistorical context.

In general, increased access to personal computers, laptops, and basic recording equipment and software since the turn of the century has radically democratized the process by which music is recorded and disseminated. Cutting a record twenty years ago usually involved booking expensive time at a professional music studio and required a substantial investment of effort, time, and money. This generally limited such opportunities to a relatively small number of particularly dedicated, gifted, moneyed, and/or well-connected individuals. Distributing a record to the public for consumption was even more difficult and was generally accomplished through recording and distribution contracts with actual record labels. Conversely, today's technological advancements and the advent of social media have enabled essentially anyone with a computer, a microphone, and some basic software to create music and upload that music onto the internet. In short, the proliferation of rudimentary home studios has afforded unprecedented numbers of young people around the world the opportunity to create and disseminate music.[13]

In Chicago, these developments have facilitated the rise of "drill music," a subgenre of gangsta rap music created and popularized by young gang members/rappers from the city's South Side that has ascended to global popularity in recent years. Drill music might be understood as the sonic distillation of Chicago's contemporary gang culture, with menacing production and gritty, nihilistic lyrics that largely revolve around the daily realities of urban gang violence; indeed, the genre's name is derived from a Chicago slang term for a gang shooting. On one level, drill music's predominant themes of gang violence, substance abuse, wanton materialism, and sexual conquest do not differ substantially from those found in other forms of popular gangsta rap from the late 1980s onward. Yet drill music's highly specific accounts of real-life violent events distinguish it from typical gangsta rap, which tends to discuss violence in abstract, impersonal terms. In contrast, drill rappers regularly and explicitly make reference to actual—and often recent—shootings and killings involving their comrades and oppositions. Their lyrical boasts and taunts are directed at identifiable, real-life enemies, not vague, nameless, and often exaggerated or imagined "haters" or "bitch-ass niggas." This unprecedented level of specificity is likely driven by the reality that these songs, unlike most traditional gangsta rap records that were recorded and released by rappers who had signed records deals and already moved out of the hood, are often recorded while these rappers and their comrades are still living in poverty and actively embroiled in deadly gang wars. In this sense, drill raps are not reflections on a harsh past contemplated from the comfort of wealth and success; they are real-time dispatches from the front lines of Chicago's gang wars. "Our beef and our music is one," as Floyd offers. "It's not separated." Montrelle and Jabari elaborate on these dynamics as follows:

RRA: So what do you think about the role that music is playing in all of this?

MONTRELLE: It's a big part, too, 'cause now they just using songs to talk shit to each other. . . . You know, Keef had a song sayin', "OTF, that's WIC City, Young Money, no Five-One, Lamron, Four-Six shit, sendin' shots at Oh-Five-One."[14] He said that, we was really throwin' down [at war], you know?

JABARI: I ain't never heard so much music that entice you to kill somebody like that. You have rappers like Tupac and Scarface talked about death, but they're talkin' about death in general. These guys . . .

RRA: Naming names?

JABARI: Namin' all types of names. Your friend just died, now they talkin' 'bout they smokin' your friend in a blunt.

But drill music is not only a reflection of Chicago's contemporary gang culture; it also plays a prominent role in *shaping* Chicago's contemporary gang culture as well. Essential to an understanding of this dynamic is a recognition of the ways in which the explosion of social media in recent years has facilitated the popularization of drill music as well as the ascendance of a number of local drill rappers to fame and stardom. Many gang members, like their adolescent and young adult counterparts the world over, are ardent consumers and producers of social media. For gang members who rap, a major appeal of these online applications is that they provide an essential platform to promote their music, for example, by sharing links to their SoundCloud accounts and YouTube videos on their Facebook profiles and in their tweets and Instagram posts. Although some of these YouTube videos simply feature a static picture or series of pictures onscreen during playback, the rising affordability of handheld video cameras and video-editing software has increasingly allowed rappers to shoot amateur music videos for their songs. These videos are typically filmed on location in the rappers' neighborhoods and feature their friends flashing gang signs and displaying firearms—in effect, providing a visual representation of the music itself.[15]

It is precisely this music-social media-video nexus that has facilitated the meteoric rise of drill music and its progenitors into the global spotlight since 2012, when the music video for "I Don't Like," a song by Chicago locals Chief Keef and Lil Reese, went viral. The song, which had more than thirty-three million views on YouTube as of mid-2019, was quickly remixed by Kanye West and helped land Keef, Reese, and a number of their counterparts recording contracts with major record labels. *Finally Rich*, the debut album for Chief Keef, the most successful member of this cohort, reached number two on *Billboard*'s Top Rap Albums charts in 2013.[16] Nearly all of Chicago's prominent drill rappers hail from the same communities, grew up with, and/or move in the same gang circles as the participants in this study, including Chief Keef, who has roots in the Parkway Gardens Homes in Greater Grand Crossing; Katie Got Bandz, who hails from the Grand Boulevard area; King Louie and Lil Jay, who both grew up in Woodlawn; Young Chop and Team 600, who hail from Washington Park; and Lil Durk and Lil Reese, who are both from Englewood. The success of these and a handful of other drill rappers have fueled aspirations of similar success among many of Chicago's young gang members, more and more of whom are trying their hand at rapping—including many of the participants in this study. In the following passages, Terrence and Cassius describe these increasingly ubiquitous dreams of rap superstardom among Chicago gang members. Terrence perceptively places the explosion of such musical aspirations within the context of declining urban drug markets and the lack of associated opportunities within the underground economy.

RRA: It seems like there's a rapper in every clique—or, shit, everybody in the clique might be a rapper. What do you think is the cause of that? Because ten years ago that wasn't the case, right?

TERRENCE: The cause of everybody wantin' to rap now 'cause, of course, Chief Keef. He actually made it, and they figure that's the easy way out now, as far as just goin' to school and all that. As far as drug dealin', the rapper now is the new drug dealer in our age. Basically, that's how people get they money now. On the South Side of Chicago, it's not too much drug dealin' goin' on. Just mostly gang-bangin' and rappin'. So that's what people be tryin' to get they money from. . . .

RRA: And then what about, like, the YouTube videos? I know that kinda goes along with it, too . . .

TERRENCE: It fall into the internet—the Facebook stuff. You know, they post they [music] videos on Facebook and everything on YouTube. Them the three main [ways] how they [distribute their music]—internet things: YouTube, Facebook, and Twitter.

RRA: What do you think about the role of social media, you know, in what's goin' on in the streets right now?

CASSIUS: These days, mu'fuckas just tryin' to live like the rappers. . . . Like, that rap shit really gettin' to mu'fuckas. So they tryin' to live like that. They tryin' to make that image, you know, like that's them, all that type of shit.

RRA: So do you think that's havin' an impact on . . .

CASSIUS: It's very impact[ful], especially on the young mu'fuckas. That's who they role models is. . . . That rap shit, it's got the biggest impact on young mu'fuckas today in Chicago.

Indeed, the popularity of local drill rappers among Chicago's young gang members has given these rappers a tremendous amount of influence on the city's streets. To a certain degree, these rappers have stepped into the power void created by the shattering of the city's traditional street gangs. Although the informal, indirect influence wielded by contemporary drill rappers stands in contrast to the official, direct authority once exercised by gang leaders, much of the power possessed by both of these groups derives—or, in the case of former gang leaders, derived—from their ability to construct and promote powerful collective identities among their devotees. For former gang leaders, such identity construction was facilitated in a very intentional and comprehensive manner, primarily through the development of sacred gang literature, symbols, and rituals.[17] Conversely, the power of drill rappers in constructing and appealing to collective identity is largely inadvertent and driven by emulation among gang members in other neighborhoods with whom these rappers and their gangs might have little or no actual contact.

Consider, for example, Jabari's account of the popularization of the "Insane" gang identity, which he credits to Lil JoJo, an eighteen-year-old rapper and member of Brick Squad, a Gangster Disciple set from Englewood, who was famously gunned down in 2012. JoJo made numerous references to being "Insane" in his music, most notably on "Put in Work" and "Real Dope," both found on his posthumously compiled mixtape, *JoJo World*.[18] He and his peers can be seen flashing the Insane hand sign in a number of music videos as well. Jabari also frames the proliferation of the Insane gang identity as a response to the spread of the "L's" identity popularized by Lil Durk, a rapper from Lamron, a Black Disciple set in Englewood and a Brick Squad rival. While initially derived from the first letters of both Lamron and "love, life, and loyalty"—the three chief principles traditionally espoused by the Black Disciples—L's was subsequently adopted as an identity by a range of other gangs who ascribed to the term their own meanings, including a number of gangs located near the South Side's elevated train tracks, known as the "L," and various Outlaw gangs for whom L represents the corresponding letter in that title. Jabari explains these dynamics as follows:

Niggas ain't start claimin' that Insane shit 'til they start hearin' about JoJo and the BDs—all that shit. 'Cause the BDs came out with L's. And then you got the Moes screamin' that L's. And then they cliqued up, now everybody just L's—you got some GDs that's L's. [Other] niggas "Die L's"—[most] GDs is "Die L's," so they Insane. All the Folks [GDs] started fallin' under the Insane act. JoJo came out like, "We Insane, woo, woo, woo." And he GD *for real*. Like, shorty had the Folks behind him. And that's how that it start pumpin' up hard.

To be clear, the conflicts between Brick Squad and Lamron and their respective allies, Tookaville and O-Block, did not start via music; indeed, they existed before any of the young rappers involved in the musical manifestations of these conflicts began gangbanging—likely before they were even born. In this respect, the music released by rappers on both sides of these conflicts, which extend to a number of their respective allies in nearby neighborhoods, serves as a reflection of ongoing gang warfare. Yet, as Jabari describes, this music has also had a profound impact on gangs outside of the actual Brick Squad–Lamron and Tookaville–O-Block conflicts being played out on record, as increasing numbers of South Side gangs have adopted the simple, slogan-like identities espoused by these rappers: Insane/I's; L's; OTF, or Only Trey Folks, a reference to the roman numeral III, the Black Disciples' symbol; WTO, or We the Opps, a rebellious embrace of the derisive "opps" term; BDK, or Black Disciple killer; GDK, or Gangster Disciple killer; and EBK, or everybody killer. These identities have functioned as the basis for new, renewed, or intensified hostilities among a number of these gangs. In short, amateur songs and videos recorded by a handful of rapping teenage gang members addressing conflicts and matters of identity specific to their own gangs have inadvertently played a role in deepening and even redrawing gang battle lines throughout much of Chicago's mid–South Side. Zeke and Rasheed describe the profound, widespread influence of local drill rappers as follows:

ZEKE: Like, last year, we wasn't really into it with them [an adjacent GD gang]. But then once what's his name—you probably know him, they call him JoJo or something—him. When he died, they wanted to get all on that like, BDK, all that stuff. . . .

RRA: So before that, it was more about, I'm into it with you just on a personal level, and now it's more gangbanging?

ZEKE: Right. . . . Like, the year—what's this, 2013? [In] 2012, it wasn't no beefin' or nothing like that. Like, 2011 and on back, we ain't shoot at them all the time. They'll come down there with they clique and we'll box [if there was an issue]. . . .

RRA: And then the JoJo stuff kinda kicked off some whole other . . .

ZEKE: Yeah, just kicked off, like, all of them wanted to be BDK now. That's really how it really got like how it is now, when JoJo died, really.

RASHEED: With this GDK, BDK shit, these mu'fuckas who into it, I don't know they ass from nothing but music. So it's like all the GDs and the BDs who wasn't even fuckin' with no music shit, they followin' [the rappers]. They followin' suit just off the strength they lookin' up [to them]. You got them bars [raps], you got niggas [followers], know what I'm sayin'? So they damn-near sendin' they whole nation off just off some personal shit, though.

Like the drill music promoted on its platforms, social media effectively serves as an extension of Chicago's gang landscape as well, both reflecting and shaping real-world gang conflicts. Indeed, the BDK and GDK slogans repopularized in drill raps became "trending terms on Twitter, showing up in thousands of tweets" as these conflicts escalated in 2012.[19] More generally, like hostile exchanges that take place in person, confrontations on social media can lead to real-world violence and add fuel to existing gang wars. As social media has become a key space within which today's young gang members fashion and present their personal and gang identities, in other words, hostile and disparaging comments made online are generally treated no differently than those made in person: Both are considered potential grounds for conflict. Indeed, social media today provides gang members with otherwise rare opportunities to communicate with their opposition in a manner beyond the physical violence that often typifies their in-person interactions. Much of these online interactions consist of denigrating remarks, boasts about enemy casualties, and threats—that is, comments that only serve to further intensify existing animosities. Social media "let the opps get in touch with you," as Marco explains. "That let the opps talk shit. 'Cause if we was face-to-face, wouldn't be no talking."[20]

In some instances, moreover, social media may play a more direct role in facilitating gang violence, in particular, through the real-time, public communication of a user's whereabouts via live streaming, the use of location "tags," the instantaneous uploading of pictures and videos, and public postings in which one's current location is referenced. Such information can be used to quickly locate rivals for the purpose of committing acts of violence. Indeed, Lil JoJo was gunned down shortly after sending a tweet openly taunting a number of rival gang members and indicating his location—in effect, stating that if these rivals were so tough and wanted to harm him, they could easily find him. Well, someone did, and social media may have helped them do so.[21] Below, Carlos describes a similar situation involving a friend of his who was killed shortly after posting his location in a social media conversation with a female counterpart, who apparently may have been the girlfriend of an enemy gang member. As Carlos explains:

> A lot of niggas gettin' whacked over that Instagram and Twitter shit, G. My homie, YG. . . . He fuckin' with a bitch, but her whole boyfriend is a opp. . . . We don't [even] know who he is, you feel me, we just know he a opp—he from that side. So, man, my homie, he was talkin' to that bitch on Instagram, tellin' her where he was and shit like, "Oh, I'm finna come see you." And all the time, the opps had rolled past while he was on the corner already. I had seen the truck, but I had just pulled off. I should've told him, "Hop in the truck with me, G." But I was goin' to do some other shit, man. Soon as I pulled off, I heard shots. And I pulled back up, he laid out. I'm like, *fuck*. So now it just been shots fired all day [they've escalated the violence against their opposition].

Like Carlos, a number of participants stated that they believed using social media to be hazardous or foolish due to the potential for making oneself a target of violence and/or due to increasing online surveillance by law enforcement. Other participants disparaged what they perceived as internet posturing, noting that online boasts and tough talk do not necessarily reflect one's capacity to actually "handle [their] business," that is, commit acts of violence when a situation calls for doing so. These criticisms, however, generally did not dissuade participants from using these social media platforms. For these young men, the ability to publicly display their identity and "let mu'fuckas know what [they] be on" clearly outweighs the potential hazards associated with the use of social media.

Like the city's gangs themselves, the gang conflicts on the South Side of Chicago today bear strikingly little resemblance to their historical counterparts—the cross-neighborhood, top-down wars that gang leaders once waged over the control of drug markets and power on the streets and in prison. Today's gang wars are distinctly local affairs driven by vendettas, not gang-nation undertakings predicated on territorial control, drug markets, money, power, or traditional gang ideologies. This violence is increasingly volatile, springing from the autonomy of individual gang members, not the strategic orders of gang leaders. Drill music and social media, moreover, have provided new avenues of expression and confrontation for gang members, stoking antagonisms, reshaping gang identities and alliances, and even helping to facilitate violence. Along with the foundational transformations in gang organization and culture described over the preceding chapters, the dramatic changes in gang violence delineated in this chapter reveal the decidedly variable nature of these phenomena.

So how do today's older, transformed gang members view contemporary violence in Chicago? Two perspectives emerged in my conversations with these individuals, both those who were interviewed for this study as well as others I have worked with. The first of these perspectives is that gang violence today is more reckless and indiscriminate than in the past. This dynamic is often framed as a by-product of the breakdown in gang leadership hierarchies, which functioned in previous eras to regulate violence and punish gang members who transgressed such regulations, for example, by killing someone without proper authorization or by hitting an unintended target during a shooting. Thus, older gang members view the autonomy and lack of accountability within today's horizontal gang structures as contributing to unrestrained violence that they perceive as victimizing increasing numbers of innocent bystanders. The second perspective is that contemporary violence in Chicago is not really gang violence at all, but is, rather, interpersonal in nature. From this viewpoint, the shattering of the city's traditional street gangs, the mixing of members from rival traditional gangs, and the violence that often takes place between individuals and groups that share common traditional gang identities collectively point to the inaccuracy of framing such violence as "gang violence." Eldridge and Paris offer their takes on these respective perspectives as follows:

ELDRIDGE: You know, they talkin' about it's the highest body total now. Nah, man, in early nineties—'91, '92? Man, it was so many bodies. And the difference that people would tell you is them people was gettin' knocked off because that's who was supposed to be gettin' knocked off, [at least] in they mind. If something happened to a certain individual or certain people without it bein' sanctioned or makin' sense, there was repercussions behind it. Versus now you got people gettin' knocked off—somebody grandmother? Come on, man, what that grandmama did to you? What the baby did to you?

PARIS: When you look at guys gettin' into it with each other right now to the extreme where they hurtin' each other and they supposed to be from the same family or from the same organization, then how can you call this a gang problem? When you got rival gang people or street organization that's gettin' money together. . . . So I think it get blown out of proportion on what's actually—it's interpersonal. It's more interpersonal violence happening than when it come to street organizations in the Chicago area. I know that firsthand because, I told you, I supervised the program. And I think if you overall look at what's happenin', it's more interpersonal—you know, wrong place, wrong time, a person got into it with somebody. It ain't like because you part of this group, I'm at you.

Both of these arguments warrant analytic evaluation. The latter argument, that violence in Chicago today does not constitute gang violence, is predicated on a narrow understanding of gang violence rooted exclusively in traditional, Chicago-specific ideologies, structures, and rivalries. Certainly, by these standards, contemporary violence in Chicago would not qualify as gang violence. Indeed, the ways in which the nature of violence today diverges from the violence of previous gang eras is a central theme of this chapter. Nonetheless, although violence today is not driven by traditional gang ideologies and antagonisms, and although violent conflicts may be sparked by interpersonal animosities and situational quarrels, the only way that the collective, ongoing vendettas that define these conflicts could *not* be understood as gang violence is through this rigid traditional interpretation. As the preceding chapters have argued, however, that framework does not apply to today's situation: Gangs on the South Side of Chicago today are different than their predecessors; so are the conflicts in which they are embroiled. As the findings in this chapter delineate, these conflicts are driven by interpersonal relationships, group dynamics, and collective grievances all firmly rooted in Chicago's contemporary gang culture. They are, in other words, gang wars. This certainly does not mean that all violence taking place in Chicago today fits the new paradigm of gang violence described in this chapter; among the study participants, however, nearly all of the serious violence with which they were involved—and, for most participants, that was quite a lot—undoubtedly does.

Assessing the veracity of the first argument, that violence in Chicago today is more reckless and indiscriminate than in the past, is less straightforward. Certainly, as described in this chapter, gang violence today is less regulated and more volatile and spontaneous than in previous eras. And there have been a number of high-profile shootings and killings in recent years that seem to support the notion that gang violence has spiraled completely out of control.[22] Yet there is little empirical evidence that gang violence today is less discriminate than in the past. The most recently available homicide report from the Chicago Police Department from 2011, for example, indicates that the percentage of the city's homicide victims that are either under the age of fourteen or over the age of fifty-five—in other words, individuals who would likely represent unintended, or at least particularly objectionable, targets in gang conflicts—actually declined by approximately one-third, from about 12 percent to 8 percent, between 1991 and 2011.[23] A quick search for appalling examples of gang violence in which children and innocent bystanders were killed during the 1990s era of gang leader–directed violence, moreover, produces no shortage of pertinent examples.[24] While Eldridge perceptively points out that rates of homicide today are substantially lower than they were in the early 1990s, whether the nature of contemporary gang violence yields greater numbers of innocent civilian casualties than in the past remains unclear.

While the perspectives shared by transformed gang members are thoughtful and merit careful consideration, the Chicago Police Department (CPD) and its affiliates have a very different take on the nature of current gang violence in Chicago, one that appears utterly divorced from reality. Until at least late 2017, for example, the CPD website featured an "Introduction to Gangs" page that included, among other dubious and outright ridiculous assertions, the claim that "African American gangs typically fight over drug trade transactions, pay-offs, unmet expectations and similar 'business' disappointments."[25] The department apparently took the page down sometime in early 2018, perhaps in response to the tremendous public backlash it received around that time over its gang database (see chapter 5).[26] Initially, it seemed possible that the department had simply neglected to update this web page since at least the early 2000s, as the emphasis on business-related violence may have been more understandable in the bygone corporate gang era of the 1990s. But in searching for the web page again in the summer of 2018, I stumbled on the Los Angeles Police Department's "Introduction to Gangs" page, which, lo and behold, contained lengthy passages that *were exactly the same as parts of CPD's statement*, including the passage quoted above.[27] Noted criminologist and gang scholar James Short Jr. argues that "every city has its own special history, and what works in one city may not work in another. There is no substitute for local knowledge, including both up-to-date information and an appreciation of history."[28] Police in Chicago and Los Angeles would appear to disagree with this assessment.

Building on the analysis presented over the preceding three chapters, the following chapter situates the prevailing dynamics of gangs and violence in Chicago more broadly, examining these phenomena within the context of contemporary conditions on the city's South Side and the experiences and perspectives of gang members themselves.

Chapter Four

UNDERSTANDING THE PERSISTENCE OF GANGS AND VIOLENCE IN CHICAGO

The analysis delineated over the preceding chapters raises a number of questions, including, perhaps most centrally: Why do gangs and violence remain such permanent fixtures on the South Side of Chicago today? After all, the realities of contemporary gang life for young gang members described to this point are tremendously bleak: Traditional gang ideologies have been abandoned, as has any sense that gangbanging is tied to some kind of grander cause, either in terms of the nation-building paradigm of the 1960s and 1970s or the outlaw-capitalist model of the 1980s and 1990s; gang membership today offers very little in terms of opportunities for basic subsistence in the underground economy, much less for more meaningful economic mobility; today's gangs are embroiled in seemingly endless violence that ostensibly serves no greater purpose beyond vengeance-seeking; and a staggering number of gang members lose their freedom, full bodily functions, friends, and their own lives to this violence. Given these grim realities, then, why do so many young people in Chicago continue to find in street gangs a compelling form of social organization? And, relatedly, why do high levels of violence persist in Chicago, especially as violence has continued to decline in most large American cities?

Like the entirety of the research presented in this book, an inductive analytic approach was employed to explore these questions, using as a starting point the conditions, experiences, and perceptions that participants described as precipitating their gang involvement as well as their accounts of the meanings and functions of these groups within their lives. The findings indicate that the persistence of these issues on the South Side of Chicago is best understood as a result of a number of closely interrelated dynamics endemic to this context, namely, marginalization and despair, poverty and economic exclusion, and pervasive community violence. What follows in this chapter is an exploration of the specific manifestations of these realities in the lives of study participants, the various linkages between these conditions and experiences, and the ways in which street gangs and violence function as responses to these dynamics in the lives of their members. The implications of these findings in relation to existing gang theory as well as to mainstream criminological and law enforcement perspectives are also discussed.

SOLIDARITY ON THE BLOCK: GANGS AS A RESPONSE TO MARGINALIZATION AND DESPAIR

In contrast to its general reputation, Chicago routinely ranks among the world's top cities in overall quality of life measures, including affordability, livability, culture, civic pride, food, architecture, and infrastructure, and it is one of the most diverse cities in the United States. Chicago is also one of the wealthiest cities in the entire world, and a number of its neighborhoods rank among the most affluent urban districts in the nation.[1] The daily experiences of many Chicagoans, however, particularly the city's low-income African American residents, are a proverbial world apart from such fanciful depictions and civic accolades. This discordant dynamic has been well documented in the veritable canon of studies on Chicago's black communities, from St. Clair Drake and Horace Cayton's *Black Metropolis* and Arnold Hirsch's *Making the Second Ghetto* to William Julius Wilson's *The Truly Disadvantaged* and Mary Pattillo's *Black on the Block*, which collectively detail the exclusion of African Americans—particularly poor and working-class blacks—from full social, political, and economic participation in city life; the effects of this exclusion on Chicago's black communities; and attempts by black Chicagoans to carve out community life in the face of these conditions.[2] Given these realities, Chicago has often been framed in Dickensian terms as a "tale of two cities" within one municipality—of "gold coast heavens and low-end hells," as one local activist characterized these savage inequalities, or, as historian Andrew Diamond describes it, "a combination of Manhattan smashed against Detroit."[3] Chicago's consistent ranking among the most racially and economically segregated cities in the country, moreover—the city ranked first in 2000 and fifth in 2010—lends additional credibility to such depictions.[4] Indeed, these dynamics have fueled a remarkable exodus of African Americans from Chicago, which lost a quarter-million black residents in less than two decades, between 2000 and 2017.[5]

It is from the latter of these "two cities"—Chicago's segregated, impoverished, and marginalized communities—that the participants in this study and the gangs that have long made the city infamous hail from. In talking about their lives, participants described confronting seemingly insurmountable circumstances—a world in which their basic material needs often go unmet and their dignity is systematically undermined. Poverty in their communities is pervasive, and patterns of racial and class segregation are as stark and entrenched as anywhere in the nation. Their families are perpetually struggling to make ends meet. Rates of unemployment in their neighborhoods are downright appalling, and those who can find employment typically work part-time in menial jobs for pitiful wages. The infrastructure in their neighborhoods is crumbling, and vacant lots and abandoned buildings outnumber occupied structures in many areas. Police-community relations are tense, if not hostile, and the police often treat the young (and not so young) people in these neighborhoods like criminals, regardless of their actual behavior. Many of their family members and friends cycle in and out of jail and prison, fodder for the expansive and expensive carceral state, while schools in their neighborhoods are shuttered at an alarming rate. Gun violence is commonplace, as is the physical and psychological trauma that it engenders, and the specter of violence constricts community life in wide-ranging ways. Mental health services and recreational facilities, however, are nearly nonexistent. Opportunities for mobility in the drug game have largely disappeared, as Latino gangs with connections to Central American cartels dominate the upper echelons of the drug trade, and black youth increasingly find themselves relegated to the bottom of both the conventional and underground economies.

These are among the distressing conditions and experiences that have shaped participants' lives as well as their views of the world and of their place within it. Crucially, they understand that not everyone lives like this—that these conditions and experiences are not universal. They interpret their life circumstances, then, as a reflection of their denigrated position in the racial and class hierarchies that shape American life, and tend to view these dynamics as the by-product of willful neglect, if not intentional social engineering: They are set up to—and, in turn, often do—fail according to conventional standards of success. For many participants, these experiences and perceptions have contributed to a profound sense of despair and alienation. Consider the following passages from Lamont and Cassius, who detail parts of their respective life struggles as well as some of the psychological effects of those experiences.

LAMONT: I had a real fucked up childhood. We grew up poor. My mama was on public assistance and everything, you know, government stuff all her life. She had six kids by the time she was twenty-three, right? So a woman trying to provide for six kids and *she's* a kid was shitty. Roaches everywhere, mices everywhere, hand-me-downs—any clothes that other people couldn't fit, we would wear. Some days I'd go to school dirty. If I did, my best friend's mom would look out for me. And it was only because my mom would wake up and go to work at six in the morning. My big brother goin' to high school, my sister gotta get us dressed, she ain't iron our clothes, we put on the clothes [from] the day before . . .

RRA: What about the community you grew up in? Did you grow up in one place or . . .

LAMONT: I grew up in several places. When I was in second and third grade, we lived at 4721 South Princeton. I don't know the name of that community, but very torn down community, very impoverished community. But then we moved to Riverdale. Riverdale was shitty—same way. And then we moved to Woodlawn, and Woodlawn was shitty. . . . [I'm just] thinkin' about my mom and how many times we been put out—the sheriff done came and set us out 'cause she didn't have all the rent money, and how wrong it was, you know?

CASSIUS: I grew up on the South Side of Chicago in poverty, you know, low income, all that type of shit. I grew up without a father. My grandma raised me. . . . When I was about eight, we used to live in [single room occupancy] hotels and shit 'cause we couldn't get no crib 'cause my OG [grandmother's] credit was fucked up. Shit, once she built her credit up, we finally got our crib right here on Sixty-Fifth and Vernon. . . .

> Sometimes I was tryin' to stay positive, but then I kept on thinkin' like, man, it's like the white mu'fuckas tryin' to put us down and shit, you know? So it really wasn't no hope, that's what I was feelin' like. And this was at an early age—I started seein' life like that at an early age—about ten. . . . 'Cause they don't really care unless it's white society and shit like that. Like, on Sixty-Third Street, it's nothing but potholes down the street. Now if you go on Madison or Chicago Avenue [downtown], shit swift as hell down the street, you ridin' good. But that's how you really just see how it's so biased.

Regarding any hopes for change in their communities, participants expressed little faith that the needs of their communities would be addressed by their elected representatives, whom they viewed as neglectful and largely corrupt. Indeed, true to form, Chicago's political elites have seemingly done everything in their power to reinforce this image, as the types of high-profile public scandals for which the city has long been infamous have continued unabated into the twenty-first century. A mere handful of recent examples includes the indictment of Ed Burke, Chicago's most powerful alderman and a fifty-year incumbent, on federal charges of attempted extortion; the revelation that another long-time alderman had been wearing a wire for federal investigators as he faced potential criminal charges himself; the resignation of successive heads of the Chicago Public Schools, the first convicted on corruption charges and the latter facing accusations of an ethics probe cover-up; the mismanagement of hundreds of incidents of student sexual abuse in the city's public schools; a series of scandals related to the city's $600 million red light camera system, including a bribery scheme, tens of thousands of unfairly or illegally issued tickets, and a $39 million class-action settlement for other mismanagement; the conviction of a South Side alderwoman, whose district cuts across five of the communities from which participants hail, and her successor (and former Chicago police officer) for unrelated cases of fraud; the year-long political cover-up following Chicago police's execution of black teenager Laquan McDonald, exposed only after a judge ordered police video footage released to the public; and, of course, the 2009 impeachment and federal conviction of former Illinois governor Rod Blagojevich for attempting to sell Barack Obama's vacated U.S. Senate seat.[6] A 2015 report by political scientists from the University of Illinois at Chicago bestowed the city with the dubious distinction as the nation's official "capital of corruption."[7]

Participants also discussed the infrequency with which local elected officials—even those who supposedly lived in their communities—visited their neighborhoods and engaged residents, as well as the lack of change in these areas in spite of the nation's election of a black president ostensibly from the South Side of Chicago.[8] They generally viewed government efforts to address violence and other issues within their communities as token gestures designed to temporarily appease fleeting media interest or maintain a façade of concern, but that ultimately revealed their political expendability. In the end, the totality of these dynamics, combined with a lifetime of material dispossession and frustration, contributed to a sense of cynicism among participants with respect to the government and the political process. Memphis, for example, describes his utter demoralization following a rare face-to-face meeting with former Chicago mayor Rahm Emanuel during which Emanuel solicited feedback from him and other participants of a subsidized employment program only to ignore their pleas to continue the program.

MEMPHIS: I talked to Rahm Emanuel exactly how I'm talkin' to you! Honest to God truth, through Better Community. We tryin' to beg him to extend this shit, bro. He said, "Alright, if we extend the program, what's gon' happen?" I say, "If y'all stop this program, what the fuck y'all think we gon' do?" I say, "To be honest, this program saved a lot of lives over these summers, mu'fuckas workin'! Y'all seen the papers, y'all see the statistics. But once y'all take this shit away, where y'all think people have to go? Right back to the streets, you know what I'm sayin', this all we know." And they shake they head, they do that shit, "Mm-hm, yeah," and don't do shit, bro. So it's a waste of fucking time talkin' to them, man. This comin' from a mu'fucka from the streets! We *tellin'* you how this shit is. Nigga, you know what's goin' on out here. Without this shit, bro, it's gon' crack out here every day.

RRA: So you were basically sayin' that the program was good this summer, but they need to keep it goin'?

MEMPHIS: Exactly. Extend the program. Why it just gotta be a summer thing? Just so y'all can make sure we live through the summer? Mu'fuckas die in the *fall*, mu'fuckas die in the *winter*. What the fuck?! So why stop this shit, you know? And they stopped it, so look where we at: right here on the block. . . .

It's so fucked up now, it's like your dreams crushed. Why? Because, man, everybody fucked up [demoralized]: They ain't gon' fuck with us [help us],

> man, we black. It's always a criticism or excuse, you know? So it's like, that shit really takin' mu'fuckas dreams and, like, demolishin' them.

Within this context of exclusion, stigmatization, and hopelessness, street gangs provide essential emotional support for their members rooted in their common experiences and concern for one another. In this sense, gangs work as informal support groups within which members collectively cope with the oppressive conditions and traumatic experiences that often pervade their lives and the various psychological effects of those lived realities. This support is rooted in a culture of acceptance and brotherly love, and participants frequently described their gangs in familial terms.[9] Indeed, very few participants—or any of the scores of other gangs members with whom I am friends and colleagues, for that matter—refer to the collectives to which they belong as "gangs." A wide range of alternate descriptors are employed in place of the term "gang," most of which emphasize group camaraderie (e.g., "my brothers," "my friends," "my niggas," "the guys") or geographic allegiance (e.g., "the hood," "the block").[10] For a number of study participants as well as countless other young people whose biological families are struggling to cope with desperate circumstances, moreover, street gangs offer the closest approximation to caring and durable relationships in their lives.[11] In the following passage, for example, Marco describes the love and emotional support that his comrades provided one another as they struggled to come to terms with the murder of their close friend at the hands of Chicago police. Tellingly, the support of his peers filled a void left by his school, family, and other potential sources of support.

> When Tre died, that messed my head up. 'Cause I never actually felt pain of losin' somebody—especially somebody that was your homie. And then, second, I never saw a dead body, especially that was your homie, though. And that messed me up, 'cause I was fifteen, man. And I saw it happen, you know, the whole lil process when he got shot. And it just messed with my head. And then that kinda drove me farther into the streets. I'll be in school, couldn't even concentrate thinking about bro, get to cryin' and leave. Go on the block where everything feel good. It's like, I don't wanna say love, but it *is*, though.

Marco continues, elaborating on the enduring importance of the supportive relationships that he shares with his gang peers as they confront and cope with difficult familial circumstances and other life challenges more generally.

When you got problems at home or something like that—like, the relationship with my brother, it wasn't no brother-to-brother relationship. He used to try to be my father, you feel me, on that mode. And then when I moved up here and got to kickin' it outside a lot, it's like these my brothers, you know, brothers I never had and stuff. . . . Not sayin' I don't love my family—I ain't say I love the streets more, but I love *bein'* in the streets more. I don't *got* no relationship with my sisters and my mama. Just last night, my sister was cryin', tellin' me how she hate me as a brother. On BD. 'Cause, man, it's just a lot of shit. And then, like, that lil argument we had at the crib—what I do? Run to the block. Forget about it. You know? In my comfort zone with my brothers, just chillin'. . . .

It's crazy. Like my homie, Boosie, who's my right-hand man. Folks be with that drillin' [shooting] shit, for real. Like, he overdo it, though—Folks a killer. His dad used to beat his ass, you know? His dad was in the Navy and shit. And then he just tellin' me—damn-near in tears tellin' me stories. That's how it be, though. It's like everybody got some lil type of story. Some worse than others, but some people get affected by something which make 'em like they is.

For many young people, the acceptance and love offered by their gang comrades, then, stands in contrast to both strained familial relations as well as their broader experiences of denigration and marginalization and their attendant struggles with alienation, despair, cynicism, self-doubt, and shame. Cedric, who lost both parents to prison at age eight, was shot at age eleven, and had been kicked out of two schools before eighth grade, distilled the psychosocial significance of gang camaraderie during his early adolescence as feeling "part of something [that] make me feel whole again." Similarly, Antonio, who also grew up in very difficult circumstances in the child welfare system, describes the acceptance he felt from his gang peers in the face of the constant rejection and stigmatization that accompanied his experiences as both a foster child and as a young black man from impoverished circumstances.

ANTONIO: I was in DCFS [Department of Child and Family Services] from three until I was, what, twenty, twenty-one. 'Cause [*pausing*] . . . I mean, I went to different family members but, you know, as a kid it was kinda difficult 'cause

I'd try to get people to try to understand what I was saying, and nobody will listen to a kid. So it was kinda difficult. So they said, oh, he's a bad kid, he's a bad kid. But I don't think I was a bad kid. . . .

RRA: So how did you first become involved in the streets?

ANTONIO: My oldest cousin, he lived on Fifty-Third and May [a gang block] . . . and he was the only one that actually really listened and took the time to really talk to me.

RRA: So what did it mean for you to be part of the block?

ANTONIO: It was more of, like, just bein' able to be out there and be surrounded by people that's in the same position as you. You don't feel no different—you don't feel inferior to them. You feel me? You go into a work zone, mu'fuckas got suit and ties and shit and you feel like, okay, I'm the black dude in the room, or I'm the uneducated dude in the room, so whatever they talkin' 'bout, I can't be a part of that 'cause I don't know about that. But if I'm out here, we talking about the same thing. . . . I mean, look, I'd rather have these niggas than not have nobody in my corner at all, man.

Not to sound racist or anything, but . . . when it comes to black American society or anything of that nature, it's more of a—you deal with it from a distance. You feel me? It's like when you got the little [stick] with the snake, you gotta hold it from a distance so it don't attack you. People deal with it at arms' length.

As this passage from Antonio suggests, young people facing such circumstances seek ways to resist internalizing their denigrated status and failure—what sociologist Pierre Bourdieu refers to as "symbolic violence."[12] Given their circumstances, however, what options do these young people have for reclaiming their dignity and constructing a positive self-image? The answer, for thousands in Chicago and millions of others across the country, lies in the construction of what sociologist Manuel Castells calls "resistance identities." Castells defines resistance identities as "generated by those actors who are in positions/conditions devalued and/or stigmatized by the logic of domination" that function through "inverting the terms of oppressive discourse."[13] For young people living in oppressive conditions in the inner city, street gangs provide a readily accessible source of resistance identity. Most centrally, within this context, resistance identities upend society's assessment of gang members' communities and the people in them as dishonored and irredeemable. As opposed to feeling embarrassed by the poverty and violence of their neighborhoods, for example, the roughness of their communities and their ability to survive under such conditions become badges of honor. Instead of feeling humiliated by being criminalized, going to prison actually functions to increase one's social capital on the streets and reinforces an affirmative outlaw persona. "The hood" and "the guys," far from constituting sources of disgrace and shame, as per conventional societal standards, instead serve as fundamental sources of identity and pride.[14]

The following passages from Lamont and Carlos offer additional examples of the centrality of this concept of resistance identity to gang membership. Within the logic of resistance identity, Lamont describes young people who have access to resources and opportunities as "lame"—the potential victims of young people like himself whose poverty has hardened them to the brutal realities of the streets. For Carlos, moreover, the entirety of one's identity is contingent on the reputation of the neighborhood gang.

RRA: Can you talk a little bit about how you first became involved with the streets? What was that process like?

LAMONT: I mean, the number one thing that really sparked it for me was really just growin' up poor. . . . Poverty brings something about where a person feels [*pausing*] . . . just sad and alone. . . . I wanted to feel like I belonged to something. And, shit, when you ain't got no money, you broke, you wanna look good, you wanna ride good, you wanna be with the big boys, you know, that's who I was around, that's who I wanted to be under. . . . In my community, it's only *one thing*—it's Black Stone.

RRA: So what did it mean for you to be part of the block?

LAMONT: I mean, shit, I ain't have to worry about nobody fuckin' with me, I'm 'a always have money in my pocket, you know? And if you fuck with me, something gon' happen to you. . . . So havin' that sense of belonging to this particular gang, it felt good because, shit, I wasn't a lame. I wasn't one of them kids that you could run up on and run in they pockets and take money out they pocket. I wasn't the kid who mama was takin' them to tap dancin' and piano lessons. My piano lesson was gettin' a pistol and gettin' a pack and servin' and poppin' at a mu'fucka if they came my way.

CARLOS: Everybody know everybody from the streets, you feel me? You know who is who, if y'all on that map. If you ain't on that map—like, say if your hood

> was from Forty-First and St. Lawrence. Everybody know the Low End, but we gon' be like, they ain't on the map, though, they radar ain't even hittin' like that. So you ain't even really on shit [about anything] over that way. . . . That's just like this map right here, shit [*pointing to a map of Chicago's neighborhoods hanging on the wall*]: Everything is what your hood is.

Within a context of acute racial and class stigma and marginalization and in the absence of conventional forms of social support and positive identification, street gangs provide desperate young people with both emotional support and resistance identities. In these ways, participants in this study described gang membership as helping them cope psychologically with the acute conditions and experiences that shape their lives as black youth from distressed urban communities and, perhaps most centrally, reclaim a positive sense of self.

HUSTLERS AND GO-GETTERS: GANGS AS A RESPONSE TO POVERTY AND ECONOMIC EXCLUSION

Participants described growing up in working-class and, even more commonly, sub-working-class families. Many reported that their parents and other caretakers worked long hours and multiple jobs in the low-wage labor market in order to make ends meet, and many described the integral roles that their extended families played in helping to raise them within such contexts of hardship. Despite these efforts, however, their families often lacked the resources to ensure that all of their basic material needs were consistently met. Indeed, many participants described living without heat or electricity for periods of time as children, being evicted from their homes, going hungry, and experiencing homelessness, among a range of other harsh experiences related to growing up in dire financial straits. For black youth on the South and West Sides of Chicago, moreover, poverty and its effects are not just personal or family problems; rather, they are *community-wide* issues that have similarly destructive and disparate effects on community life. The average poverty rate for the ten communities from which participants in this study hail is 37 percent, more than three times the national poverty rate, a reality manifest in the large tracts of vacant lots and abandoned buildings, substandard housing, crumbling infrastructure, and municipal neglect that generally characterize these neighborhoods.[15]

Among the primary contributors to this familial and communal poverty is pervasive unemployment among black Chicagoans, particularly African American youth from the city's poor neighborhoods. A 2016 report from the University of Illinois at Chicago's Great Cities Institute, for example, reveals that nearly 90 percent of working-age black teenagers in Chicago are jobless, as well as nearly 60 percent of young black adults ages twenty to twenty-four (both of these rates are even higher on the South and West Sides).[16] The average official unemployment rate in participants' communities is a staggering 25 percent, which is at least twice Chicago's citywide unemployment rate and more than six times the national rate. To situate this figure in another way, the national unemployment rate at the height of the Great Depression in 1933 was just shy of 25 percent, meaning that levels of unemployment on par with the nadir of the Great Depression exist as a daily fact of life in many of Chicago's African American neighborhoods. Of perhaps even greater consequence, the actual rate of joblessness in these communities is 68 percent, meaning that *more than two in three working-age residents of these communities lack even part-time formal employment*.[17]

Indeed, despite their near-uniform expression of an intense desire for conventional employment, participants struggled to land even unskilled, entry-level jobs: Only six of the thirty active gang members interviewed for this study were formally employed at the time of their respective interviews. Of those six with jobs, only two held relatively decent jobs, one at a nonprofit organization and another as a truck driver. The other four were working in menial and precarious positions in either fast food chains or in temporary positions through staffing agencies. In the following passage, Harold effectively summarizes participants' experiences and perspectives regarding conventional employment, incisively citing the redevelopment evident in the gentrifying neighborhood in which his interview was conducted as a counterpoint to the prevailing conditions in his own neglected and decaying neighborhood. In doing so, he connects the lack of employment opportunities in his community and the seemingly insurmountable odds of finding work as a young black man with the retreat of the public and private sectors from low-income urban African American communities and the pernicious stigma with which the residents of those communities are typically regarded. Both Harold's perceptiveness as well as his struggle to grapple with his desperate circumstances are evident in his account.

RRA: If the mayor came to you and said "How can we bring the violence down?," or if you were callin' that shot, what would be your strategy?

HAROLD: Where all these abandoneds and stuff, you could just—it's properties out here that's just—like, see what they doin' across the street [*pointing out the window at a large construction site*]? In my hood, it's a whole lot of open spots you could just build some stuff and just have people workin' in there. . . .

I don't know, man. People be discriminatin', I guess. I don't know. 'Cause I don't smoke at all—my piss clean. It's still hard, though, you know, it still be—I think they look at my background, but I ain't even got no background. . . . It's still hard to get a job, though. . . . When they see me—and I'll be presentable—I'll have a haircut, you know, dressed nice. They still—I don't know. It's just hard. Even when I fill out applications, you never get no call back or—man . . .

RRA: Why do you think that's not happening right now, like, those efforts being made to bring more jobs to the neighborhood and stuff?

HAROLD: I think 'cause the areas we in, you know, it's [an] African American neighborhood. The neighborhood known for gangbangers or something like that, so I'm thinkin' they probably won't even come [that] way. They won't be too quick to fix stuff up around [there]. So it's like, they gon' do it in a better place, like Hyde Park area or—you know?[18] Mm-mm. See, it used to be a liquor store [*again referencing the construction site outside*]. I seen that they just closed that down. That was a liquor store right there. They just—I don't know. They'll do that, though, they'll tear down liquor stores and build stuff like that. But they ain't gon' have no blacks, you know what I'm sayin'?

RRA: Do you think it's likely that people are gonna start bringing those jobs in or probably not?

HAROLD: I know I seen Obama [the] other night, he said something about they tryin' to get some jobs. But they always doin' that, they always sayin' that. But I don't [*pausing*] . . . I don't know. But I know I don't never see people get hired, though. People go to college and everything and it still be hard, you know? I don't be knowin'. Like [*pausing*] . . . I don't be knowin'.

While the shift away from open-air drug markets controlled by corporate-style street gangs has made the connection between gang membership and drug dealing less linear than in the past, the gang milieu remains the unequivocal foundation for drug trade participation in Chicago. For desperate young people on the city's South Side, the income-generating opportunities available via gang involvement, while typically rather limited, offer some reprieve to material want and exclusion from conventional employment: The opportunity to earn *some* money in the drug game often trumps the prospect of making *no* money as a perpetually unemployed young adult. For many participants and other youth, selling drugs and otherwise hustling in the streets helps to alleviate some financial pressures on their families by allowing them to provide for some of their own basic needs, if not contribute more substantially to covering household expenses like utility bills and housing costs. Indeed, many participants described their transitions into adolescence as being accompanied by decreasing financial support from their families, who often had to dedicate what few resources they had at their disposal toward supporting participants' younger siblings.[19] In the following passages, James and Roosevelt explain turning to the underground economy as young men growing up in desperate circumstances with few obvious avenues for day-to-day economic survival:

JAMES: We was going to live with my mom and this guy—got our own home and everything. It was to a point where once he left her or whatever, they stopped seeing each other, stopped talking, my mom started being depressed all the time, stressed because they was together for a long time. Everything just started going down the drain. Our house went into foreclosure because the people who was paying the mortgage [the landlord] wasn't paying it. Our heat got turned off. And this around the winter time all this happen. So we boiling hot water to keep the house warm. We got four [space] heaters on—one in all three of the rooms, one in the dining room—keep the oven on, boiling hot water to wash up. It became too hard for me so I felt like, man, if I could make some money on my own I probably could take the pressure off you and you could just take care of my younger brother. So I got to robbing people, breaking into people's houses. And then along the line I start sellin' drugs.

RRA: So around what time was this? How old were you?

JAMES: I was fourteen, fifteen around this time. . . . I mean, I ain't gonna lie, I was just that hungry. . . . I got tired of struggling. I went six months off of salami, cheese, and crackers. I got tired! And that's just what it is. I don't glorify it, but it's what you got to do to maintain. It's what you got to do to survive.

ROOSEVELT: Prior to growin' up, my mom and dad was—half my life, they was in jail. So I was mostly livin' with my auntie and my uncle, [who] raised me the

> majority of my life. And, basically, I was in the streets takin' care of myself, you know, takin' care of my youngest brothers and sisters that's under me. And comin' up, I had to do what I had to do to survive, as far as sellin' drugs. . . . You know, my auntie and my uncle, they didn't have much money to take care of us, they just had money just to feed us, really. They really couldn't do much more for us. . . .
>
> It was hard findin' jobs, 'cause wasn't nobody really hirin' you, comin' up a black male in Chicago. It was hard to get a job—real hard to get a job. . . . Most of us didn't have no choice [except to sell drugs]. . . . That's the only way you was gonna eat, that's the only way you was gonna make your money. Without that, you ain't have nothing.

In addition to the (generally limited) economic opportunities available to participants as gang members, such as selling drugs, another important factor in daily material sustenance for many of these young people is the various forms of mutual caretaking that occur between gang comrades. A number of participants, for example, described older gang members giving them small sums of money when they were young kids. Others talked about sharing food, cigarettes, and marijuana, and pooling their money together in order to procure these items. Some participants even reported living with their comrades for various periods of time. Rasheed, for example, characterized his close friend and fellow gang member—whom he lamented had recently been sentenced to ten years in prison "for some shit he ain't even do"—as "damn-near like my backbone." "If I ain't got no money, bro makin' sure I eat," Rasheed recounts. "He gon' make sure I get high, he gon' make sure I got squares and shit like that." Indeed, not only did this friend help ensure that Rasheed's daily needs were met, he even provided Rasheed with a place to live during a period of particular instability in his life when the building hallways that he "used to spend the night in for fun" with his friends had become his "domain at night" as his precarious housing situation descended into homelessness.[20]

At the same time, the economic and caretaking elements of gang membership cannot be understood in material terms alone; key to these dynamics are psychosocial issues of meaning and identity as well. In particular, adolescence—when most gang members first get involved in gangs—represents the period during which social pressures on young people to engage in conspicuous consumption typically intensify. While this is a dynamic that pervades American society more broadly, the stakes associated with projecting a particular image via consumption may be elevated within a poor and working-class urban milieu, given the generally degraded social status of youth from these areas. As middle- and upper-class status symbols like cars are almost always out of reach for these young people, conspicuous consumption within this context often revolves around designer clothing and gym shoes.[21] Having the "right" clothes, in other words, can function as a way of subverting one's marginalized socioeconomic position. "You may be poor," as the popular folk wisdom asserts, "but you don't have to look like it." Nice clothes and shoes, then, communicate that an individual is someone to be respected—even if their race, class, and neighborhood have been ascribed a lowly status within the wider society. As Susan Phillips insightfully argues in her ethnographic study of gang neighborhoods in Los Angeles, "consumption allows people to possess prestige where they sit" and to "take social power back from a system that routinely denigrates one's participation within it."[22] This is resistance identity at work. Harold's description of joining his neighborhood gang effectively illustrates the convergence of familial poverty, pervasive community unemployment, adolescent social pressures, and the economic opportunities that come with gang membership that make street gangs a vital material and psychosocial resource in the face of such conditions: "Wasn't no jobs, so I start gangbangin'. . . . I wasn't a fly guy. You know, at CVS [Chicago Vocational High School] it's no uniforms, so you had to be fly. I came in there regular 'cause my mama ain't really have no money. That's why I really started selling drugs, tryin' to fit in with people."

Beyond the subversion of racial and class stigma through consumption, the brand of outlaw capitalism rooted in the underground economy that facilitates such consumption also represents an integral source of identity for many gang members. In particular, the toughness that it takes to hustle and make money in the drug game is held up as something to aspire to and celebrate. While the rugged urban drug dealer identity might be understood within the broader cultural context of American celebrations of toughness, autonomy, and entrepreneurial spirit—think nineteenth-century cowboys "taming" the Western frontier—this identity is particularly attractive within a context of racial and class denigration and widespread exclusion from the conventional labor market.[23] Indeed, working and earning money are not only imperative for material survival; they also represent key building blocks of personal identity and self-esteem. For many black youth in impoverished communities wracked by rampant unemployment, then, there are precious few avenues for developing and sustaining such a positive self-image. Selling drugs, even in the menial roles most commonly available to gang members today, offers one of the most readily available alternatives for these young people.

Indeed, the willingness of drug-selling gang members to acknowledge, empathize, and respond, at least to some degree, to the experiences and needs of disaffected youth often casts them as local heroes in their neighborhoods—as rebels struggling against the long odds that society has stacked against them by any means necessary, not as criminals to be despised, as they are typically regarded by mainstream society. Similarly, while conventional criminology interprets the guidance that gang members provide to those coming up under them as the transmission of a criminal subculture, gang members themselves interpret these processes as acts of love and solidarity designed to help their comrades survive in an unforgiving world.[24] The reversal of value judgments integral to resistance identities prevails here again. Consider the following passage from Carlos, in which gang membership offers a means of resistance to the effects of poverty, not only in monetary or material terms but also—perhaps even more saliently—in terms of identity, belonging, and self-image.

RRA: So as a kid, what initially brought you into the streets and all that?

CARLOS: What made me wanna fuck around with it? Like I say, shit, them examples that's set upon you. I'll give you an example. You eight, nine years old, you comin' outside, you stay in the hood. Nigga, the corner store across the street, and the corner store right now, it's crackin'. You got everybody out there—niggas in new whips [cars], TVs in the whips, jewelry, Mikes [Michael Jordan gym shoes], everything. Whatever you want at that time, they got that shit and you ain't got it, you feel me? But them the niggas you can go walk up on them and ask them: "How the fuck you get that?" And they'll pull you to the side and be like, "Wop the bam, this what you gotta do."

Then when you cuffin' a lil nigga or something, G [taking someone under one's wing]—a lot of niggas don't even know what love is out here, you feel me? So when you cuff a nigga and show him how to get some money and show him a better lifestyle and shit instead of talkin' about it, then, really, ain't no stoppin' you. . . . A lot of young niggas, G, that's why they so adapted to the street. . . . You know how it go, shit: If you want something, go get it.

In sum, in the face of pervasive, unrelenting poverty and rampant joblessness and all of the ills that those realities create, street gangs provide desperate young people with opportunities to generate income in the underground economy and to participate in various forms of mutual caretaking. Beyond their obvious material implications, these aspects of gang membership also serve vital psychosocial functions for young people as well, fortifying resistance identities rooted in subversive conspicuous consumption, toughness, outlaw entrepreneurship, and collective solidarity.

BROTHERS IN ARMS AND HOOD MARTYRDOM: GANGS AS A RESPONSE TO PERVASIVE COMMUNITY VIOLENCE

The communities from which participants in this study were drawn rank among Chicago's most violent, with an average homicide rate of 46 per 100,000, nearly three times the citywide rate and eight to nine times the national rate.[25] Unsurprisingly, study participants described pervasive violence within their neighborhoods as a prominent feature of their lives growing up, and they recounted witnessing serious violence in the streets as youngsters, from beatings and robberies to kidnappings and murders. They also reported being victimized themselves by such violence, increasingly so as they entered adolescence and were thrust into navigating Chicago's volatile gang landscape. Indeed, street gangs played an integral role in much of this violence, and existing gang dynamics fueled and lent order to patterns of victimization. Given the synergy between gang and neighborhood in Chicago, for example, one is often interpreted as a proxy for the other on the streets, meaning that young people living in gang neighborhoods are often associated with the local gang by default, regardless of whether or not they are official or recognized members within their neighborhoods.[26] As described in chapter 3, moreover, the relatively small geographic territories of most street gangs and the proximity of rival groups further exacerbate the specter of violence and victimization for young people in these neighborhoods navigating this often-hazardous terrain. In short, when asked to describe the communities and social environments in which they grew up, nearly every participant described these settings primarily in terms of gangs and violence.[27]

The prominence of gangs and violence in participants' accounts of their neighborhoods offers important insights into their experiences and how their understandings of these experiences have worked to shape their worldviews. The ubiquity of such violence in the eyes of study participants, for example, contributes to a widespread view of violence as an unavoidable fact of life and of victimization as a reasonable expectation. That one's physical safety could not be taken for granted was a reality to which participants perceived the need to adapt—or suffer severe consequences. "It's Chicago—shit happens," as Cassius offers. "You can't escape the shit." Elaborating, Cassius describes his neighborhood growing up in patently stark terms:

CASSIUS: Rough. . . . Drugs, shootings, just damn-near anything. I done seen a mu'fucka get robbed right in front of me—a couple times—with a shotgun. Seein' that growin' up, you like, shit, this what it is now, you know?

RRA: So were all your friends on the same type of thing?

CASSIUS: It was kinda like the whole neighborhood—damn-near everybody was on the same shit. It was some book-bag mu'fuckas—people [who] was goin' to school and shit, straight role, all that type of shit. But it was mostly crooks. . . . Where I grew up at, it was mostly Stones, GDs, and MCs. Stones had Sixty-Fifth and shit, Vernon was the MCs and the Outlaws. So it was kinda a mixture, but every block had they own order. . . . See, Sixty-Third, that's the dividing line. Like, east and west, that's different spots [gang territories], and north and south, that's different spots. So if you was north of the train, you was the enemy. If you was south of the train, you was the enemy. Like, the train tracks is the dividing spot. And then west of King Drive, that was [one gang]. And the east, same shit.

Exacerbating the violence that pervades these communities and the sense of physical insecurity that attends such violence is the often-antagonistic nature of relations between community residents and law enforcement. Indeed, the Chicago Police Department has one of the most notorious histories of corruption, racism, and brutality of any law enforcement agency in the country, a legacy that has continued with little correction into the twenty-first century.[28] Following widespread public outrage over police dash-cam footage showing Chicago police officer Jason Van Dyke's 2014 execution of black teenager Laquan McDonald, a city-commissioned task force report concluded that "CPD's own data gives validity to the widely held belief the police have no regard for the sanctity of life when it comes to people of color."[29] These findings were echoed in a scathing Department of Justice report, which found, among other issues, that Chicago police engage in an "unreasonable" pattern of deadly force; officers admit to maintaining a strict internal code of silence; the department fails to properly investigate abuses and hold officers found guilty of misconduct accountable; officer training and supervision are deficient; and the department lacks transparency.[30] The City of Chicago paid out well over *half a billion dollars* in settlements related to police abuse and misconduct in just over a decade, from 2004 to 2015.[31]

In the eyes of participants, the police, far from fulfilling their sworn duties to protect community residents from violent victimization, instead represent an additional source of violence with which participants and their peers are forced to contend.[32] Indeed, a number of participants talked about serious acts of violence committed against themselves and their peers by police officers, including homicide. Yet their adverse experiences with law enforcement extended far beyond such relatively rare acts of severe police violence. More pervasively, participants described what amounts to the criminalization of their very existence as black youth growing up in low-income inner-city communities via routine verbal abuse, ongoing profiling and harassment, and illegal searches and orders to disperse. Strikingly, a number of participants likened the Chicago Police Department to a state-sponsored gang employing violence and coercion in the pursuit of territorial control of public space. Overall, participants reported a tremendous amount of contact with law enforcement and the criminal justice system, and half of the study's thirty youthful participants reported having adult felony convictions in their backgrounds. In the following passage, Zeke describes the traumatic effects of witnessing the murder of one of his close friends at the hands of the police.

Man, like, when I just told you I witnessed three murders, one of 'em the police did. [The person] they killed, he was like a brother to me [*voice shaking*]. Man, when that happened, that's what made me wanna just be down even more 'cause that hurted me. . . . I was walkin' up, finna [*words trailing off*] . . . then I just see him runnin' up the block. And I just see a black police detective car that's comin'. And then that's when I just heard them shots and I just seen him fall. Man [*pausing*] . . . first I thought it was a dream I was finna wake up from. But it was real. And that just put a lot of heat in my heart.

When asked if he thought the police were effective in preventing crime and violence in his neighborhood, moreover, Zeke talked about his frustration with "zero-tolerance" policing that paradoxically criminalizes community youth while simultaneously failing to prevent their victimization.

They be worryin' about little stuff, especially around my hood. They said it's zero-tolerance. They be worryin' about us walkin' in groups, [but] they just let one of our guys get poked [robbed] the other night. And they be right there in the park. I don't know if they be watchin' or not, but they be in they car, just sittin' right there.

Under these conditions of ubiquitous violence and hostile police-community relations, street gangs provide a measure of protection from the violence and physical insecurity that permeate much of the daily lives of study participants and other young people on Chicago's South Side. In particular, gang membership provides essential backup in violent and potentially violent situations as well as collective recourse in the event of personal victimization. In addition to such direct physical support, moreover, participants reported that the social recognition of belonging to a gang often serves to deter victimization, as those looking for a robbery victim or simply someone toward whom they might direct their frustrations or try to earn a reputation off of generally avoid targeting known gang members due to the presumed assurance of collective retaliation. Gang membership also provides a network of friends in allied groups who might be relied on for support in such situations as well as safe passage through their territories. Thus, within a context of pervasive community violence and acute physical insecurity, many participants viewed joining a gang not in terms of putting themselves at elevated risk for victimization, but as a means of deterring and responding to expected victimization.[33]As Lamont explains:

We grew up takin' on the older brothers' beef. . . . You inherit beef because I was in sixth or seventh, eighth grade, they was down there killin' people. Now I wanna go and walk to Sixty-First Street, I can't because of what they did. . . . Mu'fucka like, "Where you live at?" "Man, I live on Stony, but I ain't in no gang." "Whoa, whoa, whoa! You live on Stony, you Stone."[34] It ain't no—it don't *matter.* The streets dictate—unless you got on bifocals, some Urkel pants, some long socks—"You [one of the Stones] off the other end. We don't trust you 'cause you live down there with 'em."

So now, since I'm 'a get bullied on for livin' down there, I might as well get a gun and protect myself with them. 'Cause when I get jumped on, I gotta go back and tell my friends. They gon' say, "You said you wasn't with us!" You see what I'm sayin'? So you have now inherited what the people have done before you, whether they went and killed [someone] or did this or did that. Because now when you say you from Bull Town, mu'fucka like, "Aw, man, ten years ago, them niggas, they shot"—so a mu'fucka finna shoot you based on something that was ten years ago. You twenty, you was ten years old then. You ain't have nothing to do with that! But that's how it go.

Being rooted in neighborhood dynamics, safety considerations were salient regardless of the quality of participants' family lives. Cortez, for example, who reported growing up in a relatively stable two-parent working-class household, explains the inadequacy of his parents' attempts to protect him from the violence in his neighborhood and the role that the local street gang ultimately played in fulfilling that protective function.

RRA: How was your family life growing up?

CORTEZ: Family? It was pretty decent. I just really wasn't no house person like that. When I was young, I was a little sheltered. . . . I went to Catholic schools. So I guess that was my parents' way of tryin' to keep me out of trouble, but it still didn't really work that much 'cause after school, I still gotta go back to the same neighborhood and the same block.

RRA: So what about as far as violence going on—was there any of that as far as in the neighborhood, or . . .

CORTEZ: It was a lot goin' on in our neighborhood. A lot! Literally, every day. Especially on warm days when it's hot outside, that's when everything get crazy. . . . [People are] thirsty lookin' for people that don't know somebody that they know—somebody that they can just do something to real quick, and then they ain't gotta worry about nothing.

RRA: So what did it mean for you to be part of the clique or the gang or whatever?

CORTEZ: I can say I was never really worried about things happening to me. Like, I was never really worried about completely being by myself. I know if I make a phone call, I know I got ten, fifteen guys coming. You know? I know if I'm in

> the neighborhood, I know people know me by face and I know that they know who I know. So just off that strength, it's not a lot of things that I worry about. . . . A lot of problems gettin' avoided, 'cause if I didn't know the people that I did know, probably wouldn't be here right now.

Perhaps even more essential than concrete considerations of victimization and security, however, are the various psychosocial elements of these issues addressed via gang membership. Within today's relationship-centric gang culture, the ultimate measure of camaraderie is in assuming and bearing the burden of collective violence carried by one's comrades. Indeed, participation in these vendettas is how gang members on the South Side of Chicago today largely define gang membership itself: Being part of the collective means, in the most fundamental sense, embroiling oneself in the conflicts facing one's comrades. For example, Marco reports that he "started kickin' it with the guys" on his block after moving to his neighborhood as an early adolescent and, "after a while, just ended up being out there every day with them." In a process that evolved organically as these personal relationships developed via daily social contact—"it kind of transitioned without me even knowin'," as Marco puts it—Marco became enmeshed in the violent collective conflicts of his comrades and became accepted as a member of the group. "They problems became my problems," as he succinctly articulates. The following passage from Cedric similarly underscores both the centrality of intimate peer relationships and the role of violent conflicts in catalyzing and clarifying gang membership.

> It all started off just as us fighting each other [guys from a rival neighborhood]. Then somebody dies, right, and it hits that circle. And you never go back. From there on in, you're off the porch. You jumped in, you know, you in that shit. It's for real. Ain't no goin' back. . . .
>
> Around 2012, my homie Yammy died. We were close—all of us in that circle, we were real close. We all grew up together. See it's a difference: I lost big homies before, right? But it wasn't the same. He watched me grow up and he been around in the neighborhood, that's a familiar face, it hurt to see you die and leave. But somebody that been with me in the trenches, like, right next to me, stealin' and gettin' locked up with me, gettin' shot at and all that with me—right on the side of me? To lose that person, it's a lil bit more personal, if you understand what I'm

sayin'. And you go about it a different way. . . . Now it's all about revenge. Now it's all about really bein' in that shit. Like, okay, this not a joke anymore. I gotta answer to this—something gotta happen.

Contemporary gangs' emphasis on participation in violent vendettas as the cornerstone of gang membership colors gender dynamics on the streets as well, serving as a basis for the general marginalization of young women in today's gang landscape. Nearly without exception, the young men I interviewed for this research stated that their gangs do not have female members, and that the young women from their neighborhoods and/or who hang out with them are simply childhood friends and/or girlfriends. These statements reflect my own observations, both in my work and in my research as well. While hypermasculine, male-dominated street culture as well as the patriarchy embedded in American culture more generally no doubt fuel these dynamics, the focus on participation in vendettas as the organizing principle of gang life also likely plays a crucial role in these dynamics. Since the young women that hang out with these young men rarely engage in shootings against the opposition, they are typically relegated to a relatively peripheral status in terms of internal gang dynamics.[35] "I don't really consider them because they don't do the stuff we do," as Marco puts it. "I claim who from my block is who protect it." The young women, on the other hand, "only claim that because who they guy is." Montrelle echoed these sentiments, stating that "it's a few that's with us, but it's only one of them where I can say that I know if it's something went down she would be there all the way"—in other words, that she would employ lethal violence in defense of her comrades. As with Marco, this distinction represented the fundamental delimiter of insider-outsider status in the group for Montrelle as well. In this regard, then, the rest of the young women in the neighborhood were consigned to a decidedly marginal status: "They there, but they not really there," Montrelle explains.

Given the centrality of intimate personal relationships and violent vendettas to contemporary gang dynamics, developing a reputation as a "driller," that is, someone with a proven willingness to employ lethal violence against one's opposition, holds tremendous symbolic and social currency on the streets. As anthropologist George Karandinos and his colleagues argue, "value can be destructively extracted from the human body . . . by interpersonal and instrumental criminal violence when other productive resources are unavailable."[36] Yet such a proclivity for violence not only lends itself to the building of one's reputation, but, given the collective nature of these vendettas, it also serves as a means of strengthening relationships between comrades. After all, this violence is carried out in the name of brotherhood. In this sense, gang violence might be understood as a means of creating and reinforcing community. Surrounded by violence in their communities and with few viable avenues for positive identification, belonging, socioeconomic mobility, or greater purpose, violence is what many young people on Chicago's South Side have turned to in an attempt to make sense of their lives—or, stated differently, to give their lives meaning.[37] Collective violence, thus, becomes the source material for their "trenches of resistance"—the "only form of self-affirmation" readily available to those for whom "fully participating in modernity reveals its absurdity in the actual experience of everyday life," as one prominent scholar of Jihadism frames it.[38] Becoming a driller, then, represents the greatest height to which many of today's gang members feel they can realistically aspire. Harold describes this grim reality as it pertains to dispossessed black youth in Chicago as follows:

> Now, I think these young guys are tryin' to prove theyself to the older cats, like, yeah, I'm a driller—I'm a shooter. And then once they first time they shoot, they get that [response like], "Oh yeah, Folk, lil shorty a shooter—he a hitter." So everybody tryin' to prove theyself now—sixteen-, seventeen-, eighteen-year-olds, that's what they on now. Growin' up, that's what they think they gotta do to get by, I guess, in Chicago South Side—learn how to shoot. . . . And it's like, man, if something happen, ain't nobody gotta tell them nothing. They just be thirsty. They be: "Yeah? Oh, we on it! Go get 'em! Go get 'em!" . . . Lil Folks over there ain't tryin' to hear nothing [about a peace treaty]. They just wanna gangbang.

Even more tragically, perhaps the only viable means by which gang members today might achieve a more esteemed status in the eyes of their peers is through death. In other words, like the perpetration of gang violence, violent victimization within the context of gang membership is, often to an even greater degree, viewed as an honorable manifestation of solidarity. This stands in diametric opposition to the perception of nongang members—"neutrons" in traditional Chicago jargon—for whom victimization is interpreted as a sign of weakness, vulnerability, and isolation—as evidence of their status as a "lame" or a "bitch." Taking a bullet for the hood, on the other hand, serves to bolster one's reputation and earns one stripes in the streets. Gang members who pass away, moreover—almost always due to gang violence, but occasionally as a result of a police shooting or even a car accident—are venerated as hood martyrs and obsessively exalted by their surviving comrades through a variety of practices that often take on a quasi-religious quality. These practices include, for example, swearing on the name of a deceased friend during the course of routine conversation, organizing annual parties commemorating the date of a departed comrade's death and/or birthday, and naming one's gang after a fallen member.

The naming of a gang after a deceased member, in particular, means that gang members are often more celebrated in death than they are in life and clearly illustrates the efforts of gang members to cope with and make meaning of the all-too-frequent deaths of their youthful peers—a fate they recognize may soon await them as well. These gang renaming practices are nearly ubiquitous among black gangs on Chicago's South Side and can be employed in a cumulative fashion so as to accommodate for an unlimited number of deaths within a gang's ranks. The Terror Town/No Limit Muskegon Boyz, for example, a gang from the South Shore/South Chicago area made famous by drill rappers G Herbo and Lil Bibby, has adopted at least four additional aliases based on the nicknames of fallen members: Roc Block, Cobi World, Fazoland, and Pistol Gang. For study participants and other young gang members, then, participation in violence—both through perpetration *and* victimization—is a way of making sense of the brutality that surrounds them, of finding a place in an unforgiving world, even in death.[39] In the following passages, Carlos and Jabari describe the unparalleled reverence in which gang members hold their departed comrades. Note also the contrast between the meanings that Carlos ascribes to violent victimization for gang members versus for nongang members.[40]

CARLOS: Growin' up in the hood, you gotta know how to fight, shit. Mu'fuckas gon' test you every day, you feel me? Everybody gon' pull your card, G. It's either, do you got a card to pull or you just a hoe. It's either you a gangsta or a bitch, nigga. Make your mind up. . . . Some niggas go to school and be like, "I'm in this shit." Yeah, you from that hood, but you a *bitch* in your hood—you ain't nobody in your hood . . .

RRA: So what did it mean to be part of the hood?

CARLOS: If you a nobody—at the end of the day, don't nobody wanna be a nobody out here, G. That's why a lot of this shit goin' on, you feel me? So a lot of mu'fuckas dyin' over this shit. You really become somebody [when] you die, to me.

JABARI: It's all blocks now. It used to be like, okay, Seventy-Ninth is this area. Now it's everything got a "world" or "ville" or a "city" on it. Soon as somebody die, they naming they block after this person. And everybody with this block—it's different niggas on this block, different gangs and all that shit. . . .

One of my big guys [got killed]. That's why we got our name. His name was Rico, now we call ourselves Rico World. . . . Since Folks died, I'm like the heart of this shit—I keep this shit pumpin'. Not on no gangbangin', makin' noise, shootin' niggas and shit. I put in my work, but I keep it alive 'cause I'm so Rico World crazy. Like, that shit's a part of me. . . . As soon as Folks died, I made everybody put "Rico World" before they name [on their social media accounts]. I was the first one with that shit. Everybody liked how it sound, start doin' it. . . . It's just real with me. I ain't gonna be on no phony shit. I started G-Ville, Oh-Seven-Seven [Seventy-Seventh Street]. That was my other homie, Goonie. He got killed two weeks before his birthday.

Thus, within a context of ubiquitous violence and strained police-community relations, street gangs offered participants protection against the constant specter of violent victimization. In this sense, joining a gang represents a refusal to simply accept the pervasive sense of physical insecurity that often characterizes public life in impoverished urban communities. On a deeper level, participation in collective gang violence serves to strengthen relationships with one's comrades and forms an essential part of gang members' resistance identities as, paradoxically, one of the few sources of positive self-identification at the disposal of young people growing up under remarkably difficult conditions. The choices and the stakes involved, from the perspectives of gang members, are clear: Be degraded as weak and subjected to violent victimization bereft of meaning as a nobody, or find affirmation in a gang where violence and victimization are given meaning, in life as well as death.

The perspectives and experiences delineated in this chapter reveal how gang members conceive of these collectives and the relationships that constitute them, lending insight into why gangs persist as an intractable feature of Chicago's urban landscape. As young people doing their best to deal with often-desperate circumstances, participants described gang membership as serving a variety of vital material and psychosocial functions in their lives that have helped them grapple with their experiences of marginalization and despair, poverty and economic exclusion, and pervasive violence. Materially, gangs provide their members with income-generating opportunities (however limited), mutual caretaking, and assistance in violent and potentially violent situations and conflicts. Psychosocially, gangs provide youth with acceptance and love, emotional support, and, perhaps most centrally, resistance identities. These identities function as a defensive response to the impossible conditions with which young gang members are faced, as the societally ascribed indignity of being poor, black, and from the ghetto is transformed into a basis of self-affirmation; poverty and economic exclusion provide the foundation for the defiant outlaw hustler persona; and pervasive violence and physical insecurity are recast as the essential context for community-building and recognition among one's peers.

Foundational research on street gangs as well as more recent scholarship in the critical tradition typically explain gangs in ecological, material, or psychosocial terms, with each of these theoretical orientations providing important and unique insights into the development and persistence of these groups in America's inner cities.[41] Disciples of the Chicago school of sociology, including Frederic Thrasher, William Foote Whyte, Gerald Suttles, James Diego Vigil, and Sudhir Venkatesh, conceive of gangs primarily as a by-product of urban ecology, in particular, of compromised institutional functioning, collective efficacy, and social control in distressed inner-city communities.[42] Robert Merton, Martín Sánchez-Jankowski, Felix Padilla, and the early work of John Hagedorn frame street gangs chiefly as a response to poverty, joblessness, and economic exclusion, wherein gangs are understood primarily in terms of their ability to provide income-generating opportunities via the underground economy.[43] Albert Cohen, Joan Moore, David Brotherton, Robert Durán, as well as John Hagedorn in his later work, discuss gangs mainly in terms of providing young people who have been marginalized and alienated from mainstream society with a sense of belonging and identity.[44]

The findings from this study, then, support the general relevance of community conditions, material realities, and psychosocial dynamics—that is, the central explanatory elements embedded in the existing theoretical lenses described above—for understanding gangs and violence, as these elements are largely reflected in the factors that emerged inductively during the course of analysis. On the other hand, the findings also indicate that each of these existing theoretical orientations is incapable of explaining gangs and violence on its own, even within the single geographic and sociohistorical context explored in this research. In short, this research indicates that street gangs serve a variety of functions and provide a range of meanings in response to specific conditions, experiences, and perceptions in the lives of desperate young people, and the relative importance of any of these functions and meanings may vary from person to person. Thus, a more adaptable theoretical framework was constructed inductively to account for and synthesize the diversity of factors that emerged in the course of the analysis to more fully account for these phenomena within the specific context of the South Side of Chicago during the early twenty-first century. This framework and the approach from which it emerged, then, may serve as a model for exploring the often-overlapping and mutually reinforcing factors that shape gang dynamics within a particular context from the ground up—or, alternately, even for exploring these dynamics within the context of existing gang theories in ways that illuminate new possibilities for future exploration and clarification.

The experiences of gang members and the meanings they derive from their belonging in these collectives contrast sharply with the narratives and prerogatives of law enforcement and public officials as well as mainstream criminologists. While these latter groups frame gangs in terms of criminality, gang members themselves define their groups in terms of family, friendship, and neighborhood identity.[45] Tellingly, joining a gang is often referred to as "coming home" in Chicago street parlance. It is not that gang members deny that they engage in violent behavior, selling drugs, or other criminal activities; rather, it is that they do not conceive of their collectives as being criminal associations: that is not what they understand themselves to be joining; it is not why they join; it is not the primary role that gang membership plays in their lives; and it is not the meaning that they derive from their membership. Indeed, even the seemingly straightforward concept of "joining a gang" is often complicated in ways that defy simple narratives and stereotypes when examined empirically. For example, almost none of the participants in this study reported going through any type of formal initiation process; rather, their "membership" in their respective groups developed organically via long-term friendships, routine social interaction, mutual recognition, and, eventually, participation in collective violence. "Coming home," in other words, typically entailed a mutual recognition of camaraderie and common identity and struggle, not the outcome of a discrete initiation process or event.[46] "We had a lil segregated part in our building that I was raised in—it was a lil backyard," as Terrence explains. "A lot of my friends I have now, we grew up all together in the backyard." Joining the gang for Terrence and his peers, then, simply involved "gettin' older and hangin' on the front side of the building" with their older counterparts.

Police and mainstream gang researchers also consider the strong bonds between gang members to be problematic—key drivers of delinquency, criminality, and antisocial attitudes that preclude effective intervention. Accordingly, these relationships are cast and treated as needing to be weakened and/or destroyed in the service of crime control and personal rehabilitation.[47] What this crime-centric view fails to account for is the crucial material and psychosocial support that the relationships between gang members provide for young people whose lives are fraught with instability and scarcity and whose basic necessities may otherwise go unmet. To frame these relationships simply in terms of promoting deviance and criminality is to completely miss and/or disregard the lived experiences of gang members and what makes these relationships so vital in the first place. Such a view also tacitly assumes that gang membership is the sole basis for relationships between these individuals, failing to recognize that one's fellow gang members are almost always childhood friends, neighbors, and family members before they are gang comrades. Thus, while common gang membership may strengthen these relationships, it is imperative to recognize that these relationships already exist prior to such membership; indeed, they are typically the reason a young person joins a gang in the first place. "People try and make it seem like dudes grow up and they choose what organization they gon' be in," Lorenzo explains. "I didn't join a gang and make friends, I joined a gang with my friends already in it. . . . They looked at me as always bein' part of the mob."

Like other critical gang research, this study attempts to disrupt the narrow, pathologizing narratives of street gangs that dominate public discourse and mainstream criminological research and present a fuller, more humanizing picture of these groups and their members. The study findings support Brotherton's framing of street gangs as a "symptom and harbinger of something much deeper within the current social order" and likewise represent "an attempt to grapple with the roots of the phenomenon . . . to reveal fundamental contradictions that [need] to be addressed rather than some behaviors that [need] to be controlled."[48] In this sense, these findings serve a more practical, and arguably more vital, purpose, as well—namely, offering insights for addressing street gangs and reducing violence. This book's conclusion explores opportunities for possible intervention and outlines a strategy for reducing violence empirically rooted in the analysis developed throughout the course of the book. Before that, however, chapter 5 examines interventions that have *not* worked in Chicago in recent years. In particular, the failures of two highly regarded violence prevention initiatives to reduce levels of violence in the city over the last decade are explored and illuminated.

Chapter Five

A CRITICAL APPRAISAL OF VIOLENCE PREVENTION FAILURES

As discussed briefly in the introduction, levels of violence in Chicago remained relatively high and remarkably stable for more than a decade, from 2004 through 2015, during which time almost every other major U.S. city saw their rates of homicide and violent crime decline substantially: The murder rate in the nation's twenty largest cities (sans Chicago) decreased by an average of one-third over these years, while Chicago's actually increased by 5 percent.[1] Beginning in 2016, levels of violence in Chicago shot up (literally) to heights unseen since the bloody gang wars of the 1990s, before tapering off somewhat in 2017 and 2018. Nonetheless, Chicago's rate of homicide for 2016 and 2017 represents a nearly 50 percent increase over the city's average during the preceding decade. Ironically, while much was made both locally and nationally of Chicago's slight increase in homicide in 2012, that uptick, during which violence in the city was routinely regarded in the media as an "epidemic," was a proverbial blip on the radar as compared to the post-2015 increases (see figure 5.1).

Chicago has maintained its persistently high rate of homicide in spite of highly touted and ostensibly evidence-based efforts by the Chicago Police Department (CPD) and other groups to reduce violence in the city. In particular, much has been made of the CPD's use of focused deterrence strategies and the public health model employed by the Cure Violence/

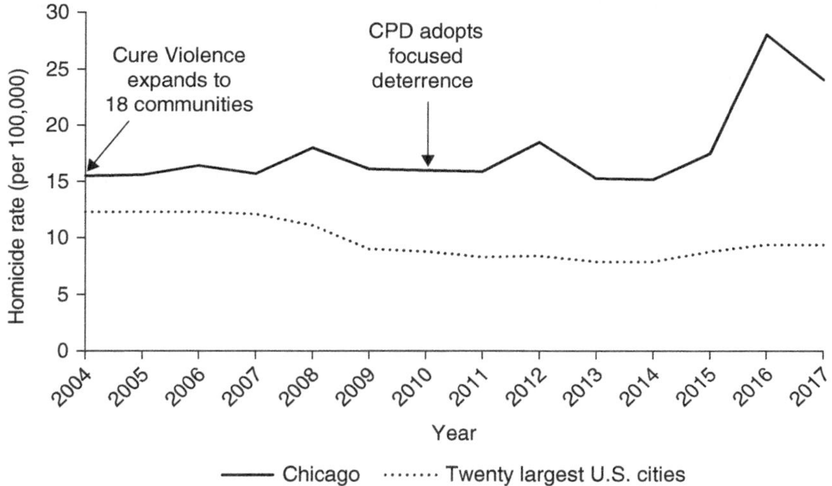

FIGURE 5.1. Homicide trends in Chicago and twenty largest U.S. cities
Source: Data from U.S. Federal Bureau of Investigation, "Crime in the U.S.," accessed July 18, 2019, https://ucr.fbi.gov/crime-in-the-u.s

CeaseFire organization. Both of these models as well as their respective architects and frontline staff have been treated with general fanfare and acclaim in local and national media, by public officials, and among researchers. Indeed, these strategies are being implemented not only in Chicago but in cities across the country and even internationally, with each being promoted as the proverbial silver bullet that holds the key to ending urban violence, whether in Chicago, Boston, or New Orleans—or, alternately, Syria or Israel-Palestine (seriously—check out the Cure Violence website). Yet despite glowing acclaim from media profiles, increasing popularity across the country and globe, and some empirical support for their efficacy in other contexts, neither of these approaches to violence prevention was ultimately capable of stemming the tide of pre-2016 violence in Chicago, during which time these efforts were in full operation. As can be seen in figure 5.1, rates of homicide in Chicago fluctuated only slightly, from a low of 15.2 to a high of 18.5 per 100,000, during the twelve years from 2004 through 2015, which encompass the timeframes of implementation for both focused deterrence and Cure Violence.

Why have these efforts ultimately failed to reduce violence in Chicago?

This chapter explores possible answers to this question. In particular, the findings from this study, described over the course of the preceding chapters, reveal a number of contradictions and inconsistencies between the assumptions underlying these models and the current nature of gang dynamics and violence on the South Side of Chicago that may help explain these failures. To be clear, the discussion in this chapter is not intended as an argument that these interventions are completely useless. Indeed, existing research indicates that they have demonstrated varying levels of success (and failure) within a variety of contexts. But the relatively high and nearly constant rate of homicide in Chicago from 2004 through 2015—to say nothing of the post-2015 spike—belies the narrative advanced by advocates of both focused deterrence and Cure Violence that these models have been effective in reducing levels of violence in Chicago, much less that their application is capable of solving all violence at any time within any context. While the relationship between these interventions and the surge in violence in Chicago since 2016 is less clear for a number of reasons, some comments on these dynamics are included here as well.

CHICAGO POLICE DEPARTMENT: FOCUSED DETERRENCE

Focused deterrence is a problem-oriented approach to policing developed in the mid-1990s by a team of researchers and police and criminal justice officials in Boston with the express goal of reducing violent offending among local youth gang members.[2] The Boston intervention, known alternately as the Boston Gun Project and Operation Ceasefire (not to be confused with Chicago's CeaseFire initiative, the original name for Cure Violence), helped reduce youth homicides in that city from an average of forty-four per year between 1991 and 1995 to twenty-six in 1996, the first year of the project, and fifteen in 1997.[3] Focused deterrence strategies that replicate or draw heavily on the Boston model have been implemented in approximately three dozen U.S. cities since the late 1990s. The model also serves as the cornerstone of the National Network for Safe Communities at John Jay College of Criminal Justice, founded in 2009 to promote and offer strategic support for the implementation of various deterrence interventions, most prominently the Group Violence Intervention based specifically on the Boston model. In addition, the U.S. Department of Justice's Project Safe Neighborhoods initiative, launched in 2001 in ninety-three federal jurisdictions throughout the country, incorporates a number of elements from the Boston model, including an emphasis on focused deterrence. Although the homicide trends in Boston largely mirrored nationwide declines in violence during the 1990s, and there has been some debate as to what proportion of this reduction can be attributed to the model specifically, evaluations of focused deterrence interventions based on the Boston model in other cities have yielded generally—though not uniformly, and not as substantially—positive results.[4]

The focused deterrence model based on the Boston Gun Project operates on a number of key assumptions about the nature of gang dynamics, gang violence, and police capacity that, taken together, constitute the conceptual and practical foundation of the intervention. Chief among these assumptions are that the vast majority of serious violent crimes in any given jurisdiction are committed by a relatively small number of individuals, that these individuals are members of street gangs or similar groups, that much of the violence in which they are embroiled is collective in nature and driven by group dynamics (e.g., gang wars), and that the individuals in these networks routinely engage in a wide range of other criminal behavior. The model further presumes that those embroiled in these gang wars are rational, that they typically do not truly want to be involved in this violence, and that they would take an "honorable exit" if presented with an opportunity to do so.[5] Given the assumption about the group-driven dynamics of gang violence, moreover, it is presumed that this dynamic can ultimately be inverted to reduce violence as well. Finally, the model assumes that local police officers both know who the most violent individuals in the community are as well as who is responsible for gang shootings when they occur.

In general, the focused deterrence model is supposed to work as follows. Local law enforcement officials identify those street gangs and individual gang members perceived to be most heavily involved in serious violence and call these individuals together for a meeting, referred to as a "call-in." During these call-ins, representatives from local and federal law enforcement agencies as well as prosecutors from the State and U.S. Attorneys offices delineate their collaborative deterrence strategy to the meetings' attendees. David Kennedy, the chief architect of the model, summarizes this message as follows:

> When a gang kills someone, or shoots guns, or terrorizes the neighborhood, this group steps in. We'll focus on everyone in the gang. We'll arrest drug dealers and

shut the markets down. We'll serve warrants. We'll call in probation and parole. Nobody's going to smoke a joint or drink in public, nobody's going to have any fun. . . . It's up to you whether you get this attention. [With] this group, no violence, no harm no foul. It's not a deal, it's a promise. Somebody else might come get you for dealing drugs, you take that chance. *We* go where the violence is.[6]

This particular form of deterrence is referred to as "pulling levers," since law enforcement and criminal justice officials "respond to incidents of serious gang violence by . . . 'pulling every lever' available on the gang or gangs in question," with levers representing an intensification of police scrutiny and a range of potential legal sanctions.[7] For those gangs or individual gang members that remain undeterred from violent behavior by the message delivered at the call-ins, these swift, sweeping, and severe responses are designed to collectively punish all members of these groups via suppressive policing and aggressive criminal prosecutions. Through the continued use of call-ins, successful prosecutions of violent gangs are advertised to other groups as examples of the high costs associated with noncompliance—that is, of continued violence—thereby reinforcing the deterrence message. Pulling levers on *all* members of a gang that persists in its use of violence, even those who may not have engaged in or even condoned the violent actions of their counterparts, represents an attempt to invert the principles of collectivism that normally work to fuel such violence in the service of preventing it: If one member shoots someone, every member will suffer the consequences of increased police attention and severe legal penalties. In theory, then, gang members will exercise social control over one another, discouraging their peers from committing acts of violence that will lead to such serious collective consequences.

The CPD piloted the pulling levers focused deterrence strategy in August 2010 on Chicago's West Side.[8] Then department superintendent Jody Weis and federal prosecutors hosted a call-in at the Garfield Park Conservatory with purported gang leaders and delivered the deterrence message. In an apparent show of contempt for the message and/or messengers, the attendees "got up and walked out." Weis summarized the message and its reception this way: "They did not like the idea at all, because they realized something one of their colleagues may do could lead to a lot of pressure on them. . . . That's what we tried to emphasize: this is group responsibility, group accountability. So you're a leader, you'd better influence your guys to behave."[9] After a young man was killed in the West Garfield Park community a few days after this initial call-in, Chicago police arrested more than sixty members of the Black Souls, the gang they deemed responsible for the killing, for crimes ranging from petty misdemeanors to various drug and weapons charges, over the course of a two-month period.[10] In 2013, moreover, nearly two dozen members of the Black Souls were indicted on sweeping conspiracy charges in state prosecutors' first use of the Illinois Street Gang and Racketeer Influenced Corrupt Organizations Law, a statute modeled after the federal RICO laws that have been used to prosecute organized crime figures and gang leaders for decades.[11]

These efforts, however, decidedly failed to reduce levels of violence in West Garfield Park, the Black Souls' base of operations. Between 2006 and 2010, the community experienced an average of fourteen homicides per year; from 2011 to 2015, that average actually *increased* slightly to just over fifteen. The homicide averages for neighboring East Garfield Park, moreover, remained exactly the same during these successive five-year periods. More generally, in spite of these interventions, West Garfield Park consistently boasts the single highest murder rate of any community in the entire city of Chicago.[12]

Weis's successor at the CPD, Garry McCarthy, was also a champion of the pulling levers focused deterrence strategy and continued its use after assuming the reins of the department in 2011 under the city's then newly elected mayor, Rahm Emanuel.[13] Indeed, a ringing endorsement of focused deterrence from McCarthy is found on the back cover of David Kennedy's book, *Don't Shoot*, a memoir and promotional vehicle for the model, where McCarthy's quote reads: "Kennedy's ideas extend beyond community policing and serve to revolutionize the entire criminal justice system." Yet a series of events that took place in 2015 during McCarthy's tenure illustrates in an even more tragic and dramatic fashion the utter failure of this strategy to curb violence among gang members in Chicago. Following an October call-in on the city's South Side, meeting attendees from the gang Killa Ward apparently followed Tracey Morgan, a member of the rival Terror Dome gang and a fellow meeting attendee, shooting at the truck in which he was traveling, killing him and wounding his mother in the process. The shooting occurred less than a mile from where the call-in was held.[14] The pulling levers threat delivered at this call-in apparently had so little effect on meeting attendees that a handful of them were not even deterred from shooting someone *immediately after leaving the call-in*. A series of retaliatory shootings that police were evidently also powerless to prevent took place in the months following Morgan's killing, resulting in the injury or death of at least a half-dozen individuals on either side of the feud. The casualties included the girlfriends of two gang members as well as Tyshawn Lee, the nine-year-old son of an alleged Killa Ward member, whose horrific execution in a South Side alley thrust violence in Chicago back into the national spotlight.[15]

More generally, these focused deterrence efforts have had no discernable impact on overall levels of homicide in Chicago: The city's average homicide rate of 16.5 per 100,000 for 2011–2015 following the implementation of focused deterrence was nearly identical to its average rate of 16.4 for 2006–2010.[16] There has certainly been no "firebreak," as has apparently occurred in other cities, in which short-term reductions in violence establish the baseline for a new, less violent equilibrium that persists going forward. Indeed, there have not even been any short-term reductions in violence in Chicago on which to build.[17]

While it is impossible to determine with certainty why focused deterrence has failed to reduce violence in Chicago, the analysis of contemporary gang dynamics and gang violence presented in the preceding chapters holds a number of potential insights regarding this matter. In particular, while the findings from this study suggest that many of the assumptions that undergird the focused deterrence model align with the realities shaping violence and policing on the city's streets today, there are at least two fundamental inconsistencies between these assumptions and realities that may have helped neutralize the model's potential efficacy in Chicago.

The first of these inconsistencies is a misalignment between the assumptions about gang dynamics embedded in the pulling levers intervention and the realities of contemporary gang dynamics, particularly among black gangs on Chicago's South Side. In particular, the notion that threats from law enforcement and criminal justice officials will cause gang members to deter their counterparts from committing acts of violence is fundamentally inconsistent with the horizontal structure of today's gangs and the fierce culture of personal autonomy that is so central to their individual and collective identities. Not only do today's gangs lack leaders capable of controlling violence, but gang members categorically reject the notion that anyone, even their closest comrades, can tell them what or what not to do with respect to violence or any other matter. Within the context of this group dynamic, the potential efficacy of any intervention relying on coercion and social control—much less some type of formal group authority—is quite likely to be limited. The utter lack of awareness of these dynamics among local law enforcement officials seems apparent from their very first call-ins, which were held with groups of alleged "gang leaders." Cassius, having heard of these call-ins, proffered the following critique, obvious to anyone with a working knowledge of gang dynamics in Chicago today: "The superintendent of the Chicago Police Department—I think they tried this methods already, like, gettin' some of the gang leaders together and shit. But it ain't too many gang leaders left."

Another problematic assumption of the focused deterrence model as it pertains to gang violence in Chicago today is that the police know who is responsible for violence when it occurs. Such knowledge is obviously an essential element of the intervention: If police do not know which gang committed a shooting or murder, they cannot follow through on their threats to pull levers on members of that gang; if they are unable to pull levers effectively, their message of deterrence rings hollow and the entire enterprise falls apart. In 2017, however, Chicago police "cleared" just 17.5 percent of the city's homicides, down slightly from 19 percent in 2016 and marking the department's worst clearance rate since at least 1990, the earliest year for which such data are available. The CPD's clearance rate for nonfatal shootings is even lower, standing at only 5 percent in 2016. Moreover, although police often frame clearing a case as "solving" a crime, this is a thoroughly misleading characterization, as clearance status is not based on a successful criminal prosecution or even the formal filing of charges, but on the mere identification of a suspect. In other words, *no suspect is even identified in more than four out of five murders and nearly 95 percent of nonfatal shootings in Chicago.*[18] According to a 2018 *Washington Post* report, between 2007 and 2016, Chicago boasted the single lowest clearance rate for homicide cases among the fifty largest cities in the country, with an average of 26 percent. By comparison, Baltimore and New Orleans, the cities with the next-worst clearance rates, cleared 35 percent of their respective homicides over the course of that decade. The overall clearance rate among the fifty cities was nearly 50 percent—twice as high as Chicago's.

The report further points out that Chicago police "solve so few homicides that vast areas stretching for miles experience hundreds of homicides with virtually no arrests."[19]

These appalling realities strongly suggest that Chicago police simply do not know who is responsible for the violence in the city, as they are consistently incapable of securing the evidence necessary to even identify suspects in shootings and killings, much less file charges against such individuals. This dynamic persists in spite of swelling budgets and technological advancements that ostensibly make policing and solving crimes easier. One factor likely contributing to these issues is that Chicago police lack legitimacy in the eyes of many residents in the city's black communities, a dynamic that tends to fuel both noncooperation with police investigations as well as vengeance-seeking.[20] Certainly, relations between police and the city's African American residents have been strained and often antagonistic for decades, owing largely to the CPD's infamous legacy of racism, corruption, and brutality, which its officers have routinely visited on the city's black citizens. While strained police-community relations likely contribute to a chronic, generalized depression of the CPD's homicide clearance rates, however, it seems unlikely that this dynamic has driven the stunning decreases in clearance rates since the early 1990s, when the department was clearing more than 60 percent of the city's homicides.[21] Indeed, a 2003 study of police demeanor, responsiveness, and performance in Chicago indicated that public perceptions—including among African Americans—actually improved on all of these measures between the early 1990s and the early 2000s, a period during which, paradoxically, the city's homicide clearance rate declined steadily.[22] These divergent trends appear to contradict the notion that declining police legitimacy is responsible for the CPD's plummeting homicide clearance rate.

A more likely source of the intensifying homicide clearance crisis in Chicago is the dramatic transformation in the nature of gang organization and gang violence on the city's South Side since the 1990s explored throughout this book. The shattering of the city's traditional black street gangs has fractured the South Side gang landscape, as long-standing alliances and enmities have been largely dismissed by younger generations of gang members, who have refashioned today's gangs and gang wars as distinctly relational, hyperlocal affairs. Relationships on the streets are more fluid, as they are not rooted in broad-based gang identities, but in personal associations and situational factors. Violence is increasingly unregulated and spontaneous, as it is driven by the impulses of youthful gang members in service of vengeance, not controlled by gang leaders for instrumental, more easily identifiable purposes—for example, the control of a particular open-air drug market. New, evolving identities rooted in informal affiliations and often driven by local drill rappers have emerged, and the city's traditional People and Folks coalitions have been effectively obsolete on the streets for nearly three decades. In short, today's gangs are not stable, hierarchical organizations with identifiable leaders and clear lines of authority. Gang animosities are fractured and diffuse, and violence is often erratic and unpredictable.

These developments have created a fluid, even dizzying, dynamic on the streets of the South Side that has likely contributed to the CPD's sinking homicide clearance rate. Within this context, how do police determine who is responsible for a shooting when the victim is the member of a gang embroiled in active conflicts with perhaps four or five other groups? How do police determine what the motive was? On which group do they then pull levers? Moreover, on which groups do they pull levers when the city may have upwards of one hundred shooting victims over the course of one summer weekend, as occurred over the Fourth of July holiday weekend in 2017?[23] How do they deploy limited policing and prosecutorial resources within a context of nearly daily shootings and killing in many areas on the South and West Sides of the city? While the CPD has apparently attempted to grapple with some of these dynamics, a department spokesman in 2015 hinted at the challenges in applying the focused deterrence strategy to a vast, fractured gang landscape within which the department has limited information, admitting that "it's very hard to keep track who is upset at who."[24]

Yet even when Chicago police have executed the pulling levers strategy in an ostensibly effective fashion, using a violent incident as a springboard for a slate of successful criminal prosecutions against a particular street gang, the effects are dubious, even on the targeted gang itself. Incredibly, the CPD and its law enforcement and prosecutorial partners were touting an early pulling levers campaign against Killa Ward at their call-ins circa 2013 as a fearsome example of the potency of their strategy. In other words, the gang whose prosecutions were being publicized at the CPD's call-ins as an example of the devastating power of pulling levers was the same group responsible for the brazen post-call-in shooting in 2015. Clearly, despite incarcerating a substantial number of their members, the pulling levers approach did not eradicate, debilitate, or even intimidate Killa Ward's membership. In the following passage, Marco, who had attended call-ins as a parole requirement, explains how one such meeting transpired. As Marco reports here, the focused deterrence message delivered at the call-ins had no effect on his and his peers' participation in violence, and they remained embroiled in a number of violent gang wars and had been involved in several shootings between his attendance at that meeting and his interview for this study.

MARCO: I had went to a parole meeting with, um, who is the head of the police?

RRA: The new one [around that time]? Garry McCarthy?

MARCO: Yeah, with him. I saw him in person, you feel me? I was like, damn, this the nigga I see on TV all the time. But I was at Washington Park. It was me and a whole bunch of other parolees, you know, from all different hoods and stuff. He was tellin' us to stop the violence because he said about some new law called accountability and stuff. And, basically, sayin' if me and you [are in the same gang, and] you went on a drill, right, and you kill somebody. I ain't got shit to do with it; I was at the crib the whole time. But I *know* you killed somebody, and I ain't sayin' nothing. And then he was tellin' us that he gon' start takin' people to jail for that. You know?

He was talkin' about a whole bunch of stuff, man. Like, he put a picture up there, right? He said, "You see this guy? He's one of the Killa Ward GDs, woo, woo, woo, woo, woo." You know, that's the area they was focused on. He had one picture. And then he had that picture, then they showed his rappie, you feel me? He was like, "This is who he's locked up with. He's also from [Killa Ward]." And then he pulled up some more pictures. And then he say, "Look at their arrest records and the locations." And I'm seein' they all within Killa Ward area, and that's how [the police] know they with the shits. And then, before I know, it's like twenty people on this board and stuff. And he's like, "If y'all block be under the radar, this is how it be for your area. So I'm tellin' y'all put down the guns because [otherwise this will happen to you]." And then he sat down, and then the head of the FBI—somebody like that—came to talk. He's like, "Hold up. My name is woo, woo, woo. I represent the FBI." Then he got to talkin' about some shit. And then somebody else came up there talkin' about the safe haven act—when you get out the joint, the lil paper you sign. He got to talkin' about that, you know? He's like, "Yeah, if you got a gun on you now, that's five years in the feds," and stuff like that.

RRA: What did you think about that?

MARCO: All they was talkin' about is how they was gonna lock our ass up, you feel me? That's all they kept talkin' about: years, years. And then dude was like, "And you know what happens when we give you life? We give you some *more* years!"

[*Marco and I both laugh*]

MARCO: He's just talkin' 'bout years and years. It really had me thinkin' like, damn, man, they got something for us. You feel me? But mu'fuckas still out here takin' these risks and shit, you know?

RRA: It hasn't stopped?

MARCO: Yeah, it hasn't stopped, shit. I don't think it's ever gon' stop, bro. That's crazy.

One additional component of the CPD's focused deterrence strategy that warrants brief discussion is its Strategic Subjects List (SSL), which the department initially compiled in 2012. The SSL is a sort of modernized version of a traditional gang database that uses an algorithm based on social network analysis and eight risk factors to create a "heat list" of individuals at high risk for being a victim or perpetrator of gun violence. Individuals on the list are assigned scores of 1–500 based on their ostensible level of risk and are ranked accordingly; police consider those with scores over 250 as warranting heightened attention. The list has been used to identify individuals and gangs for call-ins as well as what the CPD calls "custom notifications" in which police show up at the homes of individuals on the list to deliver personalized deterrence messages. The SSL has come under fire from a number of corners for a wide variety of reasons, including criticisms related to accuracy, transparency, profiling and harassment, purpose, predictive power, and efficacy.[25] While CPD superintendent Eddie Johnson claims that 1,400 individuals are responsible for driving gun violence in Chicago, for example, the SSL has nearly *400,000 entries*. Of these, more than 287,000, or 72 percent, have scores above the 250 threshold that classifies them as high-risk and meriting enhanced police scrutiny. Moreover, more than half of all black men in their twenties in Chicago are on the list, and nearly one-third of all those listed have never even been arrested or shot, leading one critic to pointedly ask, "How strategic is the Strategic Subjects List, really?"[26] An early evaluation of the SSL showed no effect on citywide homicide rates nor any predictive power related to gunshot victimization.[27]

The CPD nevertheless appears firmly committed to focused deterrence, even following Garry McCarthy's unceremonious ouster from the department in November 2015, precipitated by public outrage over video footage showing the groundless police execution of black teenager Laquan McDonald.[28] The CPD's "Gang Violence Reduction Strategy" directive, issued on the final day of 2015, prominently features focused deterrence as well as numerous references to call-ins and the SSL. Another directive related to the SSL specifically was released in July 2016.[29] Amazingly, then, Chicago's post-2015 surge in homicide has occurred while focused deterrence remained a major official policy priority of the city's police department.

So much for focused deterrence in Chicago.

CURE VIOLENCE: THE PUBLIC HEALTH MODEL

Cure Violence, formerly known as CeaseFire, is a Chicago-based organization founded in the late 1990s by Gary Slutkin, an epidemiologist and professor in the School of Public Health at the University of Illinois at Chicago and the former head of the World Health Organization's Intervention Development Unit. The cornerstone of the organization is the eponymous Cure Violence public health violence prevention model, which was piloted in the West Garfield Park community on Chicago's West Side in 2000. An internal evaluation indicated that the intervention "reduc[ed] shootings by 67% in its first year" of operation there.[30] Since that time, the model has been implemented in at least twenty-two communities in Chicago as well as in fifty other U.S. cities and more than a dozen international sites, from Central America to sub-Saharan Africa to the Middle East. The Cure Violence website boasts of the model's ability to successfully reduce essentially any type of violence within any context, noting that "cities around the world have turned to the Cure Violence Health Model to prevent violence—from sectarian violence in Iraq, to community violence in Honduras, to prison violence in England."[31] The organization also advertises that its model has undergone several independent evaluations, all of which reportedly show "large statistically significant reductions in violence."[32]

From a broader cultural perspective, Cure Violence has enjoyed intense, widespread acclaim in the national media, including a 2013 TED Talk featuring Slutkin; a 2011 award-winning documentary film, *The Interrupters*; countless flattering profiles in prominent media sources; and a slew of local, national, and international honors and awards.[33]

The Cure Violence model approaches violence prevention from a public health perspective, which means understanding and treating violence as an infectious disease, not unlike tuberculosis or cholera. On one level, this perspective challenges dominant societal views in which violent behavior is interpreted primarily in moral terms, people who behave violently are judged as bad, and violent behavior provokes often-severe punitive responses. Slutkin points out that similar judgments were levied against people infected with various diseases throughout much of human history, and people were often jailed, tortured, and killed for conditions that today are understood in medical terms. Slutkin argues, moreover, that violence shares the same three population-level characteristics of epidemic diseases: spatial clustering, discernable patterns of spreading (including acute outbreaks), and transmission between people through exposure. On the individual level, just as a person exposed to typhoid is susceptible to transmission—that is, to typhoid infection—a person exposed to violence either through observation or direct victimization is likewise at risk for transmission—in this case, adopting violent behavior. In both instances, exposure has invisible yet demonstrable physiological effects that predispose the individual to the contagion, and heightened levels of exposure increase the chances of transmission. In addition, like other contagious diseases, the spread of violence is driven by human behavior, in particular, community behavioral norms, which may include everything from handwashing habits and dietary customs to medical practices and standards of conflict resolution. Violence, then, Cure Violence maintains, is ultimately a learned behavior, and, as such, it can be unlearned.[34]

As a means of combating the epidemic of violence and fostering the unlearning of violent behavior, the Cure Violence model approaches violence prevention using the same three components public health experts use to fight other contagious diseases: "(1) detecting and interrupting ongoing and potentially new infectious events; (2) determining who are most likely to cause further infectious events from the infected population and then reducing their likelihood of developing disease and/or subsequently transmitting;

and (3) changing the underlying social and behavioral norms, or environmental conditions, that directly relate to the spread of the infection."[35] More specifically, the first element of the Cure Violence model, which involves the discovery and interruption of potentially violent incidents, is achieved through a variety of strategies, including intervening in contentious situations on the streets, working with victims of violent events and their friends and family members to prevent retaliations, and mediating ongoing group conflicts. The model's second component entails identifying those at highest risk for involvement in violence, working with them to change their understanding of violent behavior, and connecting them to resources that can help them desist from engaging in such behavior and, more generally, turn their lives around. These first two components are implemented almost exclusively with gang members embroiled in violent conflicts. The model's third component involves developing working relationships with community stakeholders to spread the message that violent behavior is unacceptable, thereby challenging prevailing norms whereby violence is conceded as inevitable, if not acceptable.

A key aspect of the Cure Violence model is the employment of former gang leaders to implement the interventions, particularly the first component, violence interruption. The rationale behind this approach is that these individuals constitute "credible messengers" among youthful gang members, the primary targets of the intervention. Like the other elements of the model, this approach of using community insiders is consistent with standard public health efforts to fight epidemic diseases throughout the world.[36]

After being piloted in West Garfield Park, the Cure Violence intervention was adopted in eighteen high-violence Chicago communities in 2004 and has been implemented in at least a handful of additional communities in the city since that time. The organization has declared its work in Chicago an unmitigated success, citing as evidence a 2008 evaluation funded by the National Institute of Justice and conducted by a team of researchers from Northwestern University.[37] Indeed, the 450-page report brims with complimentary descriptions of the program model and interventions. A close reading of the evaluation's actual findings, however, paints a decidedly more complicated picture of the program's actual efficacy. For reasons not fully elaborated in the report but having to do with access to sufficient longitudinal data, only seven of Chicago's twenty or so program sites were included in the evaluation. The outcomes reported for these seven communities were mixed, at best: Only three of these communities experienced declines in shootings that evaluators could attribute to the intervention, and only *one* saw a decrease in homicide due to the intervention. An analysis of gang-related homicides and homicide networks conducted independently and included as one of the report's appendices, moreover, concluded that Auburn Gresham "is the only CeaseFire area in which one might reasonably argue a positive program effect with some degree of confidence."[38]

These findings represent a far cry from Cure Violence's depiction of the outcomes reported in the evaluation. Indeed, even the presentation of the findings in the evaluation itself gives the impression of being engineered to cast an unduly positive light on the program. None of the mostly negative outcomes mentioned in the previous paragraph—which would seem absolutely essential to understanding the impact of the intervention—appear in the evaluation's eighteen-page executive summary. That summary highlights only a few seemingly cherry-picked "positive" outcomes, almost entirely ignoring both negative findings as well as important context, both of which qualify or cast a very different light on many of the ostensibly positive findings presented. Examinations of additional Cure Violence evaluations and the portrayals of their findings by the evaluators and/or the Cure Violence organization itself reveal a similar pattern whereby the most favorable findings are carefully selected, often decontextualized or otherwise misrepresented, and negative findings are minimized or ignored entirely.[39]

As with the CPD's focused deterrence efforts, careful analysis indicates that the effects of Cure Violence on citywide levels of violence are dubious, at best. Chicago's homicide rate remained essentially unchanged from 2004, the year that the program expanded to eighteen of the city's high-violence communities, through 2015, after which it skyrocketed. Indeed, 2004 actually marks the year during which levels of homicide in the city plateaued after falling fairly consistently from 1994 to 2003 as gang leader–directed drug wars wound down. The expansion of Cure Violence, in other words, paradoxically coincided with a break in the decade-long trend of declining homicide in Chicago and the start of a subsequent decade-long stabilization in levels of homicide. These realities stand in stark contrast to the organization's preposterous claims of "a long and continuous trend of decreasing shootings and killings starting in 2001, coinciding with the start of the CeaseFire intervention."[40] While it might be argued that Cure Violence has operated in only about one quarter of Chicago's seventy-seven communities and, therefore, could not reasonably have an impact on levels of violence in the city overall, it should be noted that collectively these communities have accounted for a staggering 64 percent of the city's homicides since 2001.[41] Substantially reducing violence in these communities, therefore, would have demonstrable citywide effects, a reality the organization itself acknowledges and even promotes.[42] Even the early foundation for the narrative of Cure Violence's efficacy, its pilot in the West Garfield Park community, is decidedly suspect: In 2001, the first year following the commencement of the Cure Violence intervention, West Garfield Park had at least 22 homicides, representing *the highest homicide rate in the entire city*, at nearly 96 per 100,000. By comparison, Chicago's citywide homicide rate for that year was less than 22 per 100,000.[43]

Like the critique of focused deterrence offered earlier, findings from this study offer insights that may shed light on the inability of Cure Violence to reduce violence in Chicago. Again, this critique is rooted primarily in exposing incongruities between various assumptions embedded in the intervention model and the prevailing realities on the streets. Perhaps most centrally, the findings from this study call into question the assumption that potentially violent events can be detected and interrupted by Cure Violence staff members. As delineated in chapter 3, gang violence today is often spontaneous, arising from the expressive impulses of young gang members as opposed to the strategic orders of gang leaders. Increasing numbers of gang shootings occur in the absence of a specific provocation, acute precipitating factor, or even an instrumental end that might pattern violence in a discernable fashion. Identifying, predicting, or, in Cure Violence parlance, detecting potentially violent events under such circumstances can be extremely difficult, if not impossible, even for outreach workers with eyes and ears on the streets. Recall, for example, the spontaneity of the shootings recounted by Marco, Carlos, and Terrence in chapter 3. The interviews for this study are filled with such examples; here are but two more to help reiterate the point.

MONTRELLE: I was chillin' with some of the guys, and we had this .45 on the block. And then one of my mans was talkin' about he wanted to go do a hit on [the opps]. And I was like, "Nah, I wanna do it." So he's like, "You sure?" I'm like, "Yeah." So I put my stuff up. And I had my hoodie on and stuff like that. We walked out on Prairie, made sure the gun was clean, make sure I had one in the head [a bullet in the chamber], just talkin' about what we was gon' do. And then he went somewhere, and I was just in the cut waitin' for them to come on the block, right by this store where they hang out at. So after that, I called another friend to make sure I had a place to run to put the gun up, just in case. . . .

MARCO: We was in the park gettin' drunk, chillin'. Opps come through, we see they ass on the corner. It's two of 'em on bikes and shit. They just get to: "Yeah, BDK, woo, woo, woo." We: "Yeah, a'ight, woo, woo, woo." They drive back to they block—they be on Seventy-Seventh and Maryland, but they be on the little side routes, though, like, Seventy-Sixth and Drexel, you know, Ingleside. So lil bro wanna blow they ass down. I'm like, "A'ight, bet." I was walkin' with my homie lil Scoop, 'cause Scoop had the gun—he had a .38 revolver. I tell lil bro, "Come walk with us to get our eyes," you know, an extra set of eyes. So he walk with us. Then I see my homie Lu-Lu walkin' up the block. The only reason why he walkin' towards the opps' shit, he gotta have a gun on him, you know? So we like, "Yeah, what's up?" We just meet up right there. I'm like, "Damn, we was on the same shit. A'ight, what's up? How we finna do this?"

The decision to "do a hit" in the first incident described by Montrelle occurred within the context of routine conversation on the block, with nothing of any particular note preceding the decision and subsequent shooting: This shooting was simply another event in a chronic conflict with a rival gang. The shooting in the second incident occurred within perhaps ten minutes of the initial, very brief, and relatively unremarkable exchange between Marco and his comrades and a couple of guys from a rival block. Amazingly, Marco describes meeting up with another friend from his block, Lu-Lu, who was also casually making his way to shoot at their enemies, perhaps due to a similar back-and-forth with these individuals. These accounts beg the question: In the absence of literally standing on the block hanging out with these guys at all times, how is it possible to detect incidents like these in order that they might be interrupted? Without being able to detect and interrupt potentially violent incidents, a linchpin of the Cure Violence model collapses.

On a related note, the autonomy of individual gang members today limits the potential efficacy of longer-term conflict mediation. Gone are the days of gang leaders controlling violence on the streets, authorizing wars, ratifying treaties, and imposing violations on those who might dare to defy such edicts. The impulsive, unilateral actions of one gang member today can and often do break established peace treaties that all other members on both sides may have supported, leading to a resumption of violent conflict that may be even more difficult to mediate in the future. For the mediation of an ongoing gang war to be successful on a long-term basis, such an intervention would likely need to convince every single person on both sides of the conflict to agree to a permanent peace. If gang members themselves are unable to do so among their own closest comrades, it seems unlikely that the efforts of a violence interrupter, however well-intentioned and honorable, would be any more effective. Although violence between rival groups may decline over time for a variety of reasons—for example, new wars to which attentions are diverted, adaptations in behavior designed to minimize contact with rivals following spates of violence, gentrification-fueled displacement—it is important to note that none of the participants in this study reported an effective, lasting peace treaty with a rival group.

An additional assumption of the Cure Violence model is that former gang leaders represent credible messengers to today's youthful gang members based on their histories as powerful gang shot-callers. According to the model's proponents, this credibility is essential to the ability of Cure Violence street workers to interrupt violence and counsel active gang members. In the documentary film *The Interrupters*, for example, former Cure Violence director Tio Hardiman states that: "Most of the violence interrupters come from the hierarchy in some of these gangs. Because can't no anybody come in and tell a guy to put his gun down."[44] Even if the detection of potentially violent events was possible—an assumption obviously called into question by the preceding discussion—the findings from this study, and even some of the material from *The Interrupters* itself, indicate that contemporary street dynamics are more complex than this logic suggests, and they challenge the foundations underlying the assumption that former gang leaders have the capacity to stop contemporary gang violence.

While a background in the streets can no doubt aid in establishing rapport with the primary targets of Cure Violence's interventions, the notion that today's youthful gang members admire and will listen to former gang leaders is decidedly questionable. Indeed, it was a crisis of legitimacy among gang leaders, whom young gang members often viewed as coercive and exploitive, that served as a key factor in precipitating the internal rebellions that shattered Chicago's black street gangs and rendered their traditional leadership structures obsolete. Thus, today's young gang members typically express a general disinterest in, if not an intense opposition to, taking advice or direction from former gang leaders. "When you make your bones, you put the work in, people acknowledge that," Paris, a longtime Cure Violence worker, explains. "It's a subculture of kids today that don't give a fuck about that." In the following passages, Rasheed and Lamont expound on the disconnect between current gang members and former gang leaders, who, even under the relatively favorable intergenerational circumstances within their particular neighborhood, wield precious little influence among young gang members today.

RASHEED: I honor that type of shit [former gang leaders working to reduce violence], 'cause they tryin' to make the difference. But, shit . . .

RRA: Do you think it's making a difference?

RASHEED: Nah, not really. They don't got no control. They don't got no control. . . . Like, mu'fuckas ain't gon'—they probably listen to 'em so far. They gon' respect 'em in front of 'em, but when he ain't around, they gon' do them [do what they want], you feel me? Vice versa: We gon' respect our big homies and all that, but, shit, we gon' do what the—ain't no tellin' what we'll do.

LAMONT: If you've been gone to jail for thirty years, you big Black Stone. I'm one of the young Moes; I'm twenty. You get home, you join CeaseFire. You haven't been in my community for thirty years. Yeah, you grew up, you put work in, you was there when the train tracks was around, they was doin' the disco, condos wasn't there, the old store was there. You could tell all them old stories, but it's been thirty years. Now you comin' in, tellin' me "CeaseFire" from somebody who I'm into it with who just came to my mama crib and stole six TVs up outta the crib and he Folks, and he this, he that. You can't cease that. Right? So to say that a person who was once a part of a mob can cease something is a lie. . . .

You know, that's how older people think. You could tell they got that plan from an older person who said, "Nah, chief and them. . . ." I wouldn't date it that far back because it's a different date and time for which all of it occurred for which respect goes along. . . . But I can't say I'm thirty, I been out of the hood for fifteen, twenty years. Shorty and them finna get a gun and go down to the other end, and *I'm* the one that stopped them from doin' that? That's amazing! How are y'all doin' that?!

The potential issues associated with looking to former gang leaders as credible messengers capable of stopping the violence among young gang members, however, can go beyond simple ineffectiveness. In fact, a number of scenes from *The Interrupters* allude to such possibilities. At a roundtable staff meeting in one of the film's early scenes, for example, a Cure Violence interrupter recounts a recent spate of shootings in which he laments his ultimate powerlessness to effectively intercede: "They kept calling me: 'Man, they shooting!' I said, 'What you want me to do? What you want me to do? . . . I might get shot!'" Indeed, this worker's fearful statements appear well justified, as the film depicts two workers who were shot in the line of duty. Another scene, edited out of the final cut of the film but included as a special feature in the film's Blu-ray release, depicts an intense confrontation between a young man and a former gang leader and Cure Violence worker whom the young man has been told ordered the murder of his father when he was a small child. While the film reports that the young man was "satisfied" with the outcome of their conversation, Hardiman points out: "It's very important as far as violence interrupters to understand that whatever you did when you were running the streets, it follows you."[45] Obviously, attempting to interrupt street violence is a hazardous task, and transforming oneself from gang leader to community worker is a monumental undertaking; to say that these endeavors are commendable and even heroic is an enormous understatement. Yet while former gang members likely represent the most qualified candidates for street intervention work, and while they are no doubt effective in this capacity in some situations, the dynamics delineated here challenge Cure Violence's insistence on their incontrovertible credibility and capacity to interrupt gang violence in Chicago today.[46]

On a broader level, a 2016 Cure Violence report argues that the ebbs and flows of violence in Chicago can be traced directly to various periods of Cure Violence expansion and contraction since the early 2000s. The report claims that the dramatic increase in homicides that began at the end of 2015, for example, was precipitated by budget cuts in March of that year that led to widespread layoffs within the organization and the shuttering of most Cure Violence community intervention sites.[47] Even if one were to accept the general argument presented in the report (which has not been peer reviewed), the reality is that the lowest level to which Chicago's murder rate had fallen since the initial 2004 Cure Violence expansion, 15.2 per 100,000 in 2014, was nearly identical to the city's 2004 homicide rate of 15.5. By comparison, rates of homicide in almost every major city fell steadily and substantially during this period without the presence of Cure Violence, including Los Angeles and New York, whose respective homicide rates declined by approximately half, to 6.7 and 3.9.[48] In his interview, Paris responded to questions about these dynamics as they pertain to Cure Violence's efficacy in reducing violence as follows:

> I understand when people like, "What's goin' on? Why it's so fucked up?" Depending on what's your measuring stick. . . . Yeah, we got seven hundred homicides. We could've had seventeen hundred. We could've had seven thousand homicides. Somebody holdin' back—some mu'fucka stoppin' that. It's someone who's doin' some work. And I'm not just sayin' Cure Violence—it's people out here doin' work. . . . So I think, theoretical, it's a great question: Well, why is it still seven hundred homicides? I'm proposin' why it ain't seven thousand? Want me to take credit for the other 6,300 that didn't happen?

On one hand, Paris raises the valid point that the violent incidents prevented through Cure Violence (or other) interventions are not captured in the city's tallies of shootings and homicides, since these potentially violent events never came to pass. Without Cure Violence, in other words, levels of violence in Chicago might be higher than they have been and currently are. This may very well be the case. The issue, however, is that Cure Violence is not marketed as an intervention designed to simply keep levels of violence in a community or city stable—or even to reduce them incrementally, for that matter. Rather, the pitch is that Cure Violence will produce "large statistically significant reductions in violence" ranging from 41 to 73 percent.[49] This has decidedly *not* been the case in Chicago, where the model has had no discernable impact on overall levels of homicide in the roughly fifteen years since its initial expansion.[50]

THE TROUBLE WITH VACUUMS

One final assumption inherent in both the focused deterrence and Cure Violence models is that these interventions are capable of reducing violence without addressing broader conditions and issues shaping life in high-violence communities, such as those described in chapter 4. This assumption is both implied within these models as well as touted explicitly by their respective architects. The notion that if we "heal the economy . . . crime will take care of itself," David Kennedy writes, "didn't survive the first five minutes in Nickerson Gardens," a notorious housing project in the Watts section of Los Angeles where Kennedy did police consultation early in his career. All that is required to eliminate violence, from his perspective, is focused deterrence: "*We know what we need to know, now, to fix it.*"[51] Cure Violence, for its part, insists that, as a learned behavior, violence must be eradicated using "behavioral change techniques that are based not on moralistic or sociological diagnoses, but on proven scientific findings." Indeed, in his TED Talk, Gary Slutkin asserts that just as public health efforts have been able to successfully "manage malaria, and reduce HIV, and reduce diarrheal diseases in places with awful economies without healing the economy," Cure Violence is likewise able to effectively reduce violence in spite of not addressing the "awful" conditions within which it is bred.[52]

The particularities of both Kennedy's and Slutkin's arguments are rooted in what their respective models assume to be the fundamental issue driving violence. Each model, however, ultimately suffers from the same general shortcoming: divorcing violence from its broader context and placing it in an explanatory vacuum of its architect's own construction.

Cure Violence promotes a seemingly neutral, "scientific" view of violence as a behavior that can be learned and unlearned by anyone within any context. While this may be true in the most general sense, such a position fails to interrogate why violent behavior is apparently learned in some settings with so much greater frequency than in others. Anyone with even the vaguest sense of the world around them knows that violence is not distributed equally throughout the human community, but, rather, that it is concentrated in specific places: regions, countries, cities, and neighborhoods.[53] The boosters of Cure Violence certainly know this, which is why their programs are in Greater Grand Crossing and Englewood on Chicago's South Side, and not on the North Side in Lincoln Park and Forest Glen (or in the city's moneyed suburbs, for that matter). Indeed, Cure Violence recognizes violence as fundamentally a community problem driven by norms that promote violent behavior as acceptable. But what creates these patterns of norms in the first place? Why is violence a norm in Grand Crossing but not in Lincoln Park? Cure Violence does not broach these issues and brazenly dismisses a century's worth of research that has established and elaborated the linkages between poverty and desperation and gangs and violence as "sociological diagnoses" that they apparently do not consider "scientific findings."[54] Ultimately, the Cure Violence model treats violence as existing in a tautological vacuum: Violence is a result of problematic community norms that create violence that create problematic community norms, and so on. Cure Violence's dismissal of important realities beyond these parameters was not lost on study participants such as Lamont, who took the organization to task for what he perceived as its narrow and reactive approach to reducing violence: "Organizations like CeaseFire only come into the community when violence erupts. Who's there in the community before violence erupts? Who's advocating for that community that the violence is about to erupt in to make sure that this community is receivin' resources so no violence *won't* erupt? Nobody!"

Even some Cure Violence workers themselves view the model's relatively narrow focus as inhibiting the intervention's ultimate efficacy, if not distracting from broader, more fundamental drivers of violence. In one scene from *The Interrupters*, for example, violence interrupter Eddie Bocanegra laments: "You have CeaseFire, and our motto is to stop the violence. In essence, it's just a Band-Aid to this big issue that's going around us. Every single day, man, they ask me for jobs." Hardiman expounds on Bocanegra's point: "The African American community and the Latino community have been beaten down so long with poor schools, lack of jobs, hopelessness, despair, a lot of people can't stick with peace if they don't have a stick that they can hold onto."[55] Incredibly, addressing "environmental conditions that directly relate to the spread of the infection" is part of Cure Violence's own model of behavioral change, albeit one that the organization clearly spurns both rhetorically and in practice in favor of a decidedly narrower approach.[56] Below, Paris makes the case that addressing broader issues of community conditions and resource deprivation represents an essential part of a properly administered public health approach. He also acknowledges that Cure Violence ultimately fails to carry out this more holistic approach in practice.

PARIS: I think if you implement the public health approach correctly, you address those [environmental] things as well. You can't be usin' public health and not fixin' the root cause of it. That's what public health look like. It's not just the surface. If I know housing is an issue—a public health issue—the public health model is gon' fix the housing issue.

RRA: Do you think that's carried out in practice, though?

PARIS: Nah, nah, nah. No. Because, again, this gon' take more resources. This gon' take more investment to fix this. . . . I think that the health approach could—I think that people allude to it, they use it because it covers a lot of different things. But to get down to the root cause of it, I think when you triage it like a physician, you assess what the needs are, and you triage each need.

Undergirding the focused deterrence model, on the other hand, is the notion that urban violence emerges from what Kennedy frames as simply a big "misunderstanding" between police and black communities, and disillusioned black youth, in particular. He elaborates: "The government is not conspiring to destroy the community, the police are not uncaring, oppressive, racist. The community does not like the drugs and the violence. Gang members and drug dealers don't want to die, don't want to go to prison, don't want—nearly any of them—to shoot people. . . . *This* is what is at the heart of America's shame of violent death and mass incarceration and unspeakable community fear and chaos. These understandings and misunderstandings and the awful stereotypes they foster and reinforce, and the awful places they push ourselves and each other."[57] Focused deterrence, Kennedy argues, can destroy these stereotypes, heal these relationships, and eliminate violence: Young people will feel as though police are taking their safety seriously; police will exercise greater discernment in whom they treat like a criminal, pleasing the wider community; and the legitimacy and authority of law enforcement will be rightfully restored. While this analysis is slightly more complex than that of Cure Violence, it ultimately falls into the same trap as its counterpart, situating the phenomenon of violence in a circular, self-perpetuating causal loop divorced from all other considerations: Violence causes police to treat entire black communities as criminal, which causes black communities to distrust police, which causes violence, which causes police to treat entire black communities as criminal, and so on.

Beyond also ignoring issues of community conditions and resources, what is ultimately left uninterrogated in this position is the societal function of police. Implicit in Kennedy's argument is that law enforcement's fundamental role in society is what we have all been told it is: to protect and serve the community. For him, therefore, the challenge at hand involves helping police better realign themselves with and fulfill this mission. But a careful consideration of the other common understanding of police functioning, that police protect law and order, actually complicates and challenges the ostensible neutrality of the protect-and-serve narrative: Police do not simply protect and serve the community; they also play a central role in creating and protecting the prevailing social order. This reframing raises questions about the exact nature of this social order and whose interests are served and whose are undermined by the strengthening of the status quo—in this case, by the wielding of police power in the service of law and order. Certainly, it is not the interests of young black gang members and other poor and desperate youth in Chicago, who find themselves on the very bottom of this highly stratified social order by nearly every conceivable measure.[58] In what ways, then, do efforts to increase "understanding" between police and black communities and to (re)assert police authority also legitimize a status quo predicated on the marginalization of poor communities of color? In what ways might this strategy actually serve to deepen inequality and undermine meaningful social change?[59] At the very least, these and similar questions must be considered with respect to any initiative aimed at further subordinating dispossessed people to a status quo that has produced their dispossession.

Proponents of focused deterrence policing and the Cure Violence public health model promote views of gang violence as an invariable phenomenon. The nature of gang violence and the group dynamics driving it, in other words, are essentially the same in any given context, according to the assumptions on which these models are based. This argument is essential to the marketing of these interventions, which are framed as universally applicable: They can be implemented anytime, anywhere, and dramatically reduce levels of violence. Such narratives are understandably attractive to law enforcement, elected officials, and the broader public, all of whom are eager for solutions to intractable problems like gang violence—especially solutions such as these, which are relatively straightforward and cheap to implement.[60]

The failures of these interventions to reduce levels of violence in Chicago, however, challenge these simplistic narratives—both that the nature of gang violence is invariable and that focused deterrence and Cure Violence are panaceas for addressing such violence. Indeed, one must look no further than Chicago to refute both notions, as the gangs and violence on the city's South Side today are dramatically different from their 1990s predecessors, and at least part of the reason that these interventions failed in Chicago is likely due to a number of inconsistencies between various assumptions embedded in their models and the realities of gang dynamics and violence as they exist on the streets today. As delineated in this chapter, among these problematic assumptions are that gang members will exercise social control over one another to prevent violence, that police know who is responsible for violence, that potentially violent events can be detected and interrupted, and that former gang leaders have the power to effectively stop violence.

But there are deeper assumptions embedded in the focused deterrence and Cure Violence models as well. In particular, proponents of these respective interventions argue that violence can ultimately be reduced to a single cause: for focused deterrence, misunderstandings that strain police–black community relations; for Cure Violence, problematic community behavioral norms. These issues, then, are situated adjacent to violence in circular explanatory vacuums that delimit the horizons of analysis and the scope of potential intervention. Accordingly, both models assume that they can eliminate violence without accounting for and addressing the broader conditions and dynamics that drive it; indeed, proponents of focused deterrence and Cure Violence do not perceive these conditions to matter much, if at all, with respect to violence. In this sense, these intervention models mirror the narrow, decontextualized, variable-centric approach of much of today's gang research. As David Brotherton points out, such narrowly focused and abstracted theorizing problematically "posits deductively an ideal-typical construct on an objective reality . . . [and] reduces a complex, holistic social problem to an identifiable, measurable and quantifiable one that can be grasped by the outsider in the service of social control and well-funded investigation."[61]

In the end, the failure of focused deterrence and Cure Violence to make a discernable impact on levels of violence in Chicago indicates that reducing gang violence is not as easy as the proponents of these models proclaim it to be—at least not in Chicago. Perhaps these interventions might be more effective under circumstances that align more closely with their respective assumptions. Perhaps they can have an incremental impact on levels of violence in Chicago. Perhaps they can play a role in part of broader efforts to reduce violence. At the very least, however, one takeaway from the preceding analysis is clear: These models are ill-suited for reducing violence in any substantive way in the fractured gang landscape of Chicago's South Side today.

So, where does that leave things? What can be done to address gangs and reduce violence in Chicago? In a critique of interventions like Cure Violence, sociologist Andrew Papachristos points out that these programs often become "too big to fail," that recognizing and admitting "the failure of such programs would leave a massive void in our approach to violence prevention, in large part because we have put all of our eggs into one basket. . . . Programs like these must succeed. And they do, regardless of what good science has to say about it."[62] Baltimore serves as a useful case in point in this regard. Baltimore launched a focused deterrence initiative in the late 1990s; the program failed, and the city has continued to suffer with one of the nation's very highest homicide rates since that time. So what did Baltimore city officials decide to do to address this violence fifteen years later, in 2014? You guessed it: bring back focused deterrence. And what happened this second time around? You (should have) guessed it: It failed again. When the city relaunched focused deterrence back in 2014, it had just hit a relatively low point in terms of homicides that year with 211 (although, to be clear, this figure still made Baltimore among the deadliest cities in America). Following focused deterrence's implementation, the city's homicide total skyrocketed to 344 homicides in 2015—an astonishing 63 percent one-year increase—followed by successive years with 318 and 343 homicides. City officials finally decided to pull the plug again in mid-2017. "We know the program works," insisted one city councilman after the program's discontinuation was announced, apparently still unable to process its utter failure.[63]

All hope, however, is not lost. The conclusion that follows takes the lessons learned from this study and outlines the parameters of an alternative way forward for addressing gangs and reducing violence in Chicago.

Conclusion

REDUCING GANG VIOLENCE FROM THE STREETS UP

As the discussion in chapter 5 indicates, our understandings of street gangs and urban violence fundamentally shape our strategies for addressing these issues. On a societal level, gangs are generally understood as criminal enterprises whose members are inherently pathological and committed to a deviant subculture of senseless violence and predatory criminality (for example, see the discussion on pages 3–6 of the introduction). This one-dimensional, sensationalistic discourse informs the view that the only logical and appropriate response to gangs involves massive surveillance, severe police suppression, increasingly harsh prison sentences, and mass incarceration for those deemed to be members of these groups. Such approaches have effectively monopolized the public response to street gangs over the last four to five decades, despite startlingly little evidence of their efficacy in reducing violence or eradicating gangs.[1] Indeed, a growing body of research reveals not only the general inadequacy of such approaches but also their often-counterproductive effects: Aggressive policing, for example, often alienates communities and pushes young people into gangs, and incarceration tends to both increase gang membership and power and further destabilize distressed neighborhoods.[2] An extensive review of existing gang research published by the Justice Policy Institute, moreover, concludes that "the official response to an emerging gang problem is rarely based on a solid understanding of gang issues or a coherent theory of what an intervention should accomplish," but, rather, on "political and institutional considerations" that provide the illusion that officials are "doing something" while simultaneously maintaining the status quo.[3]

Despite their lack of demonstrable efficacy, to say nothing of their astronomical costs, police suppression and mass incarceration remain the dominant responses to street gangs throughout the United States. In Chicago, local, state, and federal officials have made it clear that they have no intention of deviating from this course. Following the lead of the Justice Department, for example, the Chicago Crime Commission's 2018 edition of *The Gang Book* promotes a "historical conspiracy strategy" for investigating and prosecuting gang members. Touted as an adaptation of traditional conspiracy cases to the city's fractured gang landscape, the strategy involves the identification of individuals believed to be violent gang members by law enforcement officials, who then seek out evidence in support of their theories in the service of building a criminal conspiracy case. Such an approach appears to invert the purpose and process of criminal investigation, taking as its starting point not a crime that must be solved, but a group of targets to which crimes must be attributed. Even more troubling, under this strategy, "every act committed by a gang member in furtherance of the gang or faction"—what this means, exactly, is not elaborated—"whether this act is a crime or not, is an explicit act of the conspiracy."[4] Framed slightly differently, once law enforcement officials decide that someone is a "violent gang member," any and everything they and their friends do might be interpreted as part of a nefarious criminal conspiracy. Police and prosecutors, then, appear committed to a problematic investigatory and prosecutorial strategy that involves tailoring the facts—whatever they may be—to fit their a priori theories, as opposed to building theories rooted in the facts as they actually exist. Given the dramatic transformation of black street gangs on Chicago's South Side into relatively small, leaderless collectives with marginal involvement in the drug game, moreover, conspiracy cases based on outdated notions of gangs as hierarchical criminal enterprises appear to make little sense.[5]

Focused deterrence policing and the Cure Violence public health model represent the proverbial cream of the crop of alternative, "evidence-based" approaches to addressing gangs and violence. Yet both of these interventions have decisively failed to put any discernable dent in levels of violence in Chicago. I argue in chapter 5 that these failures can be attributed, in part, to the erroneous assumption that gangs and violence are invariable, and that eliminating such violence within any context, therefore, simply requires the application of one of these purportedly fail-proof strategies. Indeed, the analysis presented over the course of this book has demonstrated that street gangs and gang violence are emphatically *not* invariable, but rather are shaped in fundamental ways by the particularities of the sociohistorical contexts within which they exist within a given time and place. For a variety of reasons specific to the prevailing dynamics among Chicago's black street gangs and the nature of contemporary gang violence—most notably, today's gang culture of autonomy, the unpredictability of contemporary violence, the dubious power of former gang leaders to stop violence, and the ineffectiveness of Chicago police—these one-size-fits-all strategies were and are ill-equipped to substantively reduce violence in Chicago.

As discussed in chapter 5 as well, the failures of focused deterrence and Cure Violence are also a result of leaving untouched the desperate conditions sustaining gangs and violence on the South Side of Chicago, as delineated in chapter 4. For the architects of these models, their alleged ability to eliminate violence without addressing such conditions serves as a distinct point of pride. Yet there is an additional layer to their arguments, namely, that eliminating violence actually represents "the essential pathway to a neighborhood being able to develop, for the schools to be able to get better, for the kids to get rid of their stress disorders, for businesses to feel safe enough and well enough to be able to come into these neighborhoods."[6] While high levels of violence no doubt further compromise community life in already-distressed neighborhoods, this argument effectively treats gang violence as if it were the primary cause of racist and predatory housing policies and lending practices, global economic restructuring, the proliferation of precarious part-time and low-wage employment, disinvestment in public education, welfare state retrenchment, and the vast expansion of the criminal justice apparatus since the 1970s. At worst, then, this perspective implies that the violent pathology of the residents of these neighborhoods is to blame for all of the ills plaguing America's abandoned urban core. At best, such a position accepts the premise that the provision of basic resources and services and a decent quality of life for the millions of people living in such communities throughout the country justifiably hinges on the local homicide rate—a phenomenon, it should be noted, that proponents of both focused deterrence and Cure Violence contend is driven by a tiny fraction of these residents. In both cases, these arguments belie a perspective that improving life in these communities should be determined by the market-driven imperatives of the private sector—that the state has no proactive role to play in such a process aside from policing and incarcerating.[7]

The findings from this study, on the other hand, indicate that gangs and violence on Chicago's South Side are the products of a complex, interrelated set of conditions, experiences, and perceptions shaping the lives of poor and working-class youth in these communities, particularly those related to marginalization and despair, poverty and economic exclusion, and pervasive community violence. For young people struggling to cope with such desperate circumstances, street gangs provide a range of vital material and psychosocial supports, including opportunities to earn money, caretaking, assistance in violent and potentially violent situations and conflicts, acceptance and love, emotional support, and, perhaps most centrally, resistance identities that facilitate the reconstruction of dignity and self-esteem systematically undermined by a lifetime of marginalization and vilification. Participation in collective violence, in turn, cements bonds and strengthens community among gang comrades and gives meaning to hard lives and early deaths. Gangs and violence, in short, serve a wide range of functions and play a variety of roles in the lives of thousands of marginalized and alienated young people in Chicago. Addressing street gangs and reducing violence on the city's South Side, then, will require substantive intervention in the various conditions fueling these issues.

Building on the analysis presented throughout the preceding chapters, this conclusion outlines an approach to this work that synthesizes both theoretical considerations and concrete action. This approach is laid out in three parts: the first makes the case for understanding gangs and violence as historical phenomena, the second aims to clarify the sociopolitical dynamics that create the conditions that perpetuate gangs and violence, and, finally, the third delineates an approach to intervention. As John Hagedorn argues, "If we pay attention . . . we are likely to question what we *think we know* about gangs. This might lead us to some different conclusions about what *we think we should do* about gangs."[8] The analysis delineated here suggests no simplistic fix, nor does it fit into a neat intervention package that can be marketed around the country or globe. Indeed, while the lessons and insights presented here are likely to have relevance in other contexts, they are firmly rooted in an analysis of these dynamics as they pertain to the South Side of Chicago in the early decades of the twenty-first century.

UNDERSTANDING STREET GANGS AS HISTORICAL PHENOMENA

The research described in this book makes a case for a historical approach to understanding street gangs—that is, a recognition that these groups are not immutable monoliths, but dynamic phenomena shaped in important ways by the prevailing conditions in the communities, cities, and world in which they are situated. Changes in these conditions, then, can and often do have effects on gang organization, ideologies, and internal dynamics. This reality likely has no better illustration than the stunning ascendance of Chicago's traditional black street gangs in the late 1960s and their remarkable shattering some four decades later: The crack epidemic precipitated the full-blown corporatization of these gangs during the 1980s; its waning proved a key factor in their shattering in the early twenty-first century. Deindustrialization caused widespread occupational displacement among Chicago's black working class, leaving gangs as one of the few sources of employment for poor and working-class black youth; the end of the crack epidemic and the transformation of drug markets, in turn, caused widespread occupational displacement among this same demographic. The concentration of public housing in poor black neighborhoods and their decades-long neglect by federal and local authorities set the stage for street gangs to assume informal governance in these developments; their eventual demolition played a decisive role in the eventual breakup of those gangs. The suppressive response of Chicago's Democratic machine to black street gangs and their wider criminalization in the post–civil rights era facilitated their expansion and consolidation of power in the Illinois Department of Corrections; the federal prosecutions that moved scores of gang leaders and other gang members to the Federal Bureau of Prisons beginning in the late 1980s hastened their demise.

As indicated above and as delineated over the course of the preceding chapters, moreover, street gangs have histories of their own. The rebellions that shattered Chicago's traditional black street gangs and their reconstitution during the early twenty-first century again serve as a quintessential case in point. A holistic approach to understanding street gangs, then, must include a multilayered analysis of a gang's history, the particular sociohistorical context(s) within which the gang developed and exists, and the ways in which these histories intersect with and bear upon the group and its members.[9] A reliance on established perspectives, even those generated through rigorous empirical research, can obscure accurate readings of these groups outside of the specific context(s) within which those perspectives were developed. Studies conducted on or about Chicago's street gangs during the 1990s, for example, which stress their rigid, centralized leadership hierarchies, their emphasis on drug distribution, and the exploitation and coercion experienced by rank-and-file gang soldiers, utterly fail to describe the gangs on the city's South Side as they exist today. On the other hand, this research, including the work of Felix Padilla, Sudhir Venkatesh, John Hagedorn, and Natalie Moore and Lance Williams, provides invaluable insights into the histories of these gangs that help anchor the historical analysis presented here, both with respect to the internal rebellions that shattered these gangs as well as their profoundly divergent reconfiguration.[10]

This type of contextual, historical approach to exploring street gangs has been advocated in various fashions by a range of distinguished scholars from a variety of disciplines, including critical criminologists Joan Moore, John Hagedorn, and David Brotherton; anthropologists James Diego Vigil, Dwight Conquergood, and Laurence Ralph; sociologists Sudhir Venkatesh and Robert Durán; and historians Deborah Levenson and Andrew Diamond.[11] In spite of their important contributions, however, these scholars represent a distinct minority in the broader field of gang research and operate largely outside of mainstream currents.

Mainstream gang researchers, on the other hand, tend to treat street gangs as self-contained groups effectively divorced from the world around them. This narrow, positivist approach to research eschews any analysis of history, the prevailing social order, or even more proximate contextual factors in order to isolate and analyze a priori, generally individual-level variables of interest as they relate to gang membership and/or criminal behavior. For example, perhaps the most ubiquitous area of study in the gang literature over the last three decades or so has been the exploration of correlations between gang membership and criminality and violence (alternately framed as "patterns of offending"). The veritable deluge of research on this topic, however, has shed remarkably little light on the phenomenon of gang criminality and violence beyond the conclusion, repeated with minimal variation in scores of articles, that gang members commit offenses at higher rates than nongang members and that this dynamic is a result of gang membership.[12] There is little to no examination of discrete processes that might produce these patterns, possible differences across time and space, the potential effects of variations in gang structure or culture, the specific nature of criminal and violent behavior, or its immediate and/or structural causes.[13] There is certainly no assessment of broader contextual factors or any sense of historical perspective. Criminologist Lorine Hughes derisively labels this approach a "variables paradigm" that treats gangs and their members as "social facts to be described rather than explained. . . . none of which adequately addresses the questions of how and why."[14] Such statistical correlations, moreover, are positivistically interpreted as the discovery of universal, objective truths about gangs, which are treated as monolithic, and their members, who are reduced to amalgamations of personal risk factors and criminality.

Within the mainstream perspective, then, street gangs and their members are—to borrow the term historian Eric Wolf ironically uses to describe the scholarly neglect and one-dimensional exoticization of non-Europeans in Western society—"people without history." Indeed, the conventional gang research paradigm represents a quintessential example of the scholarly tendency to "[turn] dynamic, interconnected phenomena into static, disconnected things."[15] Echoing Wolf, David Brotherton points out that, intentionally or otherwise, these limited approaches to exploring and understanding street gangs contribute to the proliferation of superficial and often demonizing representations of these groups as "highly plastic folk devil[s] outside of history."[16]

Even much of the gang research that seeks to address questions of how and why, however, fails to incorporate a historical perspective and falls into one or more intellectual traps in assuming that gangs are monolithic, can be categorized by static typologies, or follow a uniform developmental trajectory. While insightful in their own right, many studies describing gang formation and development, organizational structures, internal gang processes, and/or the relationships of gangs and their members to their families and wider communities retain a positivist orientation and treat their findings as universal insights into these phenomena—another step closer to fully discovering the ostensibly essential nature of gangs, as it were—as opposed to recognizing them as historically contingent and subject to transformation. One study, for example, claims to provide "the definitive account of 'how gangs work.'"[17] Similarly, although such research may include contextual information, contextual factors are often treated as static background scenery, with little consideration of their historical nature, the broader sociopolitical context within which they emerged, or how these factors and/or changes in them over time shape in any substantive way forms of gang organization, intra- and intergroup dynamics, or violence.[18] In its positivistic focus on universalism, then, the empirical approach of mainstream gang research largely mirrors the focused deterrence and Cure Violence models of violence prevention described in chapter 5. The radical reconfiguration of Chicago's black street gangs presented over the course of the last five chapters demonstrates the serious shortcomings of such attempts to essentialize gangs and violence, which fail to consider, much less examine and understand, variations that develop idiosyncratically as groups of young people interact with and respond to dynamic, evolving environments.

BROADENING THE ANALYTIC SCOPE AND CLARIFYING THE SOCIOPOLITICAL PREDICAMENT

As described in the preceding chapters, the conditions and prospects confronting poor and working-class black youth on the South Side (and West Side) of Chicago today are incredibly bleak, and it is from these realities that the gang violence that continues to plague these communities in the early decades of the twenty-first century flows. Indeed, gang members themselves cast their gang involvement and the violence in their communities in precisely these terms—that is, as by-products of the oppressive conditions with which they are forced to contend: pervasive poverty, near-absolute segregation, rampant un- and underemployment, hostility from law enforcement, widespread incarceration, crumbling infrastructure, routine violence, severely underfunded schools, and the like. With a sociological perceptiveness that would make C. Wright Mills proud, they understand the challenges in their lives not just as personal problems but as manifestations of broader community conditions and social issues.[19]

But what forces are responsible for the myriad issues confronting low-income African American communities on the South Side of Chicago? How did these issues arise as such in the first place, and why do they persist? When they change, why and how does this happen? At the societal level, these issues have been largely normalized through cultural narratives and social arrangements that cast them as natural, and they are generally accepted (often subconsciously) on those terms through rationalizations such as "that's just the way things are," "there's nothing we can really do about it," and "it's their own fault."[20] The reality, however, is that these issues are not intrinsic features of human civilization. Rather, they emerge within specific historical circumstances and are produced via mechanisms embedded in the prevailing social order. Like street gangs themselves, in other words, these phenomena must be situated within a broader sociohistorical framework and examined in relation to the cultural, social, political, and economic contexts in which they have been shaped.

The dynamics that precipitated the shattering of Chicago's black street gangs discussed in chapter 1, for example, did not materialize out of thin air or by happenstance. Rather, they reflected a culmination of trends taking place both in Chicago and nationally over the last half-century. The near-wholesale demolition of Chicago's public housing projects was driven by the convergence of a wide range of factors that facilitated the deterioration of these developments and then justified their eventual clearance. Among the more notable of these factors were: the ideological and economic imperative that public housing not compete with housing in the private market, thereby restricting residence in public housing to extremely low-income tenants; cost restrictions for public housing construction that undermined quality in terms of design, materials, and craftsmanship; maintenance and security problems derived from these shortcuts that intensified over time as buildings descended into utter disrepair; grossly insufficient federal operating subsidies; decades of extraordinary managerial incompetence, corruption, and neglect; a shifting political climate in which the welfare state came under ideological assault and fiscal retrenchment; and, ultimately, widespread acceptance of the neoliberal imperative of "accumulation by dispossession" whereby the desirable real estate near the downtown Loop on which public housing was situated was privatized and commodified and its residents displaced.[21] The imprisonment of increasing numbers of gang members and other poor and working-class Chicagoans, the incarceration of gang leaders in federal prisons, and the intensification of urban policing since the 1970s most fundamentally reflect emergent strategies for containing and warehousing "a huge and growing surplus population" made obsolete by urban deindustrialization and the rise of the global finance and information economy. Within this context, political scientist Cedric Johnson argues, "the carceral state . . . has come to replace the welfare state as the chief means of managing social inequality," as the prison population has skyrocketed while programs like public housing and federal income support have been dismantled.[22]

The conditions and dynamics explored in chapter 4 that continue to fuel gangs and violence on Chicago's South Side are driven by similar prerogatives of neoliberal "pro-growth" economics, the dismantling of public services, attacks on organized labor, privatization, and the containment and displacement of "undesirables" that collectively serve the interests of investors and developers at the expense of low-income communities of color.[23] The 2016 edited volume *Chicago Is Not Broke* provides a useful blueprint with respect to a number of these dynamics. Its contributors identify nearly $10 billion dollars that have been cumulatively "stolen" from the public via corruption, bad city banking deals, and payouts from police abuse; "hidden" in tax-increment financing (TIF) district tax shelters; or "not collected" due to regressive taxation policies and inadequate municipal systems.[24] A 2018 report by the Cook County Clerk's Office, moreover, reveals that nearly one-third of all Chicago property tax revenues are diverted from the city's coffers into TIF districts, and nearly half of the $660 million in 2017 TIF revenues were funneled to fewer than 10 of the city's 143 districts—nearly all of them in wealthy, predominantly white areas.[25] So while the city cries broke as a justification for closing public schools, shuttering its mental health facilities, privatizing public housing, and its broader disinvestment in low-income neighborhoods on the South and West Sides, business is booming for the city's moneyed elite, the downtown and the North Side are thriving, and Chicago police enjoy an ever-expanding budget while having no discernable impact on levels of violence and solving ever fewer crimes.[26] While study participants may have lacked a fully elaborated analysis of the interests fueling these dynamics, they were nonetheless remarkably discerning in casting their predicament as part and parcel of the prevailing social order and their marginal place within it. Rick and Lamont, for example, explain their views on the persistence of these issues as follows:

RICK: They already resulted to reducing the population. Shit, that's what they doin' right now. They *lettin'* mu'fuckas kill each other. They *want* for the population to be reduced, man. They want mu'fuckas to kill each other. They want this to happen so they—you know, they ain't doin' nothing but making jails bigger. That's all they wanna do. So I don't even know what to tell him [the mayor, if he asked Rick about reducing the violence]. I'd probably get mad, if anything, 'cause he the reason why the shit goin' on.
RRA: So you feel like, basically, if they wanted it to stop . . .
RICK: They could've stopped this shit. They want this shit to be goin' on.

LAMONT: Police officers need jobs, judges need jobs, lawyers need jobs, prisons have to stay full. Politicians wanna stay in office, [so] there needs to be issues for people to work on. Right? So if they wanted to fix this problem, they could have been fixed it. We look at all of the other countries that we give packages of money to, to do this and do that and do this. If we gave Chicago a $10 billion package, the violence would automatically cease.

Notably, these dynamics have evolved and persisted in Chicago within a context of absolute predominance by the Democratic Party in city government for nearly a century. The vast majority of this period was dominated by the city's Democratic political machine, most famously under the mayorships of father and son Richard J. and Richard M. Daley, each of whom served over twenty years in office, from 1955 to 1976 and from 1989 to 2011, respectively.[27] While early decades of machine rule were noteworthy for the marginalization of African American political factions despite widespread black electoral support, the city's most recent mayors, Richard M. Daley and Rahm Emanuel, consolidated considerable black (and Latino) electoral support via the more substantive integration of political and civic elites of color into their governing coalitions.[28] Yet this shift has done remarkably little, if anything, to improve the quality of life in the city's poor and working-class black communities, as the Daley administration prioritized "pinstripe patronage," directing resources toward "real estate developers, lawyers, financiers, and other [businessmen]"; and Emanuel intensified this brand of elitist, "business-friendly" politics to a degree that earned him the derisive nickname "Mayor 1%."[29] As Pernell, a study participant who was schooled in the Woodlawn community's unique blend of street and formal politics, observes, Emanuel is "all about big business. If it's nothing that has to do with big business and dollars, he don't want anything to do with it."[30]

In some ways, moreover, the diversity of the Daley and Emanuel governing coalitions has likely helped facilitate the continued marginalization of Chicago's low-income communities of color. Indeed, African American bureaucrats have routinely been deployed to oversee the dismantling of public services in these communities, providing racial "cover" that has functioned "to legitimate and help impose racially charged redevelopment."[31] This has been especially true with respect to efforts to privatize public housing and public education. Vincent Lane, a black man, ran the Chicago Housing Authority (CHA) from 1988 to 1995, before it was placed under federal control. Lane implemented a series of controversial, draconian policies during his tenure, including Operation Clean Sweep, a series of predawn raids in which police conducted warrantless searches of entire project buildings. These sweeps netted few major arrests but cost the CHA $175,000 each, draining $78 million from the organization's budget annually by 1994, when they were halted by a federal judge. Lane was also a prominent advocate of public housing demolition and privatization, and, as chairman of the National Commission on Severely Distressed and Troubled Public Housing, played a vital role in pushing for passage of the HOPE VI program in 1992 that would serve as the major vehicle toward these ends in the ensuing decades.[32] More recently, the closing of forty-nine of Chicago's public schools in 2013, almost all of them in low-income African American communities, was overseen by then schools CEO Barbara Byrd-Bennett, a black woman. Both Lane and Byrd-Bennett later served time in prison for fraud and corruption, respectively.[33] Perhaps sensing these dynamics, study participant Cassius, who initially declared, "I think we need a black mayor to fix our city," quickly clarified his stance: "I ain't gon' say black mayor, but we need a mayor that really give a fuck about the black people on this side of town."

Thus, while the $10 billion figure cited earlier by Lamont in reference to a proposed government aid package for distressed communities in Chicago may be somewhat arbitrary, its enormity reveals an accurate assessment of both the scope of the challenges facing Chicago's neglected black neighborhoods as well as the reality that the amelioration of these issues will require a vast investment of public resources.[34] (Ironically, it is the exact amount *Chicago Is Not Broke* argues is being stolen, hidden, and not collected in the city due to corruption, government dysfunction, and handouts for developers and investors.) The suggestions of study participants themselves provide a useful blueprint for policy prescriptions to address the marginalization and despair, poverty and economic exclusion, and presumption of violent victimization that continue to fuel gang violence on the South and West Sides. These include a vast expansion of meaningful employment opportunities, the rebuilding of neighborhood infrastructure, better-funded schools, recreational resources, mental health services, and an end to police harassment and brutality and the criminalization of black youth. The exigencies described by study participants and their proposed solutions parallel the analyses of prominent scholars such as Mary Pattillo and Loïc Wacquant, whose research in Chicago informs their own respective calls for public "invest[ment] in poor black neighborhoods 'as is,'" and "a concerted attack on labor degradation and social desolation in the decaying hyperghetto."[35]

Adequately addressing these issues will require a massive shift in public policy involving a fundamental redistribution of resources away from the Loop, the city's upwardly mobile and predominantly white communities, and the Chicago Police Department. While the realization of such a policy agenda will unquestionably be an uphill political battle, like the discussion in the previous section that challenges the reflexive tendency to essentialize gangs and violence, the analysis delineated here confronts the tendency to reify the conditions that fuel these issues as ahistorical and naturally occurring. Thus, this is not a purely theoretical exercise, but one that is crucial to informing social action to address these issues. Gangs and violence are neither easy nor impossible to address; rather, we should recognize that doing so effectively will require the redeployment of public resources necessary to ameliorate the desperate conditions that drive them. Even more fundamentally, this will require the development of the political will to pursue an agenda aimed at transforming the highly stratified social order in Chicago. The analysis that follows, then, proceeds both from the self-evident reality that this political will does not currently exist and from the conviction that cultivating it is possible. Indeed, only in challenging the hegemonic ahistorical paradigm for understanding these issues can they be resituated where they rightfully belong: firmly within the scope of history, amenable to transformation via human action, just as they have been produced by it.

OUTLINING A STRATEGY FOR INTERVENTION: RELATIONSHIPS, RESISTANCE, AND SOCIAL MOVEMENTS

A final, essential element of this historically oriented analysis that has been intimated but not yet elucidated is that history is not simply *done to* street gangs and their members; they are not passive objects only capable of reacting to their experiences and realities in involuntary, predetermined ways. Rather, these individuals and groups possess agency as historical actors. To be certain, like all people, gang members are embedded in a web of social, political, and economic structures that shape their experiences and perspectives in fundamental ways. These realities, however, do not mechanically control their individual or collective values, cultures, ideologies, practices, or behaviors: Individually and collectively, gang members have the capacity for conscious, purposeful action. Indeed, the internal rebellions waged by young rank-and-file gang members that shattered Chicago's traditional black street gangs in the first decade of the twenty-first century and the radically divergent reconstruction of new gang forms in their wake represent prime examples of this capacity for historical agency. While these events were certainly shaped in important ways by a wide range of historical dynamics, there were no guarantees that the actors involved would respond to these evolving historical circumstances in the particular ways that they did. What ultimately happened in Chicago, then, as described in this book, was an understandable and perhaps even likely outcome of these dynamics, but certainly not the only one possible.[36]

Understanding this is vital to imagining and charting a new way forward. Just as the trajectory of black street gangs on Chicago's South Side over the last two decades was not predestined, neither is their future. Indeed, there is a unique window of opportunity for intervention today with black gangs on the city's South Side. Gang members are overwhelmingly marginalized in the underground economy and harbor few, if any, illusions about the viability of a career in the drug game. They have also rejected both the authority of former gang leaders as well as the ideologies that long gave Chicago's traditional street gangs a quasi-religious quality. In short, a number of forces that may have impeded effective intervention during previous gang eras have diminished substantially, if not entirely, in the contemporary moment. Individually and collectively, then, today's young gang members are "up for grabs" more so than at any time in nearly half a century.[37]

The remainder of this conclusion outlines a strategy for intervening with young gang members on the South Side of Chicago today rooted in both the analysis developed over the course of this book as well as the direct insights of gang members on these matters. This analysis converges on a central program around which intervention efforts might be effectively organized: specifically, one that involves engaging gang members in grassroots organizing and social movements to address the injustices that fuel gangs and violence in their communities in the first place. Such a strategy has the potential for both positive short-term effects with respect to moving young people away from gangs and violence as well as longer-term implications for challenging the conditions that underlie these issues at a more fundamental level. Indeed, as discussed in the previous section, the redistribution of resources into low-income black communities in Chicago to address these issues would represent a radical departure from the prerogatives of benign neglect, outright abandonment, containment, and displacement that have alternately characterized official city policy toward these communities for the better part of a century. Deviation from this course is unlikely in the absence of adequate social, political, and economic pressures being brought to bear on City Hall and beyond.[38]

To be certain, the notion that building collective power among poor and oppressed people to alter the systems deleteriously affecting their lives represents the essential cornerstone of both the practice and scholarship on organizing and activism, prescribed by luminaries from Frederick Douglass and Eugene Debs to Frances Fox Piven and Adolph Reed Jr.[39] Saul Alinsky, widely considered the "father "of modern community organizing, distilled this axiom as follows: "Power has always derived from two main sources, money and people. Lacking money, the Have-Nots must build power from their own flesh and blood. A mass movement expresses itself with mass tactics . . . [against] the status quo."[40] On this point, the participants in this study overwhelmingly agreed with the experts. As alluded to in the discussion above, when asked about their recommendations for addressing violence in Chicago, study participants contended that substantively reducing violence would require a broader transformation of the intolerable conditions in their communities that would necessitate a massive investment of resources, a prospect participants regarded as unlikely: If these issues had been allowed to persist for decades, why would that precedent change now? In the eyes of study participants, then, the only—or at least the most reasonable—possibility for changing this dynamic involves organizing and mobilizing around these issues in order to pressure elected officials and other powerful actors to respond to these needs. In the passages below, for example, Antonio and Marco draw on the legacy of insurgent African American social protest and collective action in describing their recommendations for reducing violence in Chicago. Indeed, although the question to which they responded was framed in terms of advice they would give the mayor to address this violence, their responses, like the passage from Rick cited earlier, reveal their complete lack of faith in the will of the political establishment to take meaningful action toward this end—at least in the absence of the proper pressure (see also the discussion on pages 113–15).

ANTONIO: When [people] say Obama's gon' help us, fuck that. I don't believe in that shit, man. He supposed to be from the same streets as everybody—as Chicago—but what the fuck is he doing? . . . So when people say, "Oh, we need a change"—get your ass up, go downtown, protest. Let these mu'fuckas know what the fuck is goin' on. But one person can't do it, man, for real. . . . You gotta use your own voice to make everybody else hear you to join in. You feel me? Think about Martin Luther King, Rosa Parks, all them, man. One person ain't enough. You gotta have of a bagillion mu'fuckas come behind you. . . . One person in a room full of thousands of people, you can't hear them. But a thousand people talkin' over one person, you ain't got no choice but to hear what the fuck they sayin', especially if they all sayin' the same thing.

RRA: So if you were the mayor of Chicago, what would you do to reduce violence in the city?

MARCO: If I was the mayor, I don't know how I would reduce violence. But what I know I would do as far as—like, okay, let me say it like this. Back in the 1960s,

> you know, black people was all together back then because we all basically had a common enemy, though, it was police brutality and shit. I always hear the old people say black people used to talk a lot and make sure everybody good, and it was, like, a *community*, you feel me? Mu'fuckas just gotta remember that. It's like people don't remember where we came from, man, and how we used to fight for our rights back then and shit. Now police do anything the fuck they want because we don't got that same drive no more. . . .
>
> I feel like the only thing that'd get everybody on the same page is if we had a common enemy, man. Like, say if you was to get into it with the police, you feel me, that'd be different than gettin' into it with [other] niggas, 'cause it's like, damn, that's the police, though—everybody hate the police, you know? That'd have to be the only way to get back on the same page—if it was back like the 1960s.

The argument presented by Antonio and Marco here, that grassroots organizing and social movements hold the key to reducing gang violence, is almost entirely absent from research on street gangs and violence.[41] Yet, as will be delineated in the following pages, this approach is highly consistent with the broader analysis presented in this book, even beyond its potential as a strategy by which the conditions that breed gangs and violence might ultimately be addressed. Meaningful and sustainable efforts toward these ends will likely involve the following elements, each of which builds on the others: building relationships, developing critical consciousness, reconstructing resistance identities, and finding common ground. The basic parameters of each of these elements will be described here in a way that offers theoretically grounded guidance on the practical matter of working with gang members to shift their energies from fighting one another toward fighting the injustices that fuel gang conflicts at the structural level.

First and foremost, any attempt to intervene with gang members today must begin with concerted efforts by community organizers, activists, social workers, and other caring and committed individuals to build meaningful relationships with them. As the findings from this study have demonstrated, there is perhaps nothing more important to black gang members on the South Side of Chicago today than personal relationships, which have superseded both traditional gang affiliations as the principal basis for gang solidarity as well as drug dealing as the primary raison d'être of gang life. These shifts bode well in terms of the potential for intervention. Developing such relationships can be challenging work, however, as these young people have often been ignored, abused, and/or exploited by those charged with helping and protecting them, including their parents, foster families, teachers, social workers, and police officers, and they can be understandably guarded in whom they place their trust. Thus, building trusting relationships with gang members can take months of persistent effort and may require demonstrations of genuine commitment and care that go beyond the parameters delineated in a job description. These relationships are also best forged on the streets, where gang members spend much of their time and where those interested in working with them are often hesitant to venture. On the other hand, most gang members are open to assistance, especially from those they feel have their best interests at heart, and most yearn for a viable alternative to gangbanging. Yet their life experiences tell them that such assistance will likely never come—hence, their reticence in placing their trust in those who say they wish to help them. In the following passage, Montrelle explains the necessity of building strong relationships with gang members, as well as the hard work required to do so, as a precondition to effectively working with them. Also evident in his remarks is that an outreach worker or activist's background in the streets means little in the absence of a long-term, caring relationship.

RRA: What have been your experiences with violence reduction programs or organizations in the community, if you've had any?

MONTRELLE: I really haven't had too many. They just think comin' to tell us—some dude will come tell us a one-time story about what he used to do. Or somebody just tellin' us not to [gangbang]. It's nothing that's really benefittin' us. It's just a moment. That's all it be. It's nothing that's really life-changing. So with these dudes now, they need to really care. They need to be out there with us. . . . That's the only way y'all could get us to change our thinking.

Consistent with this emphasis on personal relationships, however, it is unlikely that gang members will be fundamentally swayed by the types of passive, cyber-oriented organizing of groups like Black Lives Matter. A tweet by an activist announcing and encouraging participation in a downtown protest is unlikely to spur most gang members—or most other people, for that matter—into action, much less help facilitate any type of more fundamental personal transformation. Indeed, while gang members certainly sympathize with the goal of addressing police violence, none that I know are involved in Black Lives Matter in any substantive way, and questions about the group elicited little response from study participants. My sense is that this disconnect stems, at least in part, from the discrepancy between today's impersonal organizing tactics and foundational lessons from community organizing and social movements, which indicate that people become active in these efforts through involvement in neighborhood groups, local churches, and other primary groups in which they are embedded. This was the rationale for Chicagoan Saul Alinsky's strategy of creating an "organization of organizations" in his work, which facilitated the consolidation of broader membership bases by tapping into and empowering existing group networks—churches, labor unions, and the like. Similarly, Aldon Morris's seminal analysis of the civil rights movement reveals that what many consider a monolithic movement was in reality a collection of local movements rooted in networks of established groups, most notably African American churches, whose members shared close personal relationships.[42] These historical lessons appear particularly important to engaging gang members in social movements today given the intensely interpersonal focus of contemporary gang structures and ideologies. This may also help explain their indifference to Black Lives Matter and similar contemporary "movements" that have developed in the near-complete absence of meaningful face-to-face organizing efforts.[43]

Moving gang members toward prosocial collective action, moreover, will likely require the development of a new form of critical consciousness that can serve as a foundation for politicization. In *Pedagogy of the Oppressed*, his seminal work on popular education and social transformation, Paulo Freire argues that the mobilization of the dispossessed is dependent on their reinterpretation of the oppressive conditions shaping their lives and their communities as historical and changeable, rather than natural and inevitable. Freire refers to this process as *conscientização*, or conscientization, which he explains as "critical thinking by means of which people discover each other to be 'in a situation.' Only as this situation ceases to present itself as a dense, enveloping reality or a tormenting blind alley, and they can come to perceive it as an objective-problematic situation—only then can commitment exist. Humankind *emerge* from their *submersion* and acquire the ability to *intervene* in reality as it is unveiled . . . [through] the *conscientização* of the situation."[44]

As the analysis presented in chapter 4 suggests, many gang members remain "submerged" in their "situation" and conceive of it as essentially unchangeable. For Freire and other social theorists like Antonio Gramsci and Pierre Bourdieu, this is an understandable state, since people are socialized to assume the legitimacy and naturalness of the prevailing social order in which they live.[45] Yet the passages from Antonio and Marco cited earlier indicate that the seeds of a more fully formed critical consciousness that rejects the invulnerability of the unjust status quo already exist within many gang members as well. Indeed, the internal rebellions that shattered Chicago's traditional black street gangs and the subsequent, radical refashioning of these gangs were only possible through a critical consciousness among young gang members in which exploitive and coercive gang structures and practices were perceived as not only problematic but also transformable (see, especially, the quotes from James, Carlos, and Jabari on pages 36–37). In this sense, there is a precedent for both the development of critical consciousness as well as the possibility of translating that consciousness into collective action within the purview of gang members' own lived experiences. Lamont, who works with a community organization and grew up in Woodlawn, a South Side community with a long history of grassroots organizing and action, suggested conducting civic education and engagement trainings as a means of demystifying the political process and equipping gang members and other community residents with a blueprint for changing the conditions in their neighborhoods. The latent theory embedded in Lamont's recommendations largely parallels Freire's description of *conscientização*:

> You can't reduce violence until you educate the people. And a lot of times the reason why [powerful] people don't want to educate the people is because politicians get put out of office when people really learn what civic engagement is. I would create workshops where people in the community can learn civic engagement. So, me as the alderman of that community, if I'm not doin' my job, they can empower themselves to get me out of office because I want to be held accountable. Most people don't teach people how to get a gun and shoot 'em, right, because I wanna rule and do whatever that I really wanna do.

Another component of the process of politicizing gang members and moving them toward participation in social movements will involve helping them reimagine and reconstruct their resistance identities. As delineated in chapter 4, the concept of resistance identity is useful for helping elucidate many of the psychosocial functions and meanings that street gangs fulfill in the lives of their members. On one hand, these resistance identities have helped gang members reassert a sense of dignity and self-worth in the face of intolerable conditions and placed them at odds with an oppressive social structure they understand to be responsible for these conditions. On the other hand, these identities also promote internecine violence and other (self-)destructive behaviors that further imperil and marginalize young gang members and undermine the social fabric in their communities. As they are currently constructed, in other words, gang members' resistance identities situate them in opposition to the oppressive status quo, but do so in ways that are largely self-defeating.[46] Indeed, as Manuel Castells argues, resistance identities are neither inherently positive nor negative; rather, they can function in multiple, even conflicting, ways and have the capacity to evolve over time.[47] The challenge, as these dynamics pertain to addressing gang violence, then, involves helping gang members refashion their resistance identities in ways that facilitate redirecting their energies away from (self-)destructive street parochialism and gang warfare and toward prosocial collective action. Brotherton astutely frames the central question, or challenge, relating to gang resistance in terms of "whether this resistance has the potential to become transformative."[48]

Other studies of gang interventions offer some insights into what such a process might look like. In his research on the work of Christian barrio ministries with Chicano gang members in Los Angeles, for example, Edward Orozco Flores reports that these ministries promoted a "reformed barrio masculinity" among "recovering" gang members that effectively reoriented them "from the street to the household." Importantly, however, Flores notes that these interventions "did not attempt to discard all facts of gang masculinity, or masculine gang embodiment," as "reforming all facets of embodied gang masculinity was unlikely." Instead, their intervention models "allowed men to appropriate facets of gang embodiment in order to facilitate recovery from gang life and progress toward conventional manhood."[49] In another example, David Brotherton and Luis Barrios describe how reformed leaders of the Latin Kings and Queens in New York

City incorporated a variety of "nongang traditions," including radical politics, spirituality, and self-help principles, into the ideological fabric, organizational policies, and daily rituals of the gang as part of their transformation toward a prosocial community movement during the 1990s.[50] A number of the older participants in the research for this book, moreover, talked about using the traditional literature from their gangs as a guide for personal transformation. This was especially true among the older Gangster Disciples I interviewed, who were at the height of their street involvement when the gang was both the largest drug distribution organization in Chicago and simultaneously making inroads into legitimate social and political endeavors under the banner of "Growth and Development."[51] Daniel explains these dynamics as they unfolded in his life during a period of incarceration as follows:

> I read a lot of literature that these organizations write—their organization literature. And all of it is positive, instructive, uplifting words. All of 'em have laws and policies that restrict unhealthy behavior. So I was able to use that as a way of rehabilitating myself. Not to say I didn't seek God's help. I did. And I read the Bible, and I also read the Quran. But it's nothing like reading something your brothers wrote and usin' that as a daily guide. It's nothing like it. I don't know who wrote the Bible. I don't know who wrote the Quran. I know who they say did. But I know who wrote that literature—I know these people personally. You know what I'm sayin'? And I know where they got some of the stuff from. I know these guys are scholars, in a sense. But when they were writin' this, they were writin' this with people like ourselves in mind. So it was easy for me to use those words to turn my life around. And I'm glad that as I was doin' so, so were they—in deed, not just in words. So that when I returned to society and they returned to society, we were on the same page. And there was no stigma attached to tryin' to be an example of those words and not the stereotypical view of how people would view somebody from an organization called the Gangster Disciples.[52]

Each of these examples differs in important ways from the current challenge in Chicago: Unlike the ministry programs described by Flores, the goal would not be to move gang members toward "conventional manhood"; there are no leadership structures through which the gang identity reconstruction processes might be facilitated, as in Brotherton and Barrios's study; and the rejection of traditional Chicago gang ideologies—both the good and the bad—by young gang members in the early twenty-first century precludes their use as an effective blueprint for gang resocialization today. Nonetheless, these represent useful examples of processes of identity reconstruction among gang members involved in transitioning away from (self-)destruction and toward prosocial values and commitments.

As alluded to in these examples, moreover, specific elements of gang identities within a particular context may lend themselves to the creation of healthier forms of identification. For gang members on the South Side of Chicago today, these elements include their commitment to solidarity, the tremendous value they place on relationships, and their devotion to their neighborhoods. While these aspects of gang identity often manifest in limited, if not destructive, ways—solidarity and relationships, for example, often function to isolate gang members from those outside their immediate circles, and neighborhood devotion often entails shooting at members of the opposition from adjacent neighborhoods—these are not the only manifestations imaginable or possible. The identity reconstruction process, in other words, would not necessitate the wholesale repudiation of gang members' current identities—an unappealing and unlikely prospect for any group of people. In one gang study, for example, gang members were asked, "What would be the best way to get rid of your gang?" When participants responded that all of their members would have to be killed to eliminate the gang, the researcher interpreted this as evidence of the centrality of violence to gang culture—that gang members were so engrossed in violence they could not see beyond its narrow, lethal horizons. Apparently, he did not consider that participants may have been responding defiantly to a hostile question in which they and their friends were framed as something "to get rid of."[53] Realistically, who would respond well to being told that who they are and what they represent are worthless and need to be eradicated? While some elements of gang identity may indeed require outright abandonment, much of this process would instead involve helping gang members reinterpret the constituent elements of their identities and redefine how they might manifest in prosocial, transformative ways.

Finally, part of this transformation process would inevitably involve helping gang members recognize the common ground they share with members of rival gangs, in particular, their shared conditions and the common sources of those conditions—their "common enemy," as Marco put it. Political theorist Adolph Reed Jr. frames the challenge of developing social movements straightforwardly as "organizing, working ... to build support and solidarity among real people in real places around concrete objectives that they perceive as concerns."[54] As described over the course of this book, the concerns of young gang members today are myriad and severe. Importantly, however, they also cut across gangs, neighborhoods, and communities. The commonality of these concerns and the objectives designed to address them, then, constitute a potential foundation for the transcendence of gang antagonisms and the redirection of gang members' energies away from internecine violence and toward prosocial collective action.[55] In this capacity, these processes hold the potential to reduce violence even beyond the reductions that would accompany the policies, programs, and reforms secured through such efforts. They also represent a logical basis for strengthening ties between gang members and other constituent groups in their communities in the pursuit of common objectives around, among other issues, living wage employment, affordable housing, community infrastructure, neighborhood schools, and police accountability. These issues affect broad segments of residents in these communities, and therefore might serve as a foundation for deepening intracommunal relationships more generally.[56] Indeed, if these issues only affected gang members, or if gang members were the only ones that might be mobilized around them, substantive transformation on these fronts would be essentially unthinkable.

While they certainly need a great deal of cultivation, the seeds for building bridges across gang boundaries by emphasizing common concerns and interests are already present in many gang members. Indeed, the gang members interviewed for this study and many more with whom I have worked closely over the years yearn for peace. On their face, such antiviolence sentiments may seem paradoxical given gang members' direct involvement in the violence they say they wish would stop. Considering the toll that this violence takes on them, however, both as victims and perpetrators, their position is quite intelligible. To be sure, no one has more to gain from the end of gang hostilities than gang members themselves, as they are its principal victims: They are the ones who must operate on high alert anytime they are outside, even in their own neighborhoods; who cannot walk or take the bus a handful of blocks away from their homes in any direction because they are besieged by rivals; who are coping with post-traumatic stress; who face near-daily harassment and the prospect of brutality at the hands of the police; who are being shot, killed, and incarcerated at alarming rates. This reality clearly contradicts the image of gang members as irredeemably pathological so often promoted by the media, law enforcement, elected officials, and mainstream gang researchers. The truth is that, in their quiet moments of reflection, gang members almost universally talk about wanting a different life for themselves and their families. Incredibly, few gang studies or gang interventions actually ask gang members what they think about the high levels of violence in their communities, their participation in such violence, or what strategies they think might be effective in reducing this violence. This is quite remarkable given that efforts to address street gangs and reduce gang violence are, by definition, designed to directly or indirectly change the behavior of gang members.

Consider the following passage from my interview with Marco in which he describes both the burden of having to cope with the trauma associated with the constant specter of violent victimization as well as his longing for peace. In a remarkably perceptive display of empathy, moreover, he observes that he and one of his mortal enemies are, in essence, "the same nigga" and laments that they are not working together toward a mutually beneficial peace.[57]

MARCO: Being outside [gangbanging], it comes with havin' to worry about the police and the opps and stuff, so you in that mode [to use violence to defend yourself] already. So, man, I just don't see that shit stoppin', bro. I don't know. I wish it would, though. Sick of worryin', you know? Like, me and the guys, sometimes we'll just go downtown and shit, just to walk around 'cause it feel good not havin' to do this all the time [*looking behind him over each shoulder*]. You know, that's a habit—steady lookin' over your shoulder on all these cars. . . .

RRA: So how important is it to you that the violence be reduced? And why?

MARCO: It's important 'cause, man, I know how it feels to lose somebody. That shit hurt, bro. That shit ain't cool. And regardless, like, okay, it's a lot of niggas I'd like to see die, right? But I know they got loved ones, too, that's finna feel like I feel, you know? So that's the reason why it should stop.

The second reason 'cause, man, mu'fuckas got kids and stuff. I just had a lil girl, she finna be four months on Thursday. She pretty as hell. . . . And the nigga who came on my [social media] page and said "bitch-ass nigga," he got a daughter, too, you know? And it's like this: Like, we the same nigga. He tryin' to do

> [kill] me, I'm tryin' to do him. But it's like, damn, Folk. Now, in the back of my mind, I'm tryin' to change, and I can change—I want to 'cause I got something to live for. But this nigga still doin' the same shit, though. It's like, I wonder how he feel. 'Cause I'll take his ass out this shit. But it's like, damn, I don't want to, but if I have to, you feel me? Niggas be crazy, man. Like, how you got a lil girl, right, but you still doin' that type of shit, though? But even with me—I ain't no hypocrite, I be thinkin' about me, too. But [*pausing*] . . . I don't know, man.
>
> But that shit need to stop, though, for real, so people could feel safe again. 'Cause that's a good feeling. That's why we be havin' the peace treaties, man—niggas wanna feel safe and shit. But even with a peace treaty, you still gotta watch. Maybe he just want a peace treaty so we can be comfortable so we can kinda get us off our Ps and Qs so y'all could snake [betray] us, you know? . . .
>
> The violence, it ain't gon' stop. It's not, bro. I know it. I wish it would, though, 'cause it be so petty. But it's like, people just be lost, man. People be lost in they own world—they own block.

The desperation and uncertainty Marco conveys here are palpable. He does not know what the future will look like for his daughter or the daughter of his sworn enemy, both of whom may end up growing up without their fathers. He does not know how his enemy feels about the path of mutual destruction on which they have both embarked. He does not know if building connections with his enemies in the name of solidarity, peace, and social justice is possible. He does not know, moreover, if anyone cares enough to help him try to do so.

This book has described in detail the transformation of street gangs and violence on the South Side of Chicago since the 1990s and the nature of these phenomena today, situating all of these dynamics firmly within a broad historical framework. Integral to this analysis has been an examination of the desperate conditions facing young people in the city's poor and working-class black communities, as an accounting of these realities is essential to understanding not only what has taken and is taking place but also how we might move forward from here in addressing these issues.

Celebrated intervention models like focused deterrence policing and the Cure Violence public health model have failed to curb levels of violence in Chicago. These failures can be attributed to both their faulty assumptions about the invariability of gangs and violence as well as their failure to situate these issues within a broader framework that goes beyond the problematic behaviors and norms of gang members and/or the communities within which they are embedded. The findings from this study and the realities of persistently high levels of violence in Chicago indicate that attempts to reduce gang violence that do not deal more comprehensively with the conditions driving this violence are likely to achieve limited success, at best. While proponents of "universal" violence prevention models like focused deterrence and Cure Violence claim that their interventions are capable of eliminating violence without comprehensive action, their respective track records in Chicago belie this assertion. In making his case against addressing oppressive community conditions as a strategy for reducing violence, David Kennedy states that "the way we've been trying to do it" is not working.[58] This statement suggests that resources have been flooding into poor and working-class black urban neighborhoods for decades, and that violence has persisted nonetheless. The evidence, however, indicates just the opposite: These communities have typically experienced severe declines over the last half-century, as decent jobs have disappeared, poverty has increased, and abandonment and physical deterioration have intensified.[59] With these realities in mind, Kennedy's statement actually makes perfect sense: We cannot reduce violence the way we have been trying to.

But all hope for peace on the streets of Chicago is not lost, and contemporary gang dynamics and ideologies actually present crucial openings for intervention and transformation. The ultimate focus of intervention efforts should be the massive investment of public resources in low-income black communities on the city's South and West Sides aimed at addressing the intolerable conditions that continue to fuel gangs and violence, namely, marginalization and desperation, poverty and economic exclusion, and pervasive community violence. Toward these ends, community organizers, activists, social workers, and other concerned individuals can engage gang members in grassroots organizing efforts and social movements aimed at such transformation. This will likely be difficult and painstaking work that will need to occur primarily on the streets of gang members' own neighborhoods—the places they congregate and the places they care most about. The gang interventions of the 1960s, in which the commitment of a handful of gang leaders dictated the participation of thousands of gang members in the social movements of that era, are irrelevant to today's situation. The smaller scale of today's gangs and their emphasis on egalitarianism and autonomy mean that relationships with gang members today will necessarily be built on a much smaller scale. This egalitarian ethos also complements social justice goals rooted in the strengthening and expansion of democratic processes and the more equitable distribution of societal resources, potentially helping facilitate the transition from the streets to activism.

Transformed gang members will likely play an important role in this work. As discussed in chapter 5 and briefly in the preceding section, a gang background is a decidedly inadequate basis for intervention workers to exert any type of influence on young gang members today. Nonetheless, such a background may assist in building the relationships necessary to develop such influence. Coming from the same communities, having dealt with similar issues, speaking the same language—these are all factors that can help facilitate the development of meaningful relationships. Indeed, to whatever extent Cure Violence may be effective in assisting specific individuals and preventing particular instances of violence, it is likely that relationships are driving much of that efficacy. "The power of violence prevention is relationships," as Paris points out. The key question that remains, however, is what are those relationships being leveraged for? To what end? As Eldridge, another seasoned street outreach worker, puts it, "If I'm askin' you to put a gun down, I'm askin' you to put that pack [of drugs] down, what am I replacing that gun and that pack with?" The sheer enormity of the challenges facing gang members and other desperate youth in Chicago forcefully contradicts the notion that simply "increasing access" to severely inadequate resources and opportunities within the existing, highly stratified social structure or throwing a few dollars at new programming represent anything approximating a viable solution to these issues. The goal must be to challenge and eradicate the inequities that lie at the heart of the social order. Toward that end, transformed gang members can and likely must play a central role.

The analysis presented in this book is obviously derived from the experiences and perspectives of black gang members on the South Side of Chicago. While it is possible, and even likely, that some of these themes will be relevant in other contexts, the lessons from this study demonstrate that understanding the nature of gangs and violence requires a careful analysis of these phenomena as they exist within a particular time and place. Indeed, the extent to which the transformations described in this book extend beyond the black gangs on Chicago's South Side to other gangs even within the city of Chicago itself is unclear.[60] Insights into how gangs might be addressed and how violence might be reduced, then, requires a careful, contextual exploration of these dynamics, including an examination of community conditions, social policy, local politics, the perceptions and experiences of gang members themselves, the particularities of gang dynamics and gang history, the nature of violence, and issues of identity and resistance. To be certain, we need fewer narrow, deductive, one-size-fits-all violence prevention efforts that impose rigid, predetermined models on situations in which their assumptions may have no bearing. What we need are analyses and interventions developed inductively by the realities and conditions on the ground and that engage gang members where they are—in other words, from the streets up.

Appendix

NOTES ON POSITIONALITY, THE POLITICS OF REPRESENTATION, AND RESEARCH METHODOLOGY

Brief discussions of my positionality with respect to this research and the general methods employed in this study were included in the introduction. These topics, as well as issues related to the politics of representation, are treated in further detail in this appendix.

STATEMENT OF POSITIONALITY

As described in the introduction, I came to this research through my community work with gang members and other young people on the South Side of Chicago. This initial career path was shaped by my family background and various experiences growing up, some of which are outlined briefly here. I was born in São Paulo, Brazil, in the mid-1980s to American parents who were Catholic lay missionaries living and working on the fringes of a favela. Adherents to the principles of liberation theology, my parents participated in grassroots efforts to organize and support local impoverished and working-class people in their struggles for human rights under Brazil's brutal military dictatorship of that period. My parents broke bread with Miguel d'Escoto and Paulo Freire, the latter of whom my father also had the honor of introducing at a local speaking engagement. I attended my first public demonstrations when I was three weeks old. My parents had Brazilian friends who were kidnapped, tortured, and killed by government forces during these years. Yet the efforts of the people, including student and worker groups, religious leaders and laypeople, and radical political groups across the country, ultimately brought about the dissolution of the military government and a gradual return to democratic elections beginning in the mid-1980s.[1] While I was far too young to have memories of this time, this history and my parents' values and continued involvement in work around social justice certainly shaped me in important ways.

When my parents returned to the United States in 1987, they settled in a working-class, racially mixed neighborhood in Minneapolis, where I was raised. It was there that my own experiences and the experiences of my friends with gangs and violence eventually led me to my work with young people in Chicago. In fact, many of my childhood friends and their families were actually from Chicago, having migrated to Minneapolis in the 1980s and 1990s in an effort to escape the violence and despair wrought on Chicago's black community by the crack epidemic, the war on drugs, evaporating employment opportunities, and the retrenchment of the welfare state. If life in Minneapolis was better than in Chicago, however, it may not have been by very much, as rates of poverty and incarceration for African Americans living in Minnesota are six and ten times greater, respectively, than those for the state's white residents.[2] Thus, despite sharing a neighborhood and working-class upbringing, my African American peers and their families were faced with challenges from which I was afforded a degree of pigment-related protection, and many of them became involved in street gangs, selling drugs, and serious violence.

Yet while I largely managed to avoid the pitfalls of the streets that ensnared many of my comrades, gangs and violence nonetheless touched my life in profound ways, most notably, in the murder of one of my closest childhood friends when I was seventeen years old. At that point, I resolved to work with young people who, like many of the people I had grown up with, felt alienated and marginalized and lacked the resources and opportunities to help them travel a different path. As an adult, moreover, I have lost additional loved ones from my childhood, from my work in Chicago, and from my wife's family in inner-city St. Louis to murder, prison, and debilitating violent injury. It is from this background that I approached both my community work with gang members and other marginalized young people in Chicago as well as my research.

I share the broad parameters of some of my experiences not in an attempt to assert some type of street credibility—indeed, I have never been a gang member, and my experiences with gangs and violence are a proverbial drop in the bucket compared to those of many of my own friends and family—but in the service of transparency and in an attempt to accurately convey how I came to this work. Gangs and violence are not simply "areas of interest" for me; some of my closest friends, family members, and mentors are (or were) gang members, and I have loved ones who have both perpetrated and been victimized by serious violence. Though I recently moved to St. Louis, I have close friends who still live in high-violence communities in Chicago; many of them are working diligently to address this violence. From a per-capita perspective, the violence in St. Louis is even worse, and I have loved ones there dealing with these issues as well. I am currently working on a violence reduction project in East St. Louis, Illinois, moreover, the city with the single highest homicide rate in the entire country and where other members of my family reside. These issues have and continue to play a major role in my life beyond my research, but they also inform my approach to research. I care about gang members as human beings and about the communities in which they are embedded. I care about reducing violence as someone who has seen and felt its effects firsthand.

CRITICAL GANG RESEARCH AND THE POLITICS OF REPRESENTATION

Any scholarly treatment of gangs and violence, even for those with some firsthand experience with these issues, is necessarily fraught with power disparities and with the risk of exoticizing or pathologizing the study population. Here I outline and address some key considerations related to the politics of representation as they pertain to the research described in this book and situate my approach to these issues within the tradition of critical research.

First, as discussed in the introduction, gangs and violence are among the most fundamental realities shaping life for black youth on the South Side of Chicago. Indeed, this was among the key factors that initially brought me to the South Side, as I specifically wanted to work with young people who were dealing with violence and other serious issues. Thus, while depictions of Chicago are obviously full of imagery of gangs and violence, and these images are often superficial and problematic in ways I have tried to expose in this book, in a general sense, these depictions are not entirely inaccurate. The reality is that gangs and violence represent key organizers of life throughout much of the South Side, particularly for young people. Consider the following quote from the work of sociologist Loïc Wacquant, who conducted ethnographic research in the Woodlawn community, one of the same areas in which I worked and from which a number of my research participants hail. Importantly, Wacquant's research was not focused on violence, but he quickly came to the conclusion that

> the most significant brute fact of every daily [*sic*] life in the fin-de-siècle ghetto is without contest the extraordinary *prevalence of physical danger and the acute sense of insecurity* that pervades its streets. Violence is a vexed aspect of the politics of race and class in America that is difficult to broach without activating the sordid images of stereotypical media depictions of lawlessness. Yet ethnographic fieldwork conducted on Chicago's South Side convinced me that any account of the hyperghetto must start with it, because of its acute experiential salience and its wide reverberations across the social fabric.[3]

If violence does, indeed, constitute "the most significant brute fact" of daily life in many Chicago neighborhoods, from a research perspective, how can this reality be dealt with in a way that does not oversimplify and reinforce crude stereotypes about gang members and other residents of these neighborhoods? Following David Brotherton, I find Geoffrey Pearson's analytic approach to his treatment of British "hooliganism" compelling to these ends as they relate to street gangs and urban violence. In particular, Pearson argues that "the way to challenge the foundation of myth . . . is not to deny the facts of violence and disorder. Rather, it is to insist that more facts are placed within the field of vision."[4] Similarly, anthropologist George Karandinos and his colleagues argue for an approach to exploring urban violence that "unpack[s] the local ethics for interpersonal and criminal violence in their relationship to external fields of power and economic forces," thereby "render[ing] more comprehensible the emergence of contradictory destructive-and-solidary survival practices."[5]

To the best of my abilities, I have employed such an approach to the analysis presented in this book. Indeed, among the central themes of this book is that gangs and violence do not exist in a vacuum, but are shaped in fundamental ways by sociohistorical conditions—which are themselves shaped by broader considerations of culture and political economy. In their stunning photo-ethnography of homeless heroin addicts in San Francisco, Philippe Bourgois and Jeff Schonberg identify as the primary goal of their study "to clarify the relationships between large-scale power forces and intimate ways of being . . . without beatifying or making a spectacle of the individuals involved, and without reifying the larger forces enveloping them."[6] I hope to have achieved some semblance of this type of balance and sensitivity in these pages.

RESEARCH METHODOLOGY

I utilized a grounded theory methodology as my strategy of inquiry in this study.[7] Grounded theory is an approach to research that emphasizes inductive discovery rooted in the research data itself—in this case, in the experiences and perspectives of the research participants—as a foundation for the development of an explanatory framework for the phenomenon under study. This approach contrasts with deductive, positivist methodologies that tend to force research data into imposed preexisting theoretical frameworks.[8] That said, like all researchers, I approached this study with my own subjective background and worldview shaped by my experiences, perspectives, and values, as broadly described in the preceding sections of this appendix. The process of theory development in this study, then, was not purely inductive, just as no research, including deductive, positivist research, is purely objective or neutral. Nonetheless, a grounded theory approach was useful for exploring the contemporary dynamics of gangs and violence in Chicago that the existing literature was ill suited to explain, and, in turn, for formulating critiques of the shortcomings in the existing gang literature rooted in the study findings.

As discussed at various junctures throughout this book, this research grew out of my community work with gang members and other at-risk young people on the South Side of Chicago. As such, the data for this study were derived from a number of sources, primary among them in-depth, semistructured interviews with thirty-five African American gang members from the city's South Side. Each participant completed one interview lasting between one and three hours. These formal interviews were supplemented by countless conversations with many of these study participants as well as with other gang members, their families, community workers, and others, both during the research process as well as before the research began. While this study was not a formal ethnography, I also composed field notes and memos detailing my experiences in the field conducting this research, which was carried out directly in many of the neighborhoods described in these pages and from which the participants hailed. In addition, my broader experiences living and working on the South Side provided an invaluable foundation from which to undertake this research, serving as the relational basis that made interviewing gang members possible, sensitizing me to the colloquial particularities of the city's contemporary gang culture, and enriching the study's analysis through experiential contextualization. Reflections detailing some of these experiences were included to supplement the major analytic themes and narratives as they developed throughout the book. I further fleshed out emergent themes by examining what had happened and was happening in Chicago on broader social, economic, and political levels through the incorporation of additional scholarship, accounts of current events, and my own experiences as a resident and community worker. Additional data were also derived from a conference I helped convene on gang fracturing and violence at the University of Illinois at Chicago's Great Cities Institute in April 2018.[9]

My overall methodological approach was informed by the scholarship of gang researchers like John Hagedorn, David Brotherton, Joan Moore, James Diego Vigil, Sudhir Venkatesh, and Robert Durán in a number of ways, including being born out of community work and existing relationships with gang members; centering on in-depth interviews; and incorporating a critical, contextual, and historically oriented analytic lens.

Two young former gang members were trained as research assistants for this project. They aided in the development of the interview guide and the recruitment of study participants and also provided feedback on the development of the analysis. I had worked closely with both of these individuals in various capacities during the course of my community work on the South Side of Chicago. They gladly agreed to assist with the research, although both flatly refused my offer to pay them out of my own pocket for their efforts, stating that they considered any assistance they might provide on the research project simply part of the reciprocal nature of our relationships.

Their involvement in this study both assisted in its completion and also increased the rigor of the analysis.

Study participants were recruited by myself and the participatory researchers using a purposive sampling approach in which specific individuals who could speak expertly to the issues under investigation were identified and invited to participate in the study. Such individuals were identified via existing relationships with the study community of African American gang members on Chicago's South Side. Thus, this process was facilitated through the expertise of knowledgeable insiders embedded in the study community via personal involvement and/or long-term personal relationships. Accordingly, most study participants were drawn from the mid–South Side region, where these relational networks and local knowledge were strongest. On a few occasions, study participants themselves identified key individuals whom they referred to the study, based on the relevance of their knowledge and experiences to the aims of the research. Twenty participants completed formal interviews during the initial phase of data collection from 2013 to 2015. Data collection during this phase ended when the analysis reached the point of saturation, per grounded theory methodology—that is, when the development of the properties and dimensions of the major study concepts and themes and their conceptual relationships to one another were fully developed and no new themes were emerging from additional interviews. An additional fifteen interviews were conducted during a follow-up period of data collection from 2017 to 2018 that explored the perspectives of older, transformed gang members as well as the experiences of gang members in additional neighborhoods. Study participants were compensated twenty to twenty-five dollars for their participation. These funds were provided by an award from the Graduate College at the University of Illinois at Chicago, and additional funding from the Graduate College helped support me in the final year of my doctoral studies.

All interviews were audio recorded using a portable digital recording device. Interview audio files were transferred onto an encrypted computer, deleted from the recorder, and transcribed verbatim. Transcripts were verified for accuracy and then stripped of potentially identifying information, including the names of people, neighborhood-specific gangs, streets, schools, and other locations, as well as other potentially identifying details related to family life, violent events, criminal convictions, and the like. This process of de-identification was done in a way that preserved the general parameters and meanings embedded in the information that participants shared, but that also carefully concealed their identities. The audio files of the interviews were then permanently deleted from my computer, and de-identified interview transcripts were uploaded into ATLAS.ti, a qualitative data analysis program. Study data were analyzed inductively using a grounded theory process largely based on the methodology outlined by Juliet Corbin and Anselm Strauss.[10] Per grounded theory method, the data analysis process began immediately on completion of the first interview and continued throughout the data collection period and beyond. This approach facilitated the timely discovery of important concepts and themes within the data, allowing me to make practical and theoretically driven modifications to the interview guide as well as to pursue subsequent interviews with individuals who could speak to specific emergent analytic themes for additional insights. I also consulted with the participatory researchers throughout the analysis process to compare interpretations of the data and strengthen the rigor of the analysis.

A PARTIAL GLOSSARY OF CHICAGO GANG SLANG

This glossary is not exhaustive. It is weighted toward terms and references more prominent among and/or relevant to African American gangs on Chicago's South Side as well as toward the contemporary twenty-first-century gang era. Conversely, not all of these terms are exclusive to Chicago.

B A generic term for a person. Used similarly to "man," "dude," "bro," and so on.

BAR-NONE An ethos among contemporary gang members that indicates a rejection of conventional gang ideologies, allegiances, and fault lines.

BD An acronym for the Black Disciples. BDN is used as an acronym for the Black Disciple Nation. BDK is a derisive acronym for "Black Disciple killer."

BIG HOMIE An older gang leader. In plural form, the older gang members and leaders within a particular gang. This term is often customized based on gang (e.g., "big Folks" among Black Disciples and Gangster Disciples, "big Moes" among Black P Stones).

BLOW AT To shoot a gun at. "Blow down" signifies to hit someone during a shooting. Alternately, "to blow" can be a reference to smoking marijuana.

BROTHERS A proper noun used by Black P Stones, Mickey Cobras, and other gangs historically aligned with the People gang coalition in reference to fellow gang members.

BUILDINGS, THE A reference to public housing projects, particularly the high-rises that have been overwhelmingly demolished in Chicago.

. . . CRAZY An affirmation that someone wholly embodies and/or is particularly committed to something. Similar to the conventional expression "to be crazy about" something. Typically used in reference to a gang and/or neighborhood (e.g., "I'm so Low End crazy," "Shorty is Rico World crazy, for real").

CUT The narrow walking space between houses or apartment buildings. These spaces are also referred to in Chicago as "gangways." Largely consistent with this use, "cut" is also sometimes used to describe a hiding place.

DECK A division of a jail or prison.

DIE . . . Followed by a gang identity or symbol, a slogan-like statement indicating opposition to said identity or symbol (e.g., "Die Five," "Die L's").

DRILL A gang shooting.

DRILL MUSIC A brand of gangsta rap music developed and popularized by young gang members from the South Side of Chicago in the early 2010s.

DRILLER A gang member with a reputation as a shooter. Alternately referred to as a "hitter."

EAST SIDE A reference to the section of Chicago's South Side roughly encompassing the area south of Sixty-First Street and east of Cottage Grove Avenue.

EBK An acronym for "everybody killer." An ethos among contemporary gang members that indicates a rejection of conventional gang ideologies, allegiances, and fault lines.

FLIP To change one's traditional gang allegiance/identity (e.g., from Mickey Cobra to Gangster Disciple).

FOE A shorthand reference to a Four Corner Hustler. A derivative of "four." In plural form (i.e., "the Foes"), a reference to a neighborhood gang affiliated with the Four Corner Hustlers or, more broadly, the Four Corner Hustlers as a whole.

FOLKS One of two major Chicago gang coalitions formed in the Illinois Department of Corrections in the late 1970s and effectively shattered during the gang wars of the 1990s. Youthful Gangster Disciples and Black Disciples, two prominent gangs in the former Folks coalition, often still refer to their gang comrades as "Folks."

G A generic term for a person. Used similarly to "man," "dude," "bro," and so on. Originally a term used by and in reference to Gangster Disciples.

GD An acronym for the Gangster Disciples. GDN is used as an acronym for the Gangster Disciple Nation. GDK is a derisive acronym for "Gangster Disciple killer."

HEAVY A gang leader and/or big-time drug dealer. Short for "heavyweight." Used as a noun (e.g., "Dude was a heavy out here").

INSANE An emergent renegade gang identity that indicates a rejection of conventional gang ideologies, allegiances, and fault lines. Typically added in front of the name of a traditional street gang (e.g., Insane Gangster Disciple). A central element of the Insane identity involves a willingness, if not an outright desire, to engage members of one's traditional street gang in violent conflict. Gang members that claim Insane are typically hostile toward those who identify with the emergent L's identity (see below).

JOE A generic term for a person. Used similarly to "man," "dude," "bro," and so on.

KUSH A high-quality strain of marijuana, typically of the Indica variety.

L'S An emergent gang identity initially derived from the first letters of Lamron, an infamous Black Disciple set from Englewood, as well as "love, life, and loyalty"—the three chief principles traditionally espoused by the Black Disciples. L's was subsequently adopted as an identity by a range of other gangs who ascribed to the term their own meanings. Gang members that claim L's are typically hostile toward those who identify as Insane.

LACKING To be in public without a gun.

LOUD High-quality marijuana.

LOW END, THE A reference to Bronzeville, the historic black South Side ghetto, which encompasses the lower-numbered streets of the South Side and includes part or all of the Near South Side, Douglas, Oakland, North Kenwood, Grand Boulevard, and Washington Park communities. This area is also where the vast majority of Chicago's public housing once existed.

MC An acronym for the Mickey Cobras. MCN is used as an acronym for the Mickey Cobra Nation.

MOE A term used by and/or to reference members of the Black P Stones. Derived from the word "Moor," the term was associated with the refashioning of the Stones in the mid-1970s as the El Rukns, Arabic for "the cornerstones." The Stones dropped the El Rukns name in the late 1980s in favor of their traditional Black P Stone Nation moniker, but the term "Moe" has persisted.

NEUTRON A traditional Chicago gang term for an individual not affiliated with a street gang.

NOLAW An emergent renegade gang identity that indicates a rejection of conventional gang ideologies, allegiances, and fault lines. Typically added in front of the name of a traditional street gang, primarily among Black P Stones (e.g., Nolaw Black P Stone).

OG Abbreviation for original gangster. Traditionally used as a term for a respected older gang member. Today, the term is commonly used in a humorous fashion as a reference to one's mother or grandmother.

ON . . . To swear on something. A routine practice among many Chicago gang members. The object of the oath is typically determined by gang identity. For example, Black P Stones often use "on Chief" in reference to Jeff Fort, a.k.a. Chief Malik, or "on Stone." Gangster Disciples may use "on GDN" or "on the boss," a reference to the Brothers of the Struggle (BOS), a term used to refer to incarcerated GDs.

OPP A member of a rival gang. Short for "opposition." In plural form (i.e., "the opps"), it refers to a rival gang as a whole.

OTF An acronym for Only Trey Folks, a loose-knit alliance of primarily Black Disciples–affiliated gangs on the mid–South Side. It also stands for

Only the Family, the record label and clothing line of Chicago drill rapper Lil Durk.

OUTFIT, THE Chicago's mafia organization.

OUTLAW A renegade gang identity that emerged in the 1990s and indicates a rejection of conventional gang ideologies, allegiances, and fault lines. Typically added in front of the name of a traditional street gang, primarily among Gangster Disciples (e.g., Outlaw Gangster Disciple). A central element of the Outlaw identity involves a willingness, if not an outright desire, to engage members of one's traditional street gang in violent conflict.

PEOPLE One of two major Chicago gang coalitions formed in the Illinois Department of Corrections in the late 1970s and effectively shattered during the gang wars of the 1990s.

PLUGGED To be well connected, especially with regard to the illicit drug business. Alternately, to be an official member of a gang (traditional use).

PUMPKIN HEAD A beating of such severity that the victim's head swells and lumps up to resemble a pumpkin. Usually used in reference to a severe violation.

RAPPIE Partner in crime, confederate, co-conspirator. Someone who would face the same legal charge (i.e., "rap") as their comrade for a crime, although often used in a more general sense and not in reference to a specific crime.

RENEGADE An emergent renegade gang identity that indicates a rejection of conventional gang ideologies, allegiances, and fault lines. Typically added in front of the name of a traditional street gang (e.g., Renegade Mickey Cobra). A central element of the Renegade identity involves a willingness, if not an outright desire, to engage members of one's traditional street gang in violent conflict.

SAWBUCK Ten dollars. Typically used to refer to a ten-dollar bill or a ten-dollar bag of drugs.

SCORE To hit an intended target in a gang shooting.

SEND-OFF A person who is being taken advantage of, exploited, and/or manipulated. Can also be used as a verb (e.g., "to send someone off").

SERVE To sell drugs.

SERVICE A gang meeting. Used primarily by gangs historically associated with the People coalition, such as the Black P Stones and Mickey Cobras.

SEVEN, FOUR, FOURTEEN The numerical representation of the Gangster Disciple Nation, whose initials are the seventh, fourth, and fourteenth letters of the alphabet. Some other Chicago gangs use this practice with their respective initials as well (e.g., "two, four, fourteen" for the Black Disciple Nation).

SHAKE UP To perform a gang handshake.

SLOT A position of gang leadership (e.g., "He had a slot with the GDs").

THIRSTY Eager. Typically used on the streets in reference to someone's desire to either visit harm on their opposition or to pursue sexual liaisons.

VIOLATION A disciplinary measure, typically a physical beating, imposed by gang leadership in response to a member's violation of gang policies or insubordination. No longer in practice among South Side black gangs.

WILD HUNDREDS, THE A reference to the area on Chicago's far South Side distinguished by three-digit street numbers (e.g., 100th Street), especially segments of the Roseland and West Pullman communities. Referred to as the "Hundreds" for short.

WITH THE SHIT Having a propensity and reputation for violence, particularly gun violence. Sometimes used in plural form (i.e., "with the shits").

WOO, WOO, WOO All types of talk. Used similarly to blah, blah, blah, or etc., etc.

WOO WOP THE BAM All types of talk. Used similarly to blah, blah, blah, or etc., etc.

WTO An acronym for We the Opps, a rebellious identity rooted in the embrace of the derisive "opps" term. Gang members that claim WTO are typically hostile toward those who identify with the emergent L's identity.

ZIP An ounce of marijuana.

NOTES

INTRODUCTION

1. Jeffery S. Adler, *First in Violence, Deepest in Dirt: Homicide in Chicago, 1875–1920* (Cambridge, MA: Harvard University Press, 2006), 1–2.
2. This trend took off in earnest beginning in 2012. For a small sampling of the national media coverage from that year alone, see Scott Simon, "Gang Violence Smolders on Hot Chicago Streets," National Public Radio, July 28, 2012, http://www.npr.org/2012/07/28/157454927/gang-violence-smoulders-on-hot-chicago-streets; Jennifer Abbey, Candace Smith, and Matt Rosenbaum, "Chicago Gang Life: Gang Members Talk About Life on the Streets, Heartache," *Nightline*, October 19, 2012, http://abcnews.go.com/US/chicago-gang-life-gang-members-talks-life-streets/story?id=17499354#3; Scott Zamost, Drew Griffin, and Elizabeth Nunez, "Questions Surround $55 Million Program to Cut Violence in Chicago," CNN, December 3, 2012, http://www.cnn.com/2012/12/01/justice/chicago-crime-program-criticized/index.html; Peter Slevin, "Chicago Grapples with Gun Violence; Death Toll Soars," *Washington Post*, December 21, 2012, http://articles.washingtonpost.com/2012-12-21/national/36017398_1_gun-violence-homicide-rate-national-gun-debate; Sharon Cohen, "Violence, Gangs Scar Chicago in 2012," *USA Today*, December 29, 2012, https://www.usatoday.com/story/news/nation/2012/12/29/violence-gangs-chicago/1797991/.
3. Steve James, dir., *The Interrupters* (Chicago: Kartemquin Films, 2011, Blu-ray Disc, 1080p HD); Spike Lee, dir., *Chi-Raq* (New York: 40 Acres & a Mule Filmworks, 2015). Recent television shows on Chicago include Showtime's *Shameless* and *The Chi*, Fox's *The Chicago Code*, and NBC's *Chicago P.D.* Among the more famous drill rappers are Chief Keef, the late Fredo Santana, G Herbo, Katie Got Bandz, King Louie, Lil Bibby, Lil Durk, Lil Reese, Sasha Go Hard, and Team 600.

4. Phil Harris, "No Let Up in Chicago Gun Violence Despite Obama's Hometown Plea," *Guardian*, February 16, 2013, https://www.theguardian.com/world/2013/feb/16/chicago-gun-violence-barack-obama; Colleen Connolly, "'I Live on the South Side': Obama Addresses Gun Violence in Chicago," October 27, 2015, *Ward Room* (blog), NBC Chicago, https://www.nbcchicago.com/blogs/ward-room/Obama-Addresses-Hometown-Violence-in-Police-Chiefs-Conference-in-Chicago-337654961.html; "Obama on Gun Violence: 'It Happens on the Streets of Chicago Every Day,'" January 5, 2016, *Ward Room* (blog), NBC Chicago, https://www.nbcchicago.com/blogs/ward-room/Obama-on-Gun-Violence-It-Happens-on-the-Streets-of-Chicago-Every-Day-364264661.html; Stefano Esposito, "Trump Injects Chicago Crime into Debate: 'A War-Torn Country?,'" *Chicago Sun-Times*, September 27, 2016, https://chicago.suntimes.com/news/trump-injects-chicago-crime-into-debate-a-war-torn-country/.
5. Alfred Blumstein and Joel Wallman, eds., *The Crime Drop in America* (Cambridge: Cambridge University Press, 2000); Franklin E. Zimring, *The Great American Crime Decline* (Oxford: Oxford University Press, 2007); Vanessa Barker, "Explaining the Great American Crime Decline: A Review of Blumstein and Wallman, Goldberger and Rosenfeld, and Zimring," *Law & Social Inquiry* 35, no. 2 (2010): 489–516; Patrick Sharkey, *Uneasy Peace: The Great Crime Decline, the Renewal of City Life, and the Next War on Violence* (New York: Norton, 2018). There is no scholarly consensus on the causes of the unprecedented decline in rates of crime and violence in the United States during the latter half of the 1990s and early 2000s. Potential explanations include everything from increased imprisonment and policing innovations to changing demographics and economic expansion to shifts in urban ecology and youth culture to increased neighborhood civic participation.
6. Federal Bureau of Investigation, "Crime in the U.S.," accessed July 18, 2019, https://ucr.fbi.gov/crime-in-the-u.s. Homicide is not only the most severe form of violence, but it is also the most consistently reported and recorded crime across jurisdictions, making it "a reasonable proxy for violent crime in general" and providing "valuable insights into the nature and extent of this wider concern." United Nations Office on Drugs and Crime, *2011 Global Study on Homicide: Trends, Contexts, Data* (Vienna: United Nations Office on Drugs and Crime, 2011), 15.
7. Federal Bureau of Investigation, "Crime in the U.S."
8. Chicago Crime Commission, *The Gang Book*, 2nd ed. (Chicago: Chicago Crime Commission, 2012); National Gang Intelligence Center, *National Gang Threat Assessment 2009* (Washington, DC: National Gang Intelligence Center, 2009), 22; Chicago Police Department, *2011 Chicago Murder Analysis* (Chicago: Chicago Police Department, 2012), 29, https://home.chicagopolice.org/wp-content/uploads/2014/12/2011-Murder-Report.pdf.
9. For exceptions to this general trend, see John M. Hagedorn and Brigid Rauch, "Housing, Gangs, and Homicide: What We Can Learn from Chicago," *Urban Affairs Review* 42, no. 4 (2007): 435–56; Natalie Y. Moore and Lance Williams, *The Almighty Black P Stone Nation: The Rise, Fall, and Resurgence of an American Gang* (Chicago: Lawrence Hill Books, 2011); Laurence Ralph, "'As Soon as I Get Out Ima Cop Dem Jordans': The Afterlife of the Corporate Gang," *Identities: Global Studies in Culture and Power* 17, no. 6 (2010): 667–94; Laurence Ralph, *Renegade Dreams: Living Through Injury in Gangland Chicago* (Chicago: University of Chicago Press, 2014).

10. Frederic M. Thrasher, *The Gang: A Study of 1,313 Gangs in Chicago* (Chicago: University of Chicago Press, 1927); Gerald D. Suttles, *The Social Order of the Slum* (Chicago: University of Chicago Press, 1968); Gerald D. Suttles, *The Social Construction of Communities* (Chicago: University of Chicago Press, 1972); Sudhir Alladi Venkatesh, *American Project: The Rise and Fall of a Modern Ghetto* (Cambridge, MA: Harvard University Press, 2000); Sudhir Alladi Venkatesh, *Off the Books: The Underground Economy of the Urban Poor* (Cambridge, MA: Harvard University Press, 2006); John M. Hagedorn, *A World of Gangs: Armed Young Men and Gangsta Culture* (Minneapolis: University of Minnesota Press, 2008); John M. Hagedorn, *The In$ane Chicago Way: The Daring Plan by Chicago Gangs to Create a Spanish Mafia* (Chicago: University of Chicago Press, 2015).
11. Stanley Cohen, *Folk Devils and Moral Panics* (London: Paladin, 1973), 9. The concept of "moral panics" has been usefully applied to help explain the framing of a wide range of social phenomena, from music subcultures and sexual practices to drug abuse and muggings. There is also a substantive literature on moral panics as they pertain to street gangs. Marjorie S. Zatz, "Chicano Youth Gangs and Crime: The Creation of a Moral Panic," *Contemporary Crises* 11, no. 2 (1987): 129–58; Joan W. Moore, *Going Down to the Barrio: Homeboys and Homegirls in Change* (Philadelphia: Temple University Press, 1991); Richard C. McCorkle and Terance D. Miethe, *Panic: The Social Construction of the Street Gang Problem* (Upper Saddle River, NJ: Prentice Hall, 2002); Deborah T. Levenson, *Adiós Niño: The Gangs of Guatemala City and the Politics of Death* (Durham, NC: Duke University Press, 2013); John M. Hagedorn and Meda Chesney-Lind, "America's 'War on Gangs': Response to a Real Threat or Moral Panic?," in *Criminal Justice Policy*, ed. Stacy L. Mallicoat and Christine L. Gardiner (Thousand Oaks, CA: SAGE, 2014), 175–90; David C. Brotherton, *Youth Street Gangs: A Critical Appraisal* (New York: Routledge, 2015).
12. In reality, the alleged spike in violence in 2012 was well within the established range of homicide levels in Chicago over the preceding decade or so, and well below levels prior to 2004. See John M. Hagedorn, "Chicago, I Do Mind Dying," in *Oxford Textbook of Violence Prevention: Epidemiology, Evidence, and Policy*, ed. Peter D. Donnelly and Catherine L. Ward (Oxford: Oxford University Press, 2015), 219–24.
13. Chicago Crime Commission, *Gang Book*, 13.
14. CAPS—17th District Albany Park, "For those interested below is information on Gang Awareness," Facebook, July 24, 2015, https://www.facebook.com/CAPS.017/posts/636382126503679. This quote was originally taken from CPD's "Introduction to Gangs" webpage, which has since been taken down. However, the statement can still be found on the Facebook page cited here.
15. Curt Wagner, "McCarty Sees 'Crisis' in Chicago's Murder Rate," *Chicago Sun-Times*, December 30, 2016, https://chicago.suntimes.com/chicago-news/mccarthy-sees-crisis-in-chicagos-murder-rate/; B. J. Lutz and Dick Johnson, "Cops Retooling Gang Strategy," *Ward Room* (blog), NBC Chicago, March 19, 2012, https://www.nbcchicago.com/blogs/ward-room/chicago-gang-violence-police-gang-violence-143426386.html.
16. Tal Kopan, "Trump: 'We're Going to Destroy' MS-13," CNN Politics, July 28, 2017, https://www.cnn.com/2017/07/28/politics/donald-trump-ms-13/index.html; Stephen Gossett, "Trump: Chicago Is 'Like a War Zone,' Too 'Politically Correct' to Fix

'Carnage,'" *Chicagoist*, January 26, 2017, http://chicagoist.com/2017/01/26/trump_chicago_is_like_a_war_zone_to.php.

17. Richard R. Boykin, "Commentary: Tyshawn Lee's Killer Must Be Charged as a Terrorist," *Chicago Tribune*, November 9, 2015, http://www.chicagotribune.com/news/opinion/commentary/ct-tyshawn-lee-chicago-gun-violence-terrorism-perspec-20151109-story.html.
18. Kopan, "Destroy MS-13"; Gossett, "Like a War Zone."
19. Boykin, "Tyshawn Lee's Killer."
20. Whet Moser, "Mark Kirk Wants to Arrest 18,000 Chicago Gang Members at Once," *Chicago*, May 31, 2013, https://www.chicagomag.com/Chicago-Magazine/The-312/May-2013/Mark-Kirk-Wants-to-Arrest-18000-Chicago-Gang-Members-At-Once/.
21. Center for Popular Democracy, *Freedom to Thrive: Reimagining Safety & Security in Our Communities* (New York: Center for Popular Democracy, 2017), 2.
22. Tanveer Ali, "City Budget Winners and Losers: See Dept. Funding Changes Under Rahm," *DNAinfo*, October 18, 2017, https://www.dnainfo.com/chicago/20171018/albany-park/rahm-emanuel-city-budget-analysis-departments-increase-decrease; "Morning Spin: Emanuel Budget Hole Now Tops $259 Million," *Chicago Tribune*, September 26, 2017, http://www.chicagotribune.com/news/local/politics/ct-rahm-emanuel-chicago-budget-20170926-story.html.
23. Andrew Schroedter, "Chicago Police Misconduct—A Rising Financial Toll," *Better Government Association*, January 31, 2016, https://www.bettergov.org/news/chicago-police-misconduct-%E2%80%93-a-rising-financial-toll.
24. Marisa de la Torre et al., *School Closings in Chicago: Understanding Families' Choices and Constraints for New School Enrollment* (Chicago: University of Illinois at Chicago Consortium on Chicago School Research, 2015), 1–2.
25. Kari Lydersen, "Falling Through the Cracks," *Chicago Reporter*, April 25, 2015, https://www.chicagoreporter.com/falling-through-the-cracks/; Curtis Black, "Emanuel's Privatizing Mental Health Clinic in Roseland Raises Concerns," *Chicago Reporter*, November 3, 2016, https://www.chicagoreporter.com/emanuels-privatizing-mental-health-clinic-in-roseland-raises-concerns/.
26. Susan A. Phillips, *Operation Fly Trap: L.A. Gangs, Drugs, and the Law* (Chicago: University of Chicago Press, 2012), 47.
27. To be clear, however, media outlets need not rely on the guiding logic of law enforcement or elected officials to offer up sensationalistic, even reckless, portrayals of gangs and violence. In 2012, for example, music website Pitchfork posted an episode of its "Selector" video series featuring an interview with then-seventeen-year-old Chicago rapper Chief Keef. In an apparent attempt to play up and capitalize on Keef's street persona, Pitchfork set up the interview at a Manhattan gun range and recorded the teenage rapper firing a rifle at a paper target. Aside from the arguably poor taste of promoting a violent image of a teenager for entertainment purposes—indeed, a teenager already embroiled in real-life violence—Keef's participation in the interview also violated the terms of his probation stemming from a 2011 gun conviction whereby he was barred from possessing a firearm. Keef was sentenced to two months in a detention center following the interview. David Wagner, "Did Chief Keef Get Sent to Jail over Pitchfork's Gun Stunt?," *Atlantic*, January 16, 2013, https://www.theatlantic.com/entertainment/archive/2013/01/did-chief-keef-get-sent-jail-over-pitchforks-gun-stunt/319352/.

28. Federal Bureau of Investigation, "Crime in the U.S."
29. Eric Ferkenhoff and Darnell Little, "The Bleeding of Chicago," *CityLab*, February 24, 2018, https://www.citylab.com/equity/2018/02/the-bleeding-of-chicago/554141/.
30. Juan Perez Jr., "Dyett High School Hunger Strike Ends," *Chicago Tribune*, September 20, 2015, http://www.chicagotribune.com/news/local/breaking/ct-dyett-high-school-hunger-strike-ends-20150919-story.html; Lauren Harris and Kalyn Belsha, "Video: One Year After Hunger Strike, Dyett High School Opens," *Chicago Reporter*, September 1, 2016, https://www.chicagoreporter.com/video-one-year-after-hunger-strike-dyett-high-school-opens/.
31. John H. Fish, *Black Power/White Control: The Struggle of The Woodlawn Organization in Chicago* (Princeton, NJ: Princeton University Press, 1973); Adam Cohen and Elizabeth Taylor, *American Pharaoh: Mayor Richard J. Daley—His Battle for Chicago and the Nation* (New York: Little, Brown, 2000); John R. Fry, *Locked-Out Americans: A Memoir* (New York: Harper, Row, 1973); Will Cooley, "'Stones Run It': Taking Back Control of Organized Crime in Chicago, 1940–1975," *Journal of Urban History* 37, no. 6 (2011): 911–32; James A. McPherson, "The Blackstone Rangers," in *Observations of Deviance*, ed. Jack D. Douglas (New York: Random House, 1970), 170–204; Moore and Williams, *Black P Stone Nation*.
32. For a detailed exploration of these dynamics within another setting, see Robert Garot, *Who You Claim: Performing Gang Identity in School and on the Streets* (New York: New York University Press, 2010).
33. Thrasher, *The Gang*; Suttles, *Social Order of the Slum*; Suttles, *Social Construction of Communities*; Irving A. Spergel, *Street Gang Work: Theory and Practice* (Reading, MA: Addison-Wesley, 1966); Lincoln R. Keiser, *The Vice Lords: Warriors of the Streets*, fieldwork ed. (New York: Holt, Rinehart and Winston, 1979); James B. Jacobs, *Stateville: The Penitentiary in Mass Society* (Chicago: University of Chicago Press, 1977); Ruth Horowitz, *Honor and the American Dream: Culture and Identity in a Chicano Community* (New Brunswick, NJ: Rutgers University Press, 1983).
34. Venkatesh, *American Project*; Venkatesh, *Off the Books*; Sudhir Alladi Venkatesh and Steven D. Levitt, "'Are We a Family or a Business?' History and Disjuncture in the Urban American Street Gang," *Theory and Society* 29, no. 4 (2000): 427–62; Hagedorn, *World of Gangs*; Hagedorn, *In$ane Chicago Way*; John M. Hagedorn, "Race Not Space: A Revisionist History of Gangs in Chicago," *Journal of African American History* 91, no. 2 (2006): 194–208; Felix M. Padilla, *The Gang as an American Enterprise* (New Brunswick, NJ: Rutgers University Press, 1992).

    It should be noted that the term "crack epidemic" is somewhat of a misnomer, as crack cocaine use—much less addiction—was never widespread in the United States, making the insinuation of pervasiveness indicated by the term "epidemic" somewhat problematic. Craig Reinarman and Harry G. Levine have argued persuasively that the crack epidemic represented a socially constructed moral panic that elected officials used to distract from and/or justify deepening inequality, welfare state retrenchment, and the war on drugs, and that the news media used to boost ratings. Nonetheless, as Reinarman and Levine note, crack addiction was, indeed, a very serious issue within many impoverished urban communities of color during the late 1980s and early 1990s. Indeed, a great deal of scholarship, including the studies cited here, describes the devastating effects of both heavy crack use and addiction within these communities as well as the routine violence often associated with the crack trade. Since it is this particular context to which I am referring here and in other places in this book, I retain use of the term "crack epidemic." Craig Reinarman and Harry G. Levine, eds., *Crack in America: Demon Drugs and Social Justice* (Berkeley: University of California Press, 1997).

35. David and Weezy were the only participants native to Chicago who identified with a neighborhood gang but did not identify with one of these traditional street gangs. Both explained that this was due to having lived relatively "sheltered" childhoods and not becoming involved with the streets until the relatively advanced age of eighteen. In other words, this did not represent an abandonment of previously held traditional gang identities.
36. In his study of the employment experiences of black men reentering the community following incarceration, Joseph Strickland refers to such people as "transformed individuals," people "who had transformed their lives from street hoodlums to community helpers." Joseph A. Strickland, "Building Social Capital for Stable Employment: The Post Prison Experiences of Black Male Ex-Prisoners" (PhD diss., University of Illinois at Chicago, 2008), 102–3, ProQuest (UMI 3316768).
37. William Julius Wilson, *The Truly Disadvantaged: The Inner City, the Underclass, and Public Policy* (Chicago: University of Chicago Press, 1987); William Julius Wilson, *When Work Disappears: The World of the New Urban Poor* (New York: Alfred A. Knopf, 1996); Loïc Wacquant, *Urban Outcasts: A Comparative Sociology of Advanced Marginality* (Cambridge: Polity Press, 2008); Loïc Wacquant, "Urban Desolation and Symbolic Denigration in the Hyperghetto," *Social Psychology Quarterly* 73, no. 3 (2010): 215–19.
38. Chicago Public Schools, "Search Schools," 2018, https://www.cps.edu/schools/find_a_school/pages/findaschool.aspx; Sheri Cohen et al., *Healthy Chicago 2.0 Community Health Assessment: Informing Efforts to Achieve Health Equity* (Chicago: Chicago Department of Public Health, 2016), 24–26.

    It also merits mention here that, despite often being referred to monolithically, the South Side of Chicago covers a vast area comprising a diverse array of communities, including largely white, middle-class communities like Beverly and Mount Greenwood; racially diverse, middle-class communities like Hyde Park, Kenwood, and Ashburn; black, solidly middle-class communities like Calumet Heights and Washington Heights; and almost entirely Latino communities like Brighton Park, Gage Park, and the East Side. Thus, while the phrase "South Side of Chicago" tends to conjure images of the city's infamous black ghetto—and, to be certain, the phrase will be used in essentially this fashion throughout this book—it should be noted that the reality is more complex than this image might indicate.

1. THE SHATTERING OF CHICAGO'S BLACK STREET GANGS

1. Felix M. Padilla, *The Gang as an American Enterprise* (New Brunswick, NJ: Rutgers University Press, 1992); Sudhir Alladi Venkatesh, *American Project: The Rise and Fall of a Modern Ghetto* (Cambridge, MA: Harvard University Press, 2000); Sudhir Alladi Venkatesh and Steven D. Levitt, "'Are We a Family or a Business?' History and Disjuncture in the Urban American Street Gang," *Theory and Society* 29, no. 4 (2000): 427–62; Sudhir Alladi Venkatesh, *Off the Books: The Underground*

Economy of the Urban Poor (Cambridge, MA: Harvard University Press, 2006); John M. Hagedorn, *A World of Gangs: Armed Young Men and Gangsta Culture* (Minneapolis: University of Minnesota Press, 2008); John M. Hagedorn, *The In$ane Chicago Way: The Daring Plan by Chicago Gangs to Create a Spanish Mafia* (Chicago: University of Chicago Press, 2015); Laurence Ralph, "'As Soon as I Get Out Ima Cop Dem Jordans': The Afterlife of the Corporate Gang," *Identities: Global Studies in Culture and Power* 17, no. 6 (2010): 667–94; Laurence Ralph, *Renegade Dreams: Living Through Injury in Gangland Chicago* (Chicago: University of Chicago Press, 2014).

2. The extent to which this research applies to the African American gangs on Chicago's West Side is not entirely clear. Both some recent scholarship on these gangs as well as my own interviews and conversations with people knowledgeable about the dynamics on the West Side indicate that the transformations in gang culture, organization, and violence described in this book have affected black gangs on the West Side to a somewhat lesser degree. Ralph, "'Cop Dem Jordans'"; Ralph, *Renegade Dreams*.
3. Hagedorn, *World of Gangs*, 9.
4. "Mufti," an Arabic word, denotes a scholar and interpreter of Islamic law. The Black P Stones have incorporated Islamic tenets and symbolism extensively into their organizational culture, as Lamont describes later in this quote. A similar, if less pronounced, Islamic influence is evident with the Vice Lords, Mickey Cobras, and other People-allied gangs as well. See John M. Hagedorn, "Race Not Space: A Revisionist History of Gangs in Chicago," *Journal of African American History* 91, no. 2 (2006): 203; Natalie Y. Moore and Lance Williams, *The Almighty Black P Stone Nation: The Rise, Fall, and Resurgence of an American Gang* (Chicago: Lawrence Hill Books, 2011), 131–54.
5. Will Cooley, "'Stones Run It': Taking Back Control of Organized Crime in Chicago, 1940–1975," *Journal of Urban History* 37, no. 6 (2011): 911–32; Hagedorn, *In$ane Chicago Way*, 36–39.
6. Venkatesh and Levitt, "'Family or a Business'"; Ric Curtis, "The Negligible Role of Gangs in Drug Distribution in New York City in the 1990s," in *Gangs and Society: Alternative Perspectives*, ed. Louis Kontos, David C. Brotherton, and Luis Barrios (New York: Columbia University Press, 2003), 41–61.
7. Steven D. Levitt and Sudhir Alladi Venkatesh, "An Economic Analysis of a Drug-Selling Gang's Finances," *Quarterly Journal of Economics* 115, no. 3 (2000): 755–89.
8. Sudhir Alladi Venkatesh, "The Social Organization of Street Gang Activity in an Urban Ghetto," *American Journal of Sociology* 103, no. 1 (1997): 82–111; Venkatesh, *American Project*; Venkatesh and Levitt, "'Family or a Business'"; Susan J. Popkin et al., *The Hidden War: Crime and the Tragedy of Public Housing in Chicago* (New Brunswick, NJ: Rutgers University Press, 2000); Hagedorn, *In$ane Chicago Way*.
9. Federal Bureau of Investigation, "Uniform Crime Reports," accessed January 26, 2017, https://www.ucrdatatool.gov/.
10. Willie Lloyd, the former chief of the Unknown Vice Lords, passed away in 2015 at age sixty-four. Angelo Roberts, the former chief of the Four Corner Hustlers, was brutally murdered in Chicago in 1995.
11. Bruce Johnson, Andrew Golub, and Eloise Dunlap, "The Rise and Decline of Hard Drugs, Drug Markets, and Violence in Inner-City New York," in *The Crime Drop*

in America, ed. Alfred Blumstein and Joel Wallman (Cambridge: Cambridge University Press, 2000), 164–206; Venkatesh, *Off the Books*, 280–91; Randol Contreras, *The Stickup Kids: Race, Drugs, Violence, and the American Dream* (Berkeley: University of California Press, 2013), 110–11; Michael Zelenko, "If the Drug War Is Failing, Where'd All the Cocaine Go?," *Vice*, January 24, 2014, https://www.vice.com/read/if-the-drug-war-is-failing-whered-all-the-cocaine-go.

12. Office of National Drug Control Policy, *2013 Annual Report, Arrestee Drug Abuse Monitoring Program II* (Washington, DC: Executive Office of the President, 2014), 108.
13. Zelenko, "All the Cocaine."
14. R. Terry Furst et al., "The Stigmatized Image of the 'Crack Head': A Sociocultural Exploration of a Barrier to Cocaine Smoking Among a Cohort of Youth in New York City," *Deviant Behavior* 20, no. 2 (1999): 153–81.
15. Andrew Golub, Henry Brownstein, and Eloise Dunlap, *Monitoring Drug Epidemics and the Markets That Sustain Them Using ADAM II: Final Technical Report* (Washington, DC: U.S. Department of Justice, 2012), 24.
16. Benjamin Bowser, Robert Fullilove, and Carl Word, "Is the New Heroin Epidemic Really New? Racializing Heroin," *Journal of the National Medical Association* 109, no. 1 (2017): 29, 30. See also Scott Jacques and Richard Wright, *Code of the Suburb: Inside the World of Young Middle-Class Drug Dealers* (Chicago: University of Chicago Press, 2015).
17. Office of National Drug Control Policy, *2013 Annual Report*, 72, 73.
18. Hagedorn, "Race Not Space," 204, 203.
19. Danielle H. Sandler, *Externalities of Public Housing: The Effect of Public Housing Demolitions on Local Crime* (Washington, DC: U.S. Census Bureau, 2016), 2, 28. More units have been demolished since 2010, including the LeClaire Courts and Maplewood Courts.
20. Arnold R. Hirsch, *Making the Second Ghetto: Race and Housing in Chicago, 1940–1960* (Cambridge: Cambridge University Press, 1983).
21. Sandler, *Externalities of Public Housing*, 29; Mary Pattillo, *Black on the Block: The Politics of Race and Class in the City* (Chicago: University of Chicago Press, 2007), 65, 64. The Low End is a moniker for Chicago's historic South Side black ghetto, which was also home to the lion's share of the city's public housing projects prior to their wide-scale demolition over the past two decades. The area is roughly bounded by the Dan Ryan Expressway to the west, Lake Michigan and Cottage Grove Avenue to the east, Cullerton Street (2000 south) to the north, and Sixty-Third Street to the south.
22. Sandler, *Externalities of Public Housing*, 29.
23. Popkin et al., *Hidden War*; Venkatesh, *American Project*; Hagedorn, *World of Gangs*, 13–15.
24. Todd Sink and Brian Ceh, "Relocation of Urban Poor in Chicago: HOPE IV Policy Outcomes," *Geoforum* 42, no. 1 (2011): 73, 75.
25. Chicago Housing Authority, *The Plan for Transformation: An Update on Relocation* (Chicago: Chicago Housing Authority, 2011), 8. Other displaced former CHA residents moved into vacant units in other developments that had been spared from demolition, and a small percentage was able to eventually return to their original developments, which had been converted to "mixed-income" housing.

26. Popkin et al., *Hidden War*, 157–58; John M. Hagedorn and Brigid Rauch, "Housing, Gangs, and Homicide: What We Can Learn from Chicago," *Urban Affairs Review* 42, no. 4 (2007): 449–51.
27. James B. Jacobs, *Stateville: The Penitentiary in Mass Society* (Chicago: University of Chicago Press, 1977), 138–74.
28. Hagedorn, *In$ane Chicago Way*, 21. See also Venkatesh and Levitt, "'Family or a Business'"; Hagedorn, *World of Gangs*; Moore and Williams, *Black P Stone Nation*.
29. Hagedorn, *In$ane Chicago Way*, 173–74, 207.
30. Popkin et al., *Hidden War*, 57.
31. Moore and Williams, *Black P Stone Nation*, 253–55.
32. Padilla, *American Enterprise*; Levitt and Venkatesh, "Economic Analysis."
33. "On Chief" is a reference to Jeff Fort, a.k.a. Chief Malik, the cofounder and long-time chief of the Black P Stone Nation. Here, Rasheed is swearing an oath "on Chief."
34. Moore and Williams, *Black P Stone Nation*, 253.
35. See also the work of Laurence Ralph with a black gang from Chicago's West Side: Ralph, "'Cop Dem Jordans'"; Ralph, *Renegade Dreams*.
36. Hagedorn, *In$ane Chicago Way*, 11.

2. FROM STREET ORGANIZATIONS TO CLIQUES: BLACK STREET GANGS IN CHICAGO TODAY

1. Other research indicates some variation in this regard. Unlike the gangs in this study, for example, Lance Williams's long-term research with Black Stone neighborhoods in the Auburn Gresham community indicates that those gangs have retained some semblance of local leadership structure. Laurence Ralph's research with a black West Side gang indicates the same. John Hagedorn et al., *The Fracturing of Gangs and Violence in Chicago: A Research-Based Reorientation of Violence Prevention Policy* (Chicago: Great Cities Institute, University of Illinois at Chicago, 2019), 9–10; Laurence Ralph, "'As Soon as I Get Out Ima Cop Dem Jordans': The Afterlife of the Corporate Gang," *Identities: Global Studies in Culture and Power* 17, no. 6 (2010): 667–94; Laurence Ralph, *Renegade Dreams: Living Through Injury in Gangland Chicago* (Chicago: University of Chicago Press, 2014).
2. For a treatment of the tension between ideologies of brotherhood and daily realities of exploitation and coercion during the 1990s, see Felix M. Padilla, *The Gang as an American Enterprise* (New Brunswick, NJ: Rutgers University Press, 1992); Sudhir Alladi Venkatesh and Steven D. Levitt, "'Are We a Family or a Business?' History and Disjuncture in the Urban American Street Gang," *Theory and Society* 29, no. 4 (2000): 427–62.
3. It is unclear who Rasheed is referring to here when he says "they." There appear to be two likely possibilities. One is that he is referring to gang leaders who used divisive gang ideologies to maintain control of their members. The other possibility is that he is referring to society's political and economic elite, who might be viewed as cultivating divisions within marginalized communities of color as a means of thwarting unity and undermining the development of insurgent political power.
4. Although street gangs have always been dominated by young men, the organizational complexity and institutionalized nature of street gangs in Chicago has

traditionally allowed for more explicit and integral roles for women and members of a relatively wide range of ages. Sudhir Alladi Venkatesh, "The Social Organization of Street Gang Activity in an Urban Ghetto," *American Journal of Sociology* 103, no. 1 (1997): 82–111; Sudhir Alladi Venkatesh, "Gender and Outlaw Capitalism: An Historical Account of the Black Sisters United Girl Gang," *Signs: A Journal of Women in Culture and Society* 23, no. 3 (1998): 683–709; Sudhir Alladi Venkatesh, *American Project: The Rise and Fall of a Modern Ghetto* (Cambridge, MA: Harvard University Press, 2000); John M. Hagedorn, *A World of Gangs: Armed Young Men and Gangsta Culture* (Minneapolis: University of Minnesota Press, 2008); Ralph, *Renegade Dreams*.

5. See note 35 in the introduction for an explanation of the two exceptions to this trend.
6. It is not entirely unclear whether these tensions had existed beforehand and had simply been kept in check by the strength of the gang's organizational structure or if they had emerged only after its collapse.
7. Susan J. Popkin et al., *The Hidden War: Crime and the Tragedy of Public Housing in Chicago* (New Brunswick, NJ: Rutgers University Press, 2000), 51, 76; Venkatesh and Levitt, " 'Family or a Business,' " 440–41.
8. See also Natalie Y. Moore and Lance Williams, *The Almighty Black P Stone Nation: The Rise, Fall, and Resurgence of an American Gang* (Chicago: Lawrence Hill Books, 2011), 240–54; Ralph, " 'Cop Dem Jordans' "; Ralph, *Renegade Dreams*.
9. "Larry's guys" is a reference to Larry Hoover, the longtime chairman of the Gangster Disciples. Seven, four, fourteen is the numerical representation of GDN, the acronym for the Gangster Disciple Nation.
10. For an in-depth treatment of the phenomenon of switching gang identities and allegiances among Latino gangs in California, see Norma Mendoza-Denton, *Homegirls: Language and Cultural Practice Among Latina Youth Gangs* (Malden, MA: Blackwell, 2008).
11. Kathleen Kane-Willis and Scott Metzger, *Hidden in Plain Sight: Heroin's Impact on Chicago's West Side* (Chicago: Illinois Consortium on Drug Policy at Roosevelt University, 2016). For a discussion of heroin selling among a black West Side street gang, see Ralph, *Renegade Dreams*, 94, 97–99. This was also one theme that emerged during the conference I co-organized on gang fracturing and violence in Chicago at the University of Illinois's Great Cities Institute in April 2018. See Hagedorn et al., *Fracturing of Gangs*, 8, 13, 17.
12. Taking into account the high risk of incarceration, work stoppages related to conflicts over markets, and violent injury or death related to working as a street-level drug dealer, these positions were often even less profitable than minimum-wage work in the formal economy. See Steven D. Levitt and Sudhir Alladi Venkatesh, "An Economic Analysis of a Drug-Selling Gang's Finances," *Quarterly Journal of Economics* 115, no. 3 (2000): 755–89; Philippe Bourgois, *In Search of Respect: Selling Crack in El Barrio* (Cambridge: Cambridge University Press, 1995), 91–105.
13. One additional factor that may contribute to the profitability of heroin markets on Chicago's West Side is its proximity to customers in the city's white western suburbs. Indeed, Interstate 290, which runs from downtown Chicago to the western suburbs, is often referred to as "heroin highway." Kane-Willis and Metzger, *Hidden in Plain Sight*; Frank Main, "On the West Side, Maps Show Heroin ODs, Shootings Go

Hand in Hand," *Chicago Sun-Times*, March 24, 2017, https://chicago.suntimes.com/crime/on-the-west-side-maps-show-heroin-ods-shootings-go-hand-in-hand/.

14. It is common practice among urban marijuana users to smoke marijuana in cigarillos whose original contents have been emptied out and replaced with marijuana. These are typically referred to as "blunts," the namesake of a popular variety of cigarillo within the urban milieu manufactured by the brand Phillies. Swishers is another brand of cigarillos whose products are often employed to these ends.
15. Martha Ross and Nicole Prchal Svajlenka, *Employment and Disconnection Among Teens and Young Adults: The Role of Place, Race, and Education* (Washington, DC: Brookings Institution, 2016).
16. Mayor Rahm Emanuel's One Summer Chicago, *Newsroom*, 2018, http://www.onesummerchicago.org/Newsroom/.
17. Chicago Crime Commission, *The Gang Book*, 2nd ed. (Chicago: Chicago Crime Commission, 2012), 14–16. The 2018 edition of *The Gang Book* contains even less analysis of current gang dynamics but includes unfounded statements such as the claim that "loyalty has given way to income." Chicago Crime Commission, *The Gang Book*, 3rd ed. (Chicago: Chicago Crime Commission, 2018), 16.
18. The Chicago Crime Commission's 2018 edition of *The Gang Book* lists each gang's People or Folks affiliation prominently in the heading of their respective "gang profiles." Chicago Crime Commission, *Gang Book*, 3rd ed.

3. THE ANATOMY OF CONTEMPORARY GANG VIOLENCE IN CHICAGO

1. "Dropping the rakes" and "cracking the treys" denote disrespectful inversions of the Gangster Disciples' pitchfork hand sign and the Black Disciples' three-fingered salute, respectively.
2. This wartime support is typically referred to as "aid and assist" among gangs that were once part of the Folks alliance. A number of participants who identified as Black Disciples and Gangster Disciples still used this terminology.
3. Woodlawn's relative geographic isolation—as seen in figure 3.1, it is almost entirely enclosed by a variety of topographic barriers—makes the community a useful case study in this regard, as relatively few of the conflicts in which its gangs are embroiled spill outside of the community's boundaries.
4. Hyde Park's attendance zone also includes a geographically separate section of the Englewood and Auburn Gresham communities a few miles away to the southwest.
5. This prerogative first gained substantial traction in 2004 with former mayor Richard M. Daley's "Renaissance 2010" initiative. Since then, scores of neighborhood public schools have been shuttered, and more than one hundred charter schools were in operation as of early 2019. Linda Lutton, Becky Vevea, Sarah Karp, Adriana Cardona-Maguidad, and Kate McGee, "A Generation of School Closings," WBEZ, December 3, 2018, https://interactive.wbez.org/generation-school-closings/.
6. In the cases where a charter school does not immediately open to replace the closed neighborhood school all displaced students are reassigned to another neighborhood school.

7. Chicago Public Schools, "CPS School Locator," 2018, https://cps.edu/ScriptLibrary/Map-SchoolLocator/index.html.
8. See also John M. Hagedorn, "Gangs, Schools, and Social Change: An Institutional Analysis," *ANNALS of the American Academy of Political and Social Science* 673, no. 1 (2017): 190–208.
9. Susan J. Popkin et al., *The Hidden War: Crime and the Tragedy of Public Housing in Chicago* (New Brunswick, NJ: Rutgers University Press, 2000), 18.
10. To fully grasp the ideological implications of a war between a gang comprising MCs and BDs and another comprising MCs and GDs, it should be noted that both the BDs and GDs are traditional ideological enemies of the MCs. The BDs and GDs, moreover, together had once constituted the Black Gangster Disciple Nation before splitting into generally fraternal gangs and then eventually fighting a fierce war over the control of drug markets and organizational supremacy during the 1990s.
11. In the documentary film *Bastards of the Party*, Cle Sloan, a Bloods gang member, offers a strikingly similar assessment of both the dynamics that fuel gang violence in Los Angeles as well as broader patterns of collective violence: "The thing about bangin', we won't let go—we won't let go of the dead because they died for us, man. . . . The Palestinian, he doesn't care about the politics, he doesn't care about—you know, he might care something about the land. But once you kill his father, his brother, his uncle, whatever, that's what it's about. . . . It's about the man who died next to you that you love." Cle Sloan, dir., *Bastards of the Party* (Venice, CA: Fuqua Films, 2005), DVD.
12. Kanye West, "Hold My Liquor," featuring vocals by Chief Keef and Justin Vernon, track 6 on *Yeezus*, Def Jam Recordings B0018653-02, 2013, compact disc.
13. For an examination of how these developments shaped forays into music by Chicago gang members in the pre–drill music era—that is, prior to 2012—see Geoff Harkness, *Chicago Hustle and Flow: Gangs, Gangsta Rap, and Social Class* (Minneapolis: University of Minnesota Press, 2014).
14. The lyrics referenced here are from the song Chief Keef, "What I Claim," track 10 on *Bang*, Glory Boyz Entertainment, 2011, MP3 audio. OTF stands for "Only Trey Folks," or "Only the Family," a reference to a number of allied Black Disciple gangs (or gangs that are predominantly composed of Black Disciples) on Chicago's South Side, including WIC City (O-Block), Young Money, Lamron, and Four-Six. OTF is also an acronym for Only the Family, the name of rapper and Lamron affiliate Lil Durk's record label and clothing line. However, another gang with the moniker Young Money is an enemy of many of the gangs mentioned in these lyrics, thus, Keef's clarification that the Young Money gang with which he is allied is "no[t] Five-One," and that he is, instead, "sendin' shots at Oh-Five-One." These numbers are references to Fifty-First Street, along which lies the territorial heart of the enemy Young Money gang.
15. Notably, these gang signs are typically a mix of both traditional gang symbols, like the Gangster Disciples' pitchforks or the Black Disciples' "treys," and emergent forms of gang identification like Insane and L's.
16. "Finally Rich: Chief Keef," *Billboard*, http://www.billboard.com/artist/299119/ chief-keef/chart?f=335.
17. See the discussion in chapter 1. See also Dwight Conquergood, "Homeboys and Hoods: Gang Communication and Cultural Space," in *Group Communication in*

Context: Studies of Natural Groups, ed. Lawrence R. Frey (Hillsdale, NJ: Lawrence Erlbaum, 1994), 23–55; Dwight Conquergood, "Street Literacy," in *Handbook of Research on Teaching Literacy Through the Communicative and Visual Arts*, ed. James Flood, Shirley Brice Heath, and Diane Lapp, 354–75 (New York: Macmillan Library Reference), 1997; David C. Brotherton and Luis Barrios, *The Almighty Latin King and Queen Nation: Street Politics and the Transformation of a New York City Gang* (New York: Columbia University Press, 2004); John M. Hagedorn, *A World of Gangs: Armed Young Men and Gangsta Culture* (Minneapolis: University of Minnesota Press, 2008); John M. Hagedorn, *The In$ane Chicago Way: The Daring Plan by Chicago Gangs to Create a Spanish Mafia* (Chicago: University of Chicago Press, 2015).

18. Lil JoJo, *JoJo World*, self-released, 2012, MP3 audio.
19. Ben Austen, "Public Enemies: Social Media Is Fueling Gang Wars in Chicago," *Wired*, September 17, 2013, http://www.wired.com/2013/09/gangs-of-social-media/.
20. Indeed, as participants pointed out, the nature of online interaction includes a number of characteristics that may increase the likelihood of conflicts playing out on social media and escalating to the point of eventual violence, including the supremely public nature of online communications, which may make saving face an even greater priority than usual; the fact that online contact can be relatively continuous, since it is not predicated on in-person interaction; the severely limited ability of third parties to mediate confrontations, as comments are posted from the isolation of individual accounts as opposed to occurring within a conventional social context; and the relatively delayed consequences of online, versus face-to-face, confrontations, which may increase the likelihood of antagonistic behavior.
21. Austen, "Public Enemies."
22. Two prominent examples include the horrifying execution of nine-year-old Tyshawn Lee in 2015 and a 2018 shooting outside of a funeral in which six people were shot. Jeremy Gorner and Annie Sweeney, "Father of Slain 9-Year-Old Tyshawn Lee Charged with Shooting 3," *Chicago Tribune*, March 13, 2016, http://www.chicagotribune.com/news/local/breaking/ct-tyshawn-lee-father-shooting-met-20160313-story.html; Anna Spoerre and William Lee, "6 Shot While Leaving Funeral for Slain Rapper: 'Bullets Flying Everyplace,'" *Chicago Tribune*, October 23, 2018, https://www.chicagotribune.com/news/local/breaking/ct-met-chicago-funeral-shooting-20181022-story.html.
23. Chicago Police Department, *2011 Chicago Murder Analysis* (Chicago: Chicago Police Department, 2012), https://home.chicagopolice.org/wp-content/uploads/2014/12/2011-Murder-Report.pdf. Obviously, not all of these victims were the unintended targets of gang shootings, and there is no way of discerning how many of them were, given the information available in this report. Nonetheless, while this represents an admittedly imperfect measure of the level of target discrimination in gang violence, there is at least no indication that this problem has become worse since the era of leader-directed gang violence in the 1990s.
24. The September 1994 execution of eleven-year-old Black Disciple member Robert "Yummy" Sandifer, who had shot two youth and killed another in an alleged botched gang hit, by fourteen- and sixteen-year-old brothers and fellow Black Disciples at the behest of gang leaders is perhaps the most infamous example. Another high-profile incident was the October 1992 murder of seven-year-old Dantrell Davis, who

was hit by a sniper's bullet while walking to school from his building in the infamous Cabrini-Green projects. He was the third child at his elementary school to have been killed by gunfire that year alone. Nancy Gibbs, "Murder in Miniature," *Time*, September 19, 1994, http://content.time.com/time/magazine/article/0,9171,981460,00.html; Mick Dumke, "The Shot That Brought the Projects Down," *Chicago Reader*, October 12, 2012, https://www.chicagoreader.com/Bleader/archives/2012/10/12/the-shot-that-brought-the-projects-down-part-one-of-five.

25. Similarly, the Chicago Crime Commission claims that contemporary gang wars are driven by conflicts "over turf and drug markets." Chicago Crime Commission, *The Gang Book*, 3rd ed. (Chicago: Chicago Crime Commission, 2018), 192.
26. A copy of the statement is still available on the "CAPS—17th District Albany Park" Facebook page, in a post dated July 24, 2015.
27. Los Angeles Police Department, "Introduction to Gangs," 2018, http://www.lapdonline.org/get_informed/content_basic_view/23466.
28. James F. Short Jr., *Poverty, Ethnicity, and Violent Crime* (Boulder, CO: Westview Press, 1997), 204.

4. UNDERSTANDING THE PERSISTENCE OF GANGS AND VIOLENCE IN CHICAGO

1. Nate Silver, "The Most Diverse Cities Are Often the Most Segregated," *FiveThirtyEight*, May 1, 2015, https://fivethirtyeight.com/features/the-most-diverse-cities-are-often-the-most-segregated/; James Manning, "The Time Out City Life Index 2018," *Time Out*, June 13, 2018, https://www.timeout.com/things-to-do/city-life-index; Brianna Kelly, "Chicago Ranks 7th on New List of World's Best Cities," *Crain's Chicago Business*, November 27, 2018, https://www.chicagobusiness.com/tourism/chicago-ranks-7th-new-list-worlds-best-cities; Kathleen Elkins, "These Are the 10 Richest Cities in the World," CNBC, September 14, 2018, https://www.cnbc.com/2018/09/14/the-richest-cities-in-the-world.html; Stephen R. Higley, "The 2010 Higley 1000," *The Higley 1000*, February 17, 2014, https://higley1000.com/archives/638.
2. St. Clair Drake and Horace R. Cayton, *Black Metropolis: A Study of Negro Life in a Northern City* (New York: Harcourt, Brace, 1945); Arnold R. Hirsch, *Making the Second Ghetto: Race and Housing in Chicago, 1940–1960* (Cambridge: Cambridge University Press, 1983); William Julius Wilson, *The Truly Disadvantaged: The Inner City, the Underclass, and Public Policy* (Chicago: University of Chicago Press, 1987); Mary Pattillo, *Black on the Block: The Politics of Race and Class in the City* (Chicago: University of Chicago Press, 2007).
3. Kevin Covall, "Rahm Emanuel's Chicago, a Tale of Two Cities," CNN, April 3, 2014, https://www.cnn.com/2014/04/02/opinion/coval-chicagoland-rahm-emanuel/index.html. Andrew Diamond is quoted in Alana Semuels, "Chicago's Awful Divide," *Atlantic*, March 28, 2018, https://www.theatlantic.com/business/archive/2018/03/chicago-segregation-poverty/556649/. See also Andrew J. Diamond, *Chicago on the Make: Power and Inequality in a Modern City* (Berkeley: University of California Press, 2017).

Chicago was infamously profiled in one of the chapters in Jonathan Kozol's seminal 1991 examination of inequities in public education in the United States, *Savage Inequalities*. Jonathan Kozol, *Savage Inequalities: Children in America's Schools* (New York: Crown, 1991), 59.

4. Gregory Acs et al., *The Cost of Segregation: National Trends and the Case of Chicago, 1990–2010* (Washington, DC: Urban Institute, 2017).
5. Latinos, on the other hand, have continued to pour into the city, and supplanted African Americans as Chicago's second-largest demographic group in 2017. Jacqueline Serrato, "Mexicans and 'Hispanics,' Now the Largest Minority in Chicago," *Chicago Tribune*, October 13, 2017, https://www.chicagotribune.com/hoy/ct-mexicans-and-hispanics-largest-minority-in-chicago-20171013-story.html.
6. Bill Ruthhart, "How a Federal City Hall Corruption Investigation Is Dominating Chicago's Crowded Race for Mayor," *Chicago Tribune*, February 1, 2019, https://www.chicagotribune.com/news/local/politics/ct-met-chicago-mayors-race-federal-investigation-20190201-story.html; Jason Meisner and Juan Perez Jr., "Byrd-Bennett Sobs While Trying to Explain Corruption, Gets 4 1/2 Years in Prison," *Chicago Tribune*, April 28, 2017, http://www.chicagotribune.com/news/local/breaking/ct-barbara-byrd-bennett-sentence-met-20170428-story.html; Juan Perez Jr., Bill Ruthhart, and Hal Dardick, "CPS Chief Forrest Claypool Resigns After Being Accused of Ethics Probe Cover-Up," *Chicago Tribune*, December 8, 2017, http://www.chicagotribune.com/news/local/politics/ct-met-forrest-claypool-resigns-cps-20171208-story.html; David Jackson et al., "Betrayed," *Chicago Tribune*, July 27, 2018, http://graphics.chicagotribune.com/chicago-public-schools-sexual-abuse/index.html; John Byrne, "City Reaches $38.75 Million Settlement in Red Light Ticket Lawsuit," *Chicago Tribune*, July 20, 2017, http://www.chicagotribune.com/news/local/politics/ct-rahm-emanuel-red-light-tickets-lawsuit-settlement-met-20170720-story.html; Jeff Coen, "Former Chicago Alderman Sentenced to 4 Years in Prison," *Chicago Tribune*, February 18, 2009, http://articles.chicagotribune.com/2009-02-18/news/0902170689_1_alderman-arenda-troutman-hired-truck-program; Jason Meisner, "Ald. Willie Cochran Pleads Guilty—Finally—to Federal Fraud Charges for Misusing Ward's Charity Fund," *Chicago Tribune*, March 21, 2019, https://www.chicagotribune.com/news/breaking/ct-met-alderman-willie-cochran-guilty-20190320-story.html; Edward McClelland, "Rahm Emanuel's Nixon Moment: The Laquan McDonald Coverup Will Be His Legacy," *Salon*, December 2, 2015, https://www.salon.com/2015/12/02/rahm_emanuels_nixon_moment/; Monica Davey, "Blagojevich Sentenced to 14 Years in Prison," *New York Times*, December 7, 2011, https://www.nytimes.com/2011/12/08/us/blagojevich-expresses-remorse-in-courtroom-speech.html.
7. Dick Simpson et al., *Chicago: Still the Capital of Corruption* (Chicago: Department of Political Science, University of Illinois at Chicago, 2015).
8. Barack Obama's longtime former Chicago home is merely blocks away from the Washington Park and Grand Boulevard communities from which a number of the study participants hailed.
9. For members of the Black P Stones, Mickey Cobras, and other gangs associated with the historical People alliance, the term "Brother" is also used as a proper noun in reference to fellow members.

10. Older members often talk about their gangs in terms of an "organization." On the other hand, in language more consistent with stereotypical gang imagery, sometimes gang members will refer to their groups as "the mob."
11. The familial nature of street gangs is a common theme in the gang literature. See James Diego Vigil, *Barrio Gangs: Street Life and Identity in Southern California* (Austin: University of Texas Press, 1988); James Diego Vigil, *A Rainbow of Gangs: Street Cultures in the Mega-City* (Austin: University of Texas Press, 2002); Joan W. Moore, *Going Down to the Barrio: Homeboys and Homegirls in Change* (Philadelphia: Temple University Press, 1991); David C. Brotherton and Luis Barrios, *The Almighty Latin King and Queen Nation: Street Politics and the Transformation of a New York City Gang* (New York: Columbia University Press, 2004).
12. Pierre Bourdieu, *Pascalian Meditations*, trans. Richard Nice (Stanford, CA: Stanford University Press, 2000), 169–70.
13. Manuel Castells, *The Power of Identity* (Oxford: Blackwell, 1997), 8, 9.
14. For other applications of resistance identity to street gangs, see Brotherton and Barrios, *Almighty Latin King*; David C. Brotherton, *Youth Street Gangs: A Critical Appraisal* (New York: Routledge, 2015); John M. Hagedorn, *A World of Gangs: Armed Young Men and Gangsta Culture* (Minneapolis: University of Minnesota Press, 2008).
15. Suniya Farooqui, *Chicago Community Area Indicators, 2015* (Chicago: Social Impact Research Center, Heartland Alliance, 2017).
16. Teresa L. Córdova and Matthew D. Wilson, *Lost: The Crisis of Jobless and Out of School Teens and Young Adults in Chicago Illinois and the U.S.* (Chicago: Great Cities Institute, University of Illinois at Chicago, 2016).
17. Farooqui, *Chicago Community Area Indicators*.
18. A racially mixed middle- and upper-class community on the city's South Side, Hyde Park's influential stakeholders, including the University of Chicago, have long been enmeshed in efforts to gentrify adjacent black ghetto neighborhoods. See John H. Fish, *Black Power/White Control: The Struggle of The Woodlawn Organization in Chicago* (Princeton, NJ: Princeton University Press, 1973); Hirsch, *Making the Second Ghetto*; Patillo, *Black on the Block*.
19. It is not entirely clear whether the decline in familial financial support that participants reported was, in fact, related to actual reductions in such assistance or whether participants simply perceived this to be the case as their tastes became more expensive as they entered adolescence.
20. Given that such caretaking dynamics take place within a context of poverty, they parallel Russian anarcho-communist Pëtr Kropotkin's anti-Darwinian evolutionary theory of mutual aid among humans and animals seeking survival under conditions of severe hardship and strain. Pëtr Kropotkin, *Mutual Aid: A Factor of Evolution* (New York: McClure, Phillips, 1902).
21. See also Elijah Anderson, *Code of the Street: Decency, Violence, and the Moral Life of the Inner City* (New York: Norton, 1999), 74–75; Mary Pattillo, *Black Picket Fences: Privilege and Peril Among the Black Middle Class* (Chicago: University of Chicago Press, 1999), 146–66; Laurence Ralph, "'As Soon as I Get Out Ima Cop Dem Jordans': The Afterlife of the Corporate Gang," *Identities: Global Studies in Culture and Power* 17, no. 6 (2010): 667–94.
22. Susan A. Phillips, *Operation Fly Trap: L.A. Gangs, Drugs, and the Law* (Chicago: University of Chicago Press, 2012), 59.

23. See also Sudhir Alladi Venkatesh and Steven D. Levitt, "'Are We a Family or a Business?' History and Disjuncture in the Urban American Street Gang," *Theory and Society* 29, no. 4 (2000): 427–62.
24. See also Phillips, *Operation Fly Trap*, 65–66.
25. Community-level homicide rates were calculated using census population data and homicide data, respectively, from Farooqui, *Chicago Community Area Indicators*; Chicago Police Department, "Crimes—2001 to Present," 2018), https://data.cityofchicago.org/Public-Safety/Crimes-2001-to-present/ijzp-q8t2. Citywide and national homicide rates were obtained from Federal Bureau of Investigation, "Crime in the U.S," accessed November 16, 2018, https://ucr.fbi.gov/crime-in-the-u.s.
26. This dynamic may involve the ascription of a gang identity by others, self-identification by young people themselves, or some combination of these two processes within a given social context. For an in-depth treatment of the often-fluid and flexible processes of gang identification, see Robert Garot, *Who You Claim: Performing Gang Identity in School and on the Streets* (New York: New York University Press, 2010).
27. Participants' depictions of their neighborhoods as violent and gang-ridden, moreover, are likely inspired by their awareness of the nature of this research study. Additionally, violence and street gangs may figure more prominently in the minds of these research participants, who are gang members, than they would in the minds of other community residents. In other words, it is likely that asking different groups of community residents to describe these same neighborhoods would elicit a greater variety of descriptions. Nonetheless, as discussed in the appendix, violence in these communities tends to be a serious issue that affects all residents, albeit in different ways and to varying degrees.
28. The most prominent example of these dynamics from the late twentieth century was the widespread torture of black men on the city's South Side carried out under the direction of former CPD commander Jon Burge. As many as 120 black men were tortured by Burge and his colleagues into confessing to alleged crimes during the 1970s and 1980s. Micah Uetricht, "Accused Torturer Jon Burge Died Last Week, but His Legacy of Brutal, Racist Policing Lives on in Chicago," *Intercept*, September 25, 2018, https://theintercept.com/2018/09/25/jon-burge-chicago-police-torture/.
29. Police Accountability Task Force, *Recommendations for Reform: Restoring Trust Between the Chicago Police and the Communities They Serve* (Chicago: Police Accountability Task Force, 2016), 8.
30. U.S. Department of Justice, Civil Rights Division, and U.S. Attorney's Office, Northern District of Illinois, *Investigation of the Chicago Police Department* (Washington, DC: U.S. Department of Justice, 2017).
31. Andrew Schroedter, "Chicago Police Misconduct—A Rising Financial Toll," *Better Government Association*, January 31, 2016, https://www.bettergov.org/news/chicago-police-misconduct-%E2%80%93-a-rising-financial-toll.
32. While a number of participants expressed empathy for the difficult duties with which police officers are tasked, particularly those working in rough urban areas, they roundly condemned the mistreatment that they reported receiving from law enforcement officials.
33. The protective function of street gangs in the face of violence or the threat thereof is a common theme in the literature. See Frederic M. Thrasher, *The Gang: A Study*

of 1,313 Gangs in Chicago (Chicago: University of Chicago Press, 1927); Gerald D. Suttles, *The Social Order of the Slum* (Chicago: University of Chicago Press, 1968); Malcolm W. Klein, *Street Gangs and Street Workers* (Englewood Cliffs, NJ: Prentice-Hall, 1971); Scott H. Decker, "Collective and Normative Features of Gang Violence," *Justice Quarterly* 42, no. 2 (1996): 243–64; Scott H. Decker and Barrik Van Winkle, *Life in the Gang: Family, Friends, and Violence* (Cambridge: Cambridge University Press, 1996).

34. "Stony" is a reference to Stony Island Avenue, a portion of which runs along the eastern edge of the Woodlawn community and has been associated with the Black P Stones for more than half a century.
35. One recent high-profile exception to this general dynamic was the case of Gakirah Barnes, a seventeen-year-old young woman from Woodlawn, who was rumored to have been responsible for various killings before being gunned down herself in 2014. Annie Sweeney, "Tweets from Gang Members Express Grief over Violence—But Then Turn to Anger, Researchers Find," *Chicago Tribune*, April 10, 2018, https://www.chicagotribune.com/news/local/breaking/ct-met-gang-internet-banging-study-20180406-story.html.
36. George Karandinos et al., "The Moral Economy of Violence in the US Inner City: Deadly Sociability in the Retail Narcotics Economy," in *Violence at the Urban Margins*, ed. Javier Auyero, Philippe Bourgois, and Nancy Scheper-Hughes (New York: Oxford University Press, 2015), 45.
37. For a treatment of a somewhat similar dynamic, framed as the "moral economy" of violence, see the remarkable edited volume, *Violence at the Urban Margins*, especially chapters 1 and 2: Dennis Rodgers, "The Moral Economy of Murder: Violence, Death, and Social Order in Nicaragua," in *Violence at the Urban Margins*, ed. Javier Auyero, Philippe Bourgois, and Nancy Scheper-Hughes, 21–40 (New York: Oxford University Press, 2015); George Karandinos et al., "Moral Economy of Violence."
38. Castells, *Power of Identity*, 8, 22.
39. For similar treatments of the "politics of death" among gang members in Guatemala and Nicaragua, see Deborah T. Levenson, *Adiós Niño: The Gangs of Guatemala City and the Politics of Death* (Durham, NC: Duke University Press, 2013); Rodgers, "Moral Economy of Murder."
40. In a somewhat similar vein, one large-scale quantative study with middle-school adolescent students found that, despite students who identified as gang members being more likely to experience victimization and to expect future victimization, gang members "report[ed] lower fear of victimization than nongang youth," indicating that "although gang membership is not functional from an objective standpoint, as the frequency of victimization increases substantially, it may still serve its protective function from an emotive standpoint." Chris Melde, Terrance J. Taylor, and Finn-Aage Esbensen, "'I Got Your Back': An Examination of the Protective Function of Gang Membership in Adolescence," *Criminology* 47, no. 2 (2009): 581, 586.
41. To be clear, this typology is only one of many potential ways that the contributions of these various gang scholars might be classified. A more common taxonomy that approximates the one offered here, for example, would classify these theoretical orientations as social disorganization theories, strain theories, and subcultural theories. Here, my classification system strips these theoretical lenses down to what

might be considered their core elements in order to explore broader applications of these perspectives without being straightjacketed by their respective particularities. That said, some of these theories combine various ecological, material, and psychosocial elements in addition to other considerations. Others, such as Richard Cloward and Lloyd Ohlin's differential opportunity theory, do so quite explicitly. Richard A. Cloward and Lloyd E. Ohlin, *Delinquency and Opportunity: A Theory of Delinquent Gangs* (New York: Free Press, 1960).

42. Thrasher, *The Gang*; William Foote Whyte, *Street Corner Society: The Social Structure of an Italian Slum* (Chicago: University of Chicago Press, 1943); Suttles, *Social Order of the Slum*; Gerald D. Suttles, *The Social Construction of Communities* (Chicago: University of Chicago Press, 1972); Vigil, *Barrio Gangs*; Sudhir Alladi Venkatesh, "The Social Organization of Street Gang Activity in an Urban Ghetto," *American Journal of Sociology* 103, no. 1 (1997): 82–111; Sudhir Alladi Venkatesh, *American Project: The Rise and Fall of a Modern Ghetto* (Cambridge, MA: Harvard University Press, 2000).

43. Robert K. Merton, "Social Structure and Anomie," *American Sociological Review* 3, no. 5 (1938): 672–82; Martín Sánchez Jankowski, *Islands in the Street: Gangs and American Urban Society* (Berkeley: University of California Press, 1991); Felix M. Padilla, *The Gang as an American Enterprise* (New Brunswick, NJ: Rutgers University Press, 1992); John M. Hagedorn, *People and Folks: Gangs, Crime and the Underclass in a Rustbelt City* (Chicago: Lake View Press, 1988); John M. Hagedorn, "Gang Violence in the Postindustrial Era," *Crime and Justice* 24 (1998): 365–419.

44. Albert K. Cohen, *Delinquent Boys: The Culture of the Gang* (Glencoe, IL: Free Press, 1955); Moore, *Going Down to the Barrio*; Brotherton and Barrios, *Almighty Latin King*; Robert J. Durán, *Gang Life in Two Cities: An Insider's Journey* (New York: Columbia University Press, 2013); Robert J. Durán, *The Gang Paradox: Inequalities and Miracles on the U.S.–Mexico Border* (New York: Columbia University Press, 2018); Hagedorn, *World of Gangs*.

45. Indeed, mainstream gang research has increasingly assumed the logic and prerogatives of law enforcement and criminal justice officials in ways that are even more problematic. In one particularly reactionary example, a September 2017 editorial authored by two gang researchers and published in the *Wall Street Journal* encourages law enforcement agencies to label Antifa, a diffuse national antifascist and antiracist network whose members are often active participants in street protests, as a street gang. The authors note that "the gang label opens up a range of possibilities for countering Antifa," namely, suppressive policing, judicial, and prosecutorial measures. Rationalizing their position, they claim that Antifa "meet[s] the defining characteristics of a gang" as delineated in the "consensus definition" created by social scientists—an apparent allusion to the definition developed by the mainstream Eurogang research network—and proceed to describe how the group meets these criteria, which include collective identity, durability across time, a propensity for violence and other criminal activity, and a "street orientation." Apparently it did not occur to these researchers that many police departments would also easily meet these definitional criteria. David Pyrooz and James Densley, "To Deal with Antifa, Designate It a Street Gang," *Wall Street Journal*, September 17, 2017, https://www.wsj.com/articles/to-deal-with-antifa-designate-it-a-street-gang-1505672746. For an elaboration of the Eurogang definition, see Finn-Aage Esbensen and Cheryl L.

Maxson, "The Eurogang Program of Research and Multimethod Comparative Gang Research: Introduction," in *Youth Gangs in International Perspective: Results from the Eurogang Program of Research*, ed. Finn-Aage Esbensen and Cheryl L. Maxson (New York: Springer, 2012), 6.

46. Indeed, it is important to note that participation in collective violence does not entail the fulfillment of a gang-ordered shooting or random act of violence, as is often depicted in popular representations of gang "initiations." Rather, it occurs organically in the context of social interaction and the intensification of peer relationships.
47. For example, see Beth M. Huebner, Sean P. Varano, and Timothy S. Bynum, "Gangs, Guns, and Drugs: Recidivism Among Serious Young Offenders," *Criminology & Public Policy* 6, no. 2 (2007): 187–221; David C. Pyrooz, Scott H. Decker, and Vincent J. Webb, "The Ties That Bind: Desistance from Gangs," *Crime & Delinquency* 60, no. 4 (2014): 491–516; Frank M. Weerman, Peter J. Lovegrove, and Terence Thornberry, "Gang Membership Transitions and Its Consequences: Exploring Changes Related to Joining and Leaving Gangs in Two Countries," *European Journal of Criminology* 12, no. 1 (2015): 70–91.
48. Brotherton, *Youth Street Gangs*, 35.

5. A CRITICAL APPRAISAL OF VIOLENCE PREVENTION FAILURES

1. Average homicide rates for the twenty largest U.S. cities, excluding Chicago, were calculated for each year. The trend was calculated by comparing the averages of the years 2004–2007 and the years 2012–2015 for these cities and for Chicago. Federal Bureau of Investigation, "Crime in the U.S.," accessed July 18, 2019, https://ucr.fbi.gov/crime-in-the-u.s.
2. Anthony A. Braga et al., "Problem-Oriented Policing, Deterrence, and Youth Violence: An Evaluation of Boston's Operation Ceasefire," *Journal of Research in Crime and Delinquency* 38, no. 3 (2001): 195–225.
3. David M. Kennedy, "Pulling Levers: Chronic Offenders, High-Crime Settings, and a Theory of Prevention," *Valparaiso University Law Review* 31, no. 2 (1997): 449–84.
4. For the debate on the effects of the Boston Ceasefire intervention in Boston in the 1990s, see Richard Rosenfeld, Robert Fornango, and Eric Baumer, "Did Ceasefire, Compstat, and Exile Reduce Homicide?," *Criminology & Public Policy* 4, no. 3 (2005): 419–49; Richard A. Berk, "Knowing When to Fold 'Em: An Essay on Evaluating the Impact of Ceasefire, Compstat, and Exile," *Criminology & Public Policy* 4, no. 3 (2005): 451–66. For a systematic review of the effects of focused deterrence interventions, see Anthony A. Braga and David L. Weisburd, "The Effects of Focused Deterrence Strategies on Crime: A Systematic Review and Meta-Analysis of the Empirical Evidence," *Journal of Research in Crime and Delinquency* 49, no. 3 (2011): 323–58.
5. David M. Kennedy, *Don't Shoot: One Man, a Street Fellowship, and the End of Violence in Inner-City America* (New York: Bloomsbury, 2011), 71.
6. Kennedy, *Don't Shoot*, 65.
7. Kennedy, "Pulling Levers," 462.

8. It should be noted here that the discussion of focused deterrence in this chapter generally focuses on these efforts that began in 2010 and that are modeled explicitly on the original Boston model. That said, Chicago police and prosecutors have been using focused deterrence strategies since at least 2002, when the city received federal funds for the Project Safe Neighborhoods (PSN) program that continues to this day. An early evaluation of that intervention indicated that areas on the city's West Side that were initially targeted by the program experienced a 12 percent decrease in homicide attributable to the intervention the year after its commencement (homicide was trending downward throughout the city during this time as well, and less substantial declines were observed in the South Side control area and in the city as a whole). A more recent review of Chicago's PSN intervention, however, reveals both that the initial effects of the program in the original intervention area disappeared after a few years and that areas to which the program expanded following its pilot run failed to demonstrate positive program effects. Andrew V. Papachristos, Tracey L. Meares, and Jeffrey Fagan, "Attention Felons: Evaluating Project Safe Neighborhoods in Chicago," *Journal of Empirical Legal Studies* 4, no. 2 (2007): 223–72; Ben Grunwald and Andrew V. Papachristos, "Project Safe Neighborhoods in Chicago: Looking Back a Decade Later," *Journal of Criminal Law and Criminology* 107, no. 1 (2017): 131–60.
9. John Byrne and Liam Ford, "Cops, Feds Meet with Gang Leaders," *Chicago Tribune*, August 28, 2010, http://articles.chicagotribune.com/2010-08-28/news/ct-met-gangs-0829-20100828_1_gang-leaders-gang-members-gang-violence.
10. "Chicago Gang Violence: Police Chief Jody Weis Follows Through on Controversial Strategy," *HuffPost*, October 26, 2010, https://www.huffingtonpost.com/2010/10/26/chicago-gang-violence-pol_n_774402.html; National Network for Safe Communities, *Group Violence Intervention: An Implementation Guide* (Washington, DC: Office of Community Oriented Policing Services, 2016).
11. Andy Grimm, "Black Souls Gang Members Head to Trial on RICO Charges," *Chicago Sun-Times*, October 1, 2017, https://chicago.suntimes.com/news/black-souls-gang-members-head-to-trial-on-rico-charges/.
12. Homicide rates were calculated using homicide data from the Chicago Police Department and community-level census data from the City of Chicago. Chicago Police Department, "Crimes—2001 to Present," 2018, https://data.cityofchicago.org/Public-Safety/Crimes-2001-to-present/ijzp-q8t2; City of Chicago, "Community Area 2000 and 2010 Census Population Comparisons," 2018, https://www.cityofchicago.org/city/en/depts/dcd/supp_info/community_area_2000and2010census populationcomparisons.html.
13. Terry Hilliard served very briefly as interim superintendent in early 2011, between Weis's and McCarthy's tenures.
14. Jeremy Gorner, "Parolee Fatally Shot After Attending Meeting Run by Chicago Police," *Chicago Tribune*, October 16, 2015, http://www.chicagotribune.com/news/local/breaking/ct-gang-call-in-fatal-shooting-met-20151015-story.html.
15. Jeremy Gorner and Annie Sweeney, "Father of Slain 9-Year-Old Tyshawn Lee Charged with Shooting 3." *Chicago Tribune*, March 13, 2016, http://www.chicagotribune.com/news/ local/breaking/ct-tyshawn-lee-father-shooting-met-20160313-story.html.
16. Federal Bureau of Investigation, "Crime in the U.S."

17. On "firebreaks," see Kennedy, *Don't Shoot*, 97. It should be noted that one quasi-experimental study of the CPD's focused deterrence strategy indicated a 23 percent reduction in "overall shooting behavior"—shooting perpetration and victimization—among a segment of Chicago gangs whose members participated in call-ins as compared to similar groups over a one-year period following call-in attendance. It is unclear, however, whether the modest effects of call-in participation suggested in this study might persist over a longer period of time. This would appear an important consideration, especially since follow-up research on Chicago's Project Safe Neighborhoods focused deterrence intervention revealed that positive program effects observed in the few years following the start of the intervention dissipated over time, despite the continuation of the program (see chapter 5, note 8). It is also unclear why police and prosecutors have been unable to build on the apparently positive results of the more recent focused deterrence efforts that produced the 23 percent reduction noted above, efforts that were carried out with only roughly 17 percent of the city's gangs and over an evaluation period that ended in 2013. After all, police and prosecutors work at a citywide level, and proponents of focused deterrence have consistently championed the model's ability to create substantial citywide reductions in homicide, à la Kennedy's "firebreak" argument. Yet the exact opposite has happened in Chicago in recent years, as levels of homicide have skyrocketed to twenty-year highs, a trend that police and prosecutors' focused deterrence efforts have apparently been helpless to prevent. Research data based on the CPD's contemporaneous knowledge of gang dynamics and violent feuds, moreover, should be regarded with a skepticism befitting a department with the nation's lowest homicide clearance rate (see the discussion on pages 147–49). Andrew V. Papachristos and David S. Kirk, "Changing the Street Dynamics: Evaluating Chicago's Group Violence Reduction Strategy," *Criminology & Public Policy* 14, no. 3 (2015): 525–58.
18. Frank Main, "Murder 'Clearance' Rate in Chicago Hit New Low in 2017," *Chicago Sun-Times*, February 9, 2018, https://chicago.suntimes.com/news/murder-clearance-rate-in-chicago-hit-new-low-in-2017/.
19. Wesley Lowery et al., "Where Killings Go Unsolved," *Washington Post*, June 6, 2018, https://www.washingtonpost.com/graphics/2018/investigations/where-murders-go-unsolved/?noredirect=on&utm_term=.02deddoeb438.
20. Elijah Anderson, *Code of the Street: Decency, Violence, and the Moral Life of the Inner City* (New York: Norton, 1999), 34, 109, 320–23.
21. Main, "Murder 'Clearance' Rate."
22. Chicago Community Policing Consortium, *Community Policing in Chicago, Year Ten: An Evaluation of Chicago's Alternative Policing Strategy* (Chicago: Illinois Criminal Justice Information Authority, 2004).
23. "101 Shot, 14 Fatally, in July 4 Weekend Gun Violence Across Chicago," *Chicago Sun-Times*, July 6, 2017, https://chicago.suntimes.com/news/18-shot-2-fatally-in-bloody-start-to-fourth-of-july-weekend/.
24. Gorner, "Parolee Fatally Shot."
25. Some critics have likened the SSL and custom notifications to the science fiction film *Minority Report*, in which law enforcement agencies employ psychic predictions to preemptively arrest and imprison people for alleged future crimes.

26. Brianna Posada, "How Strategic Is Chicago's 'Strategic Subjects List'? Upturn Investigates," *Upturn*, June 22, 2017, https://medium.com/equal-future/how-strategic-is-chicagos-strategic-subjects-list-upturn-investigates-9e5b4b235a7c; Mick Dumke and Frank Main, "A Look Inside the Watch List Chicago Police Fought to Keep Secret," *Chicago Sun-Times*, May 18, 2017, https://chicago.suntimes.com/news/what-gets-people-on-watch-list-chicago-police-fought-to-keep-secret-watchdogs.

    Sociologist Andrew Papachristos, whose research on network analysis served as a basis for the SSL and the CPD's focused deterrence interventions, has distanced himself from these efforts, criticizing the department's lack of transparency and its emphasis on offending and suppression, as opposed to victimization and assistance. Andrew V. Papachristos, "Commentary: CPD's Crucial Choice: Treat Its List as Offenders or as Potential Victims?," *Chicago Tribune*, July 26, 2016, http://www.chicagotribune.com/news/opinion/commentary/ct-gun-violence-list-chicago-police-murder-perspec-0801-jm-20160729-story.html.
27. Jessica Saunders, Priscilla Hunt, and John S. Hollywood, "Predictions Put into Practice: A Quasi-Experimental Evaluation of Chicago's Predictive Policing Pilot," *Journal of Experimental Criminology* 12, no. 3 (2016): 347–71.
28. The video was finally released to the public due to a court order after more than a year of suppression by city and state officials.
29. The "Gang Violence Reduction Strategy" was revised again in February 2019 and retains the focused deterrence emphasis of the 2015 directive. Chicago Police Department, "Gang Violence Reduction Strategy," General Order G10–01, February 8, 2019, http://directives.chicagopolice.org/directives/data/a7a57bf0–136d1d31–16513–6d1d-382b311ddf65fd3a.html. The Strategic Subjects List was apparently rebranded in a January 2019 department directive as the Subject Assessment and Information Dashboard. This directive rescinded and replaced the July 2016 version. Chicago Police Department, "Subject Assessment and Information Dashboard (SAID)," Special Order S09–11, January 9, 2019, http://directives.chicagopolice.org/directives/data/a7a57b85–155e9f4b-50c15–5e9f-7742e3ac8b0ab2d3.html.
30. "The Model—About Us," Cure Violence, updated 2019, http://cureviolence.org/the-model/about-us/.
31. "Partners," Cure Violence, updated 2019, http://cureviolence.org/partners/.
32. "Scientific Evaluations," Cure Violence, updated 2019, http://cureviolence.org/results/scientific-evaluations/.
33. Gary Slutkin, "Let's Treat Violence Like a Contagious Disease," filmed April 2013 in Washington, DC, TEDMED video, 14:05, https://www.ted.com/talks/gary_slutkin_let_s_treat_violence_like_a_contagious_disease?language=en; Steve James, dir., *The Interrupters* (Chicago: Kartemquin Films, 2011, Blu-ray Disc, 1080p HD). A small sample of positive national and international media coverage includes Alex Kotlowitz, "Blocking the Transmission of Violence," *New York Times Magazine*, May 4, 2008, https://www.nytimes.com/2008/05/04/magazine/04health-t.html; Joel Budd, "Crime, Interrupted," *Economist*, November 19, 2008, https://www.economist.com/news/2008/11/19/crime-interrupted; Eliott C. McLaughlin, "Interrupting the Cycle of Teen Violence," CNN, September 28, 2011, http://www.cnn.com/2011/CRIME/09/27/chicago.teen.violence/index.html?iref=allsearch; Ann Givens, "On Patrol with Chicago's Last Violence Interrupters," *The Trace*, February 6, 2017,

https://www.thetrace.org/2017/02/chicago-homicides-cure-violence-interrupters/; Ana Lucia Gonzalez, "Crossing Divides: Stopping Violence Like It Was a Virus," BBC, April 27, 2018, https://www.bbc.com/news/world-us-canada-43541853; Tina Rosenberg, "Fighting Street Gun Violence as If It Were a Contagion," *New York Times*, May 8, 2018, https://www.nytimes.com/2018/05/08/opinion/fighting-street-gun-violence-as-if-it-were-a-contagion.html. For an overview of honors and awards, see "The Model – About Us," Cure Violence, updated 2019, http://cureviolence.org/the-model/about-us/.

34. Gary Slutkin, "Violence Is a Contagious Disease," in *Contagion of Violence: Workshop Summary*, rapporteurs Deepali M. Patel, Melissa A. Simon, and Rachel M. Taylor (Washington DC: National Academies Press, 2013), 94–111.
35. Slutkin, "Violence Is a Contagious Disease," 108.
36. Wesley G. Skogan et al., *Evaluation of CeaseFire-Chicago* (Evanston, IL: Northwestern University, 2008), 3-1.
37. Skogan et al., *Evaluation of CeaseFire-Chicago*.
38. Skogan et al., *Evaluation of CeaseFire-Chicago*, C-34.
39. The 2012 *Evaluation of Baltimore's Safe Streets Program* featured on the Cure Violence website serves as a useful example. The evaluation, conducted by researchers from the Johns Hopkins School of Public Health, indicated statistically significant declines in combined homicides and shooting incidents in only one of four Baltimore program sites. The evaluators offer a variety of possible explanations for these results, finally admitting that "some might infer that *Safe Streets* had no net effects on gun violence in the East Baltimore neighborhoods where it was implemented"—which is, in fact, precisely what the data indicate. Ultimately, the evaluators conclude that the intervention yielded only 2.8 fewer homicides and 17.1 fewer nonfatal shootings than would otherwise be expected across all four program sites over the course of 112 cumulative months of postintervention observation. The Department of Justice grant that funded the intervention was for $1.6 million. In a puzzling and seemingly unjustifiable decision, the evaluators also credit the intervention with similar declines in violence in areas adjacent to program sites, rationalizing this by speculating that the movement of program participants perhaps spread the effects of the intervention into nearby neighborhoods. Problematically, they do not consider interpreting declines in violence in adjacent areas as potentially indicative of broader trends in violence taking place in Baltimore during this period. Indeed, Baltimore averaged more than thirty fewer homicides per year from 2007–2011, encompassing the intervention period and one year of additional data, as compared to the five years prior to the start of the program. Being that the evaluators estimate that the program only reduced the total homicide tally in the four focus areas by less than three over an average evaluation period of more than two years, these numbers indicate that homicide was trending downward in the city more broadly for reasons unrelated to the Cure Violence intervention. While the report notes various other concurrent violence reduction efforts taking place in Baltimore, reductions in citywide levels of violence are problematically ignored in the evaluation as is the likelihood that declines in areas adjacent to program sites may not have been attributable to the intervention. Daniel W. Webster et al., *Evaluation of Baltimore's Safe Streets Program: Effects on Attitudes, Participants' Experiences, and Gun Violence* (Baltimore: Johns Hopkins Bloomberg School of Public Health, 2012).

40. Charles Ransford et al., "The Relationship Between the Cure Violence Model and Citywide Increases and Decreases in Killings in Chicago (2000–2016)," Cure Violence, September 2016, 14, http://cureviolence.org/wp-content/uploads/2017/06/2016.09.22-CV-Chicago-Memo.pdf.
41. This figure is based on homicides through 2017. Community data were missing for 386 homicides. Using address data, however, I was able to ascertain the community areas for all but 24 of these cases, all of which occurred on a border street between two communities, making it unclear which community they should be attributed to. Chicago Police Department, "Crime—2001 to Present."
42. From a recent Cure Violence report: "This model is based on proven public health techniques and is designed to have a community level effect, meaning that it does not just change individuals but also changes the entire community outcome as measured by shooting and killings. At some point, when the implementation of the model covers enough of the areas of a city with substantially high rates of lethal violence, the program is expected to have an effect on citywide levels of shootings and killings." Ransford et al., "Cure Violence Model," 2. As noted in the text, this report also credits Cure Violence with Chicago's "long and continuous trend of decreasing shootings and killings starting in 2001, coinciding with the start of the CeaseFire intervention." Here, the organization is seemingly taking credit for citywide reductions in violence when the intervention was only operating in *a single community* and ignoring the fact that homicide began declining in Chicago in 1995, six years before the program's pilot in 2000.
43. Chicago Police Department, "Crime—2001 to Present"; Federal Bureau of Investigation, "Crime in the U.S."
44. James, *Interrupters*.
45. James, *Interrupters*.
46. The film suggests a number of additional issues/challenges, especially related to difficulties navigating the code of the streets while reducing violence and the continued gang involvement of some staff members.
47. Ransford et al., "Cure Violence Model."
48. Federal Bureau of Investigation, "Crime in the U.S." One caveat here is that Cure Violence has been operating in a handful of New York neighborhoods beginning in 2009.
49. "Scientific Evaluations," Cure Violence.
50. There are a number of positive elements to the Cure Violence approach that current and former Cure Violence staff members pointed out in their interviews and with which I agree. One is that they "work with the people most likely to commit a violent act," as study participant and former Cure Violence worker Lorenzo points out. Though it is unclear the degree to which this has necessarily translated into demonstrable reductions in violence, this is an important principle. Another positive element of Cure Violence is that it serves as a pipeline of sorts for former gang members to transform their lives and their relationships to their communities. As Paris describes, "I've helped people come home from prison, change they lives, find jobs, get employment. I've had several staff members right now that went on to further they education in school as well. Even I've supervised people that went on to get they PhD degree. So, again, I live by example with demonstratin' the method of change." Indeed, I am friends with a number of current and former Cure

Violence workers whom I admire and consider to be mentors, and I have worked with others for whom I have similar admiration. While I remain decidedly unconvinced that Cure Violence is the solution to urban violence that its proponents claim it to be, I consider the work that many of these individuals do to be important and heroic and their own personal transformations to be deeply inspiring.

51. Kennedy, *Don't Shoot*, 22, 15.
52. Slutkin, "Let's Treat Violence."
53. In his ethnography of Chicago's Little Village community, Robert Vargas makes a persuasive case for zooming in even further, arguing that "violence tends to concentrate in very small geographic units or hot spots," even within neighborhoods with broader reputations for violence. Robert Vargas, *Wounded City: Violent Turf Wars in a Chicago Barrio* (New York: Oxford University Press, 2016), 5.
54. A very small sample of this literature includes Frederic M. Thrasher, *The Gang: A Study of 1,313 Gangs in Chicago* (Chicago: University of Chicago Press, 1927); Gerald D. Suttles, *The Social Order of the Slum* (Chicago: University of Chicago Press, 1968); Clifford R. Shaw and Henry D. McKay, *Juvenile Delinquency and Urban Areas*, rev. ed. (Chicago: University of Chicago Press, 1969); Donald Black, "Crime as Social Control," *American Sociological Review* 48, no. 1 (1983): 34–45; Robert J. Sampson, "Neighborhoods and Crime: The Structural Determinants of Personal Victimization," *Journal of Research in Crime and Delinquency* 22, no. 1 (1985): 7–40; Martín Sánchez Jankowski, *Islands in the Street: Gangs and American Urban Society* (Berkeley: University of California Press, 1991); John M. Hagedorn, "Gang Violence in the Postindustrial Era," *Crime and Justice* 24 (1998): 365–419; John M. Hagedorn, *A World of Gangs: Armed Young Men and Gangsta Culture* (Minneapolis: University of Minnesota Press, 2008); Anderson, *Code of the Street*; Maria Tcherni, "Structural Determinants of Homicide: The Big Three," *Journal of Quantitative Criminology* 27, no. 4 (2011): 475–96.

    Social scientists, however, are not the only ones making the case for the tackling of broader social issues as part of a vital, holistic violence reduction strategy—public health researchers and organizations, including the World Health Organization, are making many of these same arguments. The United Nations' *2011 Global Study on Homicide* finds that "higher levels of homicide are associated with low human and economic development . . . and countries with high levels of income inequality are afflicted by homicide rates almost four times higher than more equal societies," and ultimately concludes that "improvements to social and economic conditions go hand in hand with the reduction of violent crime." United Nations Office on Drugs and Crime, *2011 Global Study on Homicide: Trends, Contexts, Data* (Vienna: United Nations Office on Drugs and Crime, 2011), 10, 5; Liana B. Winett, "Constructing Violence as a Public Health Problem," *Public Health Reports* 113, no. 6 (1998): 498–507; Etienne G. Krug et al., eds., *World Report on Violence and Health* (Geneva: World Health Organization, 2002); World Health Organization, *Global Status Report on Violence Prevention 2014* (Geneva: World Health Organization, 2014).
55. James, *Interrupters*.
56. Slutkin, "Contagious Disease," 108.
57. Kennedy, *Don't Shoot*, 21.
58. For critiques of the role of policing in creating and protecting a highly stratified social order, see William Lyons, *The Politics of Community Policing: Rearranging*

the Power to Punish (Ann Arbor: University of Michigan Press, 1999); Mark Neocleous, *The Fabrication of Social Order: A Critical Theory of Policy Power* (London: Pluto Press, 2000); Loïc Wacquant, *Punishing the Poor: The Neoliberal Government of Social Insecurity* (Durham, NC: Duke University Press, 2009); Adolph Reed Jr., "How Racial Disparity Does Not Help Make Sense of Patterns of Police Violence," Nonsite.org, September 16, 2016, https://nonsite.org/editorial/how-racial-disparity-does-not-help-make-sense-of-patterns-of-police-violence.

59. For a critique of "community policing" along these lines, see Lyons, *Politics of Community Policing.*
60. Andrew V. Papachristos, "Too Big to Fail: The Science and Politics of Violence Prevention," *Criminology & Public Policy* 10, no. 4 (2011): 1053–61.
61. David C. Brotherton, *Youth Street Gangs: A Critical Appraisal* (New York: Routledge, 2015), 45.
62. Papachristos, "Too Big to Fail," 1054.
63. Kennedy, *Don't Shoot*, 101–24; Justin Fenton, "Star Criminologist Hopes to Make Difference in Return to Baltimore," *Baltimore Sun*, February 15, 2014, http://www.baltimoresun.com/news/maryland/crime/bs-md-ci-david-kennedy-ceasefire-returns-20140215-story.html; Dan Rodricks, "Baltimore Had Its Own Version of Ceasefire Before, It Could Again," *Baltimore Sun*, June 12, 2017, http://www.baltimoresun.com/news/maryland/dan-rodricks-blog/bal-baltimore-had-its-own-version-of-ceasefire-before-it-could-again-20170611-story.html.

CONCLUSION: REDUCING GANG VIOLENCE FROM THE STREETS UP

1. John E. Eck and Edward R. Maguire, "Have Changes in Policing Reduced Violent Crime? An Assessment of the Evidence," in *The Crime Drop in America*, ed. Alfred Blumstein and Joel Wallman (New York: Oxford University Press, 2000), 207–65; William Spelman, "The Limited Importance of Prison Expansion," in *The Crime Drop in America*, ed. Alfred Blumstein and Joel Wallman (New York: Oxford University Press, 2000), 97–129; Vanessa Barker, "Explaining the Great American Crime Decline: A Review of Blumstein and Wallman, Goldberger and Rosenfeld, and Zimring," *Law & Social Inquiry* 35, no. 2 (2010): 489–516; Judith Greene and Kevin Pranis, *Gang Wars: The Failure of Enforcement Tactics and the Need for Effective Public Safety Strategies* (Washington, DC: Justice Policy Institute, 2007); Jonathan Mummolo, "Militarization Fails to Enhance Police Safety or Reduce Crime but May Harm Police Reputation," *Proceedings of the National Academy of Sciences* 115, no. 37 (2018): 9181–86.

   For a partial counterargument, see Patrick Sharkey, *Uneasy Peace: The Great Crime Decline, the Renewal of City Life, and the Next War on Violence* (New York: Norton, 2018).
2. Malcolm W. Klein, *The American Street Gang: Its Nature, Prevalence, and Control* (New York: Oxford University Press, 1995); Greene and Pranis, *Gang Wars*; Victor M. Rios, *Punished: Policing the Lives of Black and Latino Boys* (New York: New York University Press, 2011); John M. Hagedorn, "Race Not Space: A Revisionist History of Gangs in Chicago," *Journal of African American History* 91, no. 2 (2006):

194–208; Deborah T. Levenson, *Adiós Niño: The Gangs of Guatemala City and the Politics of Death* (Durham, NC: Duke University Press, 2013); Benjamin Lessing, "Counterproductive Punishment: How Prison Gangs Undermine State Authority," *Rationality and Society* 29, no. 3 (2017): 257–97; Robert D. Weide, "The Invisible Hand of the State: A Critical Historical Analysis of Prison Gangs in California," *Prison Journal* (forthcoming); Bruce Western, *Punishment and Inequality in America* (New York: Russell Sage Foundation, 2006); Todd Clear, *Imprisoning Communities: How Mass Incarceration Makes Disadvantaged Neighborhoods Worse* (New York: Oxford University Press, 2007).

3. Greene and Pranis, *Gang Wars*, 67. See also Marjorie S. Zatz, "Chicano Youth Gangs and Crime: The Creation of a Moral Panic," *Contemporary Crises* 11, no. 2 (1987): 129–58.
4. Chicago Crime Commission, *The Gang Book*, 3rd ed. (Chicago: Chicago Crime Commission, 2018), 194.
5. A recent case underscores this argument. In October 2018, four alleged gang members in Englewood were charged in a federal racketeering case—for alleged crimes completely unrelated to racketeering. As a *Chicago Tribune* article notes, "Unlike traditional racketeering cases that accuse gang members of using violence to protect drug turf or other illicit enterprises, the charges against the Goonie Boss members allege they shot people simply to boost their social media brand." Apparently, the federal RICO statute, originally passed in 1970 as a tool for taking down "untouchable" Mafia bosses and dismantling organized crime syndicates, and later used to target powerful gang leaders, is now being used to prosecute impoverished young men whose alleged violence is distinguished not by its connection to any similarly meaningful illicit enterprise but by the *absence* of any such connection. Jason Meisner and Annie Sweeney, " 'It Was Killing for the Sake of Killing': Feds Charge South Side Gang Faction in 10 Killings in Englewood," *Chicago Tribune*, October 26, 2018, https://www.chicagotribune.com/news/local/breaking/ct-met-englewood-gang-murders-20181024-story.html.

   Especially taken in tandem with the Chicago Police Department's Strategic Subjects List—which, again, has more than four hundred thousand entries and includes half of all black men in their twenties in the entire city—the historical conspiracy strategy raises serious concerns about the violation of constitutional rights to freedom of association, due process, and equal protection under the law.
6. Gary Slutkin, in Steve James, dir., *The Interrupters* (Chicago: Kartemquin Films, 2011, Blu-ray Disc, 1080p HD). David Kennedy expresses a nearly identical sentiment in David M. Kennedy, *Don't Shoot: One Man, a Street Fellowship, and the End of Violence in Inner-City America* (New York: Bloomsbury, 2011), 22.
7. For a compelling example of the utter failure of reliance on the private sector to improve life in a low-income, largely African American community, see Tracy Jan's profile of Ferguson, Missouri, in the aftermath of the protests following police officer Darren Wilson's killing of black teenager Michael Brown and his subsequent nonindictment for the killing. Jan explores the deteriorating quality of life in the city's working-class black sections despite investments by various corporate development projects, which have been woefully inadequate to address the needs facing the city's low-income residents and have primarily clustered in areas of the city that were already relatively well-off and whose residents are predominantly white. A

quote from a local business owner that closes the article encapsulates both the persistence of private market-driven logic as well as its failure in Ferguson: "After the riots, a lot of corporations kind of came in, triaging the area. But everyone is still holding their breath, waiting for a champion to come along." It should be noted that the communities from which participants in this study hail are in much worse shape than Ferguson in terms of levels of poverty, segregation, and violence. Tracy Jan, "The Forgotten Ferguson," *Washington Post*, June 21, 2018, https://www.washingtonpost.com/graphics/2018/business/is-racial-discrimination-influencing-corporate-investment-in-ferguson/.

8. John M. Hagedorn, *The In$ane Chicago Way: The Daring Plan by Chicago Gangs to Create a Spanish Mafia* (Chicago: University of Chicago Press, 2015), 209.
9. David C. Brotherton, *Youth Street Gangs: A Critical Appraisal* (New York: Routledge, 2015).
10. Felix M. Padilla, *The Gang as an American Enterprise* (New Brunswick, NJ: Rutgers University Press, 1992); Sudhir Alladi Venkatesh, "The Social Organization of Street Gang Activity in an Urban Ghetto," *American Journal of Sociology* 103, no. 1 (1997): 82–111; Sudhir Alladi Venkatesh, *American Project: The Rise and Fall of a Modern Ghetto* (Cambridge, MA: Harvard University Press, 2000); Steven D. Levitt and Sudhir Alladi Venkatesh, "An Economic Analysis of a Drug-Selling Gang's Finances," *Quarterly Journal of Economics* 115, no. 3 (2000): 755–89; Sudhir Alladi Venkatesh and Steven D. Levitt, "'Are We a Family or a Business?' History and Disjuncture in the Urban American Street Gang," *Theory and Society* 29, no. 4 (2000): 427–62; Sudhir Alladi Venkatesh, *Off the Books: The Underground Economy of the Urban Poor* (Cambridge, MA: Harvard University Press, 2006); John M. Hagedorn, *A World of Gangs: Armed Young Men and Gangsta Culture* (Minneapolis: University of Minnesota Press, 2008); Hagedorn, *In$ane Chicago Way*; Natalie Y. Moore and Lance Williams, *The Almighty Black P Stone Nation: The Rise, Fall, and Resurgence of an American Gang* (Chicago: Lawrence Hill Books, 2011).
11. Joan W. Moore, *Homeboys: Gangs, Drugs, and Prison in the Barrios of Los Angeles* (Philadelphia: Temple University Press, 1978); Joan W. Moore, *Going Down to the Barrio: Homeboys and Homegirls in Change* (Philadelphia: Temple University Press, 1991); John M. Hagedorn, *People and Folks: Gangs, Crime and the Underclass in a Rustbelt City* (Chicago: Lake View Press, 1988); John M. Hagedorn, "Gang Violence in the Postindustrial Era," *Crime and Justice* 24 (1998): 365–419; Hagedorn, "Race Not Space"; Hagedorn, *World of Gangs*; Hagedorn, *In$ane Chicago Way*; David C. Brotherton and Luis Barrios, *The Almighty Latin King and Queen Nation: Street Politics and the Transformation of a New York City Gang* (New York: Columbia University Press, 2004); Brotherton, *Youth Street Gangs*; James Diego Vigil, *Barrio Gangs: Street Life and Identity in Southern California* (Austin: University of Texas Press, 1988); James Diego Vigil, *A Rainbow of Gangs: Street Cultures in the Mega-City* (Austin: University of Texas Press, 2002); Dwight Conquergood, "Homeboys and Hoods: Gang Communication and Cultural Space," in *Group Communication in Context: Studies of Natural Groups*, ed. Lawrence R. Frey (Hillsdale, NJ: Lawrence Erlbaum, 1994), 23–55; Dwight Conquergood, "Street Literacy," in *Handbook of Research on Teaching Literacy Through the Communicative and Visual Arts*, ed. James Flood, Shirley Brice Heath, and Diane Lapp (New York: Macmillan Library Reference, 1997), 354–75; Laurence Ralph, "'As Soon as I Get Out Ima Cop Dem

Jordans': The Afterlife of the Corporate Gang," *Identities: Global Studies in Culture and Power* 17, no. 6 (2010): 667–94; Laurence Ralph, *Renegade Dreams: Living Through Injury in Gangland Chicago* (Chicago: University of Chicago Press, 2014); Venkatesh and Levitt, "'Family or a Business'"; Sudhir Alladi Venkatesh, "A Note on Social Theory and the American Street Gang," in *Gangs and Society: Alternative Perspectives*, ed. Louis Kontos, David C. Brotherton, and Luis Barrios (New York: Columbia University Press, 2003), 3–11; Robert J. Durán, *Gang Life in Two Cities: An Insider's Journey* (New York: Columbia University Press, 2013); Robert J. Durán, *The Gang Paradox: Inequalities and Miracles on the U.S.–Mexico Border* (New York: Columbia University Press, 2018); Levenson, *Adiós Niño*; Andrew J. Diamond, *Mean Streets: Chicago Youths and the Everyday Struggle for Empowerment in the Multiracial City, 1908–1969* (Berkeley: University of California Press, 2009).

12. One 2016 meta-analysis of the literature, for example, includes *179 studies* on the relationship between gang membership and offending. See David Pyrooz et al., "Taking Stock of the Relationship Between Gang Membership and Offending: A Meta-Analysis," *Criminal Justice and Behavior* 43, no. 3 (2016): 365–97.

    One notable exception to these recent trends in the study of gang violence is the work of Andrew Papachristos, who has examined gang violence using network analysis techniques to explain patterns of violent victimization. Andrew V. Papachristos, "Murder by Structure: Dominance Relations and the Social Structure of Gang Homicide," *American Journal of Sociology* 115, no. 1 (2009): 74–128; Andrew V. Papachristos, David Hureau, and Anthony A. Braga, "The Corner and the Crew: The Influence of Geography and Social Networks on Gang Violence," *American Sociological Review* 78, no. 3 (2013): 417–47; Andrew V. Papachristos, Christopher Wilderman, and Elizabeth Roberto, "Tragic, but Not Random: The Social Contagion of Nonfatal Gunshot Injuries," *Social Science & Medicine* 125, no. 1 (2015): 139–50.

13. For a thoughtful critique of this literature from more than two decades ago, see James F. Short Jr., "The Level of Explanation Problem Revisited—The American Society of Criminology 1997 Presidential Address," *Criminology* 36, no. 1 (1998): 3–36.
14. Lorine A. Hughes, "Studying Youth Gangs: The Importance of Context," in *Studying Youth Gangs*, ed. James F. Short Jr. and Lorine A. Hughes (Lanham, MD: AltaMira Press, 2006), 40, 44.
15. Eric R. Wolf, *Europe and the People Without History* (Berkeley: University of California Press, 1982), 4.
16. Brotherton, *Youth Street Gangs*, iii. See also Dwight Conquergood, "The Power of Symbols," in *One City* (Chicago: Chicago Council on Urban Affairs, 1996), 11–17.
17. James A. Densley, *How Gangs Work: An Ethnography of Youth Violence* (London: Palgrave Macmillan, 2013), back cover.
18. For examples of studies in which context is described but largely divorced from the analysis, see Martín Sánchez Jankowski, *Islands in the Street: Gangs and American Urban Society* (Berkeley: University of California Press, 1991); Scott H. Decker and Barrik Van Winkle, *Life in the Gang: Family, Friends, and Violence* (Cambridge: Cambridge University Press, 1996); Jody Miller, *One of the Guys: Girls, Gangs, and Gender* (New York: Oxford University Press, 2001). Indeed, both Jankowski's and Miller's studies involved gangs in multiple cities yet both largely fail to integrate contextual factors into their analyses in any substantive fashion.

For studies in which community context is integrated elaborately into the analysis but the analysis lacks historical perspective and exploration of sociopolitical context, see the work of gang researchers from the Chicago school of sociology: Frederic M. Thrasher, *The Gang: A Study of 1,313 Gangs in Chicago* (Chicago: University of Chicago Press, 1927); William Foote Whyte, *Street Corner Society: The Social Structure of an Italian Slum* (Chicago: University of Chicago Press, 1943); James F. Short Jr. and Fred L. Strodtbeck, *Group Process and Gang Delinquency* (Chicago: University of Chicago Press, 1965); Gerald D. Suttles, *The Social Order of the Slum* (Chicago: University of Chicago Press, 1968); Gerald D. Suttles, *The Social Construction of Communities*. Chicago: University of Chicago Press, 1972).

19. C. Wright Mills, *The Sociological Imagination* (London: Oxford University Press, 1959).
20. Social theorist Antonio Gramsci refers to this dynamic as "cultural hegemony." To the extent that those victimized by this system internalize its naturalness and their marginal position within it as deserved, Pierre Bourdieu would refer to this as "symbolic violence." Antonio Gramsci, *Selections from the Prison Notebooks*, ed. and trans. Quintin Hoare and Geoffrey Nowell-Smith (New York: International Publishers, 1971); Pierre Bourdieu, *Pascalian Meditations*, trans. Richard Nice (Stanford, CA: Stanford University Press, 2000).
21. On the decline of Chicago's housing projects, see D. Bradford Hunt, *Blueprint for Disaster: The Unraveling of Chicago Public Housing* (Chicago: University of Chicago Press, 2009); Edward G. Goetz, *New Deal Ruins: Race, Economic Justice, and Public Housing Policy* (Ithaca, NY: Cornell University Press, 2013); Lawrence J. Vale, *Purging the Poorest: Public Housing and the Design Politics of Twice-Cleared Communities* (Chicago: University of Chicago Press, 2013). On accumulation by dispossession, see David Harvey, *A Brief History of Neoliberalism* (Oxford: Oxford University Press, 2005), 162–65. On how this concept relates specifically to the demolition and privatization of public housing in the United States, see John Arena, *Driven from New Orleans: How Nonprofits Betray Public Housing and Promote Privatization* (Minneapolis: University of Minnesota Press, 2012), xx–xxi, 187–88.
22. Cedric Johnson, "The Panthers Can't Save Us Now," *Catalyst* 1, no. 1 (2017): 56–85. The arguments made by Johnson and others challenge the racially reductionist framing of "mass incarceration" as "the new Jim Crow" or of police violence as an issue uniquely confronting African Americans. After all, blacks do not approximate, much less constitute, a majority of either the incarcerated or the victims of police violence in the United States. Other factors clearly seem to be at play, in particular, those related to transformations in the political economy and their effects on urban blacks and other marginalized working-class constituencies. See also Mark Neocleous, *The Fabrication of Social Order: A Critical Theory of Policy Power* (London: Pluto Press, 2000); Marie Gottschalk, *Caught: The Prison State and the Lockdown of American Politics* (Princeton, NJ: Princeton University Press, 2014); Loïc Wacquant, *Punishing the Poor: The Neoliberal Government of Social Insecurity* (Durham, NC: Duke University Press, 2009); Loïc Wacquant, "Class, Race & Hyperincarceration in Revanchist America," *Daedalus* 139, no. 3 (2010): 74–90; Adolph Reed Jr., "How Racial Disparity Does Not Help Make Sense of Patterns of Police Violence," Nonsite.org, September 16, 2016, https://nonsite.org/editorial/how-racial-disparity-does-not-help-make-sense-of-patterns-of-police-violence.

23. For critiques of how these policy prerogatives are disingenuously framed as being in the "interest of the city as a whole"—or even as being beneficial specifically to the low-income residents whose interests they directly undermine—see Adolph Reed Jr., *Stirrings in the Jug: Black Politics in the Post-Segregation Era* (Minneapolis: University of Minnesota Press, 1999); Arena, *Driven from New Orleans.*
24. Tom Tresser, ed., *Chicago Is Not Broke: Funding the City We Deserve*, 2nd ed. (Chicago: Salsedo Press, 2017).
25. Cook County Clerk's Office, "Cook County TIFs to Bring in a Record $1 Billion According to Clerk Orr; Transit TIF Revenue Doubled," July 24, 2018, https://www.cookcountyclerk.com/news/cook-county-tifs-bring-record-1-billion-according-clerk-orr-transit-tif-revenue-doubled.
26. For a scathing critique of these dynamics under former mayor Rahm Emanuel, see Kari Lydersen, *Mayor 1%: Rahm Emanuel and the Rise of Chicago's 99%* (Chicago: Haymarket Books, 2013).
27. Mike Royko, *Boss: Richard J. Daley of Chicago* (New York: E. P. Dutton, 1971); Adam Cohen and Elizabeth Taylor, *American Pharaoh: Mayor Richard J. Daley – His Battle for Chicago and the Nation* (New York: Little, Brown, 2000); Keith Koenman, *First Son: The Biography of Richard M. Daley* (Chicago: University of Chicago Press, 2013); Thomas J. Gradel and Dick Simpson, *Corrupt Illinois: Patronage, Cronyism, and Criminality* (Urbana: University of Illinois Press, 2015); Costas Spirou and Dennis R. Judd, *Building the City of Spectacle: Mayor Richard M. Daley and the Remaking of Chicago* (Ithaca, NY: Cornell University Press, 2016).

    One notable break from machine rule came with the 1983 election of Harold Washington, a progressive reformer and the city's first black mayor. See Gary Rivlin, *Fire on the Prairie: Chicago's Harold Washington and the Politics of Race* (New York: Henry Holt, 1992); Roger Biles, *Mayor Harold Washington: Champion of Race and Reform in Chicago* (Urbana: University of Illinois Press, 2018).
28. For a comprehensive treatment of the history of Chicago's Democratic machine and the city's African American community, see William J. Grimshaw, *Bitter Fruit: Black Politics and the Chicago Machine, 1931–1991* (Chicago: University of Chicago Press, 1992). On the development of diverse electoral and governing coalitions in the Daley administration, see Spirou and Judd, *Building the City*, 132–36. Emanuel has garnered less electoral support from Latino Chicagoans, since his principal challengers in each of his two mayoral runs were both Latinos with long-standing ties to the large bloc of Mexican American communities on the Southwest Side.
29. Koenman, *First Son*, 109; Lydersen, *Mayor 1%*.
30. On Woodlawn's overlapping gang and political histories, see John H. Fish, *Black Power/White Control: The Struggle of The Woodlawn Organization in Chicago* (Princeton, NJ: Princeton University Press, 1973); Cohen and Taylor, *American Pharaoh*; Moore and Williams, *Black P Stone Nation.*
31. Arena, *Driven from New Orleans*, 80. See also Reed, *Stirrings in the Jug*. Intraracial divergences in class interests have come into sharp relief recently over the plan to construct the $500 million Barack Obama Presidential Center in the Woodlawn community on the city's South Side. Middle-class homeowners, investors, developers, and business owners generally see the center as a vehicle for potentially lucrative development and improved community conditions. Emanuel, Obama's former chief of staff, has strongly backed the project. Many residents, however, most of

whom are poor and working class, fear skyrocketing rents, intensified policing, and mass displacement. The Obama Foundation has refused requests by community groups to sign a community benefits agreement that would include "rent support for residents, property-tax freezes, additional affordable housing, and a community trust fund." Obama is an undeniably iconic figure in Chicago, however, particularly among many of the city's black residents, adding further complexity to these dynamics. LeAlan M. Jones, "The Obama Center Leaves Chicago in Its Shadow," *Nation*, July 10, 2018, https://www.thenation.com/article/obama-center-leaves-chicago-communities-shadow/; Zach Mortice, "After Rahm, What Comes Next for the Obama Library?," *CityLab*, September 25, 2018, https://www.citylab.com/design/2018/09/after-rahm-what-comes-next-obama-library/571075/.

32. Popkin et al., *Hidden War*, 16–19; Venkatesh, *American Project*, 254–56; Arena, *Driven from New Orleans*, 79–80, 89–91.
33. Matt O'Connor, "Ex-CHA Chief Gets Prison," *Chicago Tribune*, August 29, 2001, https://www.chicagotribune.com/news/ct-xpm-2001-08-29-0108290314-story.html; Jason Meisner and Juan Perez Jr., "Byrd-Bennet Sobs While Trying to Explain Corruption, Gets 4 1/2 Years in Prison," *Chicago Tribune*, April 28, 2017, http://www.chicagotribune.com/news/local/breaking/ct-barbara-byrd-bennett-sentence-met-20170428-story.html.
34. Lamont's reference to a $10 billion aid package for distressed communities in Chicago echoes historical calls, which have been revived in recent years, for a domestic Marshall Plan to transform America's "dark ghettos" as well as broader policy proposals for massive public investment in jobs and infrastructure, like the Green New Deal. Ron Daniels, "A Domestic Marshall Plan to Transform America's 'Dark Ghettos': Toward a Martin Luther King–Malcolm X Community Revitalization Initiative," *Black Scholar* 37, no. 3 (2007): 10–13; Marc Morial, "Urban League's 'Main Street Marshall Plan' Incorporated in CBC's Bill," *Black Star News*, May 10, 2018, http://www.blackstarnews.com/us-politics/justice/urban-leagues-main-street-marshall-plan-incorporated-into-cbcs; Greg Carlock and Sean McElwee, "Why the Best New Deal Is a Green New Deal," *Nation*, September 18, 2018, https://www.thenation.com/article/why-the-best-new-deal-is-a-green-new-deal/; Robinson Meyer, "The Democratic Party Wants to Make Climate Policy Exciting," *Atlantic*, December 5, 2018, https://www.theatlantic.com/science/archive/2018/12/ocasio-cortez-green-new-deal-winning-climate-strategy/576514/.
35. Mary Pattillo, "Investing in Poor Black Neighborhoods 'As Is,'" in *Public Housing and the Legacy of Segregation*, ed. Margery Austin Turner, Susan J. Popkin, and Lynette Rawlings (Washington, DC: Urban Institute Press, 2009), 31–46; Wacquant, "Class, Race & Hyperincarceration," 85. Particularly pertinent to the aims of addressing gangs and reducing violence is Wacquant's proposal for "a Works-Progress Administration-style public works program aimed at the vestiges of the Black Belt [that] would help at once to rebuild its decrepit infrastructure, to improve housing conditions, and to offer economic sustenance and civic incorporation to local residents" (85).
36. Conventional scholarly views of gangs ignore these realities and discount the agency of gang members entirely. Even with respect to criminal and violent behavior, mainstream scholars view such behavior as an impersonal, mechanical by-product of gang membership, not a manifestation of individual agency. Conversely, John Hagedorn

provides numerous examples of gang agency at work among Chicago gangs during the final three decades of the twentieth century in *The In$ane Chicago Way*. Making this argument more generally, David Brotherton cautions against the "tendency toward cultural and economic determinism in gang studies." Hagedorn, *In$ane Chicago Way*; Brotherton, *Youth Street Gangs*, 49.

37. Hagedorn, *In$ane Chicago Way*, 215. See also John Hagedorn et al., *The Fracturing of Gangs and Violence in Chicago: A Research-Based Reorientation of Violence Prevention Policy* (Chicago: Great Cities Institute, University of Illinois at Chicago, 2019), 13.
38. The relative brevity of the following discussion should in no way be interpreted as an indication that the intervention outlined here might be effectively implemented with ease. While rooted in a careful, contextual analysis of the issues at hand, this discussion is intended as a strategic outline for intervention, not as the delineation of a comprehensive guide.
39. Frederick Douglass, *Frederick Douglass: Selected Speeches and Writings*, ed. Philip S. Foner and Yuval Taylor (Chicago: Chicago Review Press, 1999); Eugene V. Debs, *Eugene V. Debs Speaks*, ed. Jean Y. Tussey (New York: Pathfinder Press, 1970); Frances Fox Piven and Richard A. Cloward, *Poor People's Movements: Why They Succeed, How They Fail* (New York: Pantheon Books, 1977); Adolph Reed Jr., *Class Notes: Posing as Politics and Other Thoughts on the American Scene* (New York: New Press, 2000).
40. Saul D. Alinsky, *Rules for Radicals: A Pragmatic Primer for Realistic Radicals* (New York: Random House, 1971), 127.
41. But see Brotherton and Barrios, *Almighty Latin King*; Brotherton, *Youth Street Gangs*; Hagedorn, *World of Gangs*; Hagedorn, *In$ane Chicago Way*.
42. Saul D. Alinsky, *Reveille for Radicals* (Chicago: University of Chicago Press, 1945), 108; Aldon D. Morris, *The Origins of the Civil Rights Movement: Black Communities Organizing for Change* (New York: Free Press, 1984). See also Alinsky, *Rules for Radicals*.
43. For incisive critiques of Black Lives Matter with respect to their framing of police violence in exclusively racial terms and of the strategic issues that flow from this framing, see Johnson, "Panthers"; Reed, "Racial Disparity."
44. Paulo Freire, *Pedagogy of the Oppressed*, 30th anniv. ed., trans. Myra Bergman Ramos (New York: Continuum, 2000), 109.
45. Gramsci, *Prison Notebooks*; Bourdieu, *Pascalian Meditations*.
46. See also Philippe Bourgois, *In Search of Respect: Selling Crack in El Barrio* (Cambridge: Cambridge University Press, 1995); George Karandinos et al., "The Moral Economy of Violence in the US Inner City: Deadly Sociability in the Retail Narcotics Economy," in *Violence at the Urban Margins*, ed. Javier Auyero, Philippe Bourgois, and Nancy Scheper-Hughes (New York: Oxford University Press, 2015), 67; Robert J. Durán, *Gang Life in Two Cities: An Insider's Journey* (New York: Columbia University Press, 2013), 149–71.
47. Manuel Castells, *The Power of Identity* (Oxford: Blackwell, 1997). Similarly, John Hagedorn argues that gang members "have multiple, conflicting identities." Hagedorn, *In$ane Chicago Way*, 32. See also Hagedorn, *World of Gangs*; Levenson, *Adiós Niño*.

48. Brotherton, *Youth Street Gangs*, 74–75.
49. Edward Orozco Flores, *God's Gangs: Barrio Ministry, Masculinity, and Gang Recovery* (New York: New York University Press, 2014), 114, 180, 183.
50. Brotherton and Barrios, *Almighty Latin King.*
51. George Papajohn and John Kass, "21st Century VOTE Giving Gangs Taste of Real Power," *Chicago Tribune*, September 28, 1994, https://www.chicagotribune.com/news/ct-xpm-1994-09-28-9409280241-story.html; Neal Pollack, "The Gang That Could Go Straight," *Chicago Reader*, January 26, 1995, https://www.chicagoreader.com/chicago/the-gang-that-could-go-straight/Content?oid=886552; Rod Emery, *The Blueprint: From Gangster Disciple to Growth and Development* (Elgin, IL: Morris Publishing, 1996).
52. Daniel goes on to clarify that the prosocial overtures of the Gangster Disciples during the 1990s were not empty sloganeering or intended as diversions from some of the group's more nefarious activities, as they had been largely framed by the media, law enforcement, and elected officials. Rather, as Daniel explains, they represented the genuine vision of the organization's leadership: "I come from a community where a board member was a personal friend. So I could easily check in with him to make sure: 'Man, is this what y'all want?' And also the vice chairman was a personal friend, so it was confirmed that this is what we want. Now, they could've said, 'Nah, that ain't really what we on. We just usin' that as a ploy to get these people off our back and to get people home [from prison].' And if they had said that, I don't know what effect it would've had on me. But that's not what they said. They said, 'Man, you an example of outstanding membership.' And, I mean, I didn't need a plaque, you know? Their words were enough. Because in my mind, these were the same people that misled me—I mean, they were the template for me to be misled. I misled myself. But for them to also be the template or have that desire to be on the right path, be on the healthy path, was encouraging." Again, as Hagedorn argues, gangs are not one thing.
53. Scott H. Decker, "Collective and Normative Features of Gang Violence," *Justice Quarterly* 42, no. 2 (1996): 261.
54. Reed, *Class Notes*, viii.
55. Broad-based gang truces were accomplished during the 1960s, when the Blackstone Rangers and East Side Disciples called a truce as part of their involvement with The Woodlawn Organization's Youth Job Project, and the Vice Lords, Stones, and Disciples formed a coalition in their fight to integrate Chicago's construction industries. Contemporary gang dynamics, however, are very different than those of the 1960s. This means that gang members' involvement in prosocial collective action today will look very different than it did during that period. On this historical period of gang activism, see Fish, *Black Power/White Control*; John R. Fry, *Locked-Out Americans: A Memoir* (New York: Harper, Row, 1973); David Dawley, *A Nation of Lords: The Autobiography of the Vice Lords*, 2nd ed. (Prospect Heights, IL: Waveland Press, 1992); Hagedorn, *World of Gangs*; Diamond, *Mean Streets*; Erik S. Gellman, "'The Stone Wall Behind': The Chicago Coalition for United Community Action and Labor's Overseers, 1968–1973," in *Black Power at Work: Community Control, Affirmative Action, and the Construction Industry*, ed. David Goldberg and Trevor Griffey (Ithaca, NY: Cornell University Press, 2010), 112–33.

56. See, for example, Laurence Ralph's discussion of "why grandmothers ally with the gang" in fighting against gentrification and displacement on Chicago's West Side. Ralph, *Renegade Dreams*, 21–52.
57. Recall also another of Marco's statements, quoted earlier in the chapter, in which he called for gang unification through collective social protest around a common cause.
58. Kennedy, *Don't Shoot*, 23.
59. William Julius Wilson, *The Truly Disadvantaged: The Inner City, the Underclass, and Public Policy* (Chicago: University of Chicago Press, 1987); William Julius Wilson, *When Work Disappears: The World of the New Urban Poor* (New York: Alfred A. Knopf, 1996); Loïc Wacquant, *Urban Outcasts: A Comparative Sociology of Advanced Marginality* (Cambridge: Polity Press, 2008); Loïc Wacquant, "Urban Desolation and Symbolic Denigration in the Hyperghetto," *Social Psychology Quarterly* 73, no. 3 (2010): 215–19.
60. Black West Side gangs appear to be more heavily involved in the heroin trade and to have retained a greater degree of traditional gang uniformity and leadership at the neighborhood level than their South Side counterparts. On variation between black gangs on Chicago's West and South Sides, see the discussion on pages 67–68. Chicago's Latino gangs, on the other hand, seem to have been largely insulated from the historical factors that shattered the city's black South Side gangs: There was no public housing in Chicago's Latino communities, few if any of the gang members displaced from public housing moved to these neighborhoods, and Latino gangs control the higher levels of the city's drug trade via connections to Central American drug cartels. Indeed, Robert Vargas's recent research in Little Village, a Mexican American community on Chicago's West Side, reveals the enormous gulf between the black South Side gangs described in this book and their Latino counterparts like the Latin Kings and Two Sixers, who have maintained traditional leadership hierarchies and relatively sophisticated criminal operations. As Hagedorn points out, moreover, Chicago's Latino communities are much more stable, less impoverished, and wield greater economic and political power in the city than their African American counterparts. Hagedorn, *In$ane Chicago Way*, 210–19; Robert Vargas, *Wounded City: Violent Turf Wars in a Chicago Barrio* (New York: Oxford University Press, 2016).

    In short, gangs are not monolithic—even in Chicago today.

APPENDIX: NOTES ON POSITIONALITY, THE POLITICS OF REPRESENTATION, AND RESEARCH METHODOLOGY

1. On the brutality of Brazil's military government, see Archdiocese of São Paulo, *Torture in Brazil: A Shocking Report on the Pervasive Use of Torture by Brazilian Military Governments, 1964–1979*, 2nd ed., ed. Jaime Wright, trans. Joan Dassin (Austin: University of Texas Press, 1998). On the country's transition to democracy, see Daniel Hidalgo and Renato Lima-de-Oliviera, "Elite Contestation and Mass Participation in Brazilian Legislative Elections, 1945–2014," in *New Order and Progress: Development and Democracy in Brazil*, ed. Ben Ross Schneider, 241–67 (New York: Oxford University Press, 2016).

2. Richard S. Frase, "What Explains Persistent Racial Disproportionality in Minnesota's Prison and Jail Populations?," *Crime and Justice: A Review of Research* 38 (2009): 204.
3. Loïc Wacquant, *Urban Outcasts: A Comparative Sociology of Advanced Marginality* (Cambridge: Polity Press, 2008), 54, emphasis in original.
4. Geoffrey Pearson, *Hooligan: A History of Respectable Fears* (London: Macmillan, 1983), 236, as quoted in Brotherton, *Youth Street Gangs*, 13. While Pearson and Brotherton focus on historical comparisons in particular, the general point applies here as well.
5. George Karandinos et al., "The Moral Economy of Violence in the US Inner City: Deadly Sociability in the Retail Narcotics Economy," in *Violence at the Urban Margins*, ed. Javier Auyero, Philippe Bourgois, and Nancy Scheper-Hughes (New York: Oxford University Press, 2015), 43, 46.
6. Philippe Bourgois and Jeff Schonberg, *Righteous Dopefiend* (Berkeley: University of California Press, 2009), 5.
7. The research activities for this study were approved by and overseen by the Institutional Review Boards at the University of Illinois at Chicago and Southern Illinois University Edwardsville. Due to the nature of the research risks associated with breach of confidentiality, the IRBs granted a waiver of documentation of consent as well as a waiver of parental consent for participants under the age of eighteen.
8. Barney G. Glaser and Anselm L. Strauss, *The Discovery of Grounded Theory: Strategies for Qualitative Research* (Chicago: Aldine, 1967); Juliet Corbin and Anselm Strauss, *Basics of Qualitative Research: Techniques and Procedures for Developing Grounded Theory*, 3rd ed. (Thousand Oaks, CA: SAGE, 2008); Juliet Corbin and Anselm Strauss, *Basics of Qualitative Research: Techniques and Procedures for Developing Grounded Theory*, 4th ed. (Thousand Oaks, CA: SAGE, 2015).
9. John Hagedorn et al., *The Fracturing of Gangs and Violence in Chicago: A Research-Based Reorientation of Violence Prevention Policy* (Chicago: Great Cities Institute, University of Illinois at Chicago, 2019).
10. Corbin and Strauss, *Basics of Qualitative Research*, 3rd and 4th eds.

BIBLIOGRAPHY

"101 Shot, 14 Fatally, in July 4 Weekend Gun Violence Across Chicago." *Chicago Sun-Times.* July 6, 2017. https://chicago.suntimes.com/news/18-shot-2-fatally-in-bloody-start-to-fourth-of-july-weekend/.

Abbey, Jennifer, Candace Smith, and Matt Rosenbaum. "Chicago Gang Life: Gang Members Talk About Life on the Streets, Heartache." *Nightline*, October 19, 2012. http://abcnews.go.com/US/chicago-gang-life-gang-members-talks-life-streets/story?id=17499354#3.

Acs, Gregory, Rolf Pendall, Mark Treskon, and Amy Khare. *The Cost of Segregation: National Trends and the Case of Chicago, 1990–2010.* Washington, DC: Urban Institute, 2017.

Adler, Jeffery S. *First in Violence, Deepest in Dirt: Homicide in Chicago, 1875–1920.* Cambridge, MA: Harvard University Press, 2006.

Alinsky, Saul D. *Reveille for Radicals.* Chicago: University of Chicago Press, 1945.

Alinsky, Saul D. *Rules for Radicals: A Pragmatic Primer for Realistic Radicals.* New York: Random House, 1971.

Ali, Tanveer. "City Budget Winners and Losers: See Dept. Funding Changes Under Rahm." *DNAinfo*, October 18, 2017. https://www.dnainfo.com/chicago/20171018/albany-park/rahm-emanuel-city-budget-analysis-departments-increase-decrease.

Anderson, Elijah. *Code of the Street: Decency, Violence, and the Moral Life of the Inner City.* New York: Norton, 1999.

Archdiocese of São Paulo. *Torture in Brazil: A Shocking Report on the Pervasive Use of Torture by Brazilian Military Governments, 1964–1979.* 2nd ed. Ed. Jaime Wright. Trans. Joan Dassin. Austin: University of Texas Press, 1998.

Arena, John. *Driven from New Orleans: How Nonprofits Betray Public Housing and Promote Privatization.* Minneapolis: University of Minnesota Press, 2012.

Austen, Ben. "Public Enemies: Social Media Is Fueling Gang Wars in Chicago." *Wired*, September 17, 2013. http://www.wired.com/2013/09/gangs-of-social-media/.

Barker, Vanessa. "Explaining the Great American Crime Decline: A Review of Blumstein and Wallman, Goldberger and Rosenfeld, and Zimring." *Law & Social Inquiry* 35, no. 2 (2010): 489–516.

Berk, Richard A. "Knowing When to Fold 'Em: An Essay on Evaluating the Impact of Ceasefire, Compstat, and Exile." *Criminology & Public Policy* 4, no. 3 (2005): 451–66.

Biles, Roger. *Mayor Harold Washington: Champion of Race and Reform in Chicago*. Urbana: University of Illinois Press, 2018.

Black, Curtis. "Emanuel's Privatizing Mental Health Clinic in Roseland Raises Concerns." *Chicago Reporter*, November 3, 2016. https://www.chicagoreporter.com/emanuels-privatizing-mental-health-clinic-in-roseland-raises-concerns/.

Black, Donald. "Crime as Social Control." *American Sociological Review* 48, no. 1 (1983): 34–45.

Blumstein, Alfred, and Joel Wallman, eds. *The Crime Drop in America*. Cambridge: Cambridge University Press, 2000.

Bourdieu, Pierre. *Pascalian Meditations*. Trans. Richard Nice. Stanford, CA: Stanford University Press, 2000.

Bourgois, Philippe. *In Search of Respect: Selling Crack in El Barrio*. Cambridge: Cambridge University Press, 1995.

Bourgois, Philippe, and Jeff Schonberg. *Righteous Dopefiend*. Berkeley: University of California Press, 2009.

Bowser, Benjamin, Robert Fullilove, and Carl Word. "Is the New Heroin Epidemic Really New? Racializing Heroin." *Journal of the National Medical Association* 109, no. 1 (2017): 28–32.

Boykin, Richard R. "Commentary: Tyshawn Lee's Killer Must Be Charged as a Terrorist." *Chicago Tribune*, November 9, 2015. http://www.chicagotribune.com/news/opinion/commentary/ct-tyshawn-lee-chicago-gun-violence-terrorism-perspec-20151109-story.html.

Braga, Anthony A., David M. Kennedy, Elin J. Waring, and Anne Morrison Piehl. "Problem-Oriented Policing, Deterrence, and Youth Violence: An Evaluation of Boston's Operation Ceasefire." *Journal of Research in Crime and Delinquency* 38, no. 3 (2001): 195–225.

Braga, Anthony A., and David L. Weisburd. "The Effects of Focused Deterrence Strategies on Crime: A Systematic Review and Meta-Analysis of the Empirical Evidence." *Journal of Research in Crime and Delinquency* 49, no. 3 (2011): 323–58.

Brotherton, David C. *Youth Street Gangs: A Critical Appraisal*. New York: Routledge, 2015.

Brotherton, David C., and Luis Barrios. *The Almighty Latin King and Queen Nation: Street Politics and the Transformation of a New York City Gang*. New York: Columbia University Press, 2004.

Budd, Joel. "Crime, Interrupted." *Economist*, November 19, 2008. https://www.economist.com/news/2008/11/19/crime-interrupted.

Byrne, John. "City Reaches $38.75 Million Settlement in Red Light Ticket Lawsuit." *Chicago Tribune*, July 20, 2017. http://www.chicagotribune.com/news/local/politics/ct-rahm-emanuel-red-light-tickets-lawsuit-settlement-met-20170720-story.html.

Byrne, John, and Liam Ford. "Cops, Feds Meet with Gang Leaders." *Chicago Tribune*, August 28, 2010. http://articles.chicagotribune.com/2010-08-28/news/ct-met-gangs-0829-20100828_1_gang-leaders-gang-members-gang-violence.

Carlock, Greg, and Sean McElwee. "Why the Best New Deal Is a Green New Deal." *Nation*, September 18, 2018. https://www.thenation.com/article/why-the-best-new-deal-is-a-green-new-deal/.

Castells, Manuel. *The Power of Identity*. Oxford: Blackwell, 1997.

Center for Popular Democracy. *Freedom to Thrive: Reimagining Safety and Security in Our Communities*. New York: Center for Popular Democracy, 2017.

Chicago Community Policing Consortium. *Community Policing in Chicago, Year Ten: An Evaluation of Chicago's Alternative Policing Strategy*. Chicago: Illinois Criminal Justice Information Authority, 2004.

Chicago Crime Commission. *The Gang Book*. 2nd ed. Chicago: Chicago Crime Commission, 2012.

Chicago Crime Commission. *The Gang Book*. 3rd ed. Chicago: Chicago Crime Commission, 2018.

"Chicago Gang Violence: Police Chief Jody Weis Follows Through on Controversial Strategy." *HuffPost*, October 26, 2010. https://www.huffingtonpost.com/2010/10/26/chicago-gang-violence-pol_n_774402.html.

Chicago Housing Authority. *The Plan for Transformation: An Update on Relocation*. Chicago: Chicago Housing Authority, 2011.

Chicago Police Department. "Crimes—2001 to Present." 2018. https://data.cityofchicago.org/Public-Safety/Crimes-2001-to-present/ijzp-q8t2.

Chicago Police Department. "Gang Violence Reduction Strategy." General Order G10-01. February 8, 2019. http://directives.chicagopolice.org/directives/data/a7a57bf0-136d1d31-16513-6d1d-382b311ddf65fd3a.html.

Chicago Police Department. "Subject Assessment and Information Dashboard (SAID)." Special Order S09-11. January 9, 2019. http://directives.chicagopolice.org/directives/data/a7a57b85-155e9f4b-50c15-5e9f-7742e3ac8b0ab2d3.html.

Chicago Police Department. *2011 Chicago Murder Analysis*. Chicago: Chicago Police Department, 2012. https://home.chicagopolice.org/wp-content/uploads/2014/12/2011-Murder-Report.pdf.

Chicago Public Schools. "CPS School Locator." 2018. https://cps.edu/ScriptLibrary/Map-SchoolLocator/index.html.

Chicago Public Schools. "Search Schools." 2018. https://www.cps.edu/schools/find_a_school/pages/findaschool.aspx.

Chief Keef. "What I Claim." Track 10 on *Bang*. Glory Boyz Entertainment, 2011, MP3 audio.

City of Chicago. "Community Area 2000 and 2010 Census Population Comparisons." 2018. https://www.cityofchicago.org/city/en/depts/dcd/supp_info/community_area_2000and2010censuspopulationcomparisons.html.

Clear, Todd. *Imprisoning Communities: How Mass Incarceration Makes Disadvantaged Neighborhoods Worse*. New York: Oxford University Press, 2007.

Cloward, Richard A., and Lloyd E. Ohlin. *Delinquency and Opportunity: A Theory of Delinquent Gangs*. New York: Free Press, 1960.

Coen, Jeff. "Former Chicago Alderman Sentenced to 4 Years in Prison." *Chicago Tribune*, February 18, 2009. http://articles.chicagotribune.com/2009-02-18/news/0902170689_1_alderman-arenda-troutman-hired-truck-program.

Cohen, Adam, and Elizabeth Taylor. *American Pharaoh: Mayor Richard J. Daley—His Battle for Chicago and the Nation*. New York: Little, Brown, 2000.

Cohen, Albert K. *Delinquent Boys: The Culture of the Gang*. Glencoe, IL: Free Press, 1955.

Cohen, Sharon. "Violence, Gangs Scar Chicago in 2012." *USA Today*, December 29, 2012. https://www.usatoday.com/story/news/nation/2012/12/29/violence-gangs-chicago/1797991/.

Cohen, Sheri, Nikhil Prachand, Kirsti Bocskay, Janis Sayer, and Tina Schuh. *Healthy Chicago 2.0 Community Health Assessment: Informing Efforts to Achieve Health Equity*. Chicago: Chicago Department of Public Health, 2016.

Cohen, Stanley. *Folk Devils and Moral Panics*. London: Paladin, 1973.

Connolly, Colleen. "'I Live on the South Side': Obama Addresses Gun Violence in Chicago." *Ward Room* (blog), NBC Chicago, October 27, 2015. https://www.nbcchicago.com/blogs/ward-room/Obama-Addresses-Hometown-Violence-in-Police-Chiefs-Conference-in-Chicago-337654961.html.

Conquergood, Dwight. "Homeboys and Hoods: Gang Communication and Cultural Space." In *Group Communication in Context: Studies of Natural Groups*, ed. Lawrence R. Frey, 23–55. Hillsdale, NJ: Lawrence Erlbaum, 1994.

Conquergood, Dwight. "The Power of Symbols." In *One City*, 11–17. Chicago: Chicago Council on Urban Affairs, 1996.

Conquergood, Dwight. "Street Literacy." In *Handbook of Research on Teaching Literacy Through the Communicative and Visual Arts*, ed. James Flood, Shirley Brice Heath, and Diane Lapp, 354–75. New York: Macmillan Library Reference, 1997.

Contreras, Randol. *The Stickup Kids: Race, Drugs, Violence, and the American Dream*. Berkeley: University of California Press, 2013.

Cook County Clerk's Office. "Cook County TIFs to Bring in a Record $1 Billion According to Clerk Orr; Transit TIF Revenue Doubled." July 24, 2018. https://www.cookcountyclerk.com/news/cook-county-tifs-bring-record-1-billion-according-clerk-orr-transit-tif-revenue-doubled.

Cooley, Will. "'Stones Run It': Taking Back Control of Organized Crime in Chicago, 1940–1975." *Journal of Urban History* 37, no. 6 (2011): 911–32.

Corbin, Juliet, and Anselm Strauss. *Basics of Qualitative Research: Techniques and Procedures for Developing Grounded Theory*. 3rd ed. Thousand Oaks, CA: SAGE, 2008.

Corbin, Juliet, and Anselm Strauss. *Basics of Qualitative Research: Techniques and Procedures for Developing Grounded Theory*. 4th ed. Thousand Oaks, CA: SAGE, 2015.

Córdova, Teresa L., and Matthew D. Wilson. *Lost: The Crisis of Jobless and Out of School Teens and Young Adults in Chicago Illinois and the U.S.* Chicago: Great Cities Institute, University of Illinois at Chicago, 2016.

Covall, Kevin. "Rahm Emanuel's Chicago, a Tale of Two Cities." CNN, April 3, 2014. https://www.cnn.com/2014/04/02/opinion/coval-chicagoland-rahm-emanuel/index.html.

Curtis, Ric. "The Negligible Role of Gangs in Drug Distribution in New York City in the 1990s." In *Gangs and Society: Alternative Perspectives*, ed. Louis Kontos, David C. Brotherton, and Luis Barrios, 41–61. New York: Columbia University Press, 2003.

Daniels, Ron. "A Domestic Marshall Plan to Transform America's 'Dark Ghettos': Toward a Martin Luther King–Malcolm X Community Revitalization Initiative." *Black Scholar* 37, no. 3 (2007): 10–13.

Davey, Monica. "Blagojevich Sentenced to 14 Years in Prison." *New York Times*, December 7, 2011. https://www.nytimes.com/2011/12/08/us/blagojevich-expresses-remorse-in-courtroom-speech.html.

Dawley, David. *A Nation of Lords: The Autobiography of the Vice Lords*. 2nd ed. Prospect Heights, IL: Waveland Press, 1992.

Debs, Eugene V. *Eugene V. Debs Speaks*, ed. Jean Y. Tussey. New York: Pathfinder Press, 1970.

Decker, Scott H. "Collective and Normative Features of Gang Violence." *Justice Quarterly* 42, no. 2 (1996): 243–64.

Decker, Scott H., and Barrik Van Winkle. *Life in the Gang: Family, Friends, and Violence*. Cambridge: Cambridge University Press, 1996.

Densley, James A. *How Gangs Work: An Ethnography of Youth Violence*. London: Palgrave Macmillan, 2013.

de la Torre, Marisa, Molly F. Gordon, Paul Moore, and Jennifer Cowhy. *School Closings in Chicago: Understanding Families' Choices and Constraints for New School Enrollment*. Chicago: University of Illinois at Chicago Consortium on Chicago School Research, 2015.

Diamond, Andrew J. *Chicago on the Make: Power and Inequality in a Modern City*. Berkeley: University of California Press, 2017.

Diamond, Andrew J. *Mean Streets: Chicago Youths and the Everyday Struggle for Empowerment in the Multiracial City, 1908–1969*. Berkeley: University of California Press, 2009.

Douglass, Frederick. *Frederick Douglass: Selected Speeches and Writings*. Ed. Philip S. Foner and Yuval Taylor. Chicago: Chicago Review Press, 1999.

Drake, St. Clair, and Horace R. Cayton. *Black Metropolis: A Study of Negro Life in a Northern City*. New York: Harcourt, Brace, 1945.

Dumke, Mick. "The Shot That Brought the Projects Down." *Chicago Reader*, October 12, 2012. https://www.chicagoreader.com/Bleader/archives/2012/10/12/the-shot-that-brought-the-projects-down-part-one-of-five.

Dumke, Mick, and Frank Main. "A Look Inside the Watch List Chicago Police Fought to Keep Secret." *Chicago Sun-Times*, May 18, 2017. https://chicago.suntimes.com/news/what-gets-people-on-watch-list-chicago-police-fought-to-keep-secret-watchdogs/.

Durán, Robert J. *Gang Life in Two Cities: An Insider's Journey*. New York: Columbia University Press, 2013.

Durán, Robert J. *The Gang Paradox: Inequalities and Miracles on the U.S.–Mexico Border*. New York: Columbia University Press, 2018.

Eck, John E., and Edward R. Maguire. "Have Changes in Policing Reduced Violent Crime? An Assessment of the Evidence." In *The Crime Drop in America*, ed. Alfred Blumstein and Joel Wallman, 207–65. New York: Oxford University Press, 2000.

Elkins, Kathleen. "These Are the 10 Richest Cities in the World." CNBC, September 14, 2018. https://www.cnbc.com/2018/09/14/the-richest-cities-in-the-world.html.

Emery, Rod. *The Blueprint: From Gangster Disciple to Growth and Development*. Elgin, IL: Morris Publishing, 1996.

Esbensen, Finn-Aage, and Cheryl L. Maxson, "The Eurogang Program of Research and Multimethod Comparative Gang Research: Introduction." In *Youth Gangs in International Perspective: Results from the Eurogang Program of Research*, ed. Finn-Aage Esbensen and Cheryl L. Maxson, 1–14. New York: Springer, 2012.

Esposito, Stefano. "Trump Injects Chicago Crime into Debate: 'A War-Torn Country?'" *Chicago Sun-Times*, September 27, 2016. https://chicago.suntimes.com/news/trump-injects-chicago-crime-into-debate-a-war-torn-country/.

Farooqui, Suniya. *Chicago Community Area Indicators, 2015*. Chicago: Social Impact Research Center, Heartland Alliance, 2017.

Federal Bureau of Investigation. "Crime in the U.S." Accessed July 18, 2019. https://ucr.fbi.gov/crime-in-the-u.s.

Federal Bureau of Investigation. "Uniform Crime Reports." Accessed January 26, 2017. https://www.ucrdatatool.gov/.

Fenton, Justin. "Star Criminologist Hopes to Make Difference in Return to Baltimore." *Baltimore Sun*, February 15, 2014. http://www.baltimoresun.com/news/maryland/crime/bs-md-ci-david-kennedy-ceasefire-returns-20140215-story.html.

Ferkenhoff, Eric, and Darnell Little. "The Bleeding of Chicago." *CityLab*, February 24, 2018. https://www.citylab.com/equity/2018/02/the-bleeding-of-chicago/554141/.

"Finally Rich: Chief Keef." *Billboard*. http://www.billboard.com/artist/299119/ chief-keef/chart?f=335.

Fish, John H. *Black Power/White Control: The Struggle of The Woodlawn Organization in Chicago*. Princeton, NJ: Princeton University Press, 1973.

Flores, Edward Orozco. *God's Gangs: Barrio Ministry, Masculinity, and Gang Recovery*. New York: New York University Press, 2014.

Frase, Richard S. "What Explains Persistent Racial Disproportionality in Minnesota's Prison and Jail Populations?" *Crime and Justice: A Review of Research* 38, no. 1 (2009): 201–80.

Freire, Paulo. *Pedagogy of the Oppressed*. 30th anniv. ed. Trans. Myra Bergman Ramos. New York: Continuum, 2000.

Fry, John R. *Locked-Out Americans: A Memoir*. New York: Harper, Row, 1973.

Furst, R. Terry, Bruce D. Johnson, Eloise Dunlap, and Richard Curtis. "The Stigmatized Image of the 'Crack Head': A Sociocultural Exploration of a Barrier to Cocaine Smoking Among a Cohort of Youth in New York City." *Deviant Behavior* 20, no. 2 (1999): 153–81.

Garot, Robert. *Who You Claim: Performing Gang Identity in School and on the Streets*. New York: New York University Press, 2010.

Gellman, Erik S. "'The Stone Wall Behind': The Chicago Coalition for United Community Action and Labor's Overseers, 1968–1973." In *Black Power at Work: Community Control, Affirmative Action, and the Construction Industry*, ed. David Goldberg and Trevor Griffey, 112–33. Ithaca, NY: Cornell University Press, 2010.

Gibbs, Nancy. "Murder in Miniature." *Time*, September 19, 1994. http://content.time.com/time/magazine/article/0,9171,981460,00.html.

Givens, Ann. "On Patrol with Chicago's Last Violence Interrupters." *Trace*, February 6, 2017. https://www.thetrace.org/2017/02/chicago-homicides-cure-violence-interrupters/.

Glaser, Barney G., and Anselm L. Strauss. *The Discovery of Grounded Theory: Strategies for Qualitative Research*. Chicago: Aldine, 1967.

Goetz, Edward G. *New Deal Ruins: Race, Economic Justice, and Public Housing Policy*. Ithaca, NY: Cornell University Press, 2013.

Golub, Andrew, Henry Brownstein, and Eloise Dunlap. *Monitoring Drug Epidemics and the Markets That Sustain Them Using ADAM II: Final Technical Report*. Washington, DC: U.S. Department of Justice, 2012.

Gonzalez, Ana Lucia. "Crossing Divides: Stopping Violence Like It Was a Virus." BBC, April 27, 2018. https://www.bbc.com/news/world-us-canada-43541853.

Gorner, Jeremy. "Parolee Fatally Shot After Attending Meeting Run by Chicago Police." *Chicago Tribune*, October 16, 2015. http://www.chicagotribune.com/news/local/breaking/ct-gang-call-in-fatal-shooting-met-20151015-story.html.

Gorner, Jeremy, and Annie Sweeney. "Father of Slain 9-Year-Old Tyshawn Lee Charged with Shooting 3." *Chicago Tribune*, March 13, 2016. http://www.chicagotribune.com/news/ local/breaking/ct-tyshawn-lee-father-shooting-met-20160313-story.html.

Gossett, Stephen. "Trump: Chicago Is 'Like a War Zone,' Too 'Politically Correct' to Fix 'Carnage.'" *Chicagoist*, January 26, 2017. http://chicagoist.com/2017/01/26/trump_chicago_is_like_a_war_zone_to.php.

Gottschalk, Marie. *Caught: The Prison State and the Lockdown of American Politics*. Princeton, NJ: Princeton University Press, 2014.

Gradel, Thomas J., and Dick Simpson. *Corrupt Illinois: Patronage, Cronyism, and Criminality*. Urbana: University of Illinois Press, 2015.

Gramsci, Antonio. *Selections from the Prison Notebooks*. Ed. and trans., Quintin Hoare and Geoffrey Nowell-Smith. New York: International Publishers, 1971.

Greene, Judith, and Kevin Pranis. *Gang Wars: The Failure of Enforcement Tactics and the Need for Effective Public Safety Strategies*. Washington, DC: Justice Policy Institute, 2007.

Grimm, Andy. "Black Souls Gang Members Head to Trial on RICO Charges." *Chicago Sun-Times*, October 1, 2017. https://chicago.suntimes.com/news/black-souls-gang-members-head-to-trial-on-rico-charges/.

Grimshaw, William J. *Bitter Fruit: Black Politics and the Chicago Machine, 1931–1991*. Chicago: University of Chicago Press, 1992.

Grunwald, Ben, and Andrew V. Papachristos. "Project Safe Neighborhoods in Chicago: Looking Back a Decade Later." *Journal of Criminal Law and Criminology* 107, no. 1 (2017): 131–60.

Hagedorn, John M. "Chicago, I Do Mind Dying." In *Oxford Textbook of Violence Prevention: Epidemiology, Evidence, and Policy*, ed. Peter D. Donnelly and Catherine L. Ward, 219–24. Oxford: Oxford University Press, 2015.

Hagedorn, John M. "Gang Violence in the Postindustrial Era." *Crime and Justice* 24 (1998): 365–419.

Hagedorn, John M. "Gangs, Schools, and Social Change: An Institutional Analysis." *ANNALS of the American Academy of Political and Social Science* 673, no. 1 (2017): 190–208.

Hagedorn, John M. *The In$ane Chicago Way: The Daring Plan by Chicago Gangs to Create a Spanish Mafia*. Chicago: University of Chicago Press, 2015.

Hagedorn, John M. *People and Folks: Gangs, Crime and the Underclass in a Rustbelt City*. Chicago: Lake View Press, 1988.

Hagedorn, John M. "Race Not Space: A Revisionist History of Gangs in Chicago." *Journal of African American History* 91, no. 2 (2006): 194–208.

Hagedorn, John M. *A World of Gangs: Armed Young Men and Gangsta Culture*. Minneapolis: University of Minnesota Press, 2008.

Hagedorn, John, Roberto Aspholm, Teresa Córdova, Andrew Papachristos, and Lance Williams. *The Fracturing of Gangs and Violence in Chicago: A Research-Based*

Reorientation of Violence Prevention Policy. Chicago: Great Cities Institute, University of Illinois at Chicago, 2019.

Hagedorn, John M., and Meda Chesney-Lind. "America's 'War on Gangs': Response to a Real Threat or Moral Panic?" In *Criminal Justice Policy*, ed. Stacy L. Mallicoat and Christine L. Gardiner, 175–90. Thousand Oaks, CA: SAGE, 2014.

Hagedorn, John M., and Brigid Rauch. "Housing, Gangs, and Homicide: What We Can Learn from Chicago." *Urban Affairs Review* 42, no. 4 (2007): 435–56.

Harkness, Geoff. *Chicago Hustle and Flow: Gangs, Gangsta Rap, and Social Class*. Minneapolis: University of Minnesota Press, 2014.

Harris, Lauren, and Kalyn Belsha. "Video: One Year After Hunger Strike, Dyett High School Opens." *Chicago Reporter*, September 1, 2016. https://www.chicagoreporter.com/video-one-year-after-hunger-strike-dyett-high-school-opens/.

Harris, Phil. "No Let Up in Chicago Gun Violence Despite Obama's Hometown Plea." *Guardian*, February 16, 2013. https://www.theguardian.com/world/2013/feb/16/chicago-gun-violence-barack-obama.

Harvey, David. *A Brief History of Neoliberalism*. Oxford: Oxford University Press, 2005.

Hidalgo, Daniel, and Renato Lima-de-Oliviera. "Elite Contestation and Mass Participation in Brazilian Legislative Elections, 1945–2014." In *New Order and Progress: Development and Democracy in Brazil*, ed. Ben Ross Schneider, 241–67. New York: Oxford University Press, 2016.

Higley, Stephen R. "The 2010 Higley 1000." *The Higley 1000*, February 17, 2014. https://higley1000.com/archives/638.

Hirsch, Arnold R. *Making the Second Ghetto: Race and Housing in Chicago, 1940–1960*. Cambridge: Cambridge University Press, 1983.

Horowitz, Ruth. *Honor and the American Dream: Culture and Identity in a Chicano Community*. New Brunswick, NJ: Rutgers University Press, 1983.

Huebner, Beth M., Sean P. Varano, and Timothy S. Bynum. "Gangs, Guns, and Drugs: Recidivism Among Serious Young Offenders." *Criminology & Public Policy* 6, no. 2 (2007): 187–221.

Hughes, Lorine A. "Studying Youth Gangs: The Importance of Context." In *Studying Youth Gangs*, ed. James F. Short Jr. and Lorine A. Hughes, 37–45. Lanham, MD: AltaMira Press, 2006.

Human Rights Watch. *An Offer You Can't Refuse: How US Federal Prosecutors Force Drug Defendants to Plead Guilty*. New York: Human Rights Watch, 2013.

Hunt, D. Bradford. *Blueprint for Disaster: The Unraveling of Chicago Public Housing*. Chicago: University of Chicago Press, 2009.

Jackson, David, Jennifer Smith Richards, Gary Marx, and Juan Perez Jr. "Betrayed." *Chicago Tribune*, July 27, 2018. http://graphics.chicagotribune.com/chicago-public-schools-sexual-abuse/index.html.

Jacobs, James B. *Stateville: The Penitentiary in Mass Society*. Chicago: University of Chicago Press, 1977.

Jacques, Scott, and Richard Wright. *Code of the Suburb: Inside the World of Young Middle-Class Drug Dealers*. Chicago: University of Chicago Press, 2015.

James, Steve, dir. *The Interrupters*. Chicago: Kartemquin Films, 2011. Blu-ray Disc, 1080p HD.

Jan, Tracy. "The Forgotten Ferguson." *Washington Post*, June 21, 2018. https://www.washingtonpost.com/graphics/2018/business/is-racial-discrimination-influencing-corporate-investment-in-ferguson/.

Jankowski, Martín Sánchez. *Islands in the Street: Gangs and American Urban Society*. Berkeley: University of California Press, 1991.

Johnson, Bruce, Andrew Golub, and Eloise Dunlap. "The Rise and Decline of Hard Drugs, Drug Markets, and Violence in Inner-City New York." In *The Crime Drop in America*, ed. Alfred Blumstein and Joel Wallman, 164–206. Cambridge: Cambridge University Press, 2000.

Johnson, Cedric. "The Panthers Can't Save Us Now." *Catalyst* 1, no. 1 (2017): 56–85.

Jones, LeAlan M. "The Obama Center Leaves Chicago in Its Shadow." *Nation*, July 10, 2018. https://www.thenation.com/article/obama-center-leaves-chicago-communities-shadow/.

Kane-Willis, Kathleen, and Scott Metzger. *Hidden in Plain Sight: Heroin's Impact on Chicago's West Side*. Chicago: Illinois Consortium on Drug Policy at Roosevelt University, 2016.

Karandinos, George, Laurie Hart, Fernando Montero Castrillo, and Philippe Bourgois. "The Moral Economy of Violence in the US Inner City: Deadly Sociability in the Retail Narcotics Economy." In *Violence at the Urban Margins*, ed. Javier Auyero, Philippe Bourgois, and Nancy Scheper-Hughes, 41–72. New York: Oxford University Press, 2015.

Keiser, Lincoln R. *The Vice Lords: Warriors of the Streets*. Fieldwork edition. New York: Holt, Rinehart and Winston, 1979.

Kelly, Brianna. "Chicago Ranks 7th on New List of World's Best Cities." *Crain's Chicago Business*, November 27, 2018. https://www.chicagobusiness.com/tourism/chicago-ranks-7th-new-list-worlds-best-cities.

Kennedy, David M. *Don't Shoot: One Man, a Street Fellowship, and the End of Violence in Inner-City America*. New York: Bloomsbury, 2011.

Kennedy, David M. "Pulling Levers: Chronic Offenders, High-Crime Settings, and a Theory of Prevention." *Valparaiso University Law Review* 31, no. 2 (1997): 449–84.

Klein, Malcolm W. *Street Gangs and Street Workers*. Englewood Cliffs, NJ: Prentice-Hall, 1971.

Klein, Malcolm W. *The American Street Gang: Its Nature, Prevalence, and Control*. New York: Oxford University Press, 1995.

Koenman, Keith. *First Son: The Biography of Richard M. Daley*. Chicago: University of Chicago Press, 2013.

Kopan, Tal. "Trump: 'We're Going to Destroy' MS-13." CNN Politics, July 28, 2017. https://www.cnn.com/2017/07/28/politics/donald-trump-ms-13/index.html.

Kotlowitz, Alex. "Blocking the Transmission of Violence." *New York Times Magazine*, May 4, 2008. https://www.nytimes.com/2008/05/04/magazine/04health-t.html.

Kozol, Jonathan. *Savage Inequalities: Children in America's Schools*. New York: Crown, 1991.

Kropotkin, Pëtr. *Mutual Aid: A Factor of Evolution*. New York: McClure, Phillips, 1902.

Krug, Etienne G., Linda L. Dahlberg, James A. Mercy, Anthony B. Zwi, and Rafael Lozano, eds. *World Report on Violence and Health*. Geneva: World Health Organization, 2002.

Lee, Spike, dir. *Chi-Raq*. New York: 40 Acres & a Mule Filmworks, 2015.

Lessing, Benjamin. "Counterproductive Punishment: How Prison Gangs Undermine State Authority." *Rationality and Society* 29, no. 3 (2017): 257–97.

Levenson, Deborah T. *Adiós Niño: The Gangs of Guatemala City and the Politics of Death*. Durham, NC: Duke University Press, 2013.

Levitt, Steven D., and Sudhir Alladi Venkatesh. "An Economic Analysis of a Drug-Selling Gang's Finances." *Quarterly Journal of Economics* 115, no. 3 (2000): 755–89.

Lil JoJo. *JoJo World*. Self-released, 2012. MP3 audio.

Los Angeles Police Department. "Introduction to Gangs." 2018. http://www.lapdonline.org/get_informed/content_basic_view/23466.

Lowery, Wesley, Kimbriell Kelly, Ted Melinik, and Steven Rich. "Where Killings Go Unsolved." *Washington Post*, June 6, 2018. https://www.washingtonpost.com/graphics/2018/investigations/where-murders-go-unsolved/?noredirect=on&utm_term=.02deddoeb438.

Lutton, Linda, Becky Vevea, Sarah Karp, Adriana Cardona-Maguidad, and Kate McGee. "A Generation of School Closings." WBEZ, December 3, 2018. https://interactive.wbez.org/generation-school-closings/.

Lutz, B. J., and Dick Johnson. "Cops Retooling Gang Strategy." *Ward Room* (blog), NBC Chicago, March 19, 2012. https://www.nbcchicago.com/blogs/ward-room/chicago-gang-violence-police-gang-violence-143426386.html.

Lydersen, Kari. "Falling Through the Cracks." *Chicago Reporter*, April 25, 2015. https://www.chicagoreporter.com/falling-through-the-cracks/.

Lydersen, Kari. *Mayor 1%: Rahm Emanuel and the Rise of Chicago's 99%*. Chicago: Haymarket Books, 2013.

Lyons, William. *The Politics of Community Policing: Rearranging the Power to Punish*. Ann Arbor: University of Michigan Press, 1999.

Main, Frank. "Murder 'Clearance' Rate in Chicago Hit New Low in 2017." *Chicago Sun-Times*, February 9, 2018. https://chicago.suntimes.com/news/murder-clearance-rate-in-chicago-hit-new-low-in-2017/.

Main, Frank. "On the West Side, Maps Show Heroin ODs, Shootings Go Hand in Hand." *Chicago Sun-Times*, March 24, 2017. https://chicago.suntimes.com/crime/on-the-west-side-maps-show-heroin-ods-shootings-go-hand-in-hand/.

Manning, James. "The Time Out City Life Index 2018." *Time Out*, June 13, 2018. https://www.timeout.com/things-to-do/city-life-index.

Mayor Rahm Emanuel's One Summer Chicago. *Newsroom*, 2018. http://www.onesummerchicago.org/Newsroom/.

McCorkle, Richard C., and Terance D. Miethe. *Panic: The Social Construction of the Street Gang Problem*. Upper Saddle River, NJ: Prentice Hall, 2002.

McClelland, Edward. "Rahm Emanuel's Nixon Moment: The Laquan McDonald Coverup Will Be His Legacy." *Salon*, December 2, 2015. https://www.salon.com/2015/12/02/rahm_emanuels_nixon_moment/.

McLaughlin, Eliott C. "Interrupting the Cycle of Teen Violence." CNN, September 28, 2011. http://www.cnn.com/2011/CRIME/09/27/chicago.teen.violence/index.html?iref=allsearch.

McPherson, James A. "The Blackstone Rangers." In *Observations of Deviance*, ed. Jack D. Douglas, 170–204. New York: Random House, 1970.

Meisner, Jason. "Ald. Willie Cochran Pleads Guilty—Finally—to Federal Fraud Charges for Misusing Ward's Charity Fund." *Chicago Tribune*, March 21, 2019. https://www.chicagotribune.com/news/breaking/ct-met-alderman-willie-cochran-guilty-20190320-story.html.

Meisner, Jason, and Juan Perez Jr. "Byrd-Bennett Sobs While Trying to Explain Corruption, Gets 4 1/2 Years in Prison." *Chicago Tribune*, April 28, 2017. http://www.chicagotribune.com/news/local/breaking/ct-barbara-byrd-bennett-sentence-met-20170428-story.html.

Meisner, Jason, and Annie Sweeney. "'It Was Killing for the Sake of Killing': Feds Charge South Side Gang Faction in 10 Killings in Englewood." *Chicago Tribune*, October 26, 2018. https://www.chicagotribune.com/news/local/breaking/ct-met-englewood-gang-murders-20181024-story.html.

Melde, Chris, Terrance J. Taylor, and Finn-Aage Esbensen. "'I Got Your Back': An Examination of the Protective Function of Gang Membership in Adolescence." *Criminology* 47, no. 2 (2009): 565–94.

Mendoza-Denton, Norma. *Homegirls: Language and Cultural Practice Among Latina Youth Gangs*. Malden, MA: Blackwell, 2008.

Merton, Robert K. "Social Structure and Anomie." *American Sociological Review* 3, no. 5 (1938): 672–82.

Meyer, Robinson. "The Democratic Party Wants to Make Climate Policy Exciting." *Atlantic*, December 5, 2018. https://www.theatlantic.com/science/archive/2018/12/ocasio-cortez-green-new-deal-winning-climate-strategy/576514/.

Miller, Jody. *One of the Guys: Girls, Gangs, and Gender*. New York: Oxford University Press, 2001.

Mills, C. Wright. *The Sociological Imagination*. London: Oxford University Press, 1959.

"The Model—About Us." Cure Violence, updated 2019. http://cureviolence.org/the-model/about-us/.

Moore, Joan W. *Going Down to the Barrio: Homeboys and Homegirls in Change*. Philadelphia: Temple University Press, 1991.

Moore, Joan W. *Homeboys: Gangs, Drugs, and Prison in the Barrios of Los Angeles*. Philadelphia: Temple University Press, 1978.

Moore, Natalie Y., and Lance Williams. *The Almighty Black P Stone Nation: The Rise, Fall, and Resurgence of an American Gang*. Chicago: Lawrence Hill Books, 2011.

Morial, Marc. "Urban League's 'Main Street Marshall Plan' Incorporated in CBC's Bill." *Black Star News*, May 10, 2018. http://www.blackstarnews.com/us-politics/justice/urban-leagues-main-street-marshall-plan-incorporated-into-cbcs.

"Morning Spin: Emanuel Budget Hole Now Tops $259 Million." *Chicago Tribune*, September 26, 2017. http://www.chicagotribune.com/news/local/politics/ct-rahm-emanuel-chicago-budget-20170926-story.html.

Morris, Aldon D. *The Origins of the Civil Rights Movement: Black Communities Organizing for Change*. New York: Free Press, 1984.

Mortice, Zach. "After Rahm, What Comes Next for the Obama Library?" *CityLab*, September 25, 2018. https://www.citylab.com/design/2018/09/after-rahm-what-comes-next-obama-library/571075/.

Moser, Whet. "Mark Kirk Wants to Arrest 18,000 Chicago Gang Members at Once." *Chicago*, May 31, 2013. https://www.chicagomag.com/Chicago-Magazine/The-312

/May-2013/Mark-Kirk-Wants-to-Arrest-18000-Chicago-Gang-Members-At-Once/.

Mummolo, Jonathan. "Militarization Fails to Enhance Police Safety or Reduce Crime but May Harm Police Reputation." *Proceedings of the National Academy of Sciences* 115, no. 37 (2018): 9181–86.

National Gang Intelligence Center. *National Gang Threat Assessment 2009*. Washington, DC: National Gang Intelligence Center, 2009.

National Network for Safe Communities. *Group Violence Intervention: An Implementation Guide*. Washington, DC: Office of Community Oriented Policing Services, 2016.

Neocleous, Mark. *The Fabrication of Social Order: A Critical Theory of Policy Power*. London: Pluto Press, 2000.

"Obama on Gun Violence: 'It Happens on the Streets of Chicago Every Day.'" *Ward Room* (blog), NBC Chicago, January 5, 2016. https://www.nbcchicago.com/blogs/ward-room/Obama-on-Gun-Violence-It-Happens-on-the-Streets-of-Chicago-Every-Day-364264661.html.

O'Connor, Matt. "Ex-CHA Chief Gets Prison." *Chicago Tribune*, August 29, 2001. https://www.chicagotribune.com/news/ct-xpm-2001-08-29-0108290314-story.html.

Office of National Drug Control Policy. *2013 Annual Report, Arrestee Drug Abuse Monitoring Program II*. Washington, DC: Executive Office of the President, 2014.

Padilla, Felix M. *The Gang as an American Enterprise*. New Brunswick, NJ: Rutgers University Press, 1992.

Papachristos, Andrew V. "Commentary: CPD's Crucial Choice: Treat Its List as Offenders or as Potential Victims?" *Chicago Tribune*, July 26, 2016. http://www.chicagotribune.com/news/opinion/commentary/ct-gun-violence-list-chicago-police-murder-perspec-0801-jm-20160729-story.html.

Papachristos, Andrew V. "Murder by Structure: Dominance Relations and the Social Structure of Gang Homicide." *American Journal of Sociology* 115, no. 1 (2009): 74–128.

Papachristos, Andrew V. "Too Big to Fail: The Science and Politics of Violence Prevention." *Criminology & Public Policy* 10, no. 4 (2011): 1053–61.

Papachristos, Andrew V., David Hureau, and Anthony A. Braga. "The Corner and the Crew: The Influence of Geography and Social Networks on Gang Violence." *American Sociological Review* 78, no. 3 (2013): 417–47.

Papachristos, Andrew V., and David S. Kirk. "Changing the Street Dynamics: Evaluating Chicago's Group Violence Reduction Strategy." *Criminology & Public Policy* 14, no. 3 (2015): 525–58.

Papachristos, Andrew V., Tracey L. Meares, and Jeffrey Fagan. "Attention Felons: Evaluating Project Safe Neighborhoods in Chicago." *Journal of Empirical Legal Studies* 4, no. 2 (2007): 223–72.

Papachristos, Andrew V., Christopher Wilderman, and Elizabeth Roberto. "Tragic, but Not Random: The Social Contagion of Nonfatal Gunshot Injuries." *Social Science & Medicine* 125, no. 1 (2015): 139–50.

Papajohn, George, and John Kass. "21st Century VOTE Giving Gangs Taste of Real Power." *Chicago Tribune*, September 28, 1994. https://www.chicagotribune.com/news/ct-xpm-1994-09-28-9409280241-story.html.

"Partners." Cure Violence, updated 2019. http://cureviolence.org/partners/.
Pattillo, Mary. *Black on the Block: The Politics of Race and Class in the City.* Chicago: University of Chicago Press, 2007.
Pattillo, Mary. *Black Picket Fences: Privilege and Peril Among the Black Middle Class.* Chicago: University of Chicago Press, 1999.
Pattillo, Mary. "Investing in Poor Black Neighborhoods 'As Is.'" In *Public Housing and the Legacy of Segregation*, ed. Margery Austin Turner, Susan J. Popkin, and Lynette Rawlings, 31–46. Washington, DC: Urban Institute Press, 2009.
Pearson, Geoffrey. *Hooligan: A History of Respectable Fears.* London: Macmillan, 1983.
Perez, Juan, Jr. "Dyett High School Hunger Strike Ends." *Chicago Tribune*, September 20, 2015. http://www.chicagotribune.com/news/local/breaking/ct-dyett-high-school-hunger-strike-ends-20150919-story.html.
Perez, Juan, Jr., Bill Ruthhart, and Hal Dardick. "CPS Chief Forrest Claypool Resigns After Being Accused of Ethics Probe Cover-Up." *Chicago Tribune*, December 8, 2017. http://www.chicagotribune.com/news/local/politics/ct-met-forrest-claypool-resigns-cps-20171208-story.html.
Phillips, Susan A. *Operation Fly Trap: L.A. Gangs, Drugs, and the Law.* Chicago: University of Chicago Press, 2012.
Piven, Frances Fox, and Richard A. Cloward. *Poor People's Movements: Why They Succeed, How They Fail.* New York: Pantheon Books, 1977.
Police Accountability Task Force. *Recommendations for Reform: Restoring Trust Between the Chicago Police and the Communities They Serve.* Chicago: Police Accountability Task Force, 2016.
Pollack, Neal. "The Gang That Could Go Straight." *Chicago Reader*, January 26, 1995. https://www.chicagoreader.com/chicago/the-gang-that-could-go-straight/Content?oid=886552.
Popkin, Susan J., Victoria E. Gwiasda, Lynn M. Olson, Dennis P. Rosenbaum, and Larry Buron. *The Hidden War: Crime and the Tragedy of Public Housing in Chicago.* New Brunswick, NJ: Rutgers University Press, 2000.
Posada, Brianna. "How Strategic Is Chicago's 'Strategic Subjects List'? Upturn Investigates." *Upturn*, June 22, 2017. https://medium.com/equal-future/how-strategic-is-chicagos-strategic-subjects-list-upturn-investigates-9e5b4b235a7c.
Pyrooz, David C., Scott H. Decker, and Vincent J. Webb. "The Ties That Bind: Desistance from Gangs." *Crime & Delinquency* 60, no. 4 (2014): 491–516.
Pyrooz, David, and James Densley. "To Deal with Antifa, Designate It a Street Gang." *Wall Street Journal*, September 17, 2017. https://www.wsj.com/articles/to-deal-with-antifa-designate-it-a-street-gang-1505672746.
Pyrooz, David, Jillian J. Turanovic, Scott H. Decker, and Jun Wu. "Taking Stock of the Relationship Between Gang Membership and Offending: A Meta-Analysis." *Criminal Justice and Behavior* 43, no. 3 (2016): 365–97.
Ralph, Laurence. "'As Soon as I Get Out Ima Cop Dem Jordans': The Afterlife of the Corporate Gang." *Identities: Global Studies in Culture and Power* 17, no. 6 (2010): 667–94.
Ralph, Laurence. *Renegade Dreams: Living Through Injury in Gangland Chicago.* Chicago: University of Chicago Press, 2014.
Ransford, Charles, Tina Johnson, Brent Decker, and Gary Slutkin. "The Relationship Between the Cure Violence Model and Citywide Increases and Decreases in

Killings in Chicago (2000–2016)." Cure Violence, September 2016. http://cureviolence.org/wp-content/uploads/2017/06/2016.09.22-CV-Chicago-Memo.pdf.

Reed, Adolph, Jr. *Class Notes: Posing as Politics and Other Thoughts on the American Scene*. New York: New Press, 2000.

Reed, Adolph, Jr. "How Racial Disparity Does Not Help Make Sense of Patterns of Police Violence." Nonsite.org, September 16, 2016. https://nonsite.org/editorial/how-racial-disparity-does-not-help-make-sense-of-patterns-of-police-violence.

Reed, Adolph, Jr. *Stirrings in the Jug: Black Politics in the Post-Segregation Era*. Minneapolis: University of Minnesota Press, 1999.

Reinarman, Craig, and Harry G. Levine, eds. *Crack in America: Demon Drugs and Social Justice*. Berkeley: University of California Press, 1997.

Rios, Victor M. *Punished: Policing the Lives of Black and Latino Boys*. New York: New York University Press, 2011.

Rivlin, Gary. *Fire on the Prairie: Chicago's Harold Washington and the Politics of Race*. New York: Henry Holt, 1992.

Rodgers, Dennis. "The Moral Economy of Murder: Violence, Death, and Social Order in Nicaragua." In *Violence at the Urban Margins*, ed. Javier Auyero, Philippe Bourgois, and Nancy Scheper-Hughes, 21–40. New York: Oxford University Press, 2015.

Rodricks, Dan. "Baltimore Had Its Own Version of Ceasefire Before, It Could Again." *Baltimore Sun*, June 12, 2017. http://www.baltimoresun.com/news/maryland/dan-rodricks-blog/bal-baltimore-had-its-own-version-of-ceasefire-before-it-could-again-20170611-story.html.

Rosenberg, Tina. "Fighting Street Gun Violence as if It Were a Contagion." *New York Times*, May 8, 2018. https://www.nytimes.com/2018/05/08/opinion/fighting-street-gun-violence-as-if-it-were-a-contagion.html.

Rosenfeld, Richard, Robert Fornango, and Eric Baumer. "Did Ceasefire, Compstat, and Exile Reduce Homicide?" *Criminology & Public Policy* 4, no. 3 (2005): 419–49.

Ross, Martha, and Nicole Prchal Svajlenka. *Employment and Disconnection Among Teens and Young Adults: The Role of Place, Race, and Education*. Washington, DC: Brookings Institution, 2016.

Royko, Mike. *Boss: Richard J. Daley of Chicago*. New York: E. P. Dutton, 1971.

Ruthhart, Bill. "How a Federal City Hall Corruption Investigation Is Dominating Chicago's Crowded Race for Mayor." *Chicago Tribune*, February 1, 2019. https://www.chicagotribune.com/news/local/politics/ct-met-chicago-mayors-race-federal-investigation-20190201-story.html.

Sampson, Robert J. "Neighborhoods and Crime: The Structural Determinants of Personal Victimization." *Journal of Research in Crime and Delinquency* 22, no. 1 (1985): 7–40.

Sandler, Danielle H. *Externalities of Public Housing: The Effect of Public Housing Demolitions on Local Crime*. Washington, DC: U.S. Census Bureau, 2016.

Saunders, Jessica, Priscilla Hunt, and John S. Hollywood. "Predictions Put into Practice: A Quasi-Experimental Evaluation of Chicago's Predictive Policing Pilot." *Journal of Experimental Criminology* 12, no. 3 (2016): 347–71.

Schroedter, Andrew. "Chicago Police Misconduct—A Rising Financial Toll." *Better Government Association*, January 31, 2016. https://www.bettergov.org/news/chicago-police-misconduct-%E2%80%93-a-rising-financial-toll.

"Scientific Evaluations." Cure Violence, updated 2019. http://cureviolence.org/results/scientific-evaluations/.

Semuels, Alana. "Chicago's Awful Divide." *Atlantic*, March 28, 2018. https://www.theatlantic.com/business/archive/2018/03/chicago-segregation-poverty/556649/.

Serrato, Jacqueline. "Mexicans and 'Hispanics,' Now the Largest Minority in Chicago." *Chicago Tribune*, October 13, 2017. https://www.chicagotribune.com/hoy/ct-mexicans-and-hispanics-largest-minority-in-chicago-20171013-story.html.

Sharkey, Patrick. *Uneasy Peace: The Great Crime Decline, the Renewal of City Life, and the Next War on Violence*. New York: Norton, 2018.

Shaw, Clifford R., and Henry D. McKay. *Juvenile Delinquency and Urban Areas*. Rev. ed. Chicago: University of Chicago Press, 1969.

Short, James F., Jr. "The Level of Explanation Problem Revisited—The American Society of Criminology 1997 Presidential Address." *Criminology* 36, no. 1 (1998): 3–36.

Short, James F., Jr. *Poverty, Ethnicity, and Violent Crime*. Boulder, CO: Westview Press, 1997.

Short, James F., Jr., and Fred L. Strodtbeck. *Group Process and Gang Delinquency*. Chicago: University of Chicago Press, 1965.

Silver, Nate. "The Most Diverse Cities Are Often the Most Segregated." *FiveThirtyEight*, May 1, 2015. https://fivethirtyeight.com/features/the-most-diverse-cities-are-often-the-most-segregated/.

Simpson, Dick, Thomas J. Gradel, Melissa Mouritsen, and John Johnson. *Chicago: Still the Capital of Corruption*. Chicago: Department of Political Science, University of Illinois at Chicago, 2015.

Simon, Scott. "Gang Violence Smolders on Hot Chicago Streets." National Public Radio, July 28, 2012. http://www.npr.org/2012/07/28/157454927/gang-violence-smoulders-on-hot-chicago-streets.

Sink, Todd, and Brian Ceh. "Relocation of Urban Poor in Chicago: HOPE IV Policy Outcomes." *Geoforum* 42, no. 1 (2011): 71–82.

Skogan, Wesley G., Susan M. Hartnett, Natalie Bump, and Jill Dubois. *Evaluation of CeaseFire-Chicago*. Evanston, IL: Northwestern University, 2008.

Slevin, Peter. "Chicago Grapples with Gun Violence; Death Toll Soars." *Washington Post*, December 21, 2012. http://articles.washingtonpost.com/2012-12-21/national/36017398_1_gun-violence-homicide-rate-national-gun-debate.

Sloan, Cle, dir. *Bastards of the Party*. Venice, CA: Fuqua Films, 2005. DVD.

Slutkin, Gary. "Let's Treat Violence Like a Contagious Disease." Filmed April 2013 in Washington, DC. TEDMED video, 14:05. https://www.ted.com/talks/gary_slutkin_let_s_treat_violence_like_a_contagious_disease?language=en.

Slutkin, Gary. "Violence Is a Contagious Disease." In *Contagion of Violence: Workshop Summary*, rapporteurs Deepali M. Patel, Melissa A. Simon, and Rachel M. Taylor, 94–111. Washington, DC: National Academies Press, 2013.

Spelman, William. "The Limited Importance of Prison Expansion." In *The Crime Drop in America*, ed. Alfred Blumstein and Joel Wallman, 97–129. New York: Oxford University Press, 2000.

Spergel, Irving A. *Street Gang Work: Theory and Practice*. Reading, MA: Addison-Wesley, 1966.

Spirou, Costas, and Dennis R. Judd. *Building the City of Spectacle: Mayor Richard M. Daley and the Remaking of Chicago*. Ithaca, NY: Cornell University Press, 2016.

Spoerre, Anna, and William Lee. "6 Shot While Leaving Funeral for Slain Rapper: 'Bullets Flying Everyplace.'" *Chicago Tribune*, October 23, 2018. https://www.chicagotri

bune.com/news/local/breaking/ct-met-chicago-funeral-shooting-20181022-story.html.

Strickland, Joseph A. "Building Social Capital for Stable Employment: The Post Prison Experiences of Black Male Ex-Prisoners." PhD diss., University of Illinois at Chicago, 2008. ProQuest (UMI 3316768).

Suttles, Gerald D. *The Social Construction of Communities*. Chicago: University of Chicago Press, 1972.

Suttles, Gerald D. *The Social Order of the Slum*. Chicago: University of Chicago Press, 1968.

Sweeney, Annie. "Tweets from Gang Members Express Grief over Violence—But Then Turn to Anger, Researchers Find." *Chicago Tribune*, April 10, 2018. https://www.chicagotribune.com/news/local/breaking/ct-met-gang-internet-banging-study-20180406-story.html.

Tcherni, Maria. "Structural Determinants of Homicide: The Big Three." *Journal of Quantitative Criminology* 27, no. 4 (2011): 475–96.

Thrasher, Frederic M. *The Gang: A Study of 1,313 Gangs in Chicago*. Chicago: University of Chicago Press, 1927.

Tresser, Tom, ed. *Chicago Is Not Broke: Funding the City We Deserve*. 2nd ed. Chicago: Salsedo Press, 2017.

Uetricht, Micah. "Accused Torturer Jon Burge Died Last Week, but His Legacy of Brutal, Racist Policing Lives on in Chicago." *Intercept*, September 25, 2018. https://theintercept.com/2018/09/25/jon-burge-chicago-police-torture/.

United Nations Office on Drugs and Crime. *2011 Global Study on Homicide: Trends, Contexts, Data*. Vienna: United Nations Office on Drugs and Crime, 2011.

U.S. Department of Justice, Civil Rights Division, and U.S. Attorney's Office, Northern District of Illinois. *Investigation of the Chicago Police Department*. Washington, DC: U.S. Department of Justice, 2017.

Vale, Lawrence J. *Purging the Poorest: Public Housing and the Design Politics of Twice-Cleared Communities*. Chicago: University of Chicago Press, 2013.

Vargas, Robert. *Wounded City: Violent Turf Wars in a Chicago Barrio*. New York: Oxford University Press, 2016.

Venkatesh, Sudhir Alladi. *American Project: The Rise and Fall of a Modern Ghetto*. Cambridge, MA: Harvard University Press, 2000.

Venkatesh, Sudhir Alladi "Gender and Outlaw Capitalism: An Historical Account of the Black Sisters United Girl Gang." *Signs: A Journal of Women in Culture and Society* 23, no. 3 (1998): 683–709.

Venkatesh, Sudhir Alladi. "A Note on Social Theory and the American Street Gang." In *Gangs and Society: Alternative Perspectives*, ed. Louis Kontos, David C. Brotherton, and Luis Barrios, 3–11. New York: Columbia University Press, 2003.

Venkatesh, Sudhir Alladi. *Off the Books: The Underground Economy of the Urban Poor*. Cambridge, MA: Harvard University Press, 2006.

Venkatesh, Sudhir Alladi. "The Social Organization of Street Gang Activity in an Urban Ghetto." *American Journal of Sociology* 103, no. 1 (1997): 82–111.

Venkatesh, Sudhir Alladi, and Steven D. Levitt. " 'Are We a Family or a Business?' History and Disjuncture in the Urban American Street Gang." *Theory and Society* 29, no. 4 (2000): 427–62.

Vigil, James Diego. *Barrio Gangs: Street Life and Identity in Southern California*. Austin: University of Texas Press, 1988.

Vigil, James Diego. *A Rainbow of Gangs: Street Cultures in the Mega-City*. Austin: University of Texas Press, 2002.

Wacquant, Loïc. "Class, Race & Hyperincarceration in Revanchist America." *Daedalus* 139, no. 3 (2010): 74–90.

Wacquant, Loïc. *Punishing the Poor: The Neoliberal Government of Social Insecurity*. Durham, NC: Duke University Press, 2009.

Wacquant, Loïc. "Urban Desolation and Symbolic Denigration in the Hyperghetto." *Social Psychology Quarterly* 73, no. 3 (2010): 215–19.

Wacquant, Loïc. *Urban Outcasts: A Comparative Sociology of Advanced Marginality*. Cambridge: Polity Press, 2008.

Wagner, Curt. "McCarty Sees 'Crisis' in Chicago's Murder Rate." *Chicago Sun-Times*, December 30, 2016. https://chicago.suntimes.com/chicago-news/mccarthy-sees-crisis-in-chicagos-murder-rate/

Wagner, David. "Did Chief Keef Get Sent to Jail over Pitchfork's Gun Stunt?" *Atlantic*, January 16, 2013. https://www.theatlantic.com/entertainment/archive/2013/01/did-chief-keef-get-sent-jail-over-pitchforks-gun-stunt/319352/.

Webster, Daniel W., Jennifer Mendel Whitehill, Jon S. Vernick, and Elizabeth M. Parker. *Evaluation of Baltimore's Safe Streets Program: Effects on Attitudes, Participants' Experiences, and Gun Violence*. Baltimore: Johns Hopkins Bloomberg School of Public Health, 2012.

Weerman, Frank M., Peter J. Lovegrove, and Terence Thornberry. "Gang Membership Transitions and Its Consequences: Exploring Changes Related to Joining and Leaving Gangs in Two Countries." *European Journal of Criminology* 12, no. 1 (2015): 70–91.

Weide, Robert D. "The Invisible Hand of the State: A Critical Historical Analysis of Prison Gangs in California." *Prison Journal* (forthcoming).

West, Kanye. "Hold My Liquor." Featuring vocals by Chief Keef and Justin Vernon. Track 6 on *Yeezus*. Def Jam Recordings B0018653-02, 2013, compact disc.

Western, Bruce. *Punishment and Inequality in America*. New York: Russell Sage Foundation, 2006.

Whyte, William Foote. *Street Corner Society: The Social Structure of an Italian Slum*. Chicago: University of Chicago Press, 1943.

Wilson, William Julius. *The Truly Disadvantaged: The Inner City, the Underclass, and Public Policy*. Chicago: University of Chicago Press, 1987.

Wilson, William Julius. *When Work Disappears: The World of the New Urban Poor*. New York: Alfred A. Knopf, 1996.

Winett, Liana B. "Constructing Violence as a Public Health Problem." *Public Health Reports* 113, no. 6 (1998): 498–507.

Wolf, Eric R. *Europe and the People Without History*. Berkeley: University of California Press, 1982.

World Health Organization. *Global Status Report on Violence Prevention 2014*. Geneva: World Health Organization, 2014.

Zamost, Scott, Drew Griffin, and Elizabeth Nunez. "Questions Surround $55 Million Program to Cut Violence in Chicago." CNN, December 3, 2012. http://www.cnn.com/2012/12/01/justice/chicago-crime-program-criticized/index.html.

Zatz, Marjorie S. "Chicano Youth Gangs and Crime: The Creation of a Moral Panic." *Contemporary Crises* 11, no. 2 (1987): 129–58.
Zelenko, Michael. "If the Drug War Is Failing, Where'd All the Cocaine Go?" *Vice*, January 24, 2014. https://www.vice.com/read/if-the-drug-war-is-failing-whered-all-the-cocaine-go.
Zimring, Franklin E. *The Great American Crime Decline*. Oxford: Oxford University Press, 2007.

INDEX

Page numbers followed by the letters *f* or *t* indicate figures or tables, respectively.

accumulation by dispossession, 176, 241n21
activism, 7, 182, 195, 245n55
activists, 7, 110–11, 182, 84–85, 194
against the grain (ATG), 62. *See also* gang identity: renegade
alderman, 113, 187
Alinsky, Saul, 7–8, 182, 186
Antifa, 229n45
Arena, John, 242n23
Auburn Gresham (Chicago community), 13f, 155, 219n1, 221n4
Austin (Chicago community), 11t, 13f, 14t

Baltimore: Cure Violence in, 234n39; focused deterrence in, 167; homicide clearance rate, 147; homicide rate, 6, 167
Barnes, Gakirah, 228n35
bar-none, 55–56, 88. *See also* gang identity: renegade
Barrios, Luis, 188–90
BDK. *See* Black Disciples: BDK
BDs. *See* Black Disciples
Black Disciples, 10, 11t, 16, 87–88, 90–92, 101, 116; and aid and assist, 221n2; BDK, 102–3, 157; and cliquing up, 30–31, 54–59, 55t, 70, 87–88, 222n10; egalitarian ideology of, 50–51; federal prosecutions of, 32; and "first Demetrius," 50–51, 72; and gang shattering, 88, 222n10; and relations between neighborhoods, 30, 47, 88, 222n14; and Sandifer killing, 223–24n24; traditional structure of, 50–51, 72, 88; traditional symbolism of, 101–2, 221n1, 222n15; and war with Gangster Disciples, 22, 78, 86, 222n10
Black Lives Matter, 185–86, 244n43
Black P Stones, 3, 10, 11t, 16, 40, 59, 87, 101, 118, 129–30; and cliquing up, 30, 54–57, 55t, 127; and division of labor, 19; egalitarian ideology of, 52–53, 159; federal prosecutions of, 31, 32t; and "flipping," 62–64; and gang shattering, 34, 37–38, 51–53, 159, 219n1; history of, 8, 17–19, 228n34, 245n55; Islamic influence on, 18–19, 217n4; and Lords,

Black P Stones (*continued*)
Stones, and Disciples coalition, 245n55; role of women in, 19; traditional structure of, 17–19, 30, 34, 219n33; traditional symbolism of, 19, 217n4, 219n33, 225n9
Black Souls, 16; federal prosecution of, 32t; and focused deterrence, 145. *See also* Illinois Street Gang and Racketeer Influenced Corrupt Organizations Law
Blackstone Rangers. *See* Black P Stones
Blagojevich, Rod, 113
Bloods, 222n11
Bocanegra, Eddie, 163
Boston, 141; focused deterrence in, 142–43, 230n4, 231n8; homicide rate, 6, 142–43
Boston Gun Project. *See* Boston: focused deterrence in
Bourdieu, Pierre, 117, 187, 241n20
Bourgois, Philippe, 201, 220n12
Boykin, Richard, 4
Brazil, 197–98
Brick Squad, 101–2
Bronzeville, 7, 27–28. *See also* Low End, the
Brotherton, David, 136, 139, 166, 173–74, 188–90, 200, 202, 243–44n36
Brown, Michael, 238–39n7
Burge, Jon, 227n28
Burke, Ed, 113
Byrd-Bennett, Barbara, 179

Cabrini-Green, 27, 223–24n24
Castells, Manuel, 117, 188
Cayton, Horace, 110
CeaseFire. *See* Cure Violence
central leadership. *See* gang structure: central leadership
Chatham (Chicago community), 11t, 13f; effects of CHA demolitions on, 29
Chicago Crime Commission: and Chicago Police Department, 77; and historical conspiracy strategy, 169; and portrayal of Chicago gangs, 4, 76–77, 221n17, 224n25
Chicago Housing Authority (CHA): demolitions by, 27–31, 33–35, 57, 83, 172, 176, 179, 218n25; deterioration within, 176; and gangs' rise to power, 172; as lucrative drug markets, 24, 28, 33–34, 86; and Operation Clean Sweep, 179; and privatization, 176–77, 179; and racial segregation, 27–28, 172, 218n21
Chicago Is Not Broke (book), 177, 180
Chicago Police Department, 6, 169–70; budget of, 4–5, 177, 180; and Chicago Crime Commission, 77; and civil damages, 5, 128, 177; corruption in, 113, 127–28, 227n28; and disruption of drug markets, 27, 33, 67, 85; and focused deterrence, 6, 15, 140–42, 144–52, 155, 231n8, 232n17, 233n26, 233n29; and gang suppression, 18, 128–29, 179, 238n5; homicide clearance rates of, 147–49, 232n17; and online surveillance, 104; and police–community relations, 8–9, 111, 127–29, 135, 148, 175, 180; and portrayal of gangs and violence, 3–4, 107–8, 245n52; Third District Offices of, 82f; and violence, 113, 115, 127–28, 134, 177, 180, 191–92, 227n28, 227n32
Chicago Public Schools, 12, 115, 163, 175, 223–24n24, 224–25n3; attendance zones, 81–83, 82f; and charter school privatization, 83, 221n5, 221n6; gang dynamics in, 29–30, 81–83, 82f; and scandals and mismanagement, 113; and school closings, 5, 7, 83–85, 111, 177, 179, 221n5, 221n6
Chief Keef (rapper), 7, 92, 98–100, 211n3, 214n27, 222n14
CityLab, 6
civil rights movement, 183–84, 186, 195–96
Clarence Darrow Homes, 27
clique. *See* gang structure: clique
cliquing up. *See* gang alliances
Cloward, Richard, 228–29n41
cocaine, 20, 25; declining popularity of, 23–25; falling price of, 23. *See also* crack cocaine epidemic
Cohen, Albert, 136

community organizing. *See* organizing
Conquergood, Dwight, 173
conscientização. *See* gang intervention: *conscientização* and
Cook County, 4, 177
Cook County Jail, 61–62, 74–75, 78
Corbin, Juliet, 204
corruption. *See* Chicago Police Department: corruption; political corruption
crack cocaine epidemic, 16, 31, 67–68, 85, 198; decline in, 23–26, 34–36, 42–43, 65, 71, 172; and "epidemic" as misnomer, 215–16n34; as impetus for gang wars, 10, 21–22, 78–79, 86; rise of, 9–10, 19–20, 25, 172
Crips, 75; Rollin 60s, 11t, 75–76
culture of autonomy. *See* gang culture: of autonomy
culture of obedience. *See* gang culture: of obedience
Cure Violence: in Baltimore, 234n39; in Chicago, 6, 15, 141–42, 141f, 152, 154–61, 165–66, 169–70, 193–94, 235n42; and credible messengers, 154, 158–60; evaluations of, 152, 154–55, 234n39, 235n42; as facilitator of personal transformation, 235–36n50; media acclaim of, 153; and public health model, 152–54, 156–58, 161–64, 166, 170–71, 235–36n50; and relationships, 195; as too big to fail, 167; as universal intervention, 15, 141–42, 152, 165–66, 170, 175, 193–94

Daley, Richard J., 7–8, 178
Daley, Richard M., 178–79, 221n5, 242n28
Dan Ryan Expressway, 66, 218n21
Davis, Dantrell, 223–24n24
Debs, Eugene V., 182
deductive research, 166, 196, 201
deindustrialization, 6, 177; effects on Chicago gangs, 9, 16, 25–26, 172
Democratic machine, Chicago, 7–8, 172, 178, 242n27, 242n28
Department of Child and Family Services, 116
Department of Justice, U.S., 128, 142–43, 169, 234n39
d'Escoto, Miguel, 197
despair, 66–72, 112–21, 132–36, 163, 171, 192–94
Detroit, 110–11; homicide rate, 6
Diamond, Andrew, 110–11, 173
differential opportunity theory, 228–29n41
Douglass, Frederick, 182
downtown. *See* Loop, the (Chicago's central business district)
Drake, St. Clair, 110
drill. *See* gang violence
drill music, 105, 211n3, 222n13; influence of on Chicago gang life, 98–103, 105, 149; and music videos, 99–102, 222n15; and power of drill rappers, 100–103, 149; promotion of via social media, 98–100, 103, 105; as reflection of Chicago gang life, 97–98, 105; rise of, 1, 99–100
drug cartels, 70, 111, 246n60
drug game: and decline of markets, 23–28, 66–68, 85–86, 96, 100, 121–22, 172; gang wars over, 10, 21–22, 28–29, 33–34, 78, 85–86, 90, 94, 104–5, 220n12, 222n10; and mobile markets, 25, 66–67, 85; and open-air markets, 19–20, 24–25, 66–67, 85–86, 96, 121, 149; predominance of Latino gangs in, 70, 111, 246n60; relationships and access to, 69–71. *See also* gang culture: outlaw-capitalist
Durán, Robert, 136, 173, 202
Dyett High School, Walter H., 7, 83

East Garfield Park (Chicago community), 13f, 145
East Side Disciples. *See* Gangster Disciples
East Side of Chicago, 29, 67
East St. Louis, 199
EBK, 88, 102. *See also* gang identity: renegade
El Rukns. *See* Black P Stones

Emanuel, Rahm, 7, 114–15, 145, 178–79, 242n28, 242–43n31
employment programs, 8, 71–72, 114
Englewood (Chicago community), 11t, 13f, 78, 99, 101, 162, 221n4, 238n5; effects of CHA demolitions on, 29; heroin in, 67
Eurogang research, 229–30n45
everybody killer. *See* EBK

Facebook, 99–100
Federal Bureau of Prisons: gang leaders in, 31–36, 43–44, 172, 177
federal gang prosecutions, 31–33, 35, 172; in Los Angeles, 5
Ferguson, Missouri, 238–39n7
First Presbyterian Church, 8
Flores, Edward Orozco, 188–90
focused deterrence: in Baltimore, 167; in Boston, 142–43, 230n4, 231n8; call-ins, 143–47, 149–52, 232n17; in Chicago, 6, 15, 140–42, 141f, 144–52, 155–56, 169–70, 193–94, 233n26, 233n29; evaluations of, 143, 230n4, 231n8, 232n17; and "firebreaks," 146, 232n17; model, 142–44, 161–62, 164–67, 170–71, 193–94; pulling levers, 144–47, 149–50; as universal intervention, 15, 141–42, 165–66, 170, 175, 193–94
Foes. *See* Four Corner Hustlers
Folks gang coalition, 22, 76–77, 149, 221n18, 221n2
Forest Glen (Chicago community), 13f, 162
Fort, Jeff, 31, 219n33
foster care, 116–17, 185
Four Corner Hustlers, 10, 11t, 16, 217n10; and cliquing up, 55t; federal prosecutions of, 32t; war with Unknown Vice Lords, 22, 217n10
Four-Six, 98, 222n14
41st–Cottage Grove, 27
Fredo Santana, 211n3
Freire, Paulo, 186–87, 197
Fry, John, 8

gang alliances: basis for, 29–31, 56, 58–59, 80–81, 100–103, 148–49; benefits of, 80–81, 84; and cliquing up, 30–31, 54–59, 55t, 80–82, 84–85, 87–88; drawbacks of, 84–85; formal, 17; informal, 47, 80; and People and Folks coalitions, 22, 76–77, 149, 217n4, 221n18, 221n2, 225n9; tenuousness of, 47, 84–85, 88, 93; in traditional Chicago gangs, 17, 58–59, 64, 80, 148
gang culture: of autonomy, 46–55, 58, 60, 63, 91–94, 105, 146–7, 157–58, 170, 195; complexities of, 18–19; of egalitarianism, 48–54, 73, 93, 195; as familial, 115–18; and institutionalized gangs, 18–19, 44, 219–20n4; of Los Angeles versus of Chicago, 75–76; of obedience, 18–21, 35–36, 48–49, 74–75; outlaw-capitalist, 6–7, 9–10, 16, 19–22, 25–28, 33–34, 39, 65, 78–79, 109; as relationship-oriented, 30–31, 52–59, 81, 88–91, 115–17, 125, 131–35, 138, 184–85, 190; socialization into, 17, 49–50, 52–53, 189–90; tensions and contradictions within, 26–27, 33–37, 43–45, 49, 61–63, 92–94, 104, 188–90
gang identity: declining importance of traditional, 29–31, 54–64, 87–88; fallen comrades and, 57, 134–35; and "flipping," 30–31, 60, 62–64, 220n10; influence on drill rappers of, 100–103, 105, 149; neighborhood and, 8, 57–58, 126, 129–30, 227n26; as personal matter, 60–64; as quasi-religion, 17–19, 44–45, 134–35, 181–82; reconstruction of, 184, 188–90; renegade, 61–64, 76–77, 88, 101–2; as resistance identity, 117–19, 123–26, 133–36, 171, 184, 188–90, 196; social media and, 103–4, 135; traditional Chicago, 17–19, 44–45, 59–60, 74–75
gang ideology. *See* gang culture
gang initiations: as "coming home," 137–38; lack of formality in, 131, 137–38; in Los Angeles, 76; role of collective violence in, 131–32, 138, 230n46
gang intervention, 8–9; and civic education and engagement, 187; community investment and, 121, 171,

178–83, 194; *conscientização* and, 186–87; employment opportunities and, 71–73, 114–15, 121; finding common ground as, 190–93, 245n55; gang suppression, 4, 168–69; ground-up, 171–72, 182, 195–96; historical conspiracy strategy, 169, 238n5; identity reconstruction and, 188–90; opportunity for, 181–82; relationships as foundation for, 184–86; 194–95; social movements and, 182–95, 245n55; weakening gang relationships and, 138. *See also* Cure Violence; focused deterrence
Gangland (TV show), 5–6
gang membership: and economic opportunities, 121–26; and emotional support, 115–17; as fluid, 8, 137–38; functions and meanings of, 109–39, 171, 175, 188–90; and mutual caretaking, 123, 226n20; neighborhood as proxy for, 8, 126, 129–30; protective function of, 129–31, 228n40; and resistance identity, 117–19, 123–26, 133–36, 171, 184, 188–90, 196; as rooted in relationships, 115–17, 137–38; solidarity and, 117–18, 125–26; violence as delimiter of, 131–32, 138
gang research: as antidote to stereotype, 3, 5–6, 14–15, 76–77, 107–8, 110, 137–39, 168–69, 173–75, 192; in Chicago, 3, 6–7, 9–10, 18, 35–36, 173; critical, 139, 173, 199–202; critiques of mainstream, 137–39, 166, 173–75, 184, 190, 192, 229–30n45, 240–41n18; and gang theory, 135–39, 171–75, 181, 228–29n41; need for historical, 172–75, 240–41n18, 243–44n36; "variables paradigm," 174
gangs: in California, 220n10; as folk devils, 174; Latino gangs in Chicago, 47–48, 58, 70, 111, 246n60; in Los Angeles, 5, 11t, 12, 18, 75–76, 108, 124, 222n11; as more than one thing, 18–19, 44–45, 189, 245n52, 244n47; in New York City, 20, 188–90; as "people without history," 174; on West Side of Chicago, 10–12, 217n2, 219n1, 246n60
Gangster Disciples, 3–4, 10, 11t, 16, 59, 80, 84, 91, 150; and aid and assist, 221n2; and cliquing up, 31, 54–57, 55t, 70, 87–88, 127, 222n10; federal prosecutions of, 32t; and "flipping," 62–64; and gang shattering, 33–34, 60–64, 74–75, 88, 222n10; GDK, 102–3; Growth and Development, 189, 245n52; history of, 8; Insane, 10, 11t, 61–64, 101–2; and Lords, Stones, and Disciples coalition, 245n55; Outlaws, 10, 11t, 61, 127; traditional structure of, 17–18, 61, 74–75, 220n9; traditional symbolism of, 17–19, 75, 220n9, 221n1, 222n15; and war with Black Disciples, 22, 78, 86, 222n10
gang structure: central leadership, 9–10, 17, 19–20, 33–34, 47, 74; clique, 46–64; corporate-style, 9–10, 25–27, 44–45, 90; cross-neighborhood federation/nation, 9–10, 17–19, 21, 33–34, 46–49, 59–60, 90, 96, 103, 105, 109; egalitarian, 48–54, 73; factions, 41–42, 47, 61, 76, 169; hierarchical, 7, 16–22, 25–27, 32–37, 74–75; inequality within, 20–22, 35–36, 40–41; local governance, 47–48, 75; role of women, 17–19, 56–57, 132, 219–20n4; sets, 17, 20, 28, 31, 33–34, 41–42, 47, 57–60, 80, 87–88, 101; shattering of, 35–43; street organization, 16–22, 46–47, 74–75; symbolic leadership, 50–51, 72; weakening of, 23–35
gang territories: CHA demolitions and, 28–31, 57; conflicts over, 28–29, 85–86, 94, 96; and drug markets, 19–20, 86; proximity of, 79–82, 82f, 126–27; and restriction of movement, 8, 29–30, 80–81, 126, 129–30, 191–92; size of, 41–42, 47, 80, 126; splintering of, 41–42, 47, 79–80
gang theory. *See* gang research: gang theory

gang violence: CHA demolitions and, 28–29; Chicago's reputation for, 1, 3–6, 109; cliquing up and, 80–81, 84–85; control of drug markets and, 21–22, 29, 33–34, 78–79, 85–87; as delimiter of gang membership, 131–32, 138; drill music and, 98, 102–3, 105; expressive, 90, 96; and extortion, 22; as foundation for solidarity, 47, 89–91, 131–35; gang leader-directed, 19, 21, 35–37, 78–79; instrumental, 21–22, 40–41; and internal rebellions, 36–43, 58–59; interpersonal animosities and, 88–90; and intragang conflict, 33–34, 41–42, 58–59, 62–64, 87–88; as meaning-giving, 132–35; parochial, 79–83, 82f, 105; personal autonomy and, 91–94, 105; relationships and, 88–91, 131–35; situational, 29, 89; social media and, 103–5, 223n20; stereotypes of, 4, 86, 107–8; traditional gang ideologies and, 28–30, 87, 90; transformed members' views of, 105–6; as unavoidable, 96, 126–27, 129–31; as unpredictable, 94–96, 149, 156–57; as vendettas, 90–91, 94–95, 105–6, 131–33; victimization as honorable, 133–35. *See also* Cure Violence; focused deterrence; violations
Garfield Park Conservatory, 144
Garot, Robert, 215n32, 227n26
GDs. *See* Gangster Disciples
gentrification, 7–8, 120, 158, 226n18, 242–43n31, 246n56
G Herbo, 134, 211n3
ghetto, 7, 27, 136, 200, 216n38, 218n21, 226n18, 243n34; hyperghetto, 180, 200
Gramsci, Antonio, 187, 241n20
Grand Boulevard (Chicago community), 11t, 13f, 99, 225n8. *See also* Bronzeville; Low End, the
Greater Grand Crossing (Chicago community), 11t, 13f, 82f, 99, 162
Green New Deal, 243n34
grounded theory, 201–4
Group Violence Intervention, 142. *See also* focused deterrence

Hagedorn, John, 9, 18, 32, 44, 136, 171, 173, 202, 244n47, 245n52, 246n60; *The In$ane Chicago Way*, 243–44n36
Hardiman, Tio, 158, 160, 163
Harkness, Geoff, 222n13
Harold Ickes Homes: demolition of, 27; as a "war zone," 33–34
heroin, 25, 201; predominance of in West Side markets, 67–68, 220n13; rise of in open-air markets, 19–20; selling of among West Side gangs, 220–21n11, 246n60
Hilliard, Terry, 231n13
Hirsch, Arnold, 110
homelessness, 112, 119, 123, 201
homicide rate: in Baltimore, 6, 167, 234n39; in Boston, 6, 142–43; in Chicago, 2, 2f, 22, 105, 107, 109, 140–42, 141f, 146, 152, 155–56, 160–61, 169, 193, 213n12, 232n17, 235n42; in Detroit, 6; in East Garfield Park, 145; in East St. Louis, 199; and inequality, 236n54; in largest U.S. cities, 109, 140, 141f; in Los Angeles, 2, 2f, 6, 161; in New York City, 2, 2f, 6, 161; in participants' communities, 12, 14t, 126; as proxy for violent crime, 212n6; in San Francisco, 6; in St. Louis, 6; in the United States, 212n5; in West Garfield Park, 145, 156
Hoover, Larry, 62, 74, 220n9
HOPE VI, 179
Horowitz, Ruth, 9
Hughes, Lorine, 174
Human Rights Watch, 32t
hunger strike, 7
Hyde Park (Chicago community), 13f, 82f, 121, 216n38, 226n18
Hyde Park Academy High School, 82f, 83, 221n4

I's. *See* Insane
Ida B. Wells Homes, 27

Illinois Consortium on Drug Policy, 67
Illinois Department of Corrections: contemporary gang dynamics in, 61–62; and decline of prison gang politics, 56, 79; expansion of gangs in, 32, 172; incarceration of gang leaders in, 20, 32, 78; and People and Folks gang coalitions, 22; and power of incarcerated gang leaders, 10, 20–22, 32, 78, 104–5; and removal of gang leaders, 31–32, 32t, 44, 172, 177
Illinois Street Gang and Racketeer Influenced Corrupt Organizations Law, 145
incarceration. *See* prison
inductive research, 109–10, 137, 196, 201, 204
Industrial Workers of the World, 89–90
Insane, 61–62, 76–77, 222n15; Gangster Disciples, 10, 11t, 55, 61–64, 88, 101–2; as oppositional to L's, 101–2. *See also* gang identity: renegade
Instagram, 99, 104
Interrupters, The (documentary), 153, 158, 160, 163, 235n46

Jacobs, James, 9; *Stateville*, 32
Jihadism, 133
John Jay College of Criminal Justice, 142
Johnson, Cedric, 176–77, 241n22, 244n43
Johnson, Eddie, 151
"jumping off the porch," 49, 131. *See also* gang initiations

Karandinos, George, 132–33, 200
Katie Got Bandz (rapper), 99, 211n3
Keiser, Lincoln, 9
Kennedy, David, 143–45, 162, 164, 194, 232n17, 238n6
Killa Ward, 145–46, 149–50
King, Martin Luther, Jr., 184
King Louie (rapper), 99, 211n3
Kirk, Mark, 4
Kozol, Jonathan, 224–25n3
Kropotkin, Pëtr, 226n20

"L" (Chicago's public train system), 65–66, 101, 127, 159
L's, 62, 102, 222n15; Black Disciples origins, 101; multiple meanings of, 101–2; as oppositional to Insane, 101–2. *See also* gang identity: renegade
Lakefront Properties, 27
Lake Michigan, 13f, 82f, 218n21
Lamron, 98, 101–2, 222n14
Lane, Vincent, 179
Latin Folks, 22
Latin Kings: in Chicago, 3, 246n60; in New York City, 188–89
law enforcement, 19, 23, 75, 165, 171, 191, 212n5, 229n45, 232n25; as "common enemy," 183–84; and gang suppression, 4, 168–69; and narratives of precision, 5–6; perspective of on gangs, 110, 137–38, 229n45; and portrayal of gangs and violence, 3–5, 192; and relations with black communities, 8, 164–66; self-interest of, 3; as shapers of media perspectives, 5–6, 214n27; societal functions of, 164–65, 176–78, 241n22; and violence, 183–86, 238n7, 241n22, 244n43; and zero-tolerance policing, 129
LeClaire Courts, 218n19
Lee, Tyshawn, 146, 223n22
Levenson, Deborah, 173
Levine, Harry, 215–16n34
Levitt, Steven, 20, 220n12
liberation theology, 197
Lil Bibby, 134, 211n3
Lil Durk, 99, 101, 211n3, 222n14
Lil Jay, 99
Lil JoJo, 101–4
Lil Reese, 99, 211n3
Lincoln Park (Chicago community), 13f, 162
Little Village (South Lawndale–Chicago community), 13f, 236n53, 246n60
Lloyd, Willie, 22, 217n10
Loop, the (Chicago's central business district), 13f, 113, 176–77, 180, 183, 192

Los Angeles: gang intervention in, 188; gangs in, 5, 11t, 12, 18, 75–76, 108, 124, 222n11; homicide rate in, 2, 2f, 6, 161; Watts section in, 162
Los Angeles Police Department, 108, 162
Low End, the, 27–28, 110–11, 118–19, 218n21. *See also* Bronzeville

Madden Park Homes, 27
mandatory minimum prison sentences, 31
Manhattan, 111, 214n27. *See also* New York City
Maplewood Courts, 218n19
marginalization: in drug game, 26–27, 40–41, 65–73, 181; societal, 12, 14t, 65, 71–73, 110–21, 124–26, 132–36, 165, 170–71, 175–84, 194; in traditional gangs, 26–27, 35–37, 40–41
marijuana, 19, 73, 123, 221n14; as alternative to crack cocaine, 24, 65, 68, 85; consumption of as coping mechanism, 66, 68–69; Kush, 39; loud, 42; meager profitability of for dealers, 25, 65, 68–69, 71; popularity of, 24, 68; theft and retribution in supply chain, 39–40
Marshall Plan, 243n34
McCarthy, Garry, 4, 145, 150–52, 231n13
McDonald, Laquan, 113, 127–28, 152
MCs. *See* Mickey Cobras
Mendoza-Denton, Norma, 220n10
mental health services: closing of public clinics, 5, 177; hospitalizations, 12; lack of, 5, 111, 180
Merton, Robert, 136
Mickey Cobras, 10, 11t, 16, 91; and cliquing up, 54–55, 55t, 58–59, 70, 87–88, 127, 222n10; federal prosecutions of, 32t; and gang shattering, 58–59, 87–88, 222n10; Islamic influence on, 217n4; traditional symbolism of, 21, 217n4, 225n9
Mills, C. Wright, 175
Minneapolis, 7, 27, 198
Moes. *See* Black P Stones
Moore, Joan, 136, 173, 202
Moore, Natalie, 34, 40, 173
moral panic, 3–4, 213n11; crack cocaine epidemic as, 215–16n34; gangs and violence in Chicago as, 4–6, 140, 211n2, 213n12
Morgan, Tracey, 145–46
Morris, Aldon, 186

narratives of precision. *See* law enforcement: narratives of precision
National Commission on Severely Distressed and Troubled Public Housing, 179
National Institute for Drug Abuse, 24
National Institute of Justice, 154
National Network for Safe Communities, 142
nation packs, 20–21
Near North Side (Chicago community), 13f, 27
neutrons, 133–34
New Breeds, 16; federal prosecutions of, 32t
New City (Chicago community), 11t, 13f, 14t; heroin in, 67
New Orleans, 141; homicide clearance rate, 147
New York City: Cure Violence in, 235n48; drug organizations, 20; homicide rate, 2, 2f, 6, 161; Latin Kings and Queens, 188–89
New York Police Department, 5
Nickerson Gardens, 162
Nolaw, 61. *See also* gang identity: renegade
No Limit Muskegon Boyz. *See* Terror Town
North Side of Chicago, 7, 13f, 27, 162, 177
Northwestern University, 154

Obama, Barack, 1, 4, 6, 113–14, 121, 183, 225n8, 242–43n31
O-Block, 57, 98, 102, 222n14
Ohlin, Lloyd, 228–29n41
One Summer Chicago, 72. *See also* employment programs
Only the Family. *See* OTF
Only Trey Folks. *See* OTF

Operation Ceasefire. *See* focused deterrence: in Boston
organizing, 182–87, 190–91, 194; historical gang, 58
OTF, 98, 102, 222n14. *See also* Black Disciples
Outlaw, 61, 127; Gangster Disciples, 10, 11t, 55t, 61; and L's, 101. *See also* gang identity: renegade
outlaw capitalism, 118, 124–26, 136. *See also* gang culture: outlaw-capitalist

Padilla, Felix, 9, 35–36, 136, 173
Papachristos, Andrew, 167, 233n26, 240n12
Parks, Rosa, 184
Parkway Gardens Homes, 99. *See also* O-Block
Pattillo, Mary, 27, 110, 180
peace treaty, 93–94, 133, 157–58, 193
Pearson, Geoffrey, 200
People gang coalition, 22, 76–77, 149, 217n4, 221n18, 225n9
personal autonomy. *See* gang culture: of autonomy
Phillips, Susan, 5, 124
"pinstripe patronage," 178
Pitchfork (website), 214n27
Piven, Frances Fox, 182
Plan for Transformation, 27. *See also* Chicago Housing Authority (CHA): demolitions by
police. *See* Chicago Police Department; law enforcement
political corruption, 113, 176–77, 179–80
politics of representation, 199–201
Popkin, Susan, 33–34
positivist research, 173–75, 201
poverty, 171, 180; in communities, 12, 14t, 28, 111, 117–20, 175, 194; and drill music, 98; in participants' families, 111–12, 116–19, 122–26; and resistance identity, 117–18, 124–26, 136; as structural determinant of violence, 162–63, 236n54
Prairie Avenue Courts, 27
prison: and commonness in participants' communities, 8–9, 111, 116, 123, 175 191–92; Cure Violence as facilitating reentry from, 235–36n50; explosion of, 9, 111; and length of sentences, 31, 33, 43, 168; as predominant response to gangs, 31–32, 168–69, 171; and resistance identity, 118; solitary confinement in, 32; "supermax," 32; as surplus population management, 176–78, 241n22; war on drugs and, 16, 31
Project Safe Neighborhoods, 142–43; in Chicago, 231n8, 232n17. *See also* focused deterrence
"pumpkin head," 64
"putting in work," 43, 69–70, 135

Racketeer Influenced and Corrupt Organizations Act. *See* RICO Act
Ralph, Laurence, 173, 217n2, 219n1, 220n11, 246n56
Randolph Towers. *See* Washington Park Homes
Raymond Hilliard Homes, 28
Reed, Adolph, Jr., 182, 190–91, 241n22, 242n23, 244n43
Reinarman, Craig, 215–16n34
Renaissance 2010, 221n5. *See also* Chicago Public Schools: school closings
Renegade, 61, 76–77. *See also* gang identity: renegade
renegade gang identities. *See* gang identity: renegade
resistance identity, 117, 171; consumption as, 123–24; marginalization and, 117–19; outlaw persona as, 118, 124–25; reconstruction of, 184, 188–90; violence and, 132–35. *See also* gang identity: as resistance identity
RICO Act, 31–32, 43, 145, 238n5
robbery, 37–38, 40–42, 63, 122, 127, 129
Roberts, Angelo, 22, 217n10
Robert Taylor Homes, 20, 27, 30, 78, 86
Rollin 60s Crips. *See* Crips: Rollin 60s
Roosevelt University, 67
Roseland (Chicago community), 11t, 13f, 78
rustbelt cities, homicide rate in, 6. *See also* deindustrialization

Sánchez-Jankowski, Martín, 136
Sandifer, Robert. *See* Black Disciples: Sandifer killing
San Francisco, 201; homicide rate, 6
São Paulo, 197
Scarface (rapper), 98
Schonberg, Jeff, 201
Section 8, 28–29
"send-off," 50, 103
Shakur, Tupac, 98
Short, James, Jr., 108, 240n13
Sloan, Cle, 222n11
Slutkin, Gary, 152–53, 162
snitching, 33, 51, 93
social disorganization theory, 228–29n41
social media: as facilitator of violence, 103–4, 223n20; gang members' use of, 97, 99–105, 135, 192, 238n5; and identity, 103–4, 135; music promotion via, 97, 99–101
social movements, 182–95
social work, 7–9
social workers, 184–85, 194
South Shore (Chicago community), 11t, 13f, 75–76, 82f, 134
South Side of Chicago, 13f; Barack Obama and, 4, 114, 225n8, 242–43n31; diversity of communities in, 216n38; and drill music, 1, 98–103; high levels of violence in, 6, 149, 180; traditional gangs of, 10, 16
Spanish Growth and Development, 22
Spergel, Irving, 9
Stateville Correctional Center, 32. *See also* Illinois Department of Corrections
Stateway Gardens, 27
"stickup era," 40
St. Louis, 198–99; homicide rate, 6, 199
strain theory, 228–29n41
Strategic Subjects List, 151–52, 232n25, 233n26, 233n29, 238n5
Strauss, Anselm, 204
street gangs. *See* gang alliances; gang culture; gang identity; gang initiations; gang intervention; gang membership; gang research; gangs; gang structure; gang territories; gang violence
Strickland, Joseph, 216n36
study participants' communities: blight in, 7, 12, 111–13, 119–21, 194, 243n35; disinvestment in, 5, 12, 27–28, 71–72, 83, 111–15, 119–21, 163–64, 170–71, 175–81, 194–95; gangs in, 117–19, 127, 129–32; poverty in, 12, 14t, 28, 111, 117–20, 175, 194; schools in, 12, 29–30, 81–85, 82f, 111, 115, 175, 221n6; unemployment in, 12, 14t, 25, 28, 65–66, 71–73, 111, 120–22, 124–25, 175, 180, 243n35; violence in, 8–10, 12, 14t, 79–85, 96, 117–18, 126–36, 191–93, 227n27
subcultural theory, 125, 228–29n41
Suttles, Gerald, 9, 136
symbolic violence, 117, 241n20

tax-increment financing districts, 177
Team 600, 99, 211n3
TED Talk, 153, 162
Terror Dome, 145–46
Terror Town, 57, 134
Thrasher, Frederic, 136; *The Gang*, 9, 48
Tookaville, 102
tough-on-crime policies, 31, 168
Trump, Donald, 4
truth-in-sentencing, 31
Tupac. *See* Shakur, Tupac
Twitter, 99–100, 103–4, 185–86
Two Sixers, 246n60

unemployment: of African Americans in Chicago, 25, 71–72, 120, 163; community levels of, 9, 12, 14t, 16, 25, 28, 65–66, 111, 120, 124–25, 175, 180, 243n35; as comparable to Great Depression, 120; participants' experiences of, 10, 65–66, 71–73, 120–23
United Nations Office on Drugs and Crime, 236n54
University of Chicago, 82f; and development and gentrification, 7–8, 226n18; school of sociology at, 136, 241n18

University of Illinois at Chicago, 9, 113, 120, 152, 202–203

Van Dyke, Jason, 127–28. *See also* McDonald, Laquan
Vargas, Robert, 236n53, 246n60
Venkatesh, Sudhir, 9, 20, 35–36, 136, 173, 202, 220n12
Vice Lords, 3, 16; and cliquing up, 55t; federal prosecutions of, 32t; Islamic influence on, 217n4; and Lords, Stones, and Disciples coalition, 245n55; Traveling Vice Lords, 32; Unknown Vice Lords, 22, 217n10; and war with Four Corner Hustlers, 22, 217n10
Vigil, James Diego, 136, 173, 202
violations: abolition of, 53, 64, 88, 93, 157–58; grounds for, 18, 21, 37, 88; inconsistent application of, 35; resistance to, 37, 93; as tool of discipline and coercion, 21, 53, 93
violence. *See* gang violence; study participants' communities: violence; violations

Wacquant, Loïc, 180, 200, 241n22, 243n35
Wall Street Journal, 229n45
war on drugs, 16, 31, 198, 215–16n34
Washington, Harold, 242n27
Washington Park (Chicago community), 7, 11t, 13f, 82f, 99, 150, 225n8; heroin in, 67. *See also* Low End, the
Washington Park Homes, 27
Washington Post, 147
Weis, Jody, 144–45, 231n13
Wendell Phillips High School, 83
West, Kanye, 99
West Garfield Park (Chicago community), 13f; and Cure Violence, 152, 154, 156; focused deterrence in, 145; homicide rate in, 145, 156
West Pullman (Chicago community), 11t, 13f
West Side of Chicago, 11t, 13f; CHA demolitions, 27–28; and Cure Violence, 152, 154, 156; and focused deterrence, 144–45, 231n8; and gang differences from South Side, 217n2, 219n1, 246n60; and high levels of violence, 6, 149, 180; poverty and disinvestment in, 119–20, 175, 177, 180, 194, 246n56; and predominance of heroin markets, 67–68, 220n11, 220–21n13, 246n60; traditional gangs of, 10–12, 16
We the Opps. *See* WTO
Whyte, William Foote, 136
WIC City. *See* O-Block
"Wild Hundreds," the, 78
Williams, Lance, 34, 40, 173, 219n1
Wilson, Darren, 238–39n7
Wilson, William Julius, 110
Wolf, Eric, 174
Woodlawn (Chicago community), 7–8, 11t, 13f, 99, 187; community conditions in, 112, 200; contemporary gang dynamics in, 81–83, 82f, 221n3, 228n35; and gentrification, 7–8, 226n18, 242–43n31; and grassroots politics, 7–8, 179, 187; and historical gang dynamics, 8, 228n34
Woodlawn Organization, The, 7–8, 226n18, 245n55
World Health Organization, 152, 236n54
WTO, 102. *See also* gang identity: renegade

Young Chop, 99
Young Money: Fifty-First Street gang, 98, 222n14; OTF-affiliated gang, 98, 222n14
YouTube, 99–100